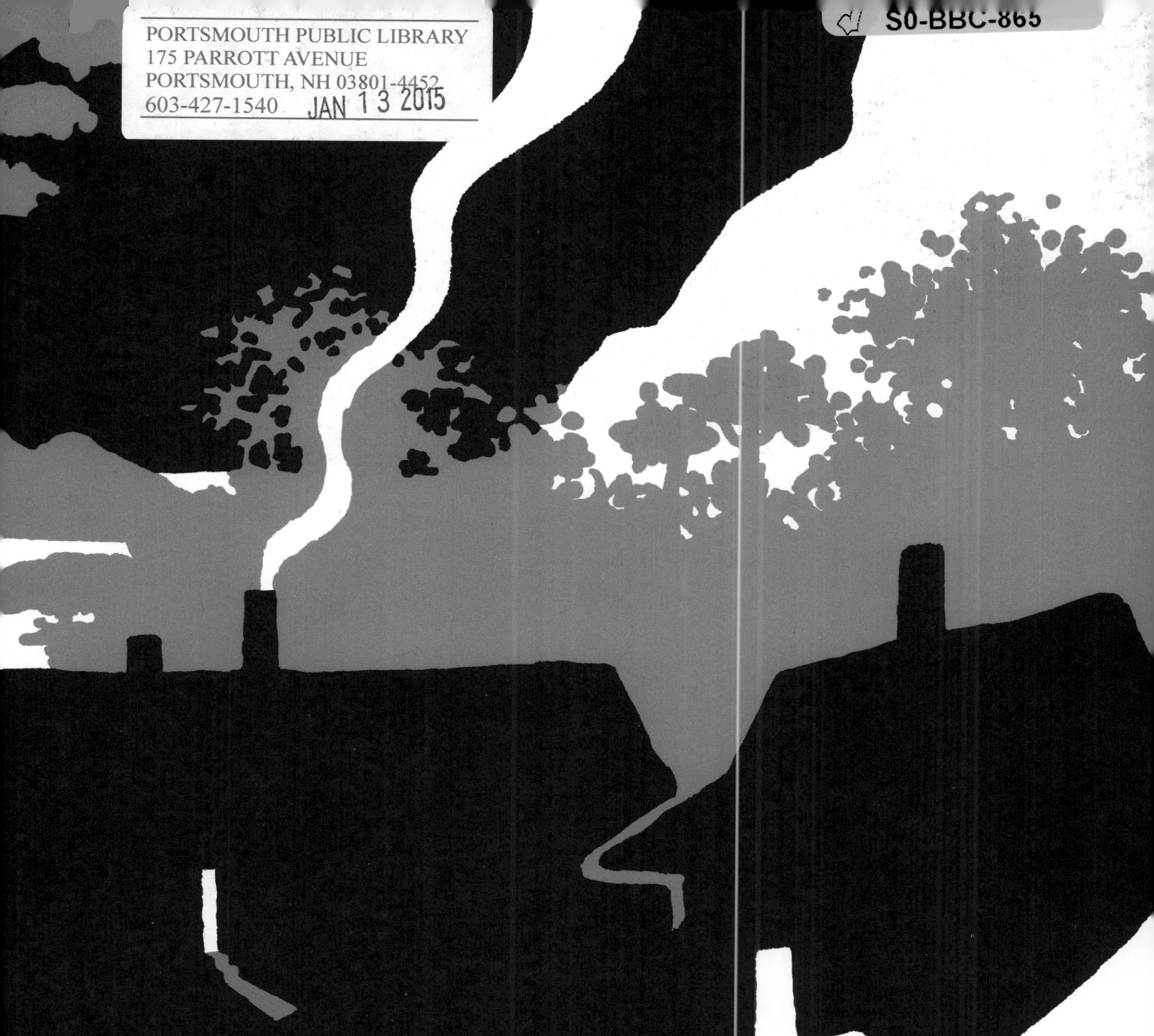

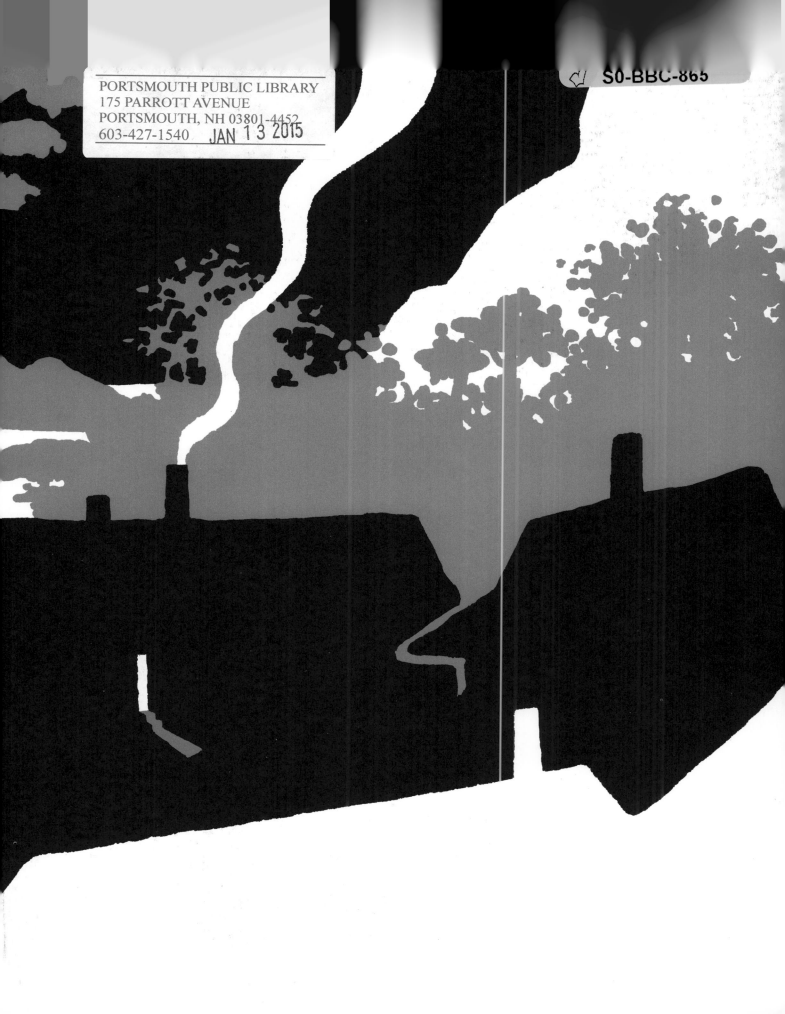

Kerascoët & Hubert
Beauty

Story and colors : Hubert
Art : Kerascoët

NBM
ComicsLit

ISBN 9781561638949
Initially published in French as *Beauté* © Dupuis, 2011-13 by
Hubert, Kerascoët
All rights reserved
© 2014 NBM for the English translation
LC control number: 2014943195
Translation by Joe Johnson
Lettering by Ortho

1st printing, October 2014

NBMPUB.COM

Comicslit is an imprint
and trademark of

NANTIER · BEALL · MINOUSTCHINE
Publishing inc.
new york

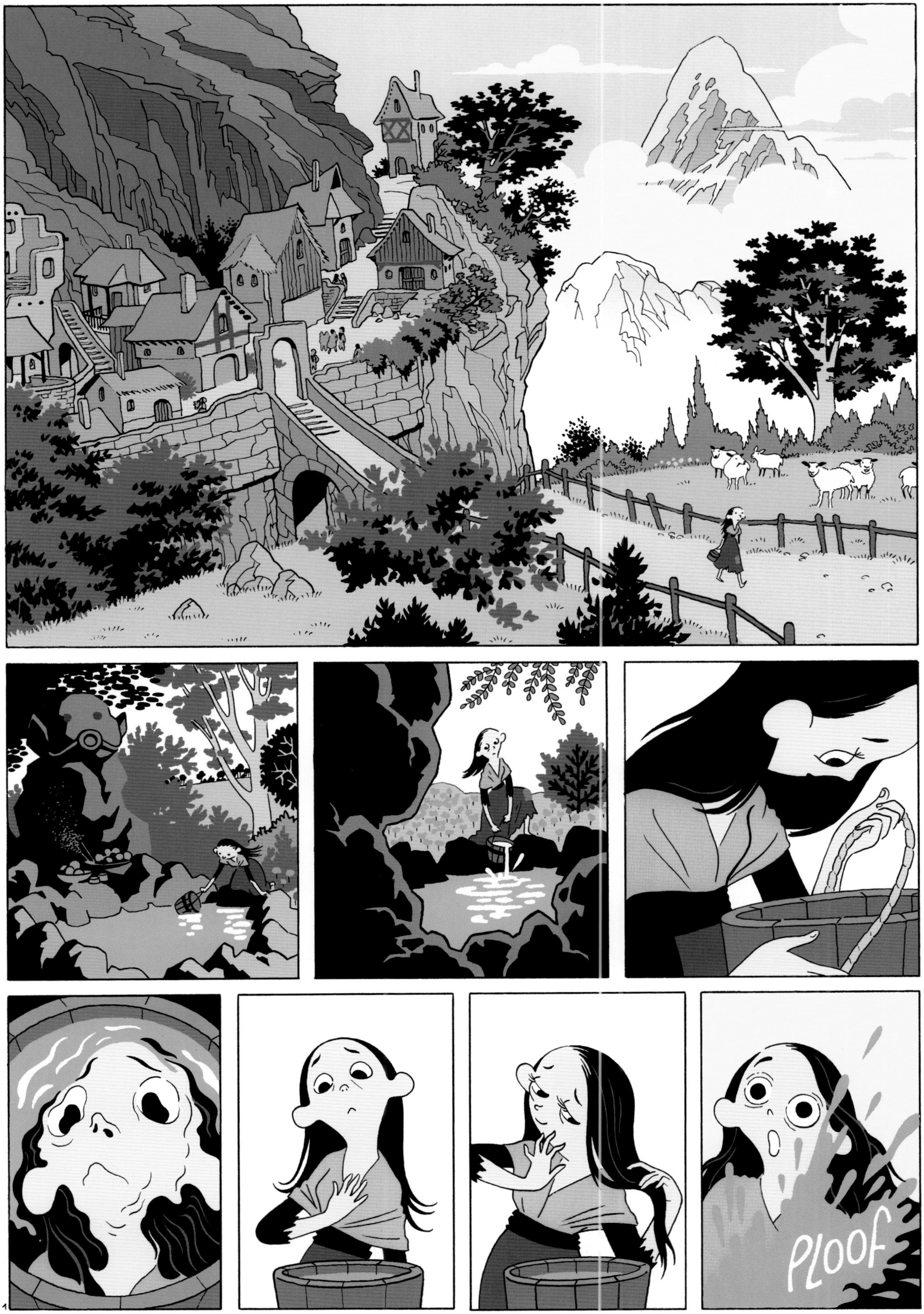
PLOOF

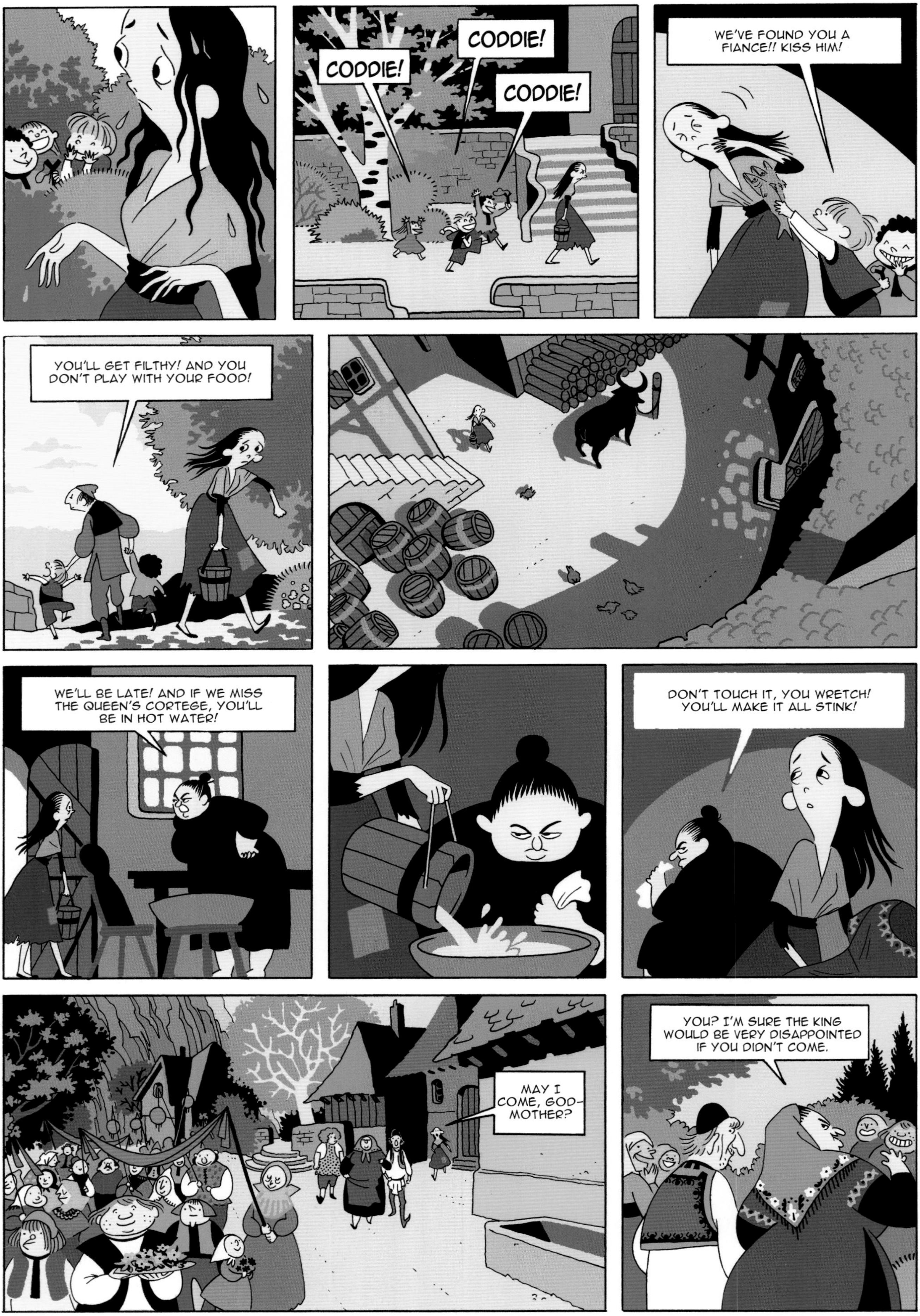
CODDIE!
CODDIE!
CODDIE!
WE'VE FOUND YOU A FIANCE!! KISS HIM!
YOU'LL GET FILTHY! AND YOU DON'T PLAY WITH YOUR FOOD!
WE'LL BE LATE! AND IF WE MISS THE QUEEN'S CORTEGE, YOU'LL BE IN HOT WATER!
DON'T TOUCH IT, YOU WRETCH! YOU'LL MAKE IT ALL STINK!
MAY I COME, GOD-MOTHER?
YOU? I'M SURE THE KING WOULD BE VERY DISAPPOINTED IF YOU DIDN'T COME.

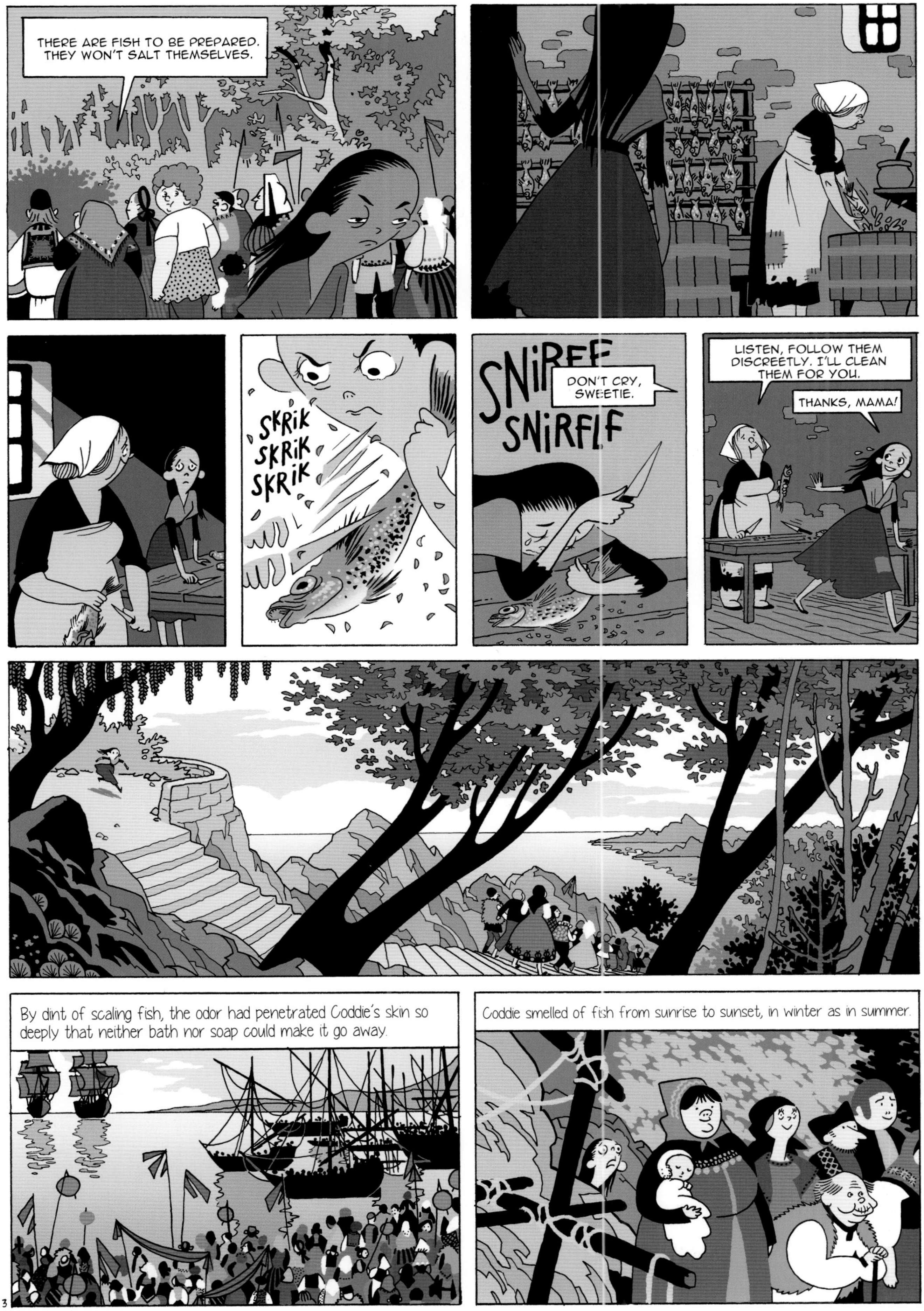
THERE ARE FISH TO BE PREPARED. THEY WON'T SALT THEMSELVES.
SKRIK SKRIK SKRIK
SNIRFF
DON'T CRY, SWEETIE.
SNIRFLF
LISTEN, FOLLOW THEM DISCREETLY. I'LL CLEAN THEM FOR YOU.
THANKS, MAMA!
By dint of scaling fish, the odor had penetrated Coddie's skin so deeply that neither bath nor soap could make it go away.
Coddie smelled of fish from sunrise to sunset, in winter as in summer.

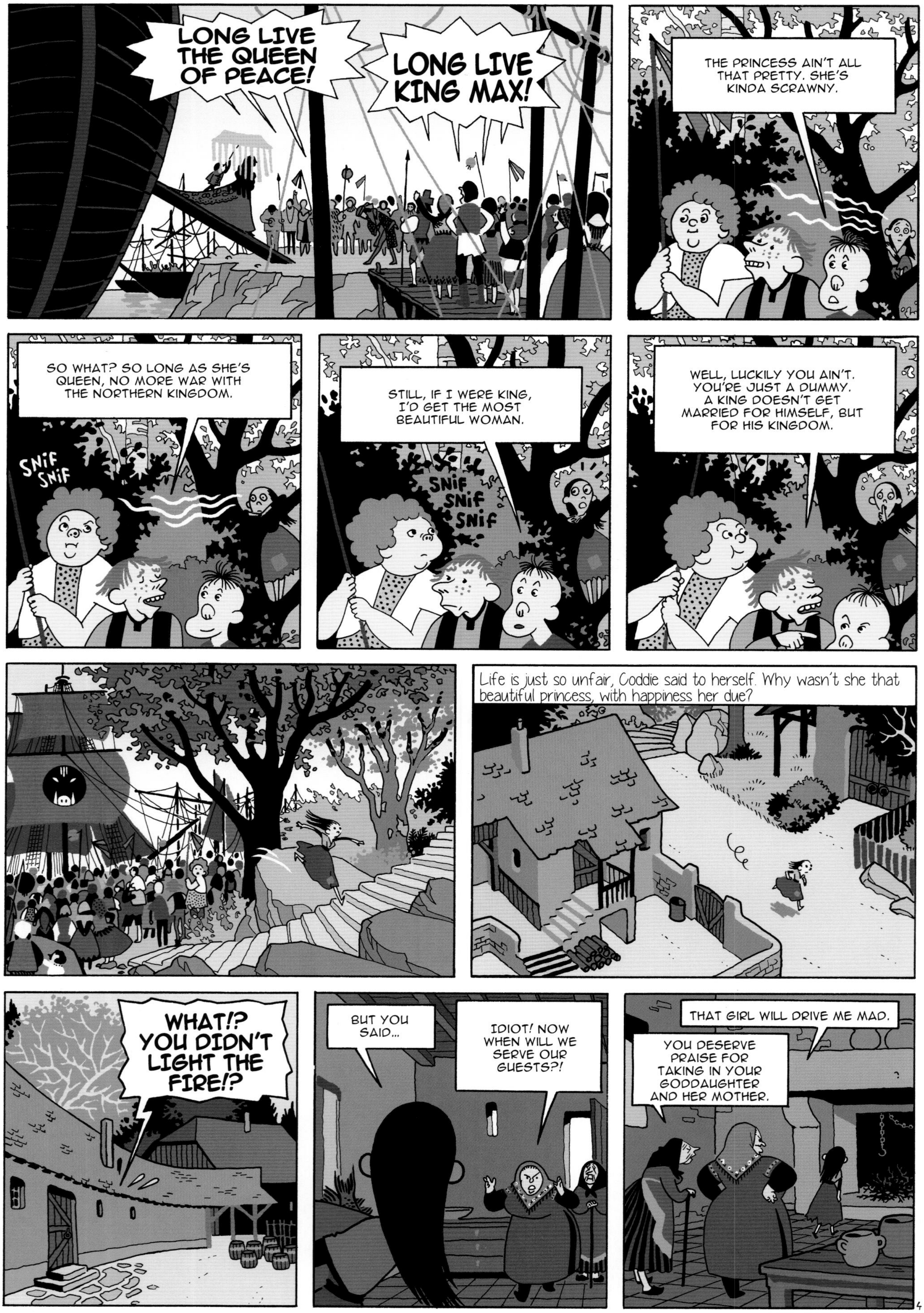
LONG LIVE THE QUEEN OF PEACE!
LONG LIVE KING MAX!
THE PRINCESS AIN'T ALL THAT PRETTY. SHE'S KINDA SCRAWNY.
SO WHAT? SO LONG AS SHE'S QUEEN, NO MORE WAR WITH THE NORTHERN KINGDOM.
SNIF SNIF
STILL, IF I WERE KING, I'D GET THE MOST BEAUTIFUL WOMAN.
SNIF SNIF SNIF
WELL, LUCKILY YOU AIN'T. YOU'RE JUST A DUMMY. A KING DOESN'T GET MARRIED FOR HIMSELF, BUT FOR HIS KINGDOM.
Life is just so unfair, Coddie said to herself. Why wasn't she that beautiful princess, with happiness her due?
WHAT!? YOU DIDN'T LIGHT THE FIRE!?
BUT YOU SAID...
IDIOT! NOW WHEN WILL WE SERVE OUR GUESTS?!
THAT GIRL WILL DRIVE ME MAD.
YOU DESERVE PRAISE FOR TAKING IN YOUR GODDAUGHTER AND HER MOTHER.

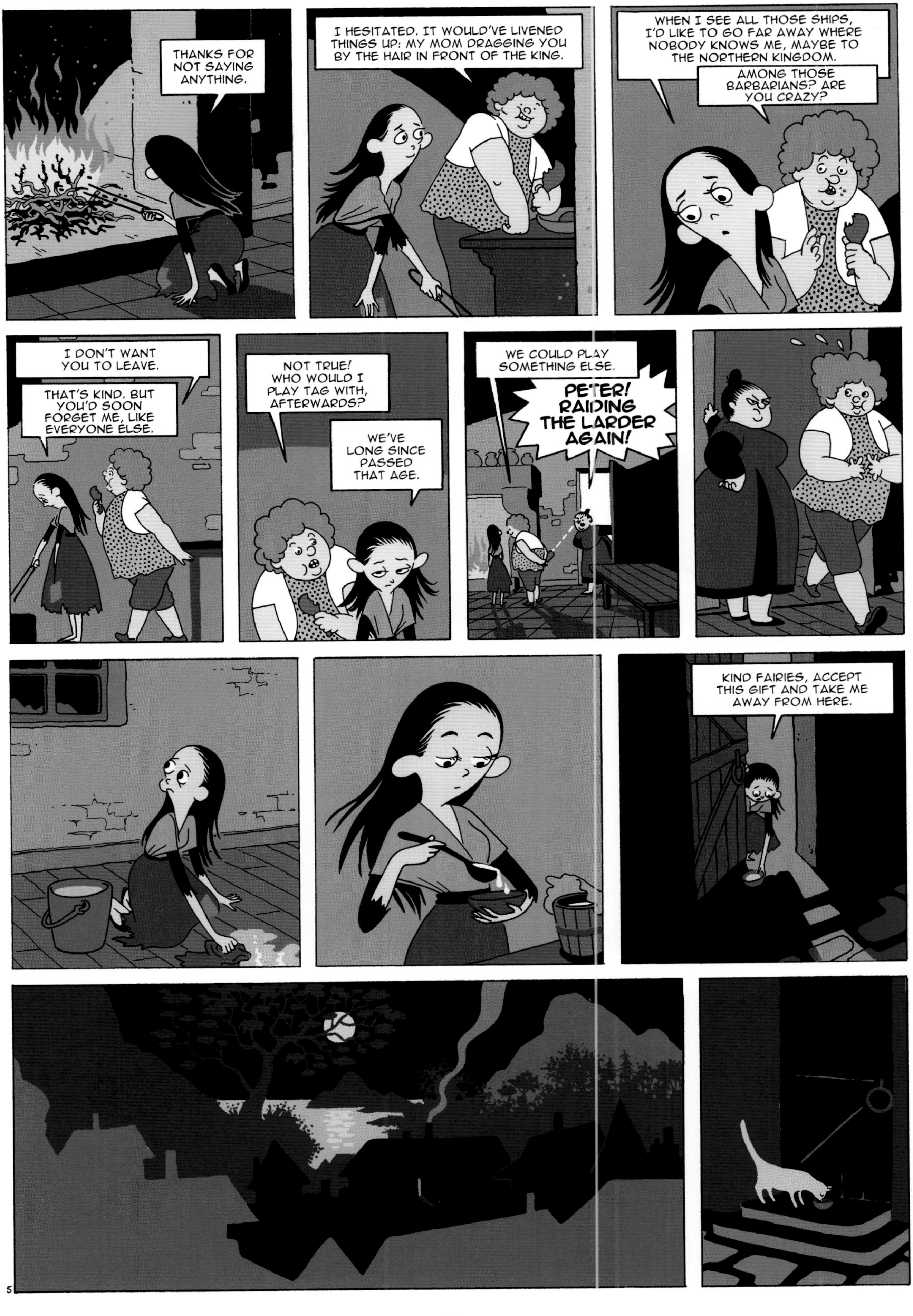
THANKS FOR NOT SAYING ANYTHING.
I HESITATED. IT WOULD'VE LIVENED THINGS UP: MY MOM DRAGGING YOU BY THE HAIR IN FRONT OF THE KING.
WHEN I SEE ALL THOSE SHIPS, I'D LIKE TO GO FAR AWAY WHERE NOBODY KNOWS ME, MAYBE TO THE NORTHERN KINGDOM.
AMONG THOSE BARBARIANS? ARE YOU CRAZY?
I DON'T WANT YOU TO LEAVE.
THAT'S KIND. BUT YOU'D SOON FORGET ME, LIKE EVERYONE ELSE.
NOT TRUE! WHO WOULD I PLAY TAG WITH, AFTERWARDS?
WE'VE LONG SINCE PASSED THAT AGE.
WE COULD PLAY SOMETHING ELSE.
PETER! RAIDING THE LARDER AGAIN!
KIND FAIRIES, ACCEPT THIS GIFT AND TAKE ME AWAY FROM HERE.

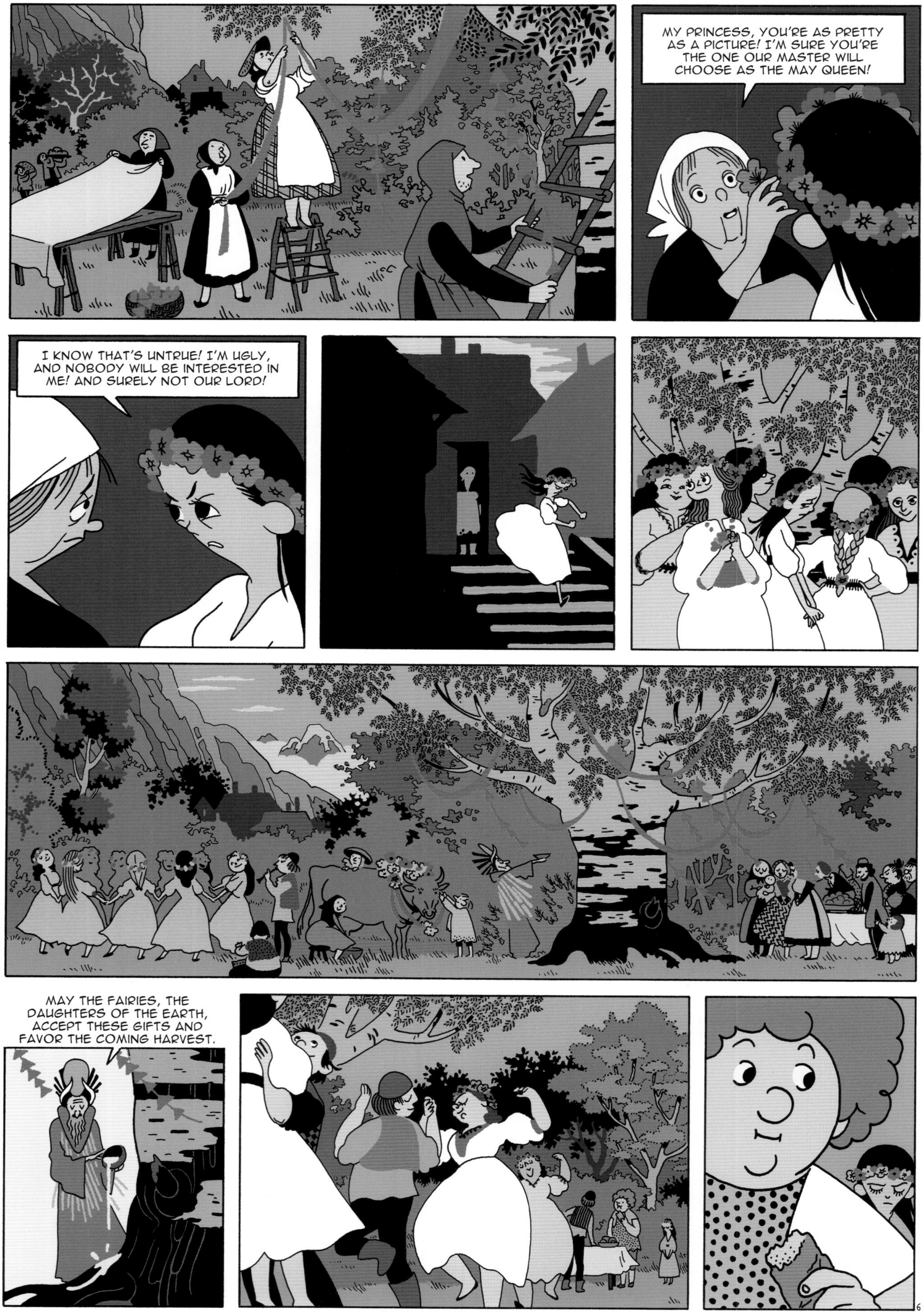
MY PRINCESS, YOU'RE AS PRETTY AS A PICTURE! I'M SURE YOU'RE THE ONE OUR MASTER WILL CHOOSE AS THE MAY QUEEN!
I KNOW THAT'S UNTRUE! I'M UGLY, AND NOBODY WILL BE INTERESTED IN ME! AND SURELY NOT OUR LORD!
MAY THE FAIRIES, THE DAUGHTERS OF THE EARTH, ACCEPT THESE GIFTS AND FAVOR THE COMING HARVEST.
6

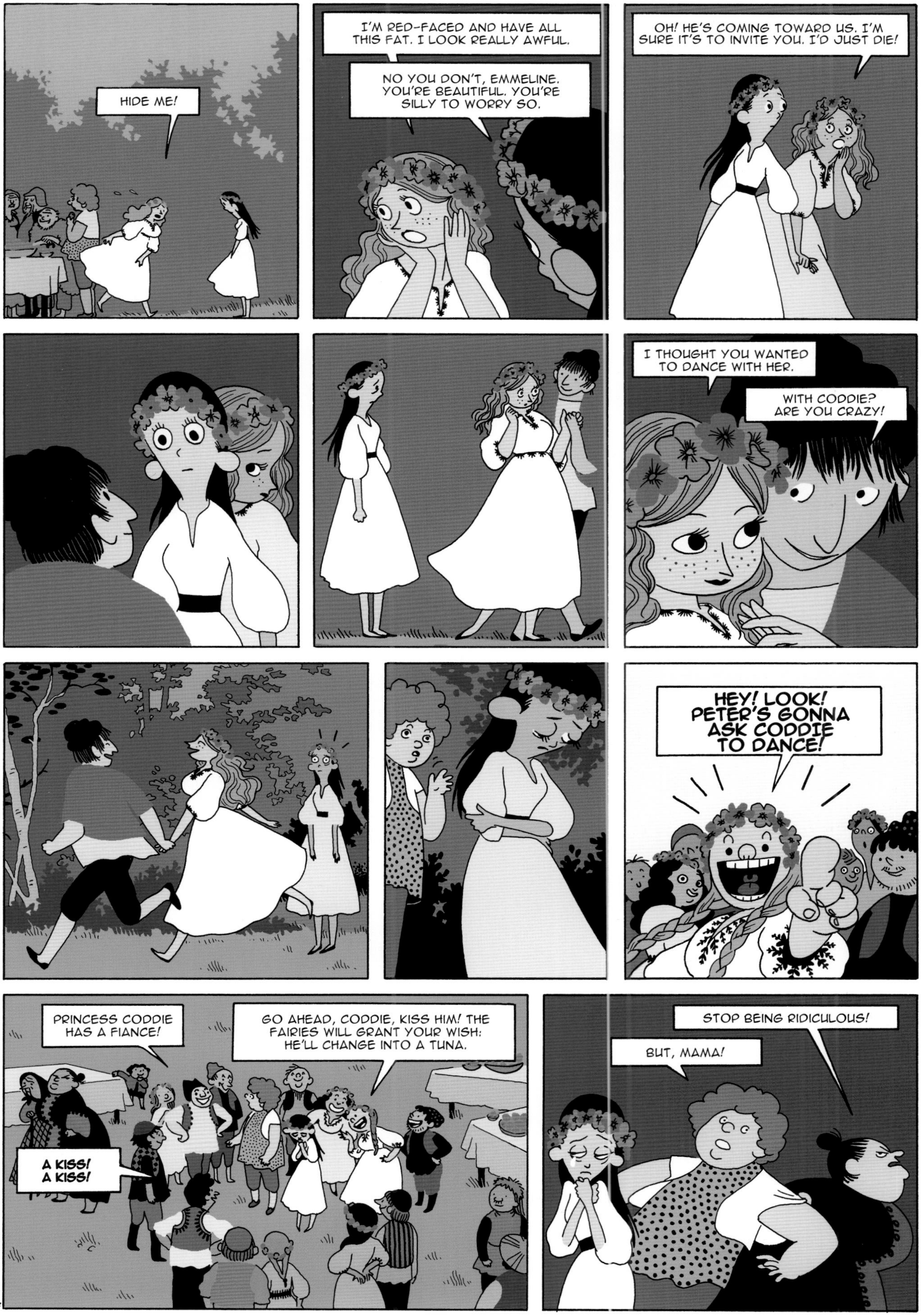
HIDE ME!
I'M RED-FACED AND HAVE ALL THIS FAT. I LOOK REALLY AWFUL.
NO YOU DON'T, EMMELINE. YOU'RE BEAUTIFUL. YOU'RE SILLY TO WORRY SO.
OH! HE'S COMING TOWARD US. I'M SURE IT'S TO INVITE YOU. I'D JUST DIE!
I THOUGHT YOU WANTED TO DANCE WITH HER.
WITH CODDIE? ARE YOU CRAZY!
HEY! LOOK! PETER'S GONNA ASK CODDIE TO DANCE!
PRINCESS CODDIE HAS A FIANCE!
GO AHEAD, CODDIE, KISS HIM! THE FAIRIES WILL GRANT YOUR WISH: HE'LL CHANGE INTO A TUNA.
A KISS! A KISS!
STOP BEING RIDICULOUS!
BUT, MAMA!

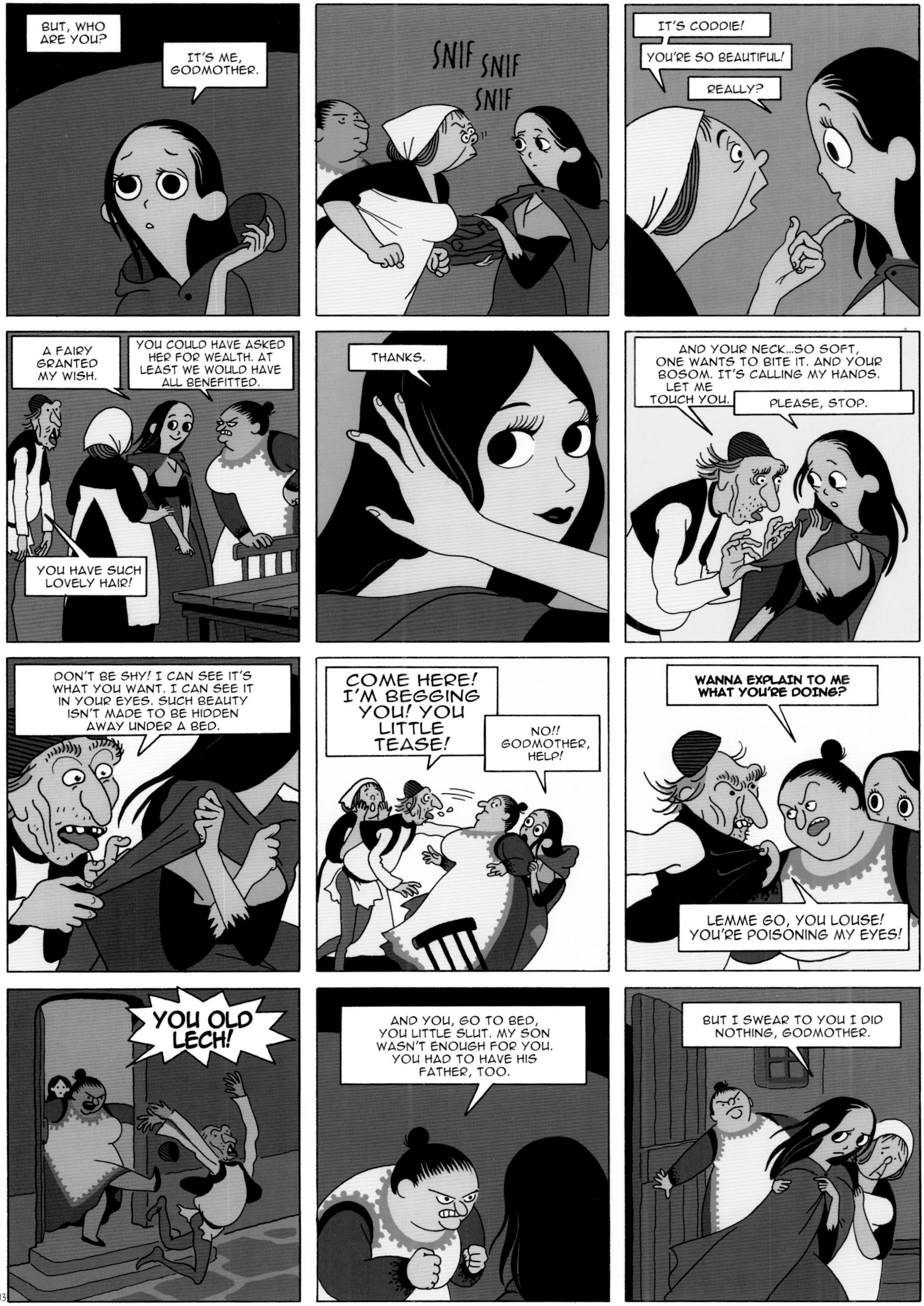
BUT, WHO ARE YOU?
IT'S ME, GODMOTHER.
SNIF SNIF SNIF
IT'S CODDIE!
YOU'RE SO BEAUTIFUL!
REALLY?
A FAIRY GRANTED MY WISH.
YOU COULD HAVE ASKED HER FOR WEALTH. AT LEAST WE WOULD HAVE ALL BENEFITTED.
YOU HAVE SUCH LOVELY HAIR!
THANKS.
AND YOUR NECK...SO SOFT, ONE WANTS TO BITE IT. AND YOUR BOSOM. IT'S CALLING MY HANDS. LET ME TOUCH YOU.
PLEASE, STOP.
DON'T BE SHY! I CAN SEE IT'S WHAT YOU WANT. I CAN SEE IT IN YOUR EYES. SUCH BEAUTY ISN'T MADE TO BE HIDDEN AWAY UNDER A BED.
COME HERE! I'M BEGGING YOU! YOU LITTLE TEASE!
NO!! GODMOTHER, HELP!
WANNA EXPLAIN TO ME WHAT YOU'RE DOING?
LEMME GO, YOU LOUSE! YOU'RE POISONING MY EYES!
YOU OLD LECH!
AND YOU, GO TO BED, YOU LITTLE SLUT. MY SON WASN'T ENOUGH FOR YOU. YOU HAD TO HAVE HIS FATHER, TOO.
BUT I SWEAR TO YOU I DID NOTHING, GODMOTHER.

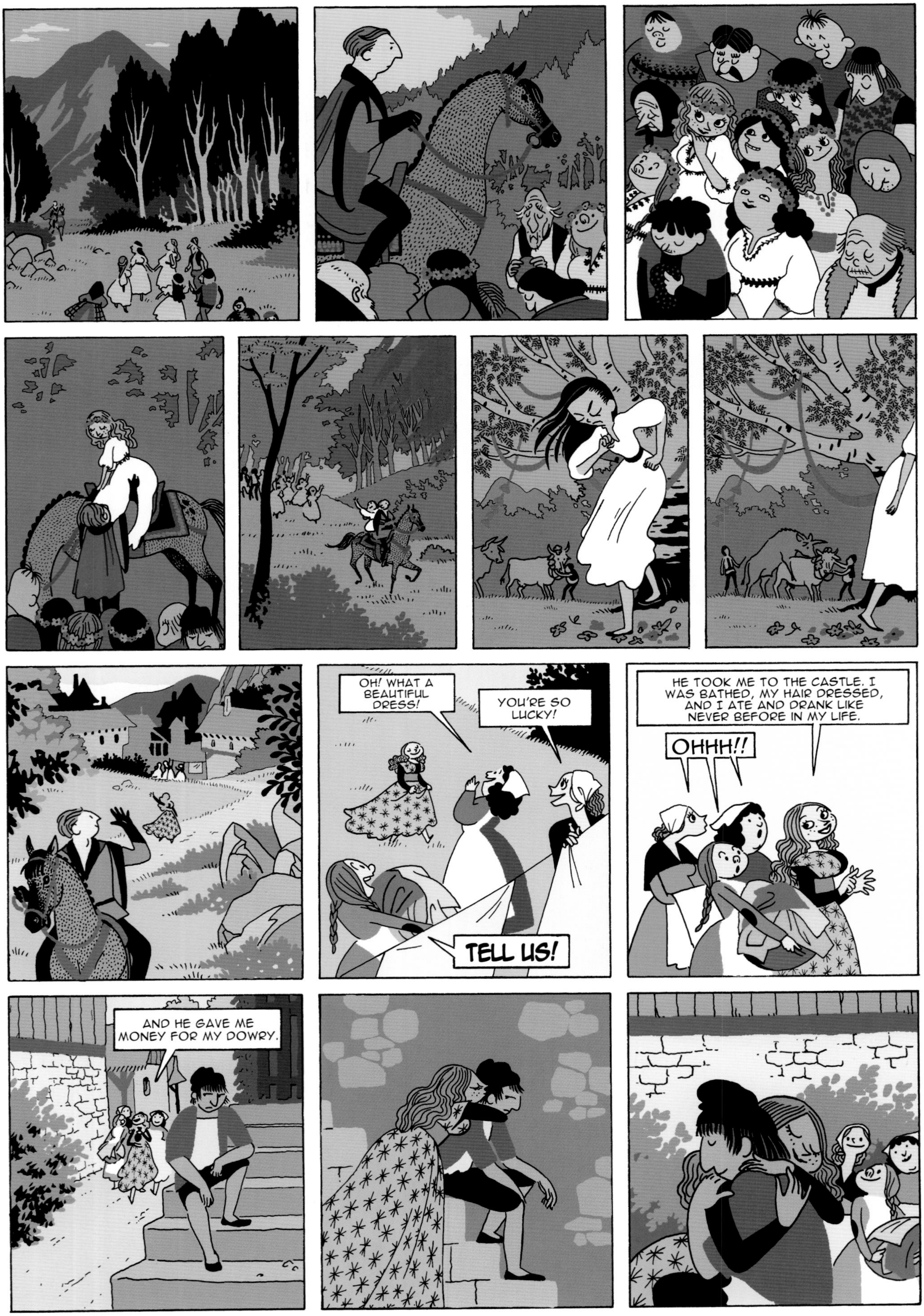
OH! WHAT A BEAUTIFUL DRESS!
YOU'RE SO LUCKY!
TELL US!
HE TOOK ME TO THE CASTLE. I WAS BATHED, MY HAIR DRESSED, AND I ATE AND DRANK LIKE NEVER BEFORE IN MY LIFE.
OHHH!!
AND HE GAVE ME MONEY FOR MY DOWRY.

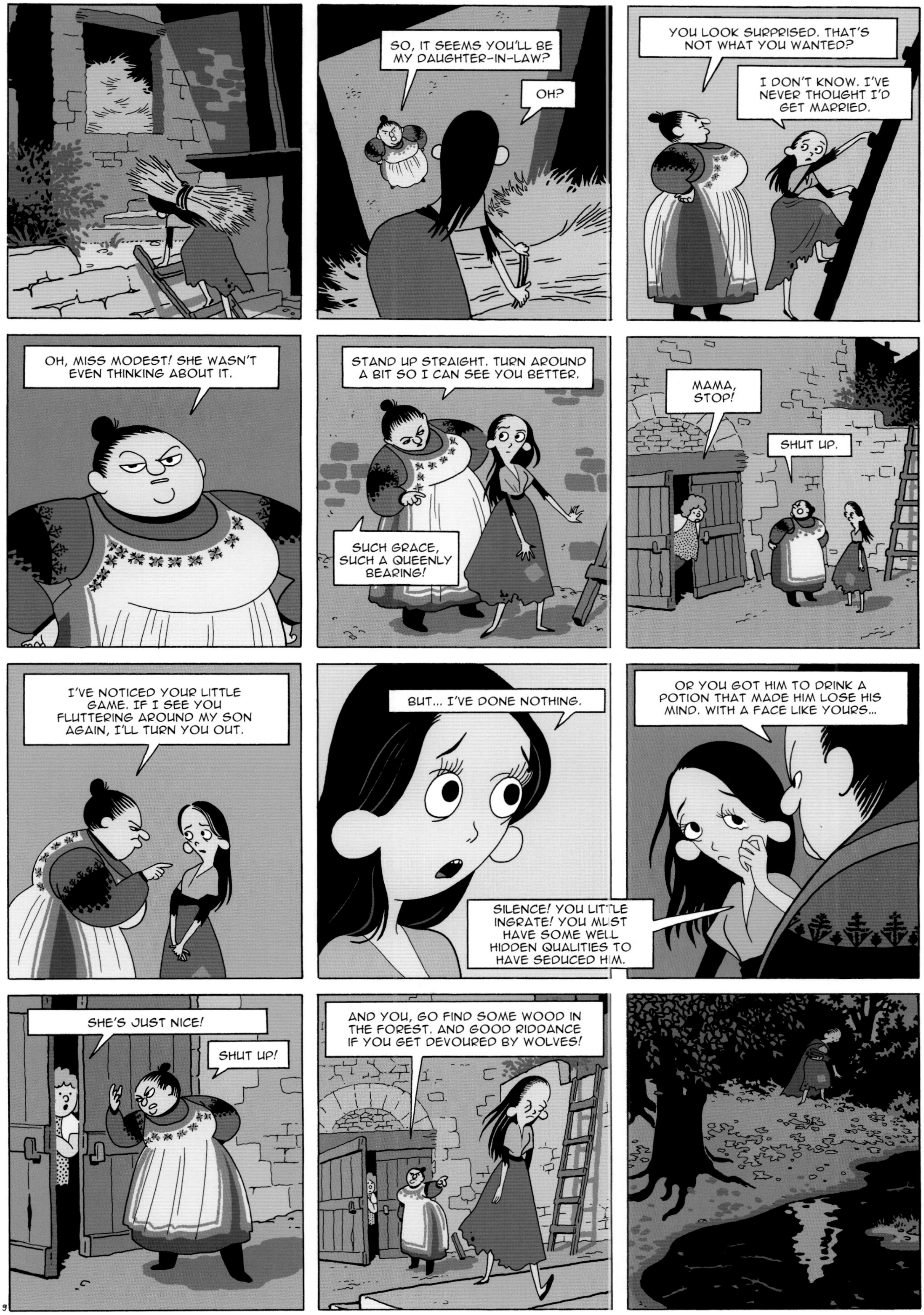

SO, IT SEEMS YOU'LL BE MY DAUGHTER-IN-LAW?
OH?
YOU LOOK SURPRISED. THAT'S NOT WHAT YOU WANTED?
I DON'T KNOW. I'VE NEVER THOUGHT I'D GET MARRIED.
OH, MISS MODEST! SHE WASN'T EVEN THINKING ABOUT IT.
STAND UP STRAIGHT. TURN AROUND A BIT SO I CAN SEE YOU BETTER.
SUCH GRACE, SUCH A QUEENLY BEARING!
MAMA, STOP!
SHUT UP.
I'VE NOTICED YOUR LITTLE GAME. IF I SEE YOU FLUTTERING AROUND MY SON AGAIN, I'LL TURN YOU OUT.
BUT... I'VE DONE NOTHING.
SILENCE! YOU LITTLE INGRATE! YOU MUST HAVE SOME WELL HIDDEN QUALITIES TO HAVE SEDUCED HIM.
OR YOU GOT HIM TO DRINK A POTION THAT MADE HIM LOSE HIS MIND. WITH A FACE LIKE YOURS...
SHE'S JUST NICE!
SHUT UP!
AND YOU, GO FIND SOME WOOD IN THE FOREST. AND GOOD RIDDANCE IF YOU GET DEVOURED BY WOLVES!

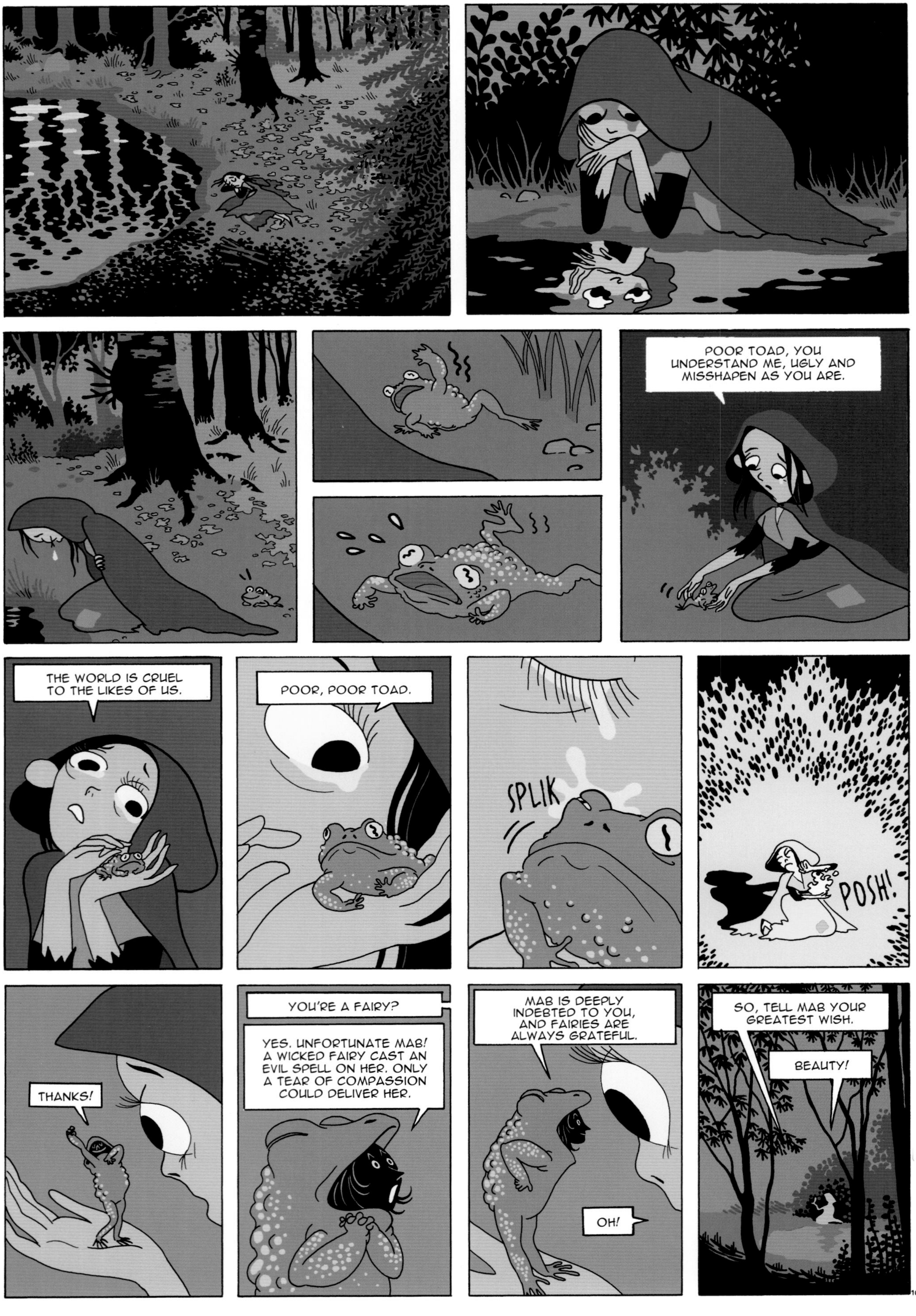
POOR TOAD, YOU UNDERSTAND ME, UGLY AND MISSHAPEN AS YOU ARE.
THE WORLD IS CRUEL TO THE LIKES OF US.
POOR, POOR TOAD.
SPLIK
POSH!
THANKS!
YOU'RE A FAIRY?
YES. UNFORTUNATE MAB! A WICKED FAIRY CAST AN EVIL SPELL ON HER. ONLY A TEAR OF COMPASSION COULD DELIVER HER.
MAB IS DEEPLY INDEBTED TO YOU, AND FAIRIES ARE ALWAYS GRATEFUL.
OH!
SO, TELL MAB YOUR GREATEST WISH.
BEAUTY!
10

IT'S TRUE NATURE HASN'T SPOILED YOU.

I KNOW! I'M UGLY! THE UGLIEST GIRL IN THE WORLD!

THE OTHER GIRLS ALL HAVE SOMETHING NICE, THEY ALL HAVE ADMIRERS, AND NOBODY'S INTERESTED IN ME. IT'S NOT FAIR!

INDEED. AND YOU WANT MAB TO FIX THAT, DON'T YOU?

OH YES!

ALAS, MAB CANNOT CHANGE BEAUTY. UGLY YOU WERE BORN, UGLY YOU WILL REMAIN. THE FAIRIES WOULD HAVE HAD TO HOVER OVER YOUR CRADLE, BUT YOU'RE NOT A KING'S DAUGHTER.

OH.

BUT IF MAB CANNOT CHANGE YOUR NATURE, SHE CAN CHANGE THE PERCEPTION OF IT.

WOULD I BE BEAUTIFUL?

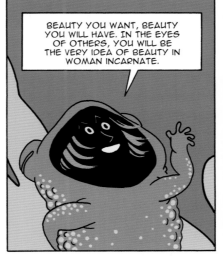

BEAUTY YOU WANT, BEAUTY YOU WILL HAVE. IN THE EYES OF OTHERS, YOU WILL BE THE VERY IDEA OF BEAUTY IN WOMAN INCARNATE.

THROUGH THIS ENCHANTMENT, YOU WILL ECLIPSE THE MOST LOVELY MORTAL WOMAN EVER BORN.

13

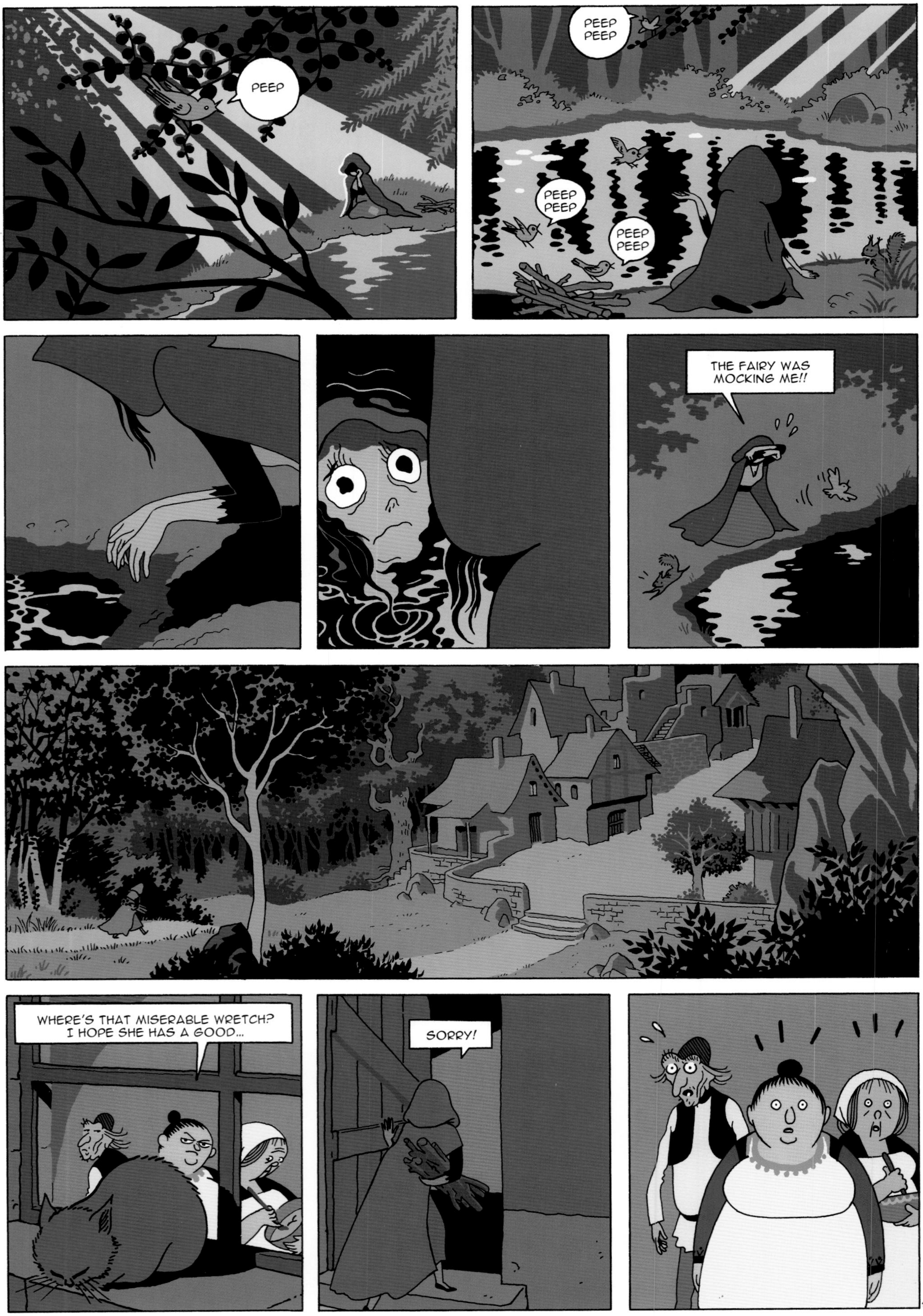
PEEP
PEEP PEEP
PEEP PEEP
PEEP PEEP
THE FAIRY WAS MOCKING ME!!
WHERE'S THAT MISERABLE WRETCH? I HOPE SHE HAS A GOOD...
SORRY!
12

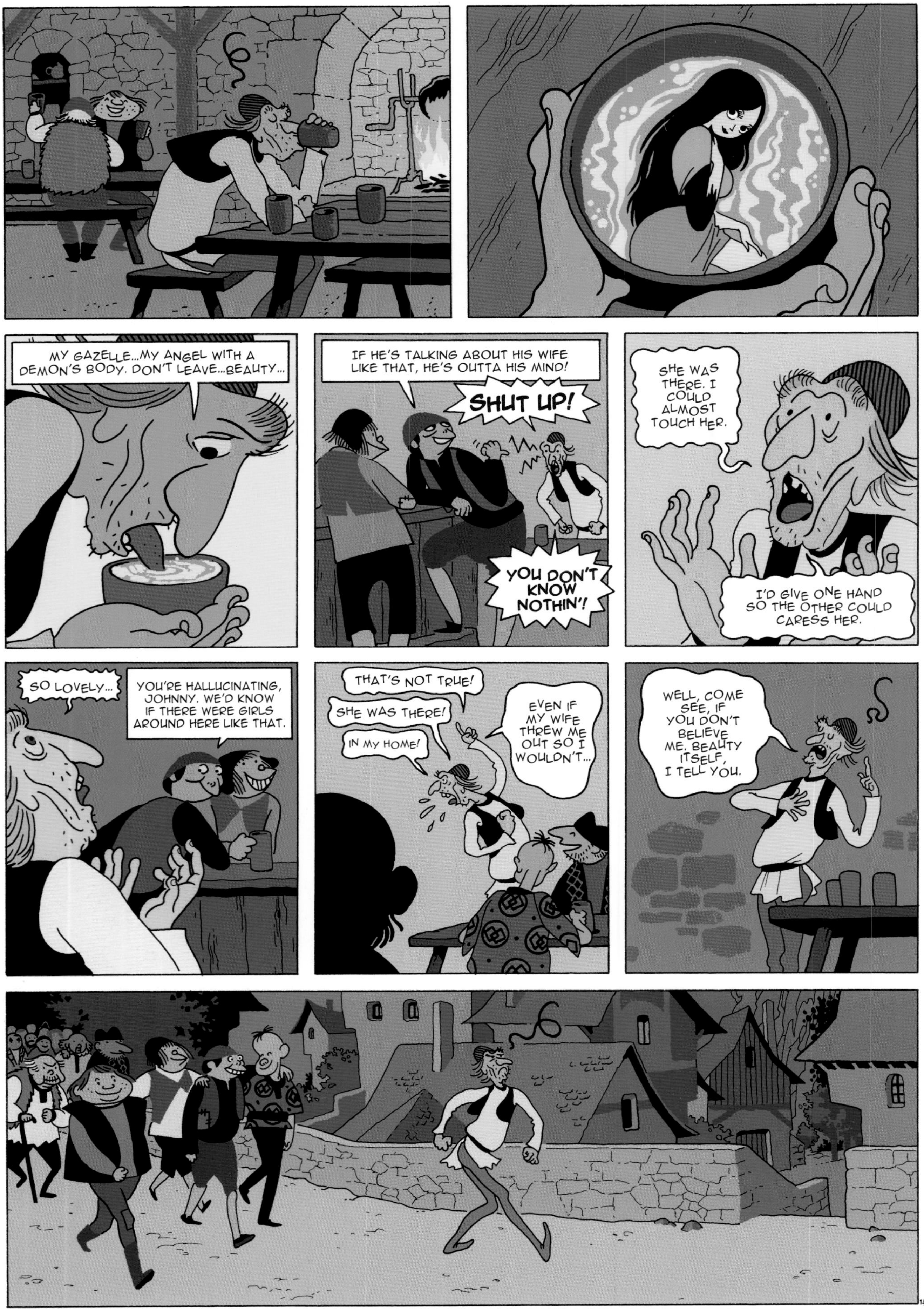
MY GAZELLE...MY ANGEL WITH A DEMON'S BODY. DON'T LEAVE...BEAUTY...
IF HE'S TALKING ABOUT HIS WIFE LIKE THAT, HE'S OUTTA HIS MIND!
SHUT UP!
YOU DON'T KNOW NOTHIN'!
SHE WAS THERE. I COULD ALMOST TOUCH HER.
I'D GIVE ONE HAND SO THE OTHER COULD CARESS HER.
SO LOVELY...
YOU'RE HALLUCINATING, JOHNNY. WE'D KNOW IF THERE WERE GIRLS AROUND HERE LIKE THAT.
THAT'S NOT TRUE!
SHE WAS THERE!
IN MY HOME!
EVEN IF MY WIFE THREW ME OUT SO I WOULDN'T...
WELL, COME SEE, IF YOU DON'T BELIEVE ME. BEAUTY ITSELF, I TELL YOU.
14

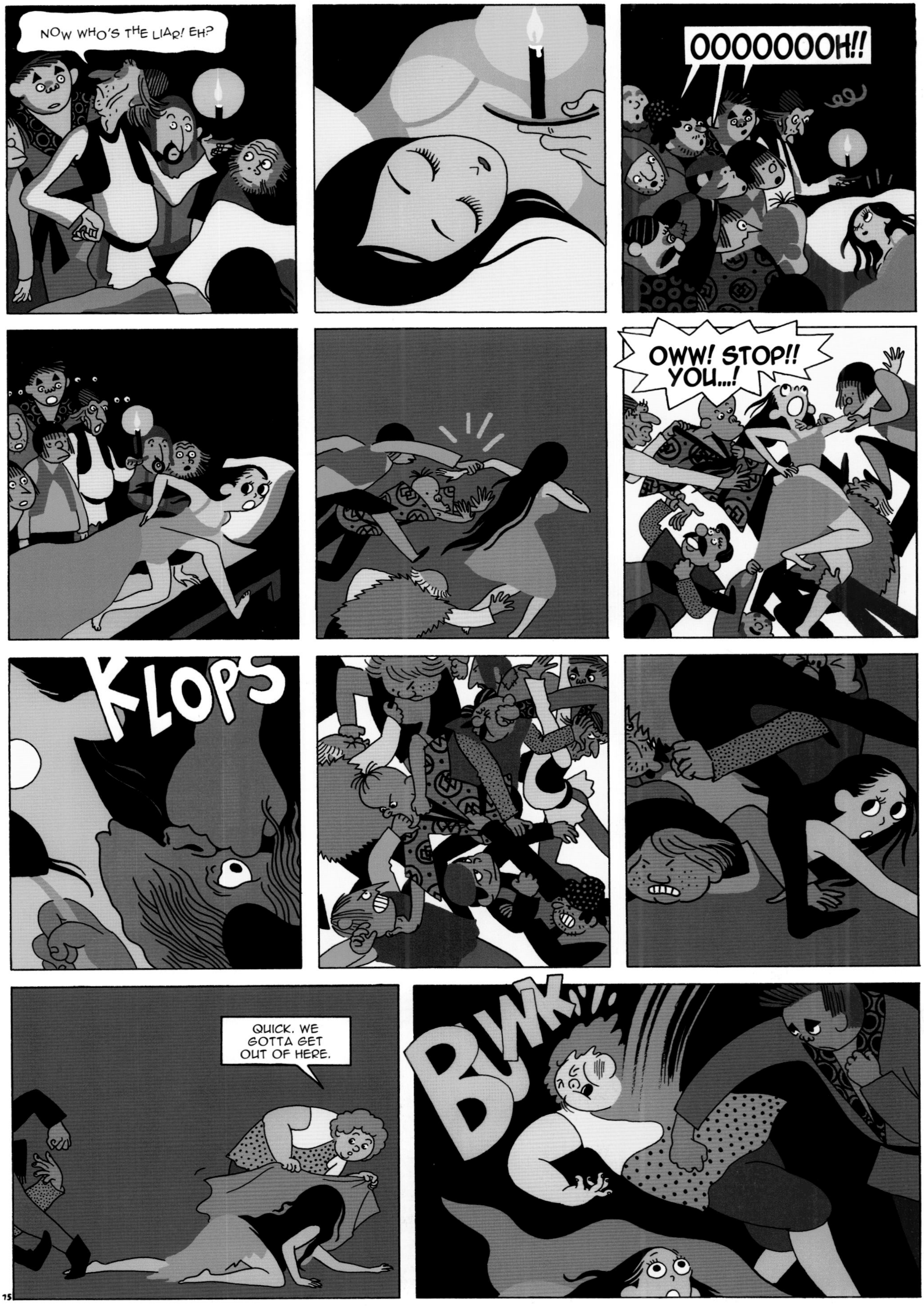
NOW WHO'S THE LIAR! EH?
OOOOOOOH!!
OWW! STOP!! YOU...!
KLOPS
QUICK. WE GOTTA GET OUT OF HERE.
BUNK!!

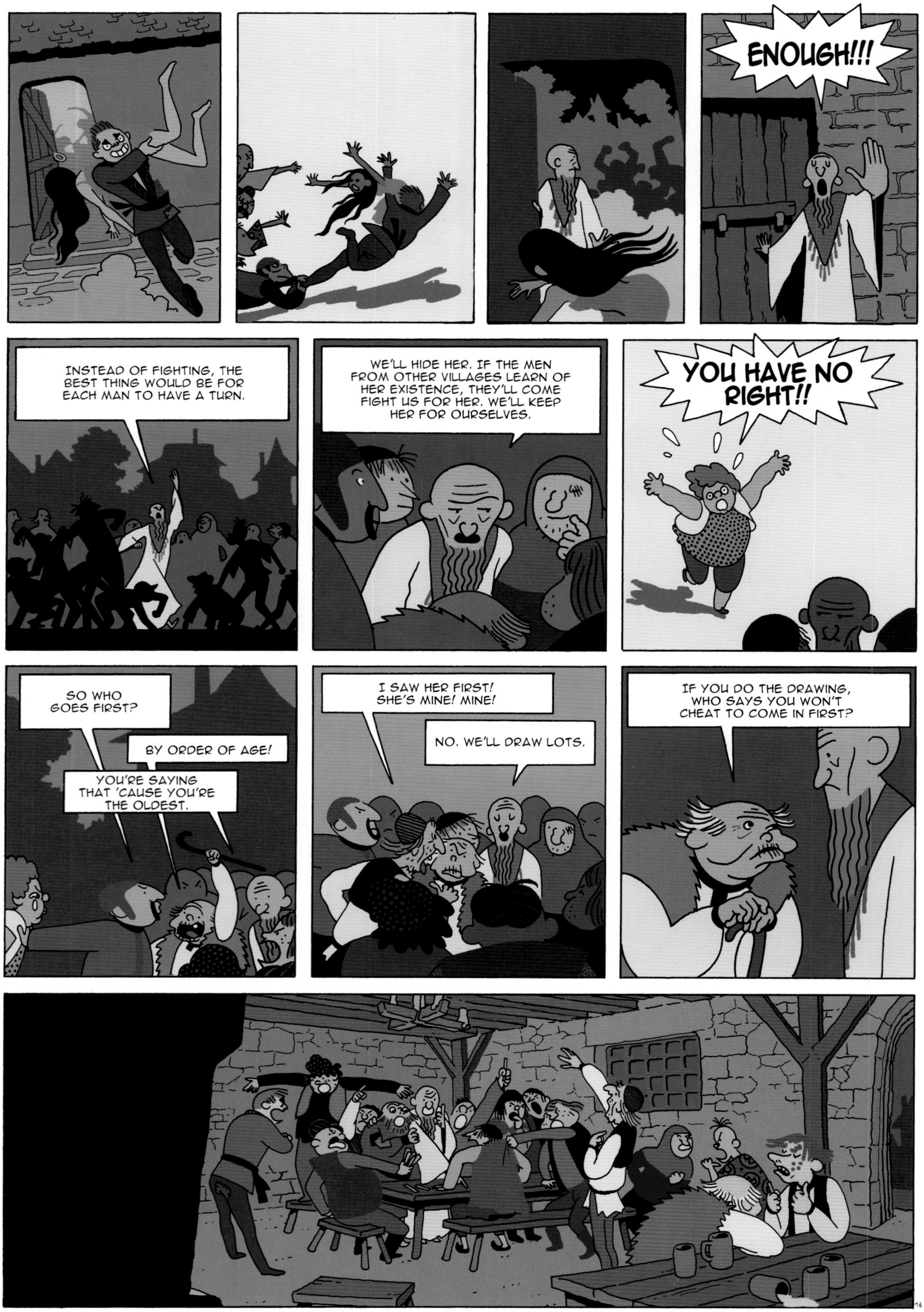

ENOUGH!!!
INSTEAD OF FIGHTING, THE BEST THING WOULD BE FOR EACH MAN TO HAVE A TURN.
WE'LL HIDE HER. IF THE MEN FROM OTHER VILLAGES LEARN OF HER EXISTENCE, THEY'LL COME FIGHT US FOR HER. WE'LL KEEP HER FOR OURSELVES.
YOU HAVE NO RIGHT!!
SO WHO GOES FIRST?
BY ORDER OF AGE!
YOU'RE SAYING THAT 'CAUSE YOU'RE THE OLDEST.
I SAW HER FIRST! SHE'S MINE! MINE!
NO. WE'LL DRAW LOTS.
IF YOU DO THE DRAWING, WHO SAYS YOU WON'T CHEAT TO COME IN FIRST?

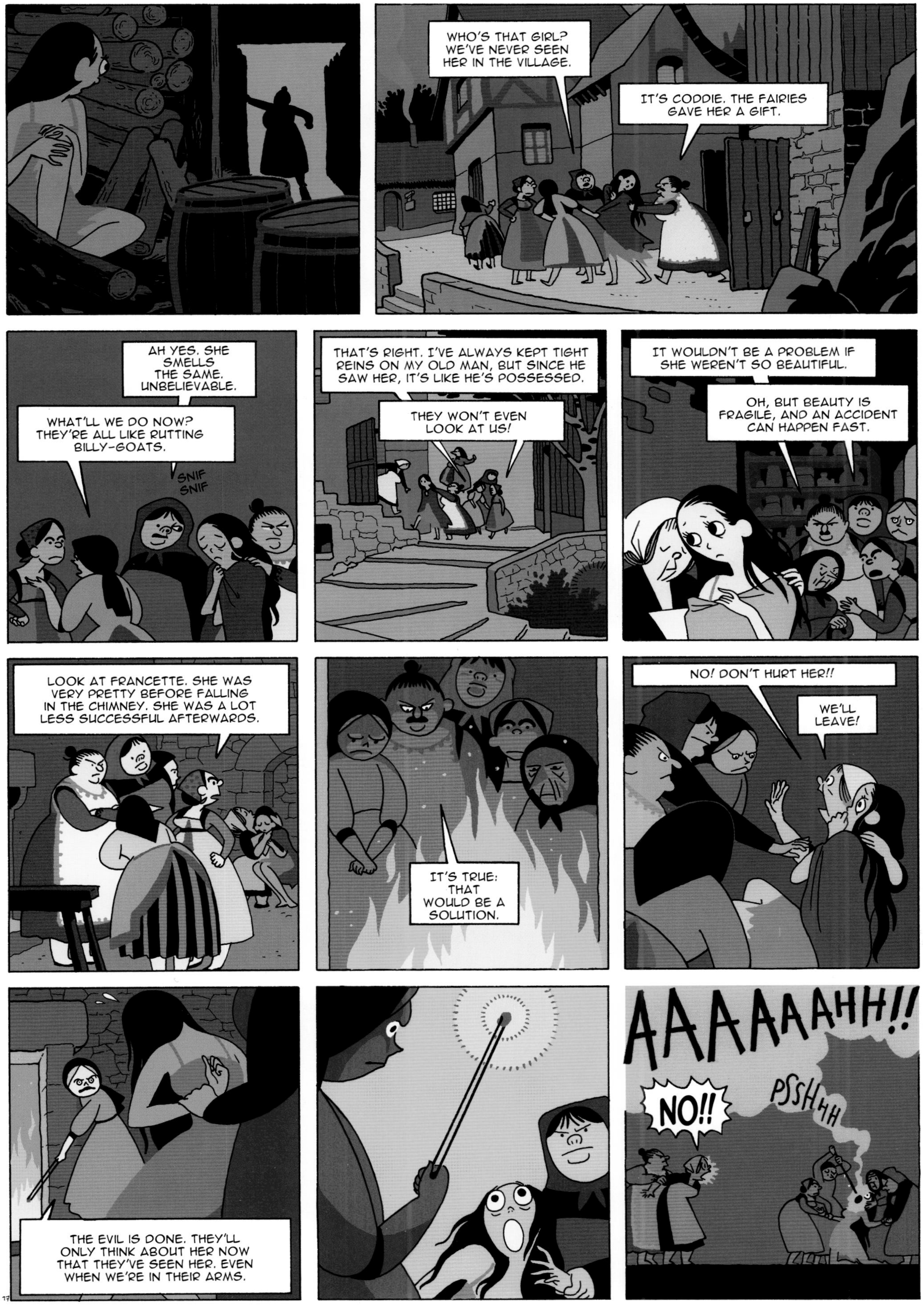

WHO'S THAT GIRL? WE'VE NEVER SEEN HER IN THE VILLAGE.
IT'S CODDIE. THE FAIRIES GAVE HER A GIFT.
AH YES. SHE SMELLS THE SAME. UNBELIEVABLE.
WHAT'LL WE DO NOW? THEY'RE ALL LIKE RUTTING BILLY-GOATS.
SNIF SNIF
THAT'S RIGHT. I'VE ALWAYS KEPT TIGHT REINS ON MY OLD MAN, BUT SINCE HE SAW HER, IT'S LIKE HE'S POSSESSED.
THEY WON'T EVEN LOOK AT US!
IT WOULDN'T BE A PROBLEM IF SHE WEREN'T SO BEAUTIFUL.
OH, BUT BEAUTY IS FRAGILE, AND AN ACCIDENT CAN HAPPEN FAST.
LOOK AT FRANCETTE. SHE WAS VERY PRETTY BEFORE FALLING IN THE CHIMNEY. SHE WAS A LOT LESS SUCCESSFUL AFTERWARDS.
IT'S TRUE: THAT WOULD BE A SOLUTION.
NO! DON'T HURT HER!!
WE'LL LEAVE!
THE EVIL IS DONE. THEY'LL ONLY THINK ABOUT HER NOW THAT THEY'VE SEEN HER. EVEN WHEN WE'RE IN THEIR ARMS.
AAAAAAHH!!
NO!!
PSSHHH

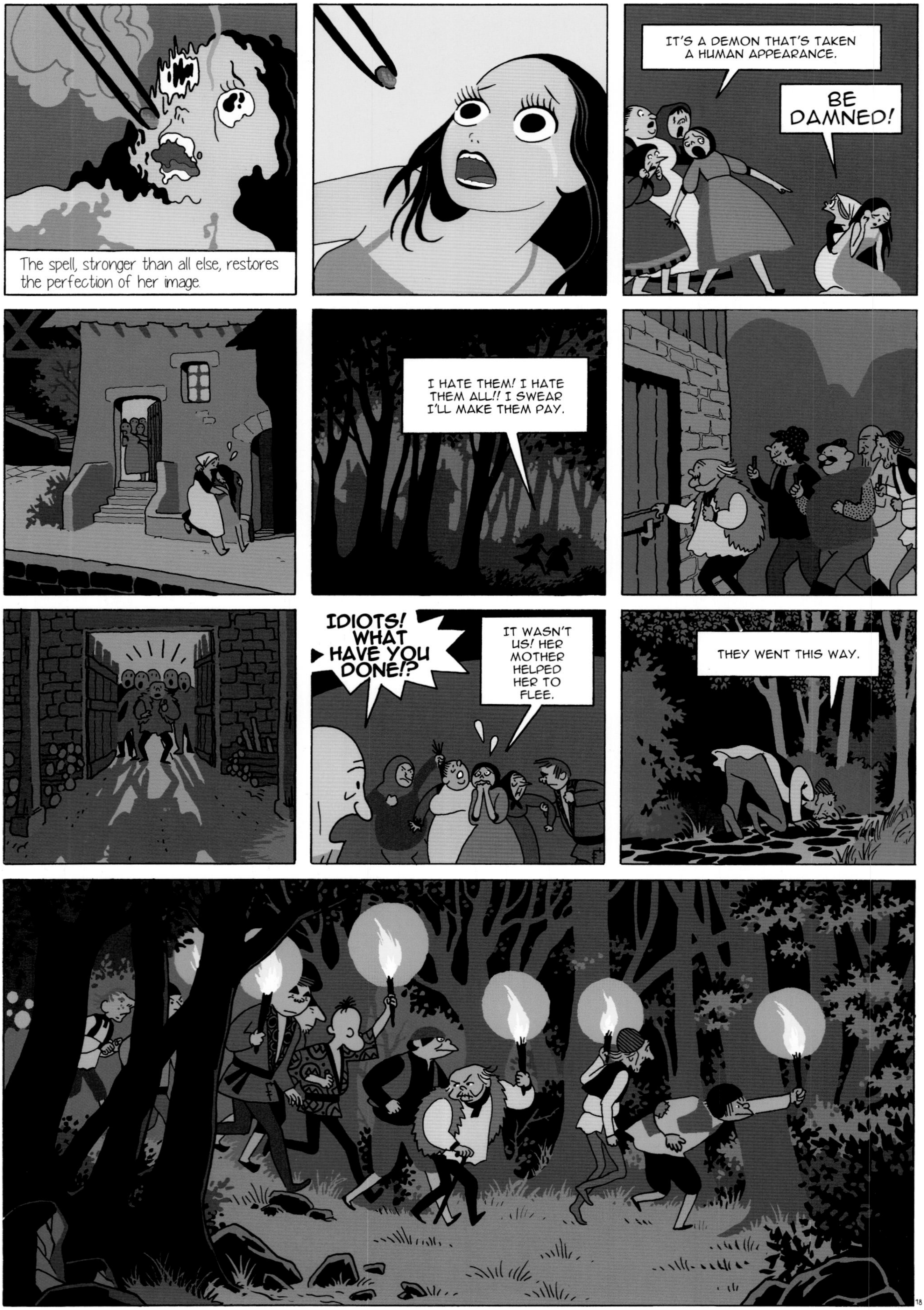
The spell, stronger than all else, restores the perfection of her image.
IT'S A DEMON THAT'S TAKEN A HUMAN APPEARANCE.
BE DAMNED!
I HATE THEM! I HATE THEM ALL!! I SWEAR I'LL MAKE THEM PAY.
IDIOTS! WHAT HAVE YOU DONE!?
IT WASN'T US! HER MOTHER HELPED HER TO FLEE.
THEY WENT THIS WAY.
18

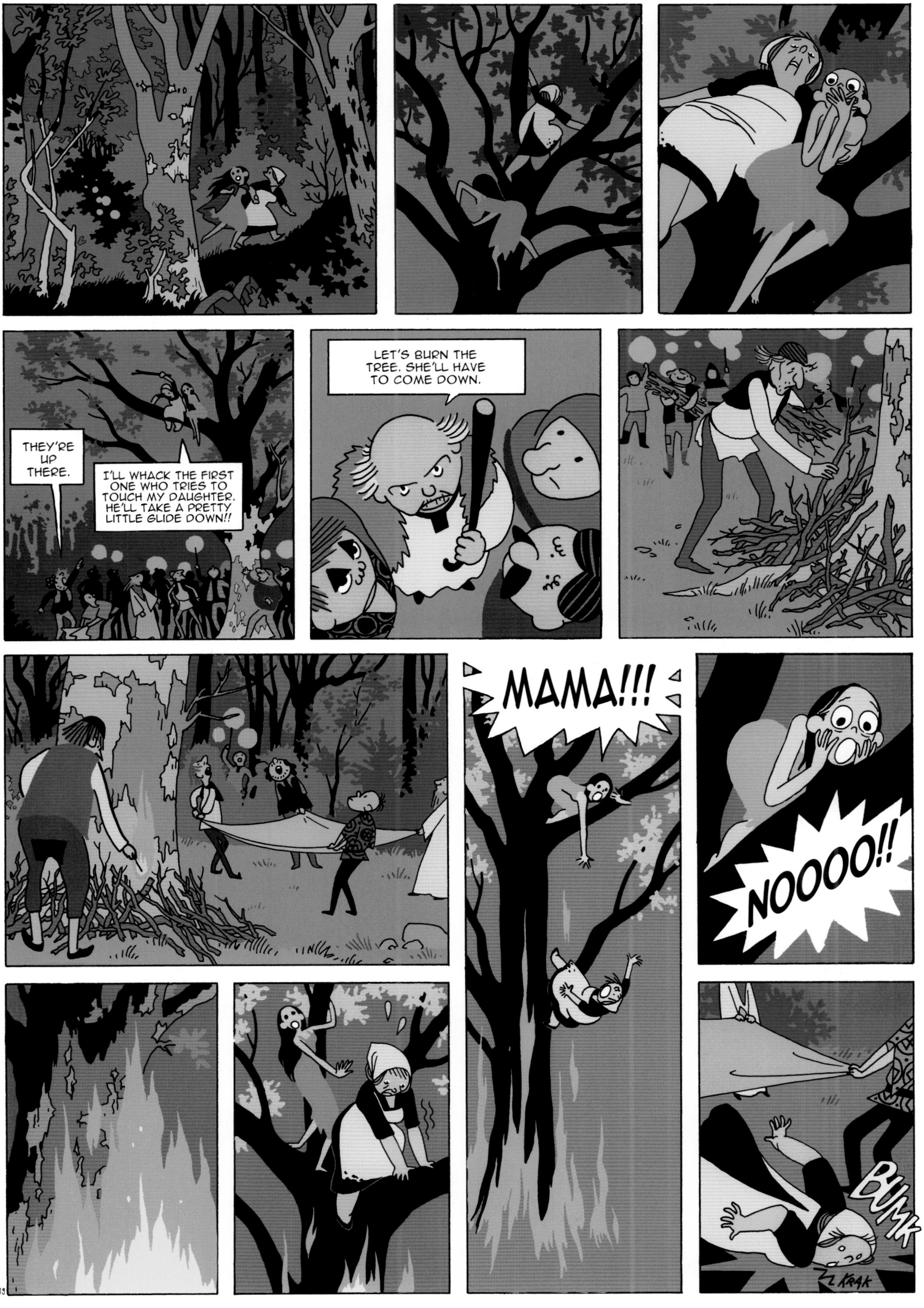
THEY'RE UP THERE.
I'LL WHACK THE FIRST ONE WHO TRIES TO TOUCH MY DAUGHTER. HE'LL TAKE A PRETTY LITTLE GLIDE DOWN!!
LET'S BURN THE TREE. SHE'LL HAVE TO COME DOWN.
MAMA!!!
NOOOO!!
BUMK
KRAK

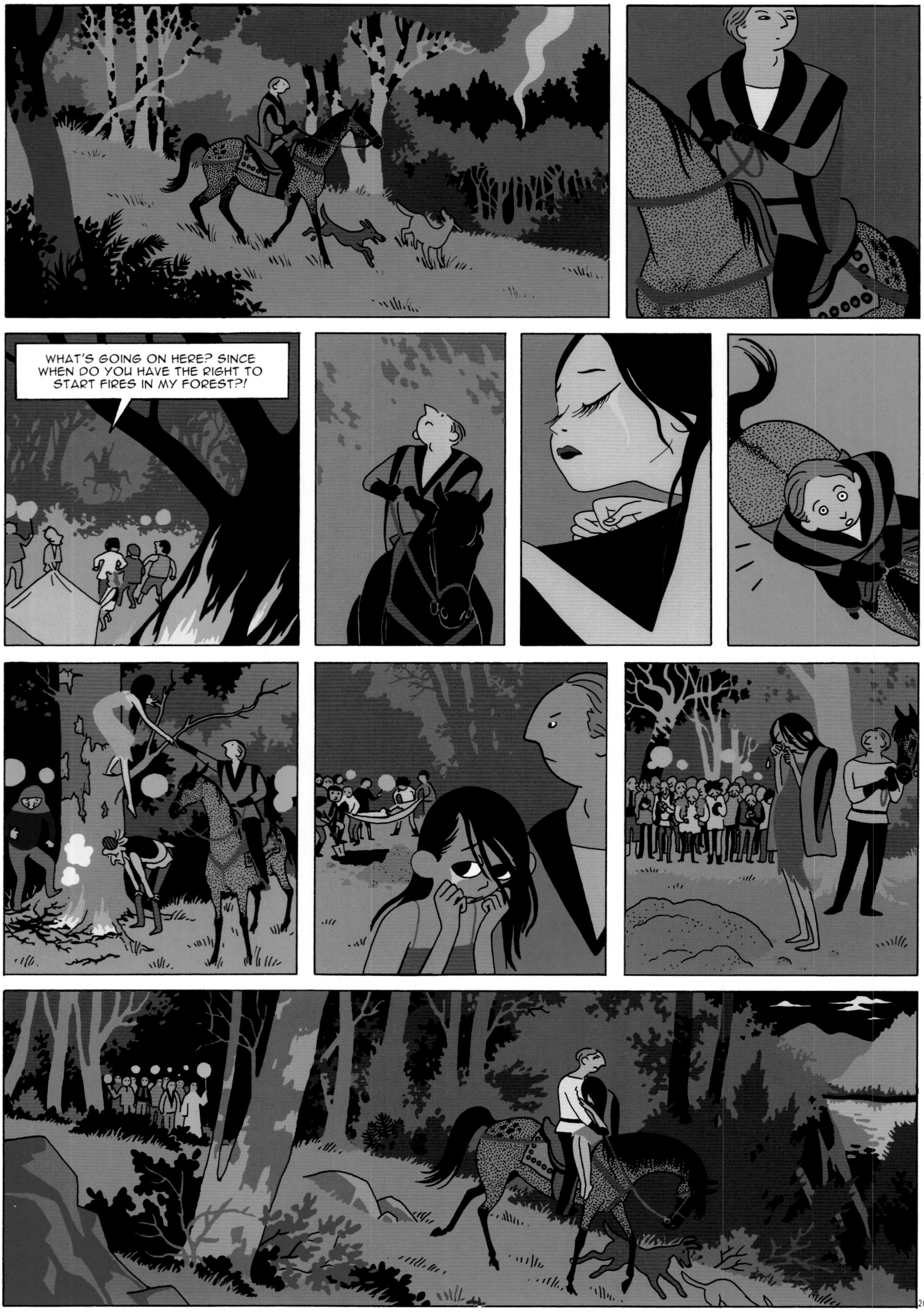
WHAT'S GOING ON HERE? SINCE WHEN DO YOU HAVE THE RIGHT TO START FIRES IN MY FOREST?!

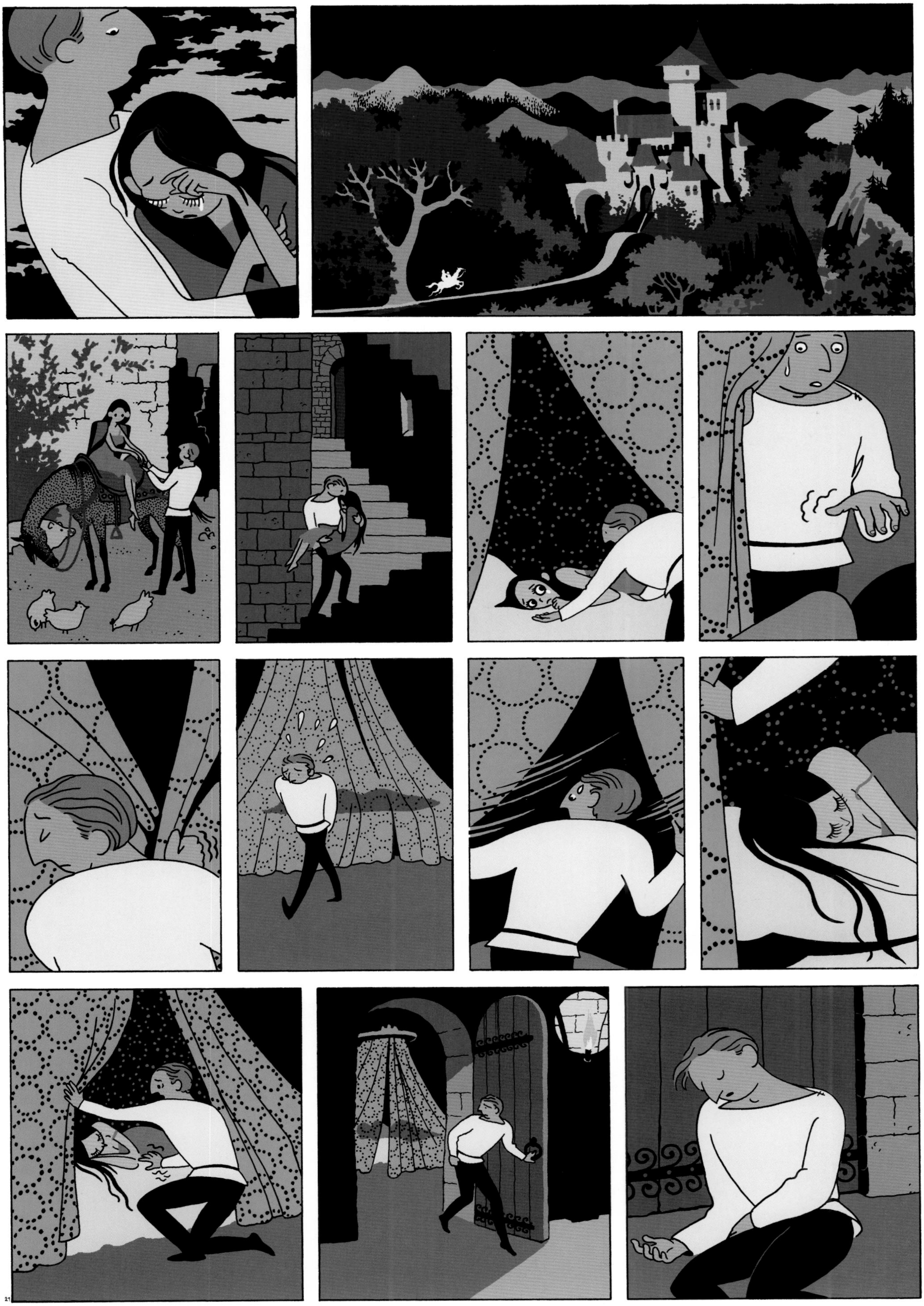

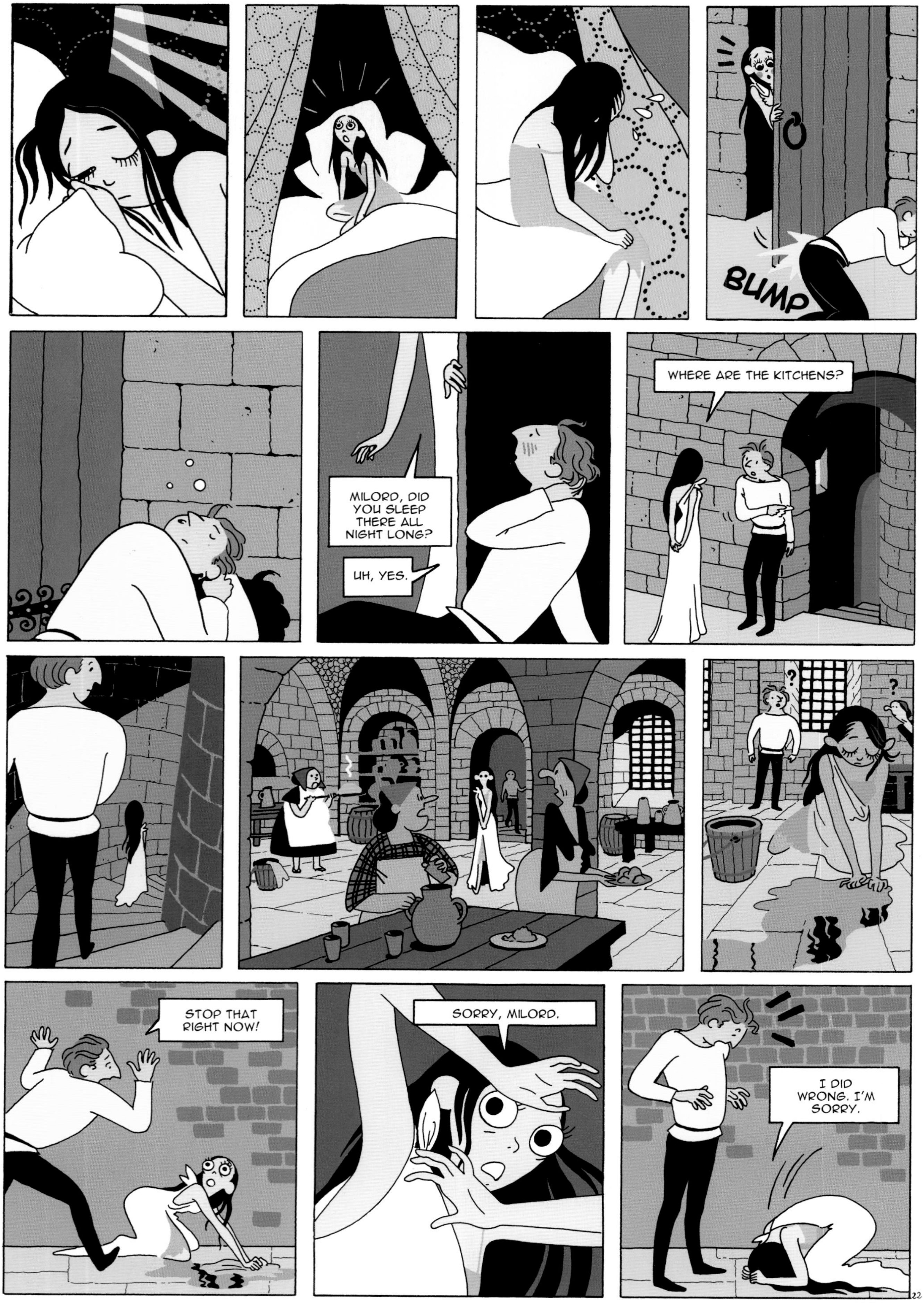
BUMP
MILORD, DID YOU SLEEP THERE ALL NIGHT LONG?
UH, YES.
WHERE ARE THE KITCHENS?
STOP THAT RIGHT NOW!
SORRY, MILORD.
I DID WRONG. I'M SORRY.

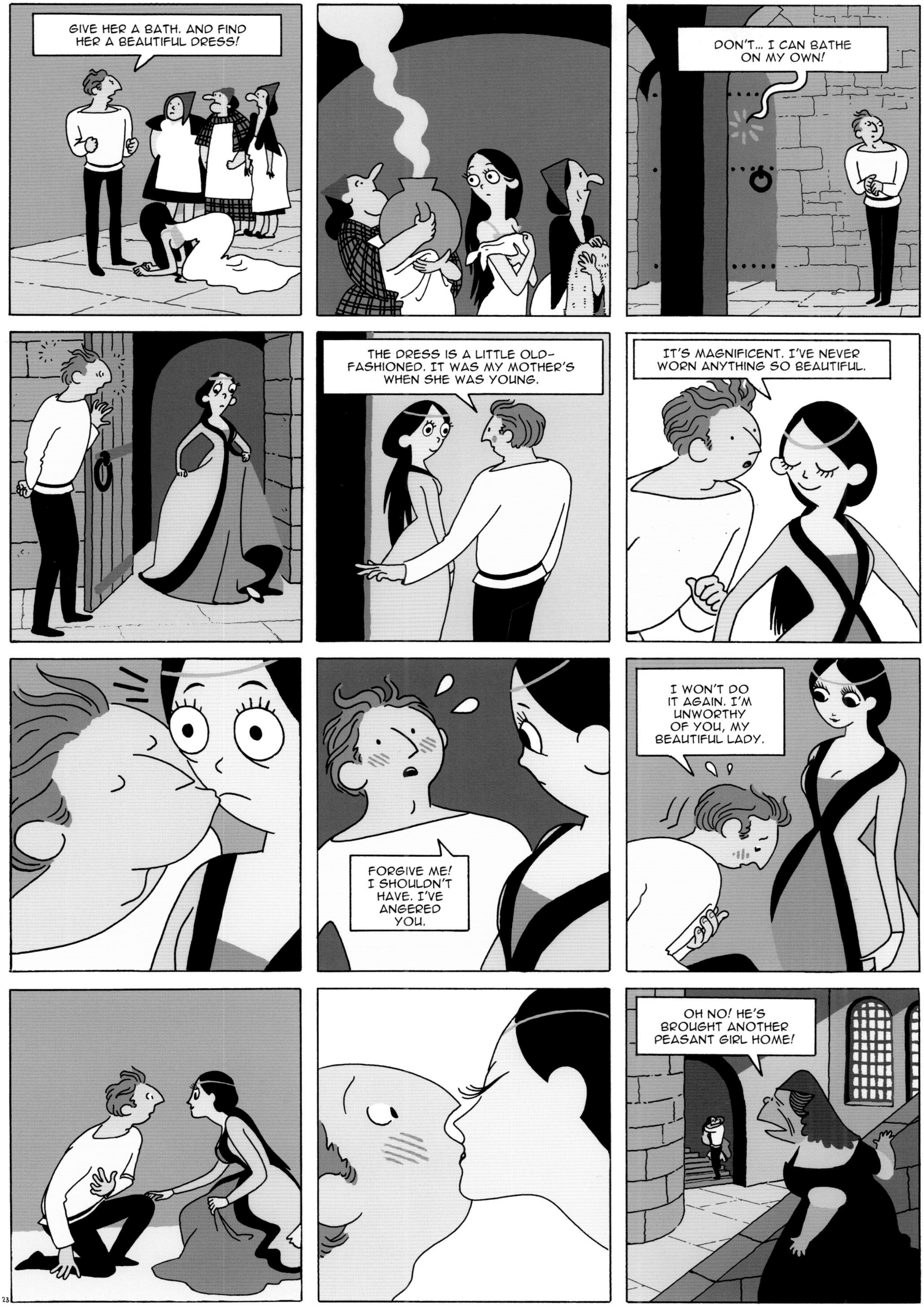
GIVE HER A BATH. AND FIND HER A BEAUTIFUL DRESS!
DON'T... I CAN BATHE ON MY OWN!
THE DRESS IS A LITTLE OLD-FASHIONED. IT WAS MY MOTHER'S WHEN SHE WAS YOUNG.
IT'S MAGNIFICENT. I'VE NEVER WORN ANYTHING SO BEAUTIFUL.
FORGIVE ME! I SHOULDN'T HAVE. I'VE ANGERED YOU.
I WON'T DO IT AGAIN. I'M UNWORTHY OF YOU, MY BEAUTIFUL LADY.
OH NO! HE'S BROUGHT ANOTHER PEASANT GIRL HOME!

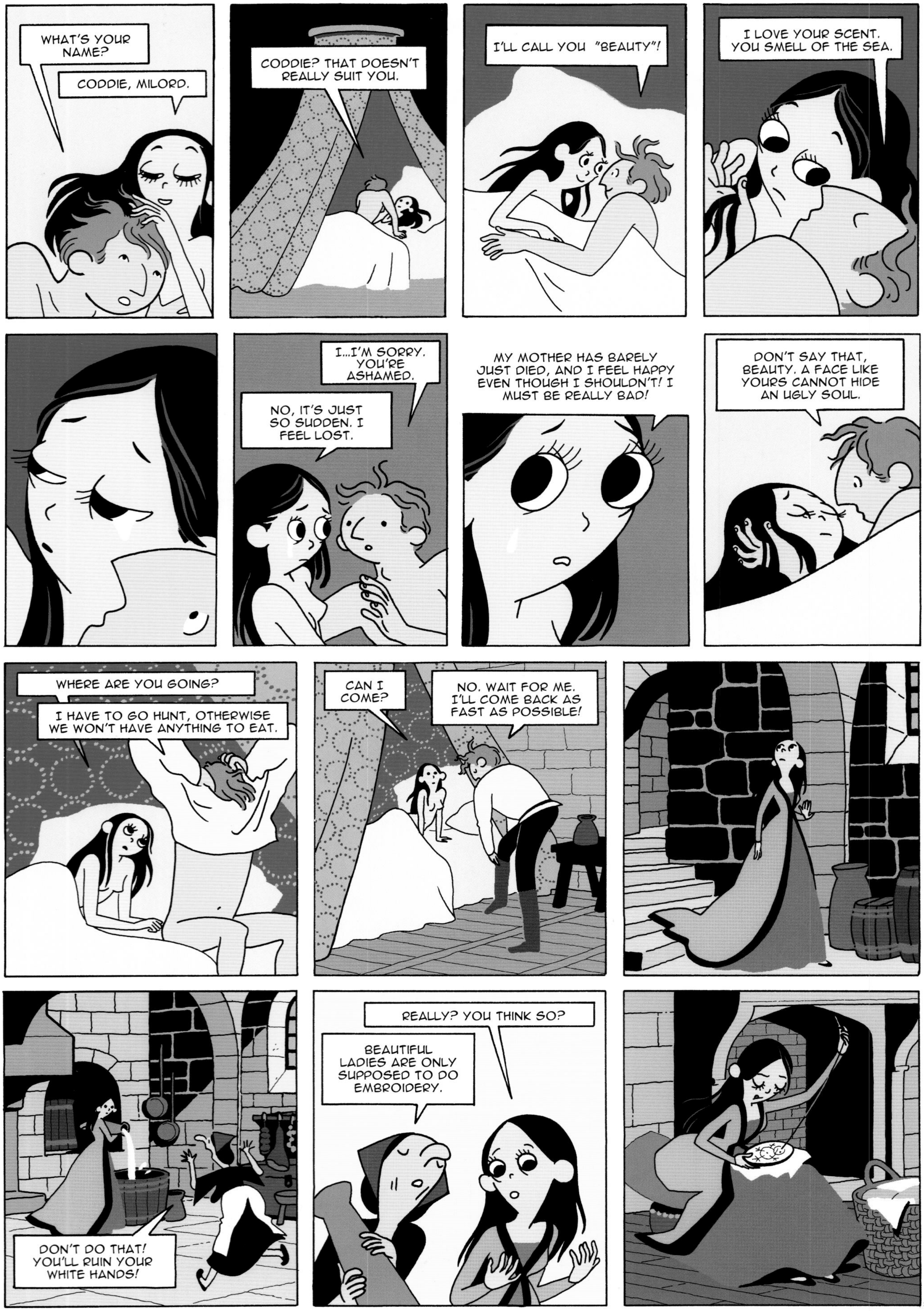
WHAT'S YOUR NAME?
CODDIE, MILORD.
CODDIE? THAT DOESN'T REALLY SUIT YOU.
I'LL CALL YOU "BEAUTY"!
I LOVE YOUR SCENT. YOU SMELL OF THE SEA.
I...I'M SORRY. YOU'RE ASHAMED.
NO, IT'S JUST SO SUDDEN. I FEEL LOST.
MY MOTHER HAS BARELY JUST DIED, AND I FEEL HAPPY EVEN THOUGH I SHOULDN'T! I MUST BE REALLY BAD!
DON'T SAY THAT, BEAUTY. A FACE LIKE YOURS CANNOT HIDE AN UGLY SOUL.
WHERE ARE YOU GOING?
I HAVE TO GO HUNT, OTHERWISE WE WON'T HAVE ANYTHING TO EAT.
CAN I COME?
NO. WAIT FOR ME. I'LL COME BACK AS FAST AS POSSIBLE!
DON'T DO THAT! YOU'LL RUIN YOUR WHITE HANDS!
REALLY? YOU THINK SO?
BEAUTIFUL LADIES ARE ONLY SUPPOSED TO DO EMBROIDERY.
24

WHY DO YOU STARE AT ME LIKE THAT?
IS SOMETHING WRONG WITH ME?
NO!
IS IT MY HAIR? IS MY HAIRDO MESSED UP?
NO!
MY EARS STICK OUT, I KNOW.
BUT HOW CAN YOU SAY THAT? THEY'RE ADORABLE.
MY CHIN THEN? IT'S UGLY, UH?
NO! IT'S... IT'S...
WELL, WHAT THEN?
YOU'RE NICE.
NOTHING! YOU'RE PERFECT!
I'M NOT NICE. I DON'T HAVE WORDS TO EXPRESS...
FORGIVE ME, BEAUTY.
STOP.

25

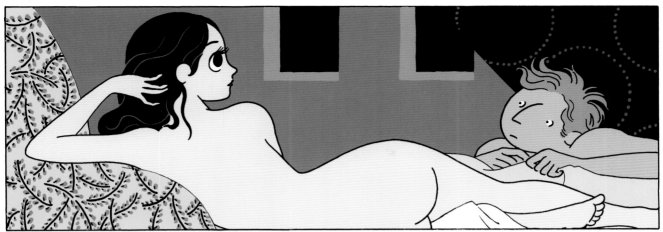

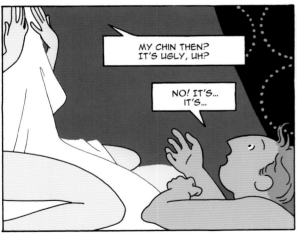

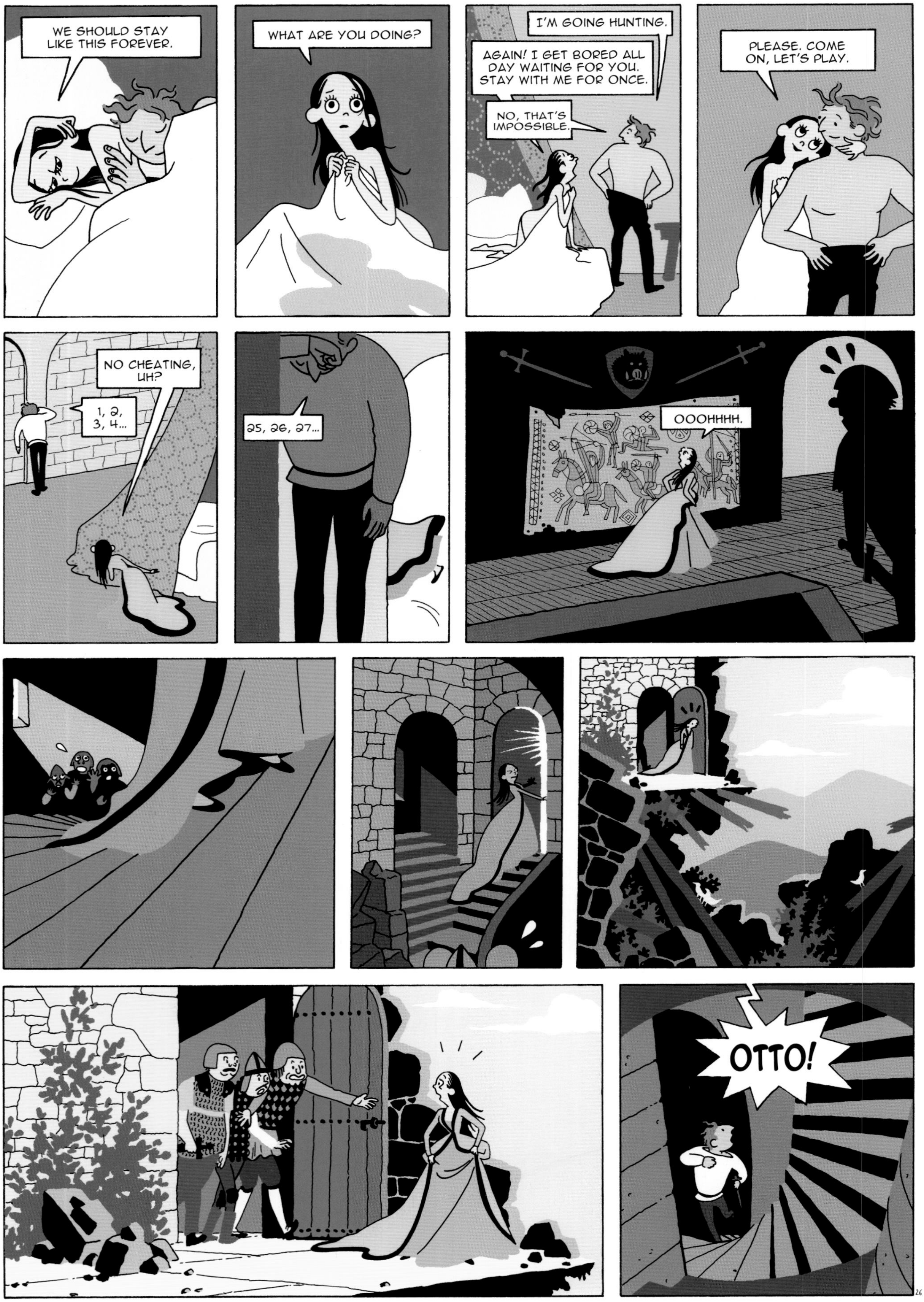
WE SHOULD STAY LIKE THIS FOREVER.
WHAT ARE YOU DOING?
I'M GOING HUNTING.
AGAIN! I GET BORED ALL DAY WAITING FOR YOU. STAY WITH ME FOR ONCE.
NO, THAT'S IMPOSSIBLE.
PLEASE. COME ON, LET'S PLAY.
NO CHEATING, UH?
1, 2, 3, 4...
25, 26, 27...
OOOHHHH.
OTTO!

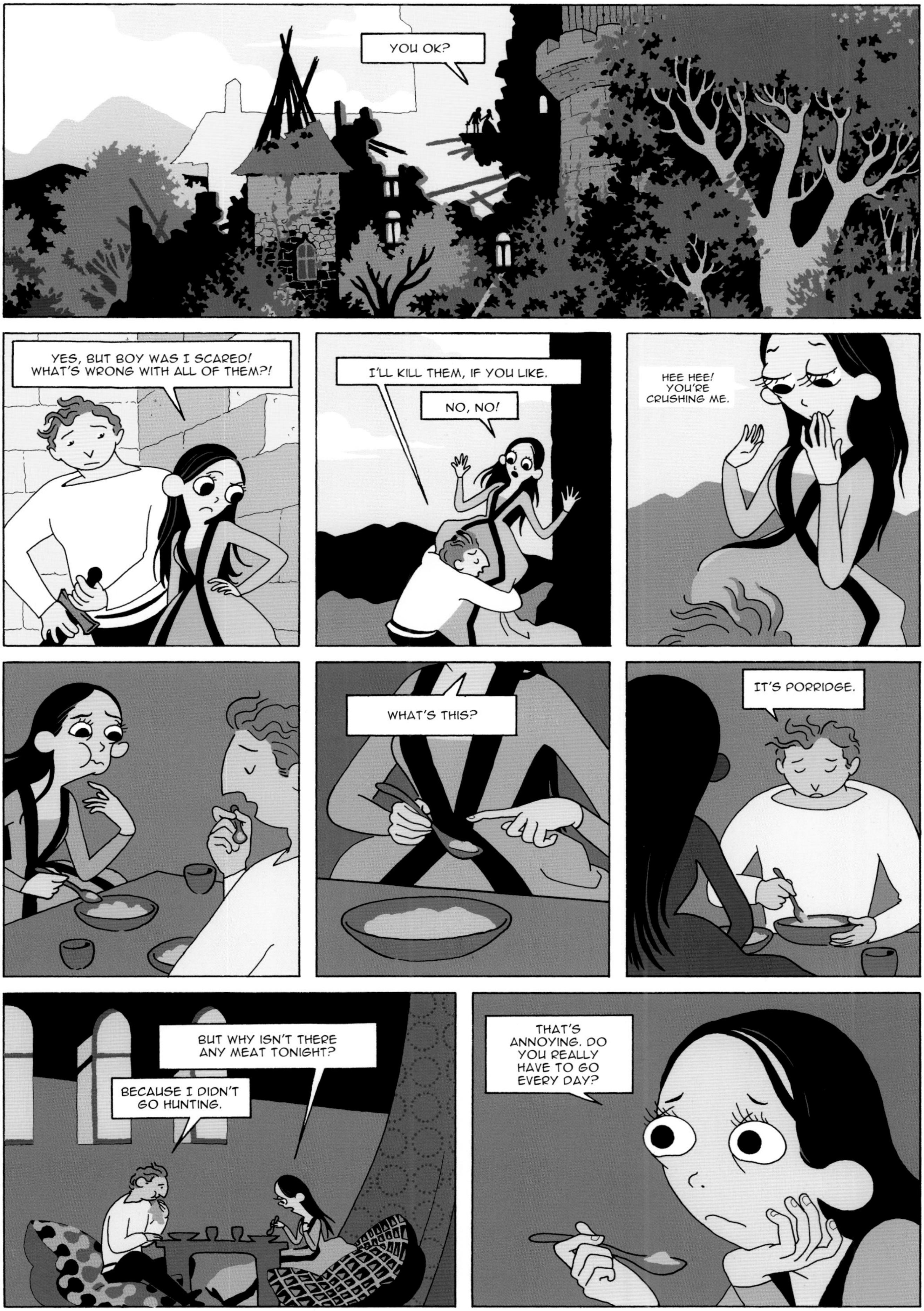
YOU OK?
YES, BUT BOY WAS I SCARED! WHAT'S WRONG WITH ALL OF THEM?!
I'LL KILL THEM, IF YOU LIKE.
NO, NO!
HEE HEE! YOU'RE CRUSHING ME.
WHAT'S THIS?
IT'S PORRIDGE.
BUT WHY ISN'T THERE ANY MEAT TONIGHT?
BECAUSE I DIDN'T GO HUNTING.
THAT'S ANNOYING. DO YOU REALLY HAVE TO GO EVERY DAY?

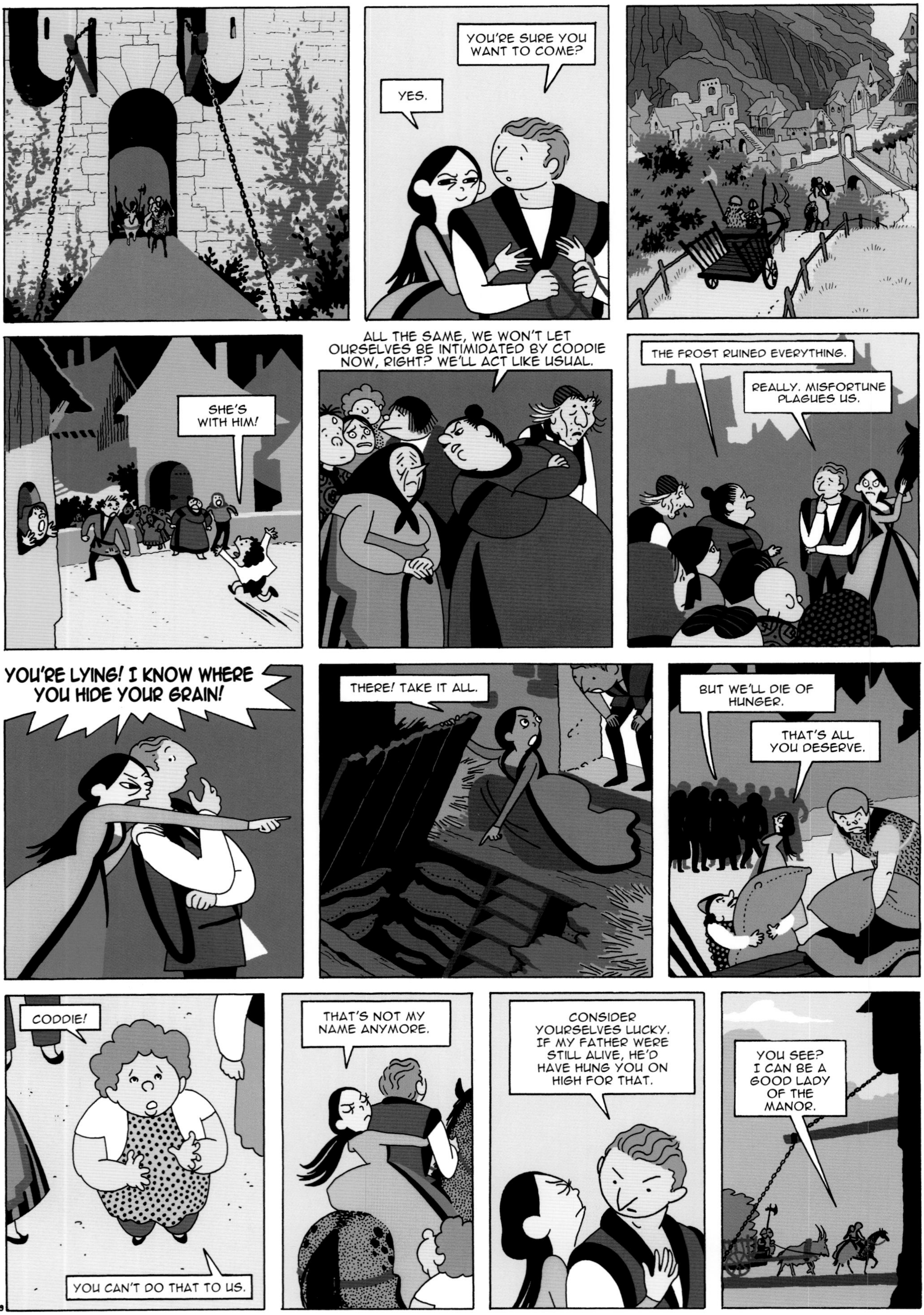

YOU'RE SURE YOU WANT TO COME?
YES.
SHE'S WITH HIM!
ALL THE SAME, WE WON'T LET OURSELVES BE INTIMIDATED BY CODDIE NOW, RIGHT? WE'LL ACT LIKE USUAL.
THE FROST RUINED EVERYTHING.
REALLY. MISFORTUNE PLAGUES US.
YOU'RE LYING! I KNOW WHERE YOU HIDE YOUR GRAIN!
THERE! TAKE IT ALL.
BUT WE'LL DIE OF HUNGER.
THAT'S ALL YOU DESERVE.
CODDIE!
YOU CAN'T DO THAT TO US.
THAT'S NOT MY NAME ANYMORE.
CONSIDER YOURSELVES LUCKY. IF MY FATHER WERE STILL ALIVE, HE'D HAVE HUNG YOU ON HIGH FOR THAT.
YOU SEE? I CAN BE A GOOD LADY OF THE MANOR.

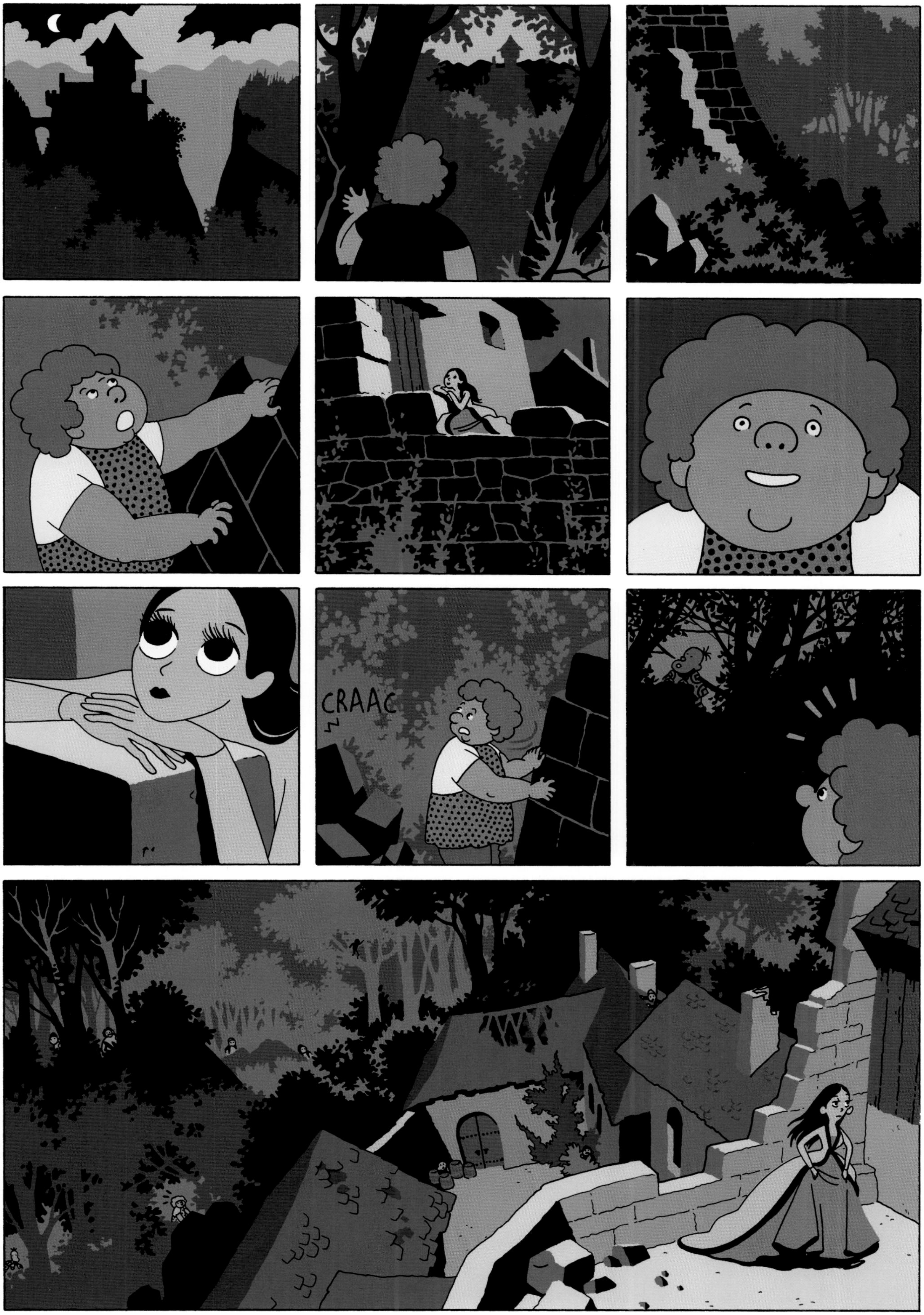
CRAAC

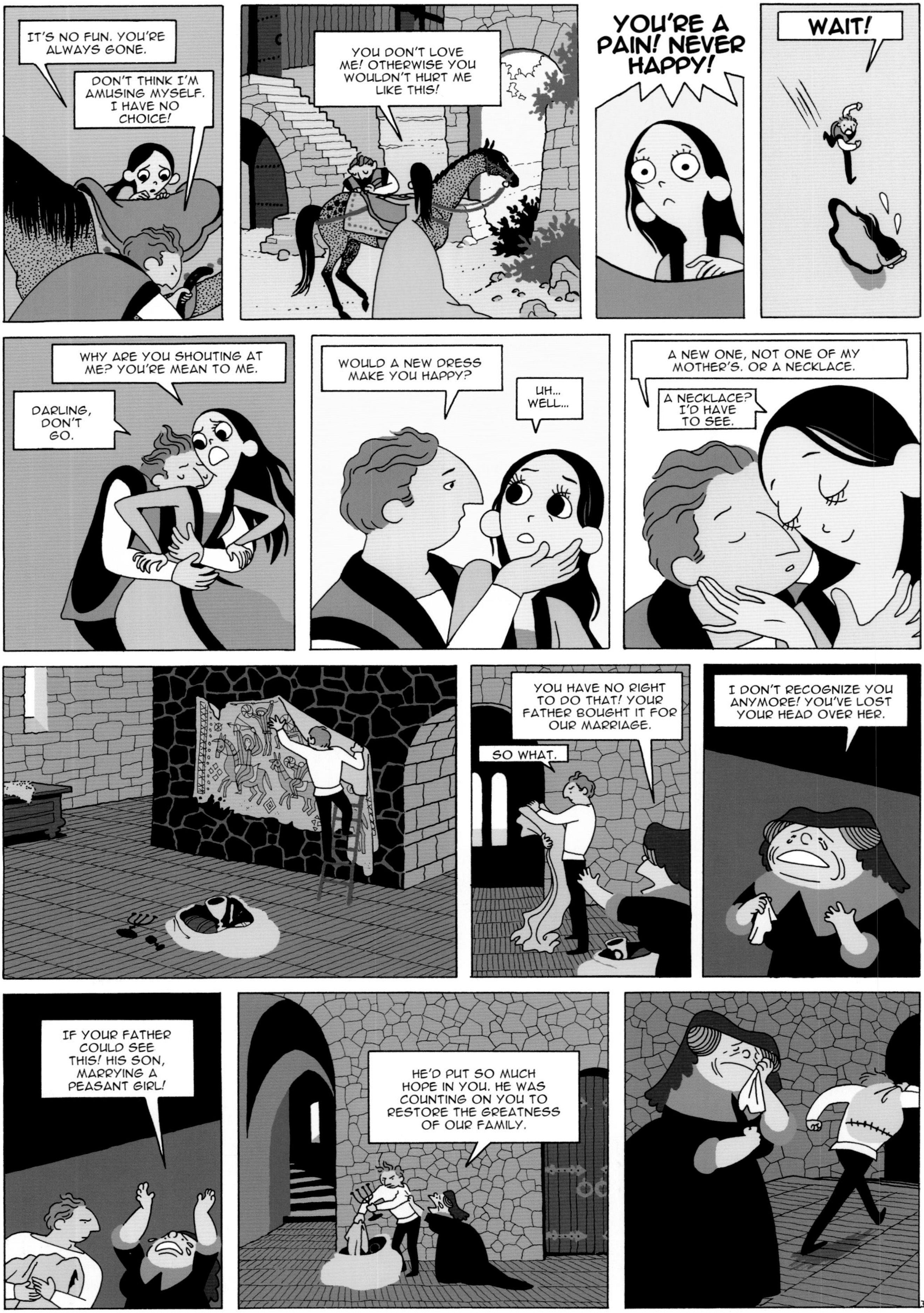
IT'S NO FUN. YOU'RE ALWAYS GONE.
DON'T THINK I'M AMUSING MYSELF. I HAVE NO CHOICE!
YOU DON'T LOVE ME! OTHERWISE YOU WOULDN'T HURT ME LIKE THIS!
YOU'RE A PAIN! NEVER HAPPY!
WAIT!
WHY ARE YOU SHOUTING AT ME? YOU'RE MEAN TO ME.
DARLING, DON'T GO.
WOULD A NEW DRESS MAKE YOU HAPPY?
UH... WELL...
A NEW ONE, NOT ONE OF MY MOTHER'S. OR A NECKLACE.
A NECKLACE? I'D HAVE TO SEE.
YOU HAVE NO RIGHT TO DO THAT! YOUR FATHER BOUGHT IT FOR OUR MARRIAGE.
SO WHAT.
I DON'T RECOGNIZE YOU ANYMORE! YOU'VE LOST YOUR HEAD OVER HER.
IF YOUR FATHER COULD SEE THIS! HIS SON, MARRYING A PEASANT GIRL!
HE'D PUT SO MUCH HOPE IN YOU. HE WAS COUNTING ON YOU TO RESTORE THE GREATNESS OF OUR FAMILY.

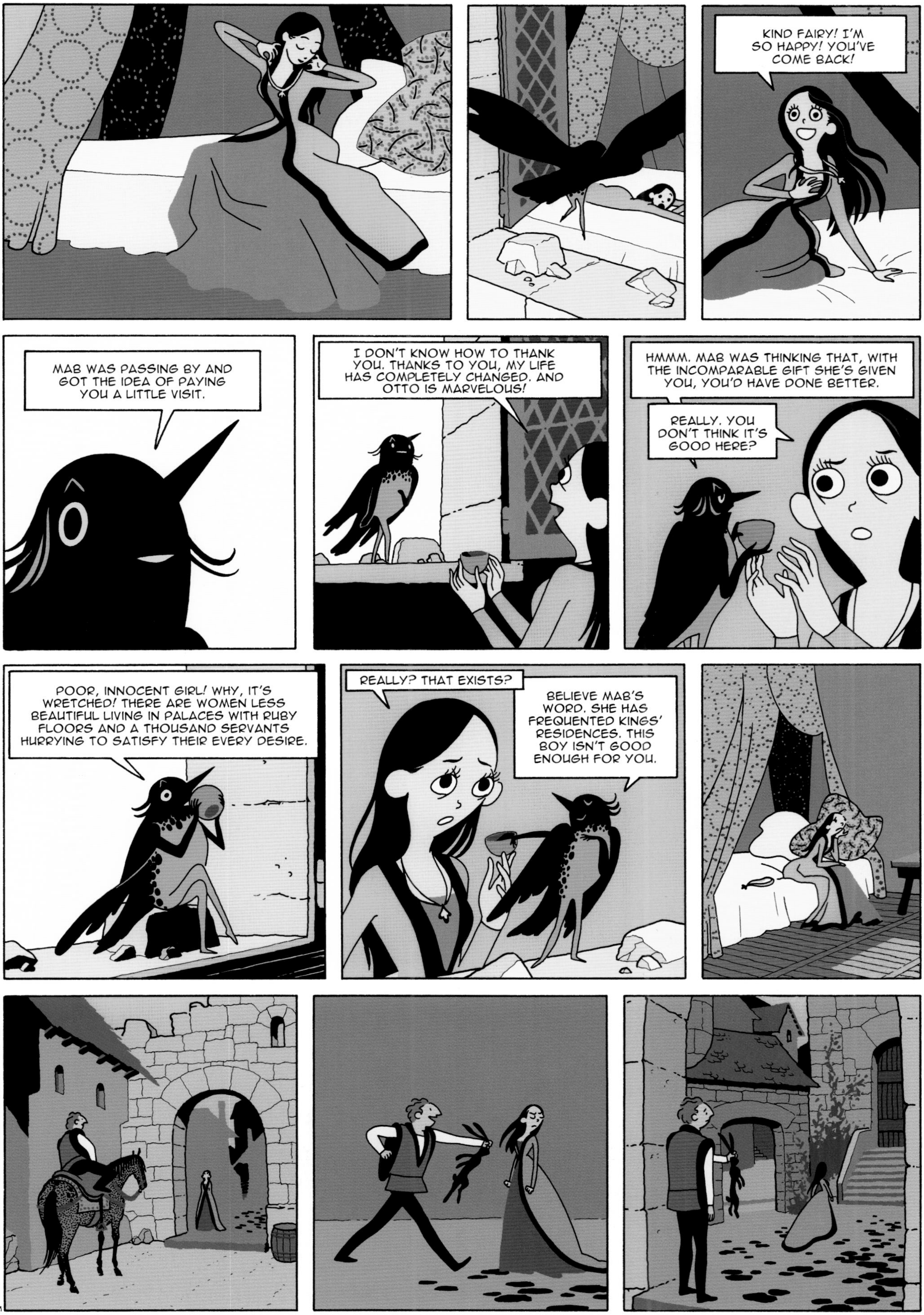
KIND FAIRY! I'M SO HAPPY! YOU'VE COME BACK!
MAB WAS PASSING BY AND GOT THE IDEA OF PAYING YOU A LITTLE VISIT.
I DON'T KNOW HOW TO THANK YOU. THANKS TO YOU, MY LIFE HAS COMPLETELY CHANGED. AND OTTO IS MARVELOUS!
HMMM. MAB WAS THINKING THAT, WITH THE INCOMPARABLE GIFT SHE'S GIVEN YOU, YOU'D HAVE DONE BETTER.
REALLY. YOU DON'T THINK IT'S GOOD HERE?
POOR, INNOCENT GIRL! WHY, IT'S WRETCHED! THERE ARE WOMEN LESS BEAUTIFUL LIVING IN PALACES WITH RUBY FLOORS AND A THOUSAND SERVANTS HURRYING TO SATISFY THEIR EVERY DESIRE.
REALLY? THAT EXISTS?
BELIEVE MAB'S WORD. SHE HAS FREQUENTED KINGS' RESIDENCES. THIS BOY ISN'T GOOD ENOUGH FOR YOU.
31

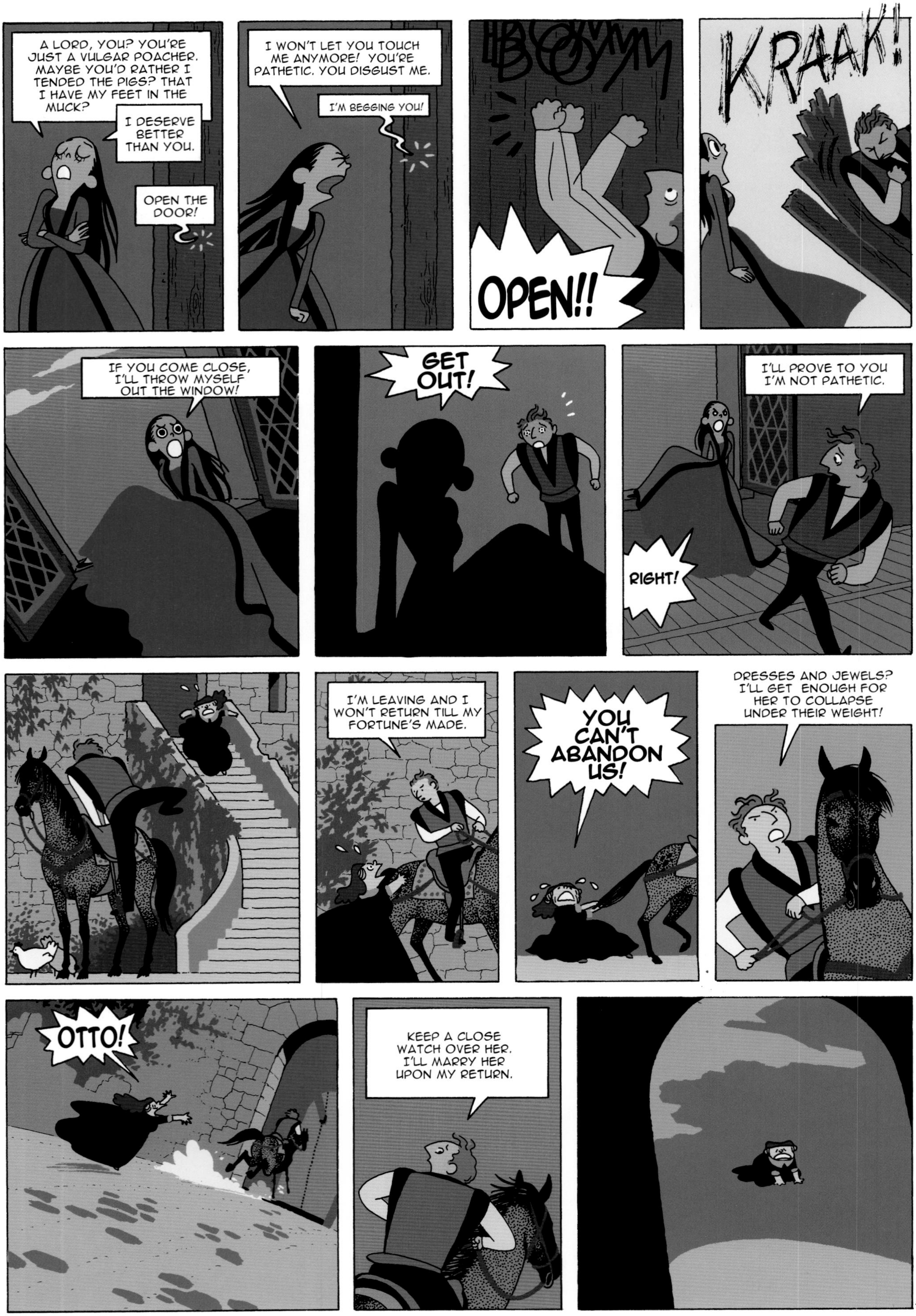
A LORD, YOU? YOU'RE JUST A VULGAR POACHER. MAYBE YOU'D RATHER I TENDED THE PIGS? THAT I HAVE MY FEET IN THE MUCK?
I DESERVE BETTER THAN YOU.
OPEN THE DOOR!
I WON'T LET YOU TOUCH ME ANYMORE! YOU'RE PATHETIC. YOU DISGUST ME.
I'M BEGGING YOU!
BOOM
OPEN!!
KRAAK!
IF YOU COME CLOSE, I'LL THROW MYSELF OUT THE WINDOW!
GET OUT!
I'LL PROVE TO YOU I'M NOT PATHETIC.
RIGHT!
I'M LEAVING AND I WON'T RETURN TILL MY FORTUNE'S MADE.
YOU CAN'T ABANDON US!
DRESSES AND JEWELS? I'LL GET ENOUGH FOR HER TO COLLAPSE UNDER THEIR WEIGHT!
OTTO!
KEEP A CLOSE WATCH OVER HER. I'LL MARRY HER UPON MY RETURN.

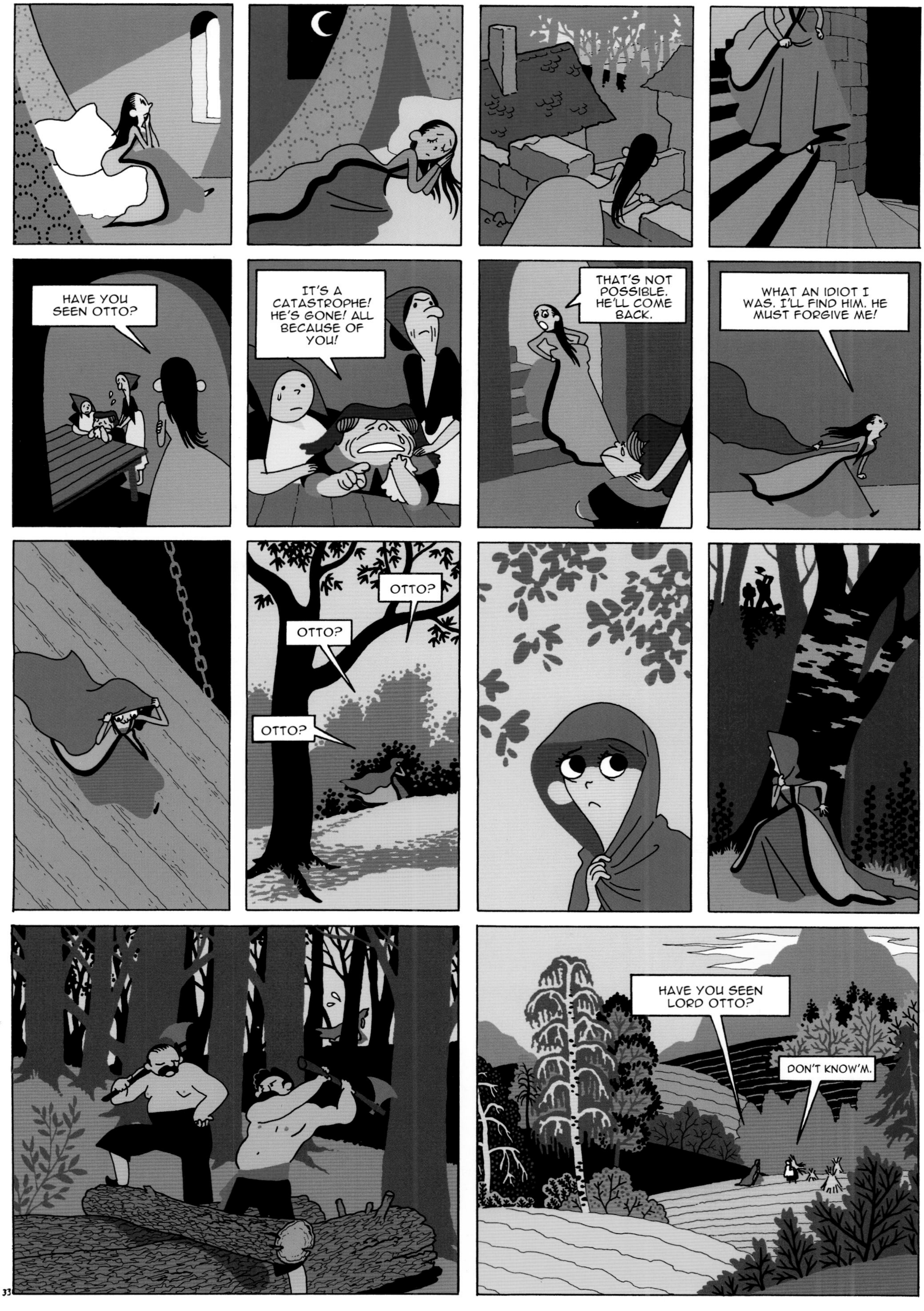

HAVE YOU SEEN OTTO?
IT'S A CATASTROPHE! HE'S GONE! ALL BECAUSE OF YOU!
THAT'S NOT POSSIBLE. HE'LL COME BACK.
WHAT AN IDIOT I WAS. I'LL FIND HIM. HE MUST FORGIVE ME!
OTTO?
OTTO?
OTTO?
HAVE YOU SEEN LORD OTTO?
DON'T KNOW'M.

SO, YOU LEFT HIM. AND NONE TOO SOON.

GOOD FAIRY, TELL ME WHERE HE IS!

MAB KNOWS, BUT WON'T SAY. THAT WOULDN'T BE DOING YOU ANY FAVOR.

I'M BEGGING YOU.

IT'S ALL FOR THE BEST.

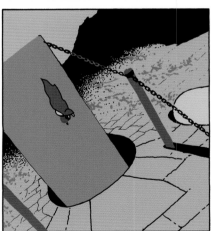

HAS HE COME BACK?

NO.

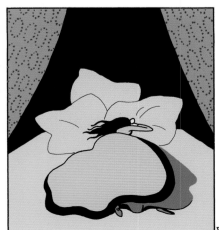

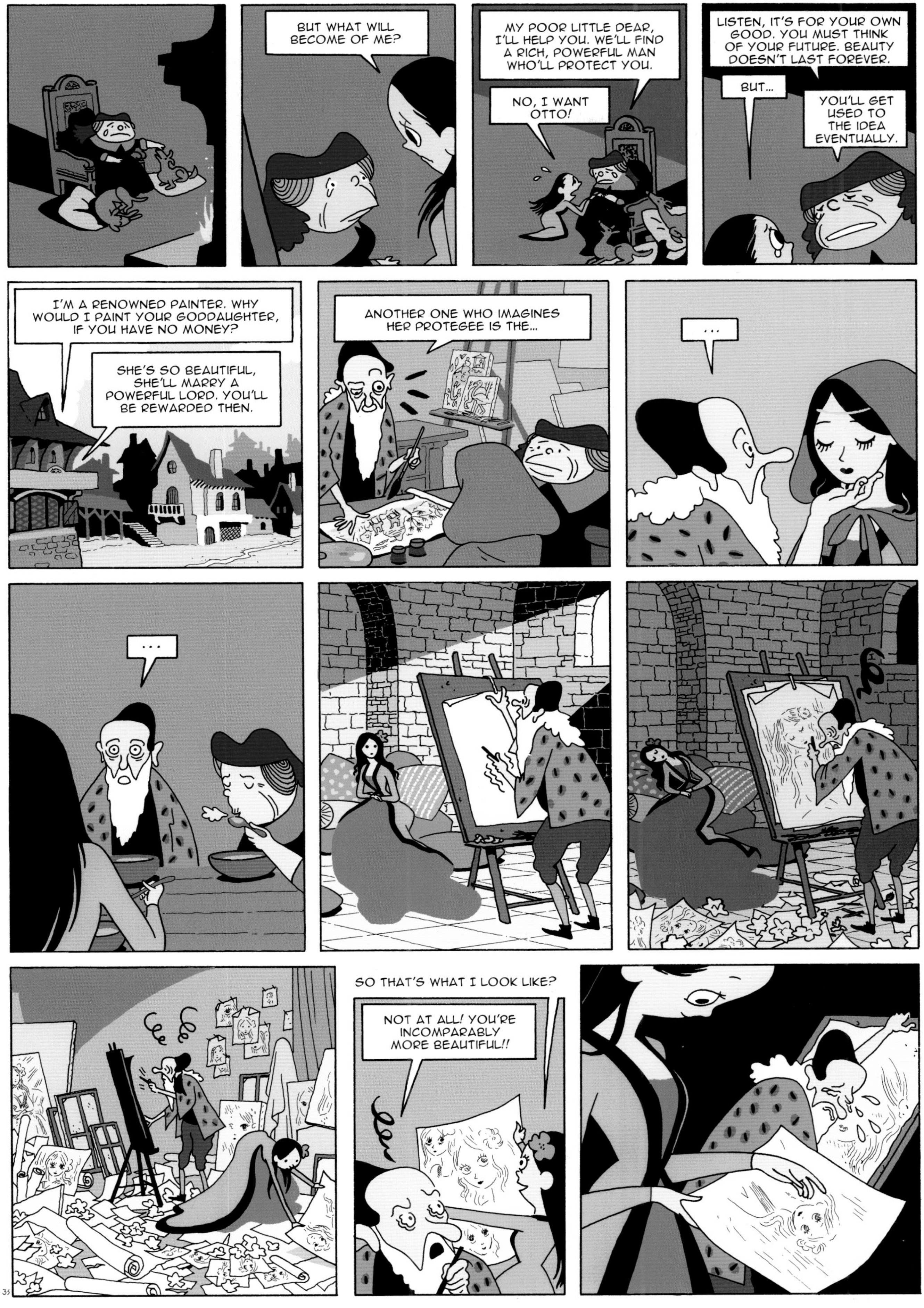
BUT WHAT WILL BECOME OF ME?
MY POOR LITTLE DEAR, I'LL HELP YOU. WE'LL FIND A RICH, POWERFUL MAN WHO'LL PROTECT YOU.
NO, I WANT OTTO!
LISTEN, IT'S FOR YOUR OWN GOOD. YOU MUST THINK OF YOUR FUTURE. BEAUTY DOESN'T LAST FOREVER.
BUT...
YOU'LL GET USED TO THE IDEA EVENTUALLY.
I'M A RENOWNED PAINTER. WHY WOULD I PAINT YOUR GODDAUGHTER, IF YOU HAVE NO MONEY?
SHE'S SO BEAUTIFUL, SHE'LL MARRY A POWERFUL LORD. YOU'LL BE REWARDED THEN.
ANOTHER ONE WHO IMAGINES HER PROTEGEE IS THE...
...
...
SO THAT'S WHAT I LOOK LIKE?
NOT AT ALL! YOU'RE INCOMPARABLY MORE BEAUTIFUL!!

YOU'RE NOT FINISHING ANYTHING!
YOU CAN SEE: IT'S AWFUL!!
OH, I THINK YOU'RE A LITTLE HARD ON YOURSELF.
IT GIVES A FORETASTE. THAT SHOULD BE SUFFICIENT TO WHET CURIOSITY.
SUFFICIENT? THAT COULDN'T BE SUFFICIENT! BEAUTY INCARNATE IS THERE BEFORE MY EYES, AND I'M INCAPABLE OF PAINTING IT.
I'M GOOD FOR NOTHING!
AH, ARTISTS...
MISTER PAINTER?
YOOHOO!!
ARE YOU THERE?
?
IT'S MY FAULT! I KILLED HIM!
COME NOW, DON'T BE AN IDIOT. YOU'VE GOT NOTHING TO DO WITH IT.
?...
AH, THIS ONE SHOULD DO THE JOB.
WITH THIS, I SHOULD BE ABLE TO CONVINCE FOLKS TO PAY US A LITTLE VISIT. AND ONCE THEY'VE SEEN YOU...

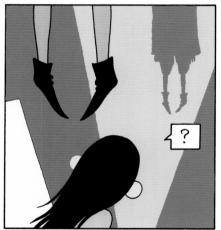

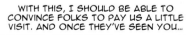

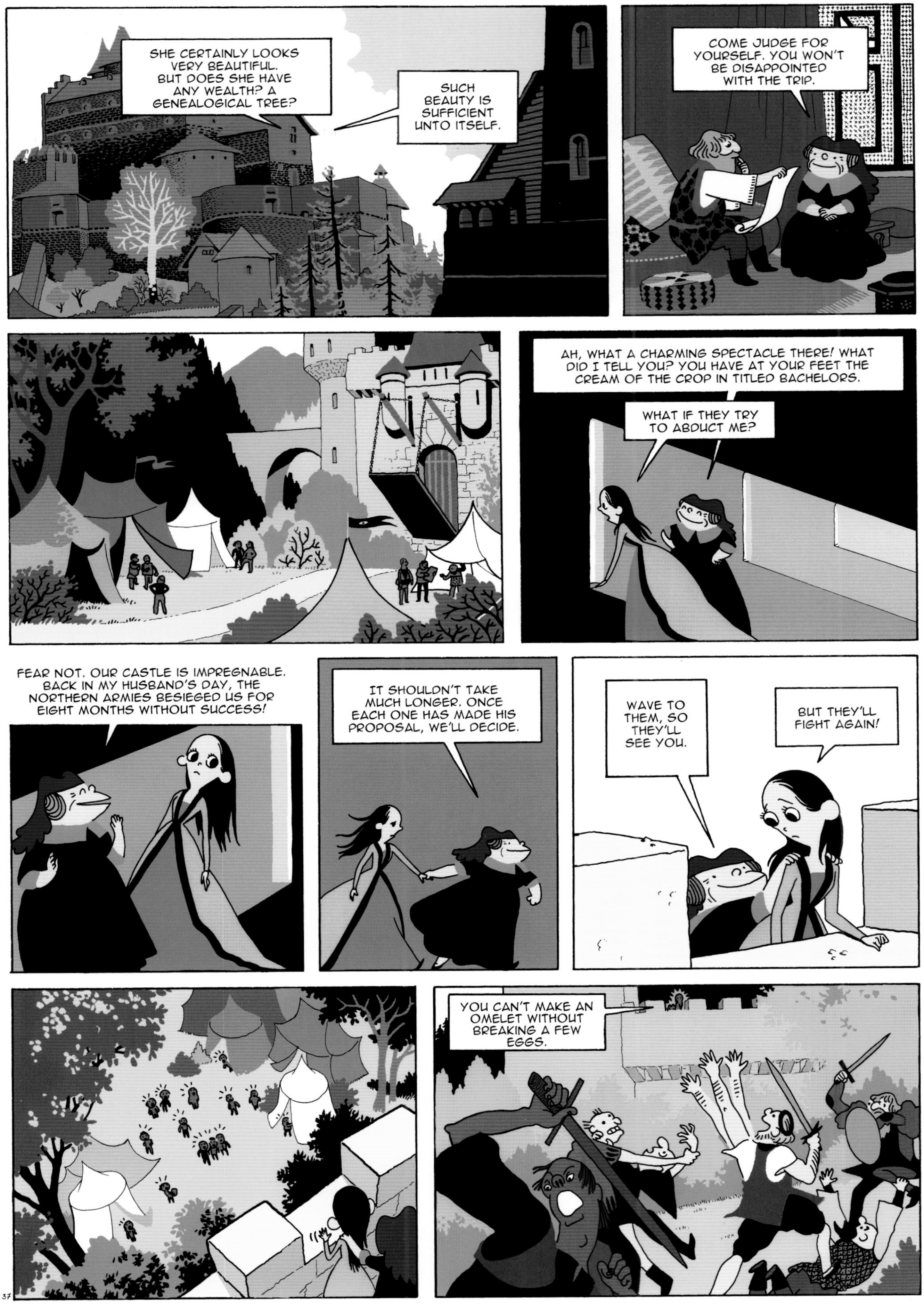
SHE CERTAINLY LOOKS VERY BEAUTIFUL. BUT DOES SHE HAVE ANY WEALTH? A GENEALOGICAL TREE?
SUCH BEAUTY IS SUFFICIENT UNTO ITSELF.
COME JUDGE FOR YOURSELF. YOU WON'T BE DISAPPOINTED WITH THE TRIP.
AH, WHAT A CHARMING SPECTACLE THERE! WHAT DID I TELL YOU? YOU HAVE AT YOUR FEET THE CREAM OF THE CROP IN TITLED BACHELORS.
WHAT IF THEY TRY TO ABDUCT ME?
FEAR NOT. OUR CASTLE IS IMPREGNABLE. BACK IN MY HUSBAND'S DAY, THE NORTHERN ARMIES BESIEGED US FOR EIGHT MONTHS WITHOUT SUCCESS!
IT SHOULDN'T TAKE MUCH LONGER. ONCE EACH ONE HAS MADE HIS PROPOSAL, WE'LL DECIDE.
WAVE TO THEM, SO THEY'LL SEE YOU.
BUT THEY'LL FIGHT AGAIN!
YOU CAN'T MAKE AN OMELET WITHOUT BREAKING A FEW EGGS.

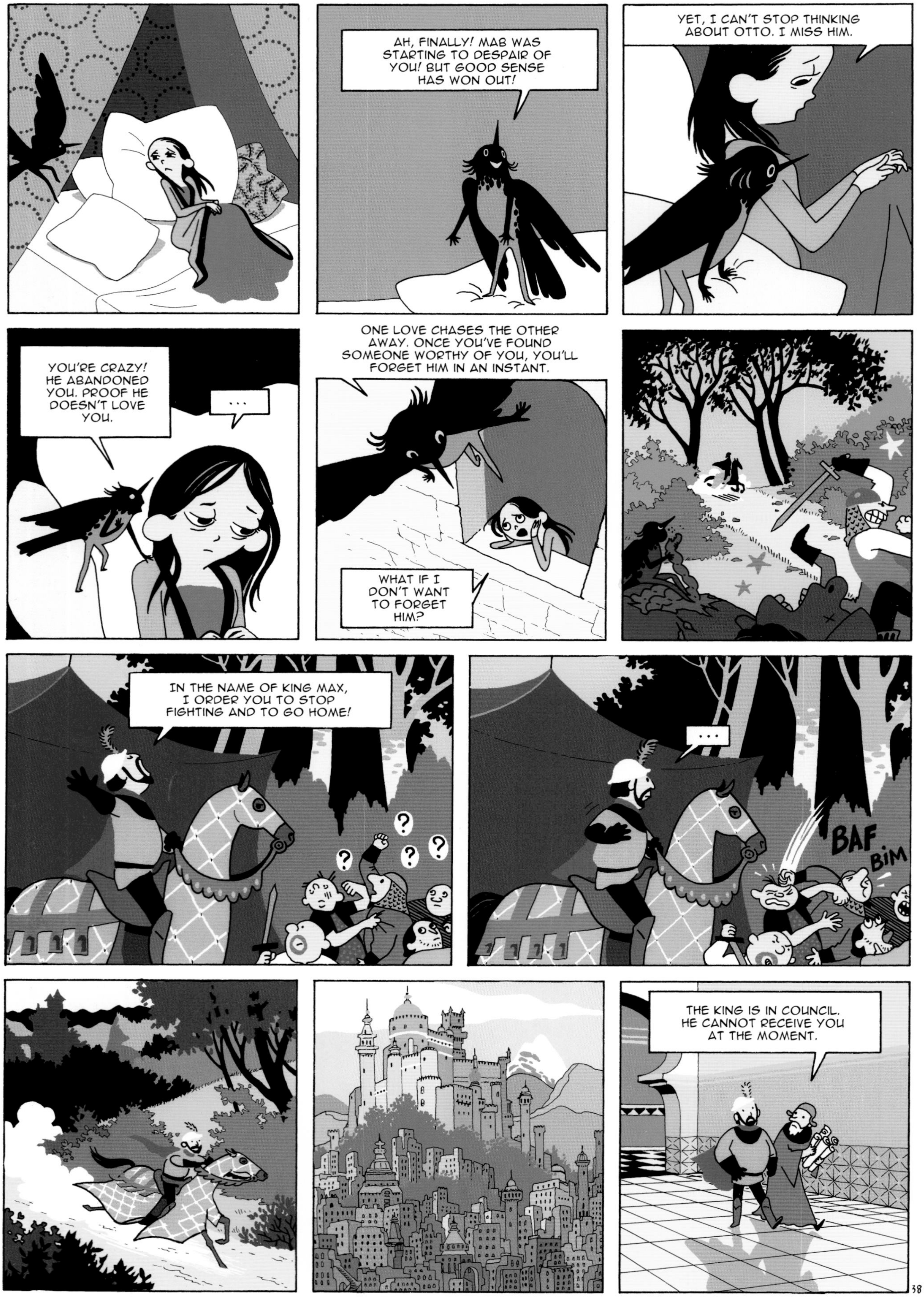
AH, FINALLY! MAB WAS STARTING TO DESPAIR OF YOU! BUT GOOD SENSE HAS WON OUT!
YET, I CAN'T STOP THINKING ABOUT OTTO. I MISS HIM.
YOU'RE CRAZY! HE ABANDONED YOU. PROOF HE DOESN'T LOVE YOU.
...
ONE LOVE CHASES THE OTHER AWAY. ONCE YOU'VE FOUND SOMEONE WORTHY OF YOU, YOU'LL FORGET HIM IN AN INSTANT.
WHAT IF I DON'T WANT TO FORGET HIM?
IN THE NAME OF KING MAX, I ORDER YOU TO STOP FIGHTING AND TO GO HOME!
...
BAF
BIM
THE KING IS IN COUNCIL. HE CANNOT RECEIVE YOU AT THE MOMENT.
38

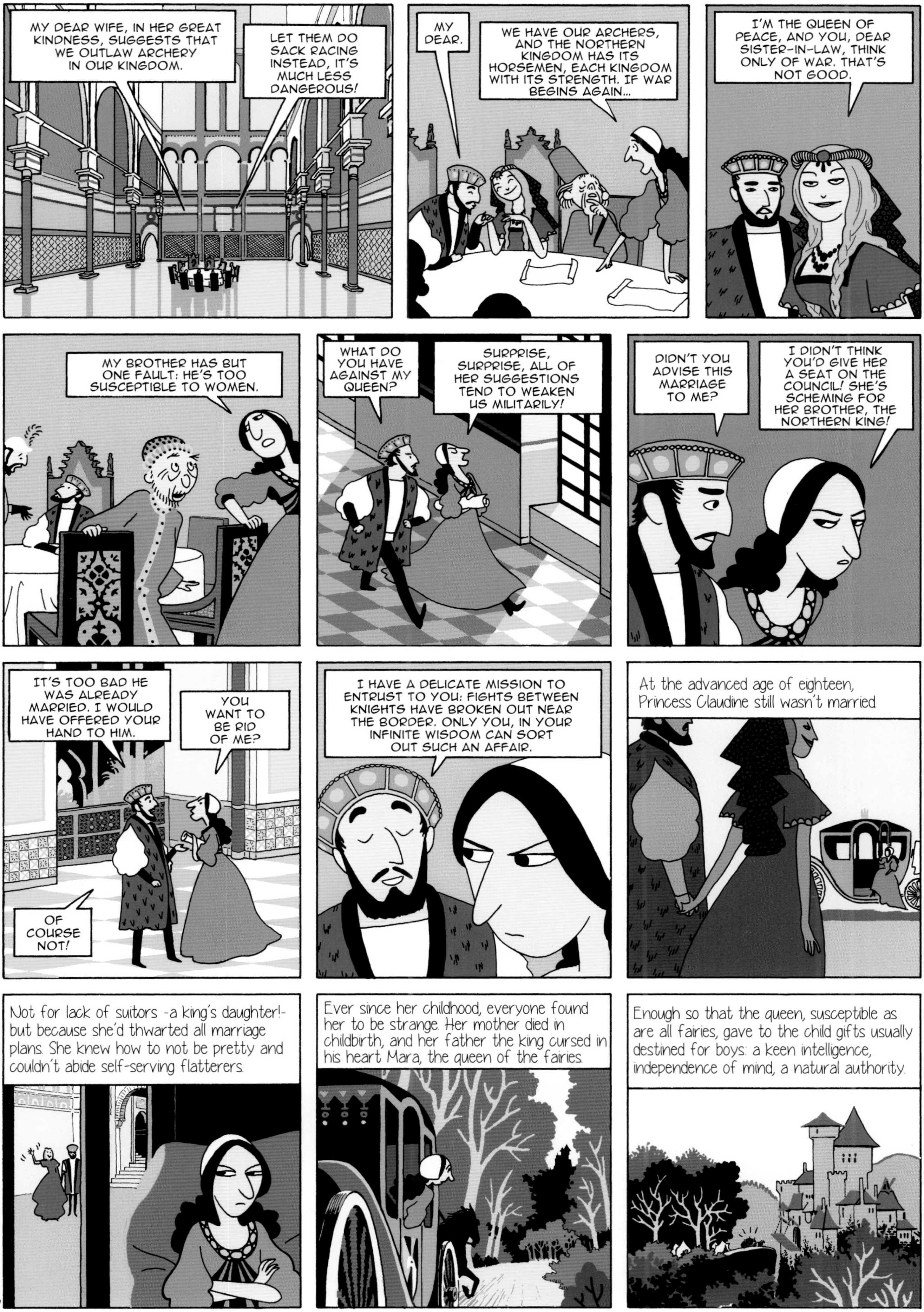
MY DEAR WIFE, IN HER GREAT KINDNESS, SUGGESTS THAT WE OUTLAW ARCHERY IN OUR KINGDOM.
LET THEM DO SACK RACING INSTEAD, IT'S MUCH LESS DANGEROUS!
MY DEAR.
WE HAVE OUR ARCHERS, AND THE NORTHERN KINGDOM HAS ITS HORSEMEN, EACH KINGDOM WITH ITS STRENGTH. IF WAR BEGINS AGAIN...
I'M THE QUEEN OF PEACE, AND YOU, DEAR SISTER-IN-LAW, THINK ONLY OF WAR. THAT'S NOT GOOD.
MY BROTHER HAS BUT ONE FAULT: HE'S TOO SUSCEPTIBLE TO WOMEN.
WHAT DO YOU HAVE AGAINST MY QUEEN?
SURPRISE, SURPRISE, ALL OF HER SUGGESTIONS TEND TO WEAKEN US MILITARILY!
DIDN'T YOU ADVISE THIS MARRIAGE TO ME?
I DIDN'T THINK YOU'D GIVE HER A SEAT ON THE COUNCIL! SHE'S SCHEMING FOR HER BROTHER, THE NORTHERN KING!
IT'S TOO BAD HE WAS ALREADY MARRIED. I WOULD HAVE OFFERED YOUR HAND TO HIM.
YOU WANT TO BE RID OF ME?
OF COURSE NOT!
I HAVE A DELICATE MISSION TO ENTRUST TO YOU: FIGHTS BETWEEN KNIGHTS HAVE BROKEN OUT NEAR THE BORDER. ONLY YOU, IN YOUR INFINITE WISDOM CAN SORT OUT SUCH AN AFFAIR.
At the advanced age of eighteen, Princess Claudine still wasn't married.
Not for lack of suitors -a king's daughter!- but because she'd thwarted all marriage plans. She knew how to not be pretty and couldn't abide self-serving flatterers.
Ever since her childhood, everyone found her to be strange. Her mother died in childbirth, and her father the king cursed in his heart Mara, the queen of the fairies.
Enough so that the queen, susceptible as are all fairies, gave to the child gifts usually destined for boys: a keen intelligence, independence of mind, a natural authority.

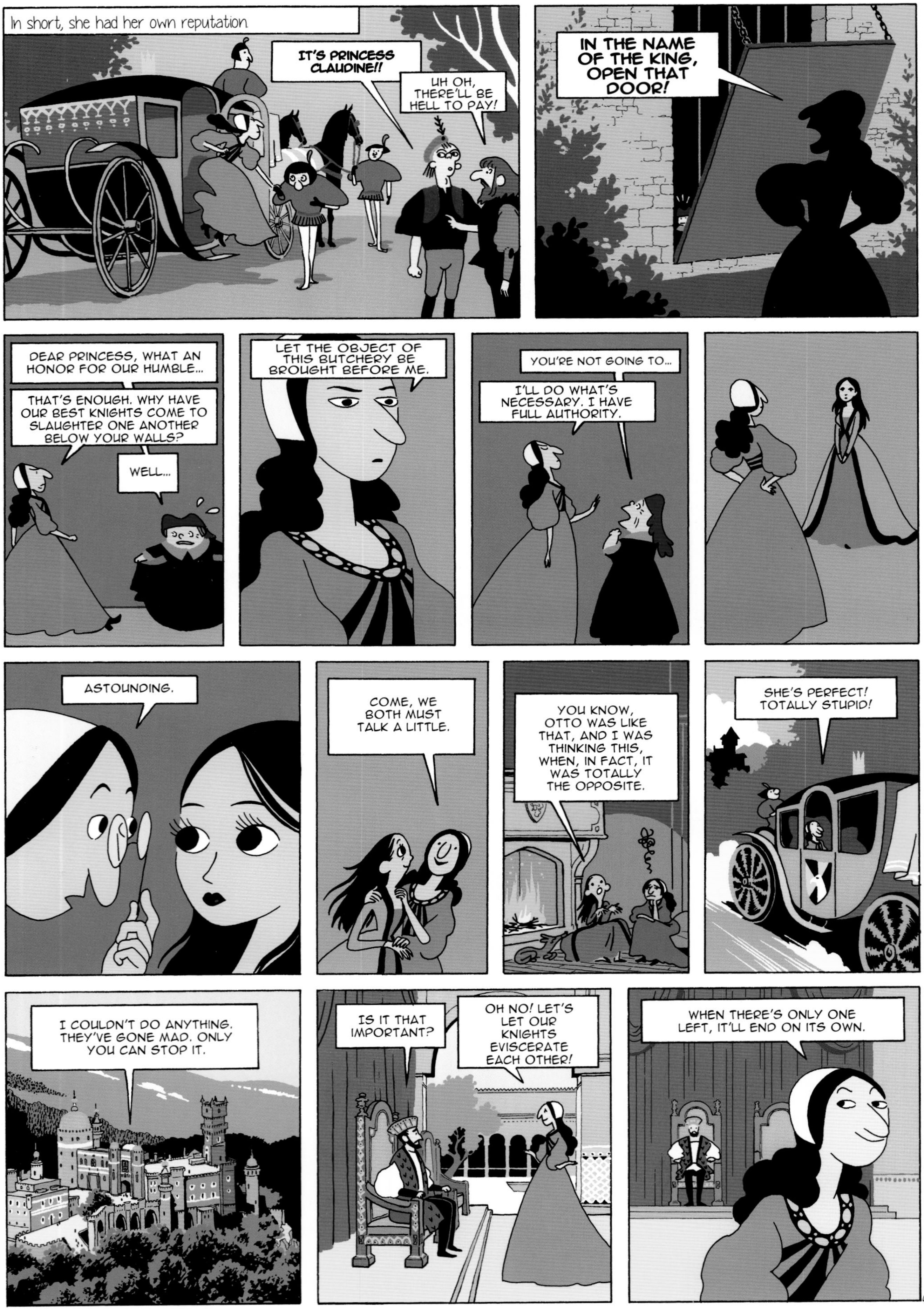
In short, she had her own reputation.
IT'S PRINCESS CLAUDINE!!
UH OH, THERE'LL BE HELL TO PAY!
IN THE NAME OF THE KING, OPEN THAT DOOR!
DEAR PRINCESS, WHAT AN HONOR FOR OUR HUMBLE...
THAT'S ENOUGH. WHY HAVE OUR BEST KNIGHTS COME TO SLAUGHTER ONE ANOTHER BELOW YOUR WALLS?
WELL...
LET THE OBJECT OF THIS BUTCHERY BE BROUGHT BEFORE ME.
YOU'RE NOT GOING TO...
I'LL DO WHAT'S NECESSARY. I HAVE FULL AUTHORITY.
ASTOUNDING.
COME, WE BOTH MUST TALK A LITTLE.
YOU KNOW, OTTO WAS LIKE THAT, AND I WAS THINKING THIS, WHEN, IN FACT, IT WAS TOTALLY THE OPPOSITE.
SHE'S PERFECT! TOTALLY STUPID!
I COULDN'T DO ANYTHING. THEY'VE GONE MAD. ONLY YOU CAN STOP IT.
IS IT THAT IMPORTANT?
OH NO! LET'S LET OUR KNIGHTS EVISCERATE EACH OTHER!
WHEN THERE'S ONLY ONE LEFT, IT'LL END ON ITS OWN.
40

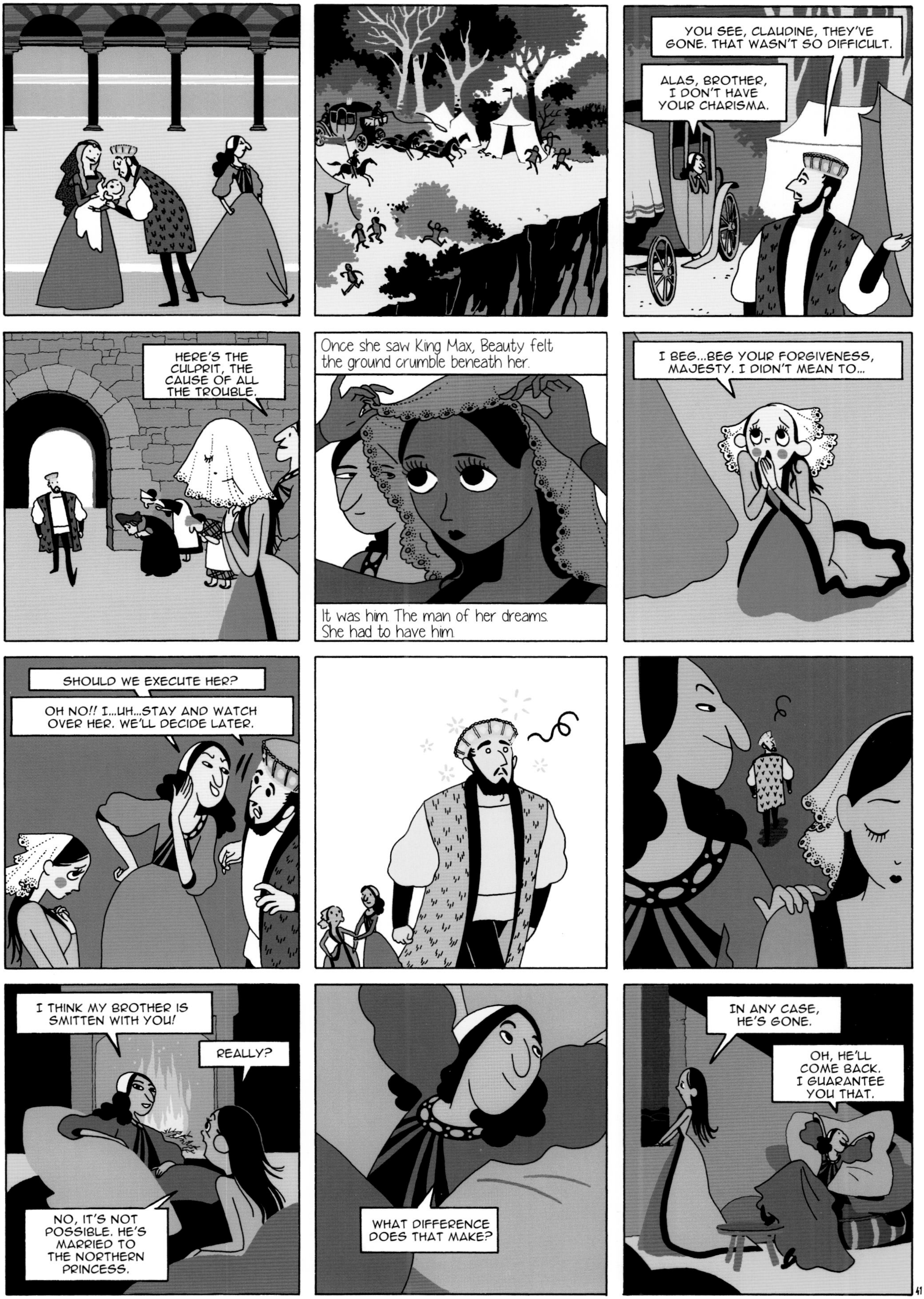

YOU SEE, CLAUDINE, THEY'VE GONE. THAT WASN'T SO DIFFICULT.
ALAS, BROTHER, I DON'T HAVE YOUR CHARISMA.
HERE'S THE CULPRIT, THE CAUSE OF ALL THE TROUBLE.
Once she saw King Max, Beauty felt the ground crumble beneath her.
It was him. The man of her dreams. She had to have him.
I BEG...BEG YOUR FORGIVENESS, MAJESTY. I DIDN'T MEAN TO...
SHOULD WE EXECUTE HER?
OH NO!! I...UH...STAY AND WATCH OVER HER. WE'LL DECIDE LATER.
I THINK MY BROTHER IS SMITTEN WITH YOU!
REALLY?
NO, IT'S NOT POSSIBLE. HE'S MARRIED TO THE NORTHERN PRINCESS.
WHAT DIFFERENCE DOES THAT MAKE?
IN ANY CASE, HE'S GONE.
OH, HE'LL COME BACK. I GUARANTEE YOU THAT.
41

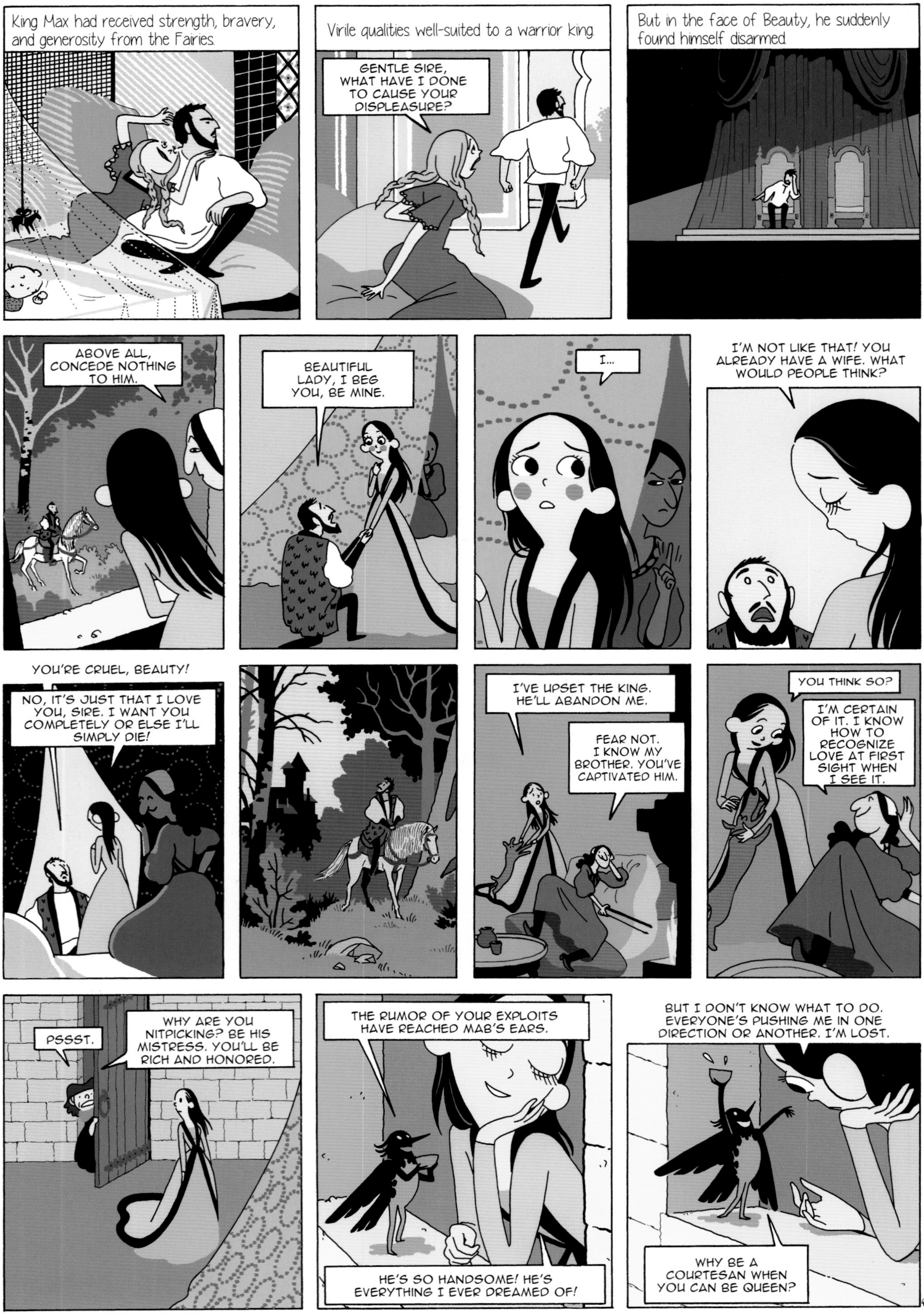
King Max had received strength, bravery, and generosity from the Fairies.
Virile qualities well-suited to a warrior king.
GENTLE SIRE, WHAT HAVE I DONE TO CAUSE YOUR DISPLEASURE?
But in the face of Beauty, he suddenly found himself disarmed.
ABOVE ALL, CONCEDE NOTHING TO HIM.
BEAUTIFUL LADY, I BEG YOU, BE MINE.
I...
I'M NOT LIKE THAT! YOU ALREADY HAVE A WIFE. WHAT WOULD PEOPLE THINK?
YOU'RE CRUEL, BEAUTY!
NO, IT'S JUST THAT I LOVE YOU, SIRE. I WANT YOU COMPLETELY OR ELSE I'LL SIMPLY DIE!
I'VE UPSET THE KING. HE'LL ABANDON ME.
FEAR NOT. I KNOW MY BROTHER. YOU'VE CAPTIVATED HIM.
YOU THINK SO?
I'M CERTAIN OF IT. I KNOW HOW TO RECOGNIZE LOVE AT FIRST SIGHT WHEN I SEE IT.
PSSST.
WHY ARE YOU NITPICKING? BE HIS MISTRESS. YOU'LL BE RICH AND HONORED.
THE RUMOR OF YOUR EXPLOITS HAVE REACHED MAB'S EARS.
HE'S SO HANDSOME! HE'S EVERYTHING I EVER DREAMED OF!
BUT I DON'T KNOW WHAT TO DO. EVERYONE'S PUSHING ME IN ONE DIRECTION OR ANOTHER. I'M LOST.
WHY BE A COURTESAN WHEN YOU CAN BE QUEEN?
42

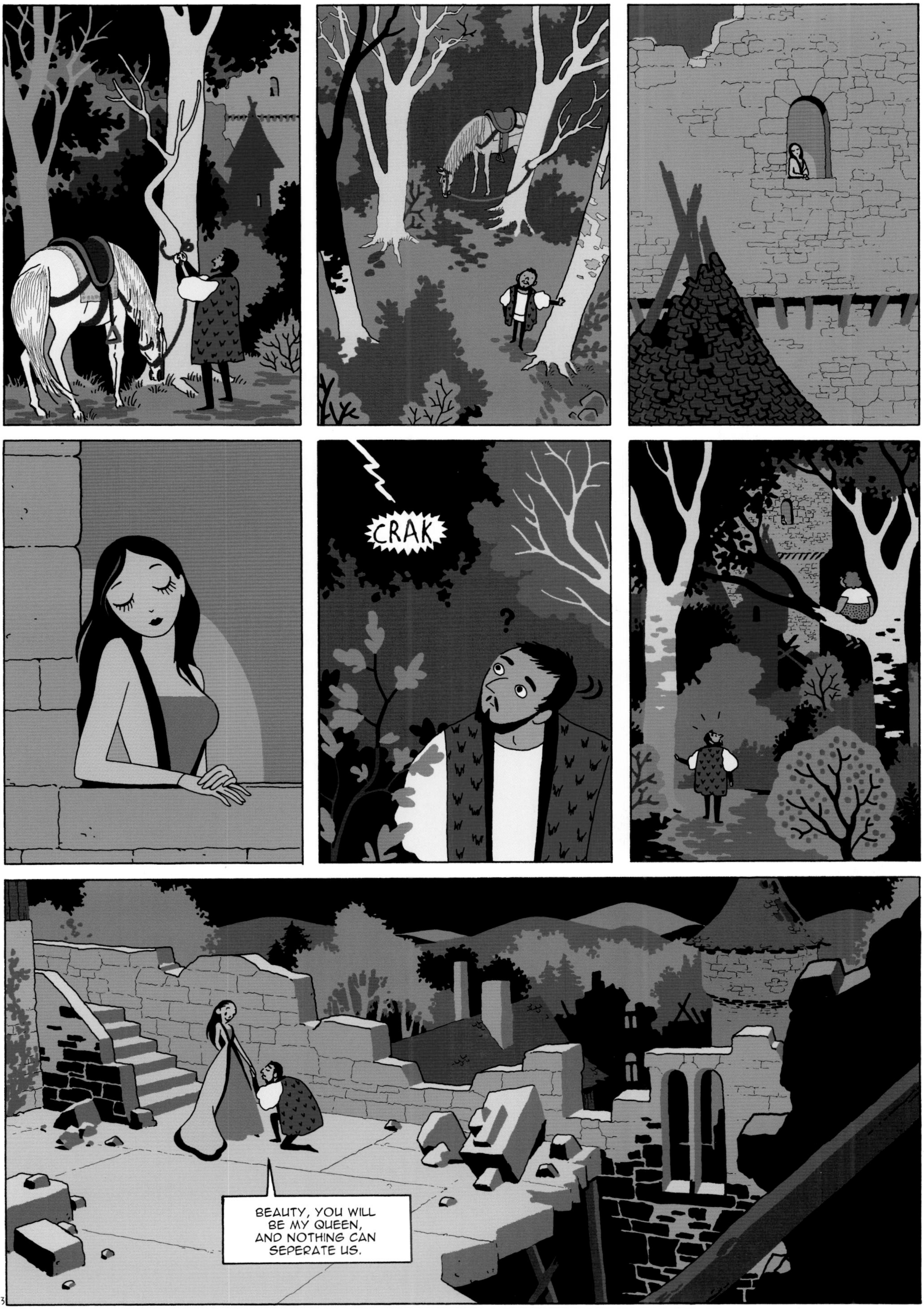
CRAK
?
BEAUTY, YOU WILL BE MY QUEEN, AND NOTHING CAN SEPERATE US.
43

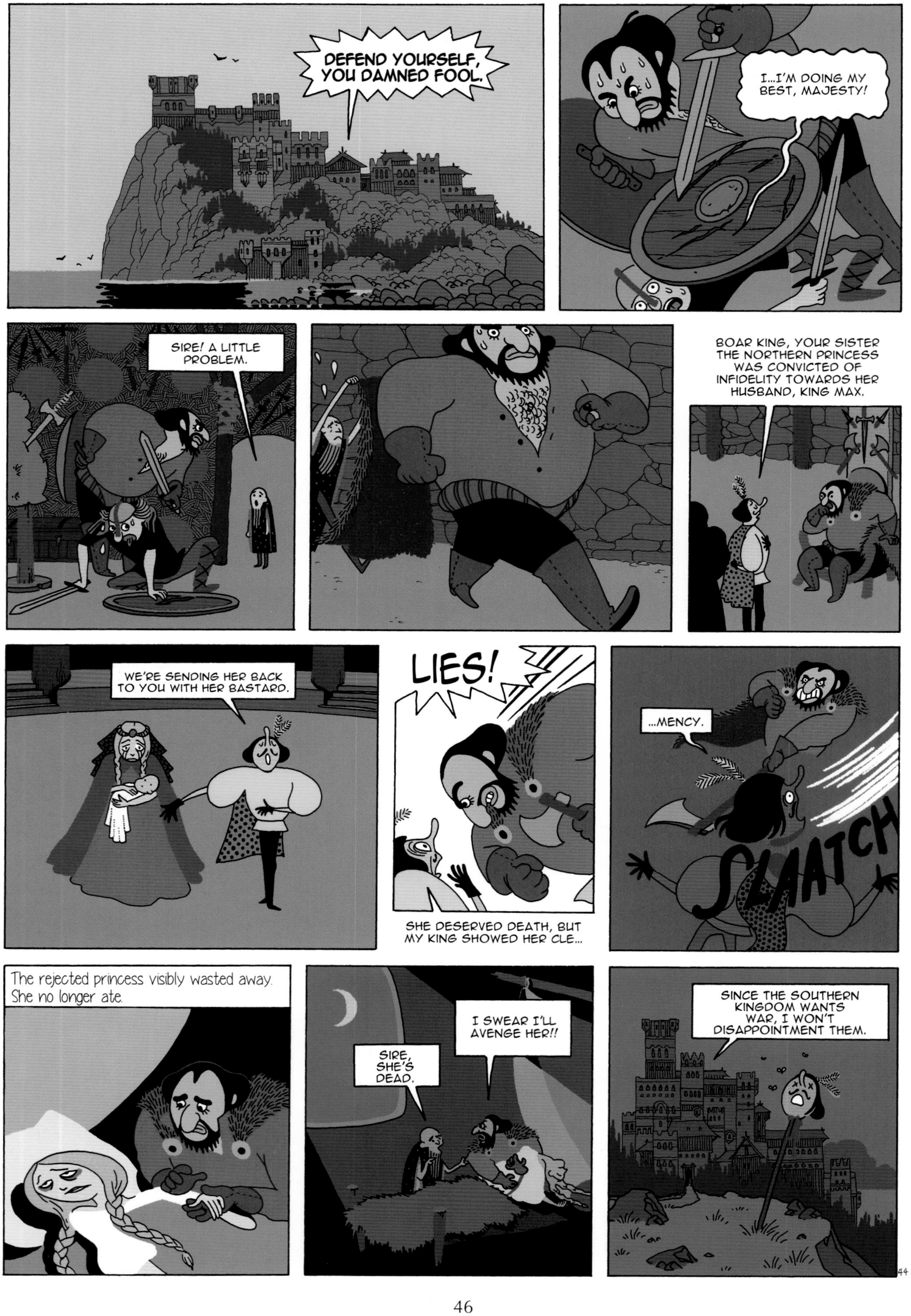
DEFEND YOURSELF, YOU DAMNED FOOL.
I...I'M DOING MY BEST, MAJESTY!
SIRE! A LITTLE PROBLEM.
BOAR KING, YOUR SISTER THE NORTHERN PRINCESS WAS CONVICTED OF INFIDELITY TOWARDS HER HUSBAND, KING MAX.
WE'RE SENDING HER BACK TO YOU WITH HER BASTARD.
LIES!
SHE DESERVED DEATH, BUT MY KING SHOWED HER CLE...
...MENCY.
SLAATCH
The rejected princess visibly wasted away. She no longer ate.
I SWEAR I'LL AVENGE HER!!
SIRE, SHE'S DEAD.
SINCE THE SOUTHERN KINGDOM WANTS WAR, I WON'T DISAPPOINTMENT THEM.
44

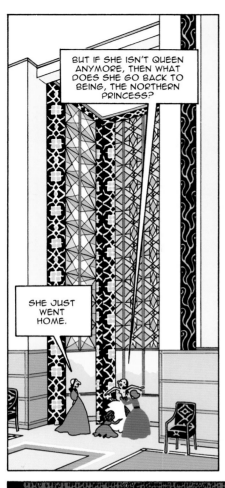

BUT IF SHE ISN'T QUEEN ANYMORE, THEN WHAT DOES SHE GO BACK TO BEING, THE NORTHERN PRINCESS?

SHE JUST WENT HOME.

IT ALL FRIGHTENS ME A LITTLE. I'M ONLY A PEASANT GIRL.

FEAR NOT. YOUR SUBJECTS WILL ADORE YOU. HOW COULD IT BE OTHERWISE?

I'M SO AFRAID OF DOING SOMETHING I SHOULDN'T.

I'LL BE HERE TO GUIDE YOU. TRUST ME.

YOU'RE REALLY GOOD TO ME. YOU'RE A TRUE FRIEND.

WHY YES, OF COURSE.

MAY MARA, QUEEN OF THE FAIRIES, BLESS THE UNION OF THIS MAN AND THIS WOMAN.

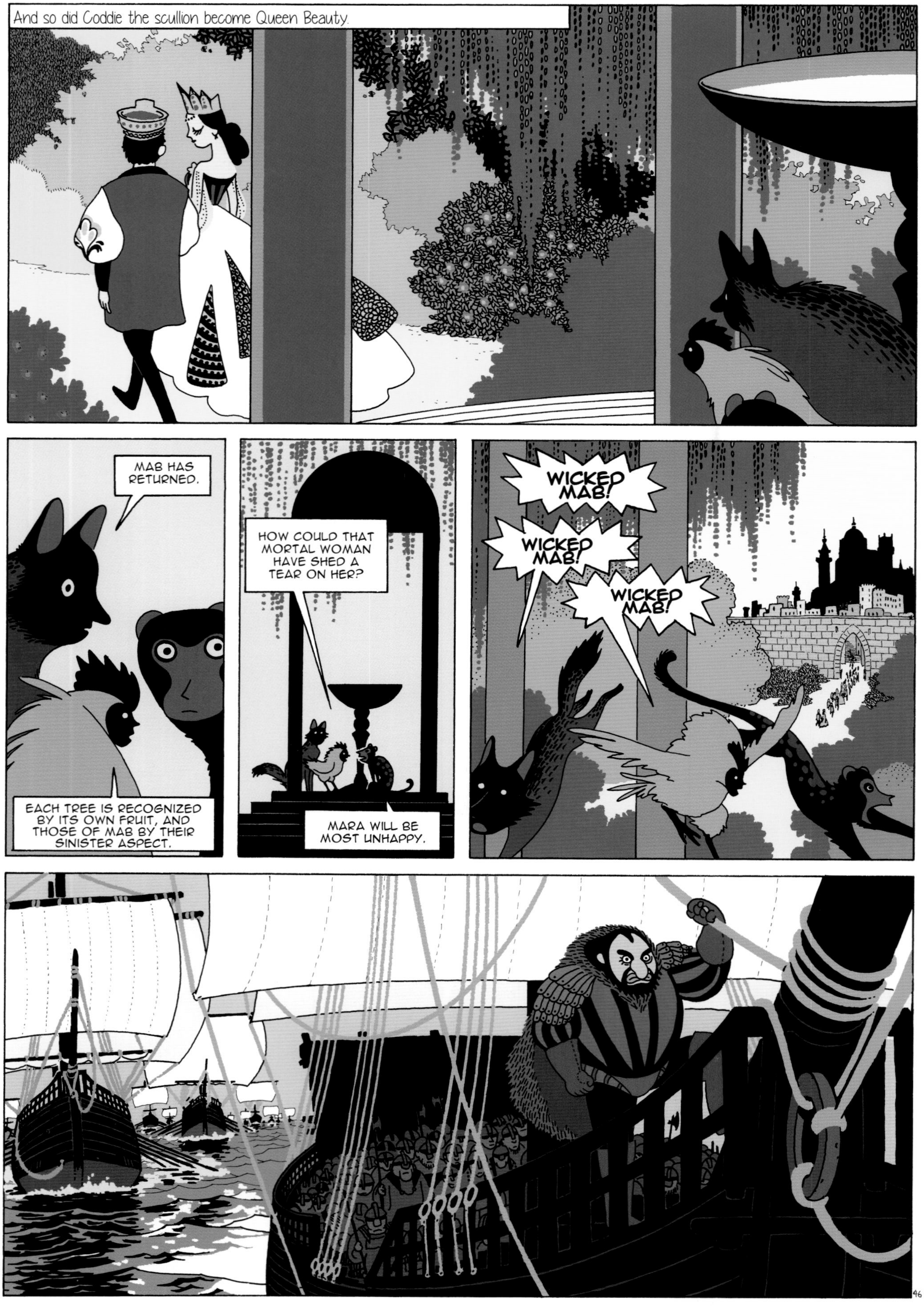
And so did Coddie the scullion become Queen Beauty.
MAB HAS RETURNED.
EACH TREE IS RECOGNIZED BY ITS OWN FRUIT, AND THOSE OF MAB BY THEIR SINISTER ASPECT.
HOW COULD THAT MORTAL WOMAN HAVE SHED A TEAR ON HER?
MARA WILL BE MOST UNHAPPY.
WICKED MAB!
WICKED MAB!
WICKED MAB!
46

2 ~ THE INDECISIVE QUEEN

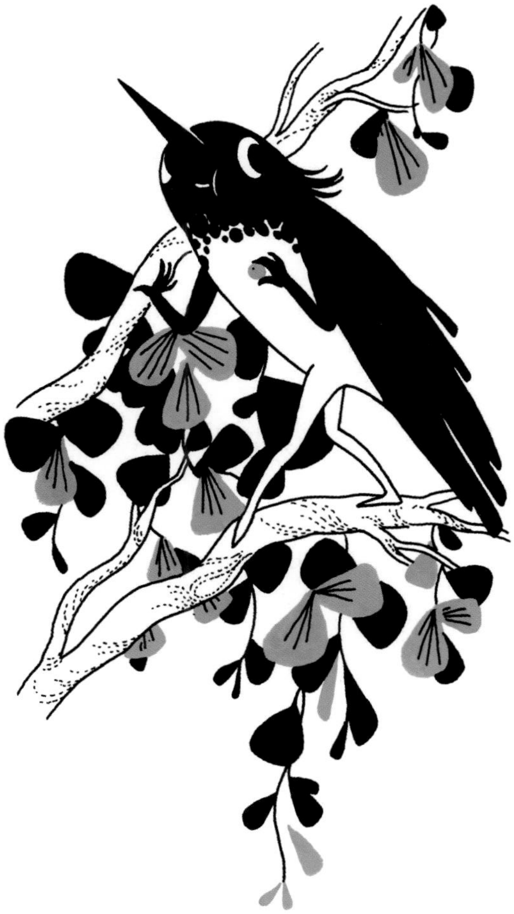

Walking arm in arm with King Maxence, Beauty felt completely beautiful for the first time. She was so happy! Everything would be perfect from now on.

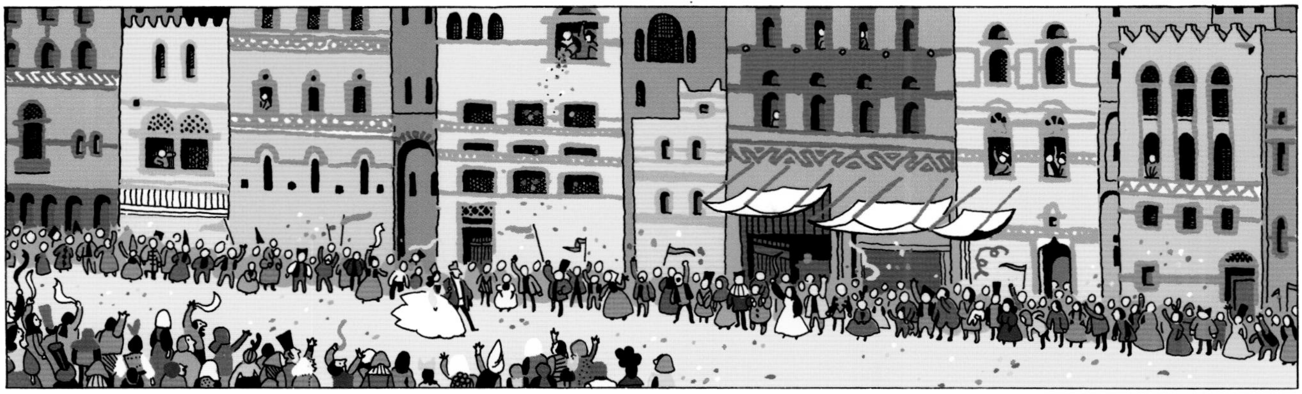

In her heart, she thanked Mab, the kind fairy who had given her such a marvelous gift.

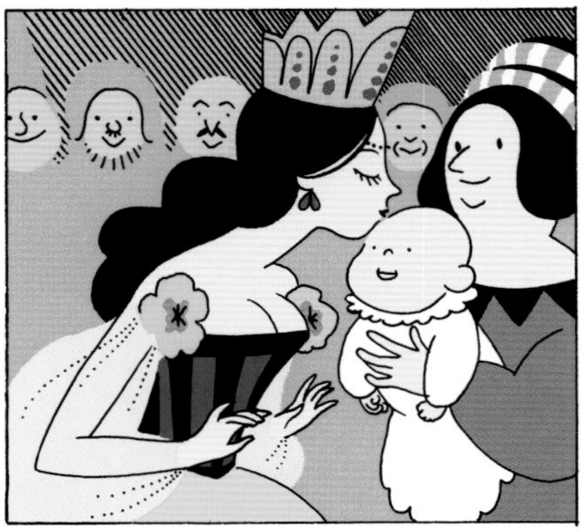

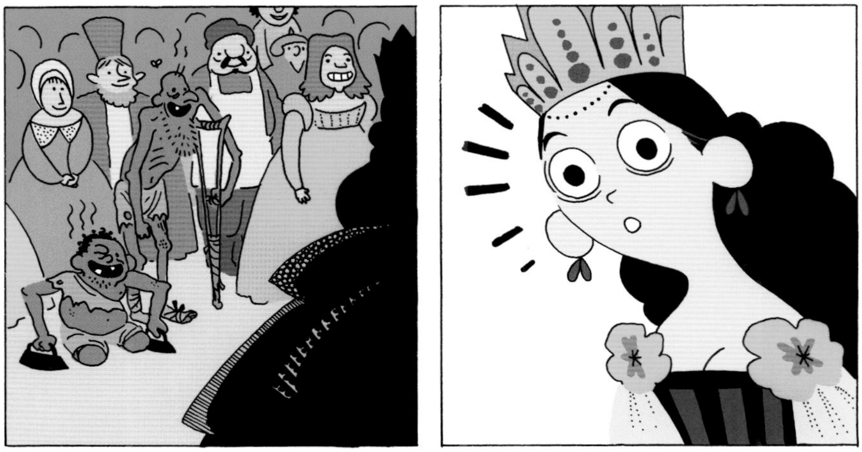

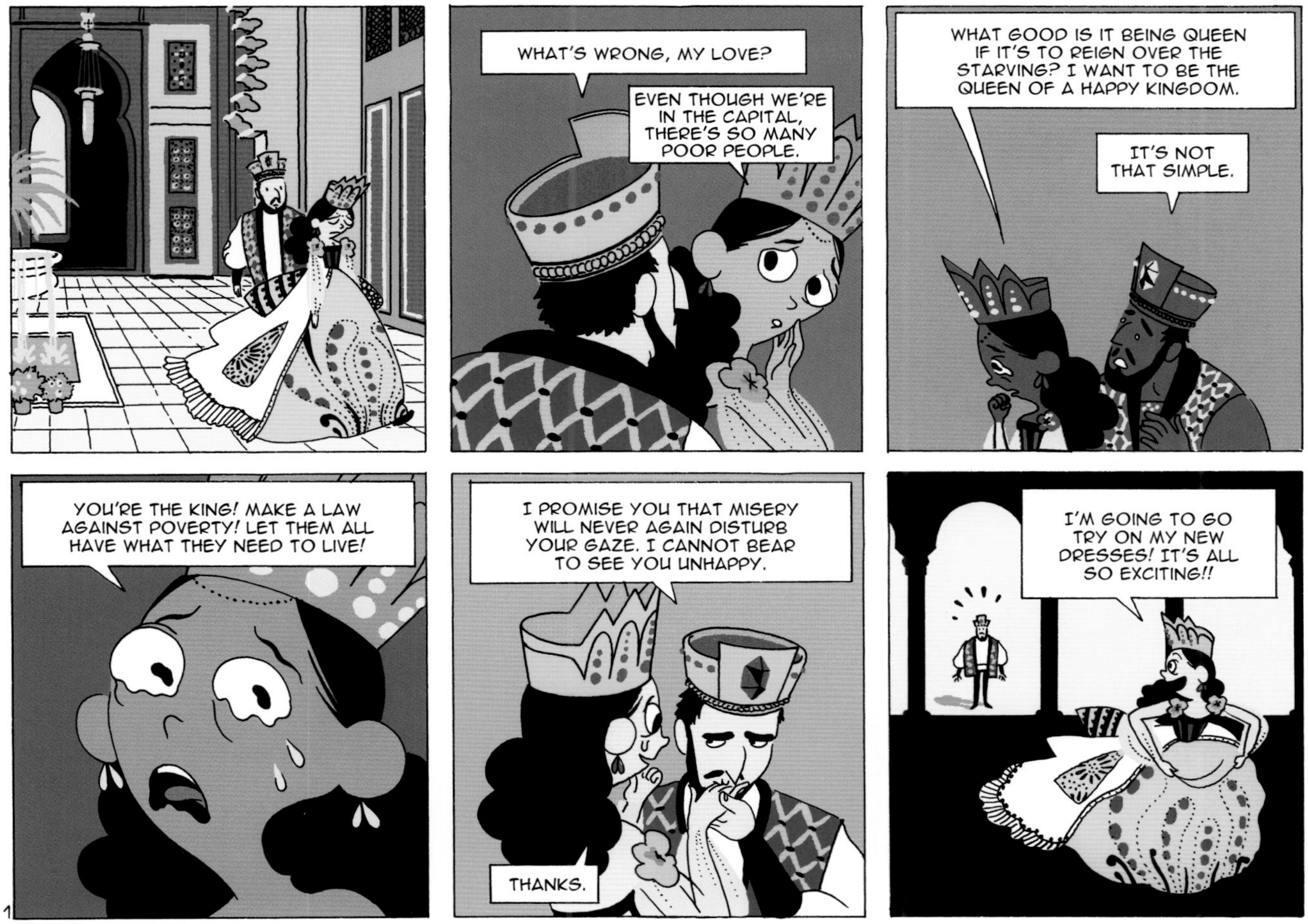
WHAT'S WRONG, MY LOVE?
EVEN THOUGH WE'RE IN THE CAPITAL, THERE'S SO MANY POOR PEOPLE.
WHAT GOOD IS IT BEING QUEEN IF IT'S TO REIGN OVER THE STARVING? I WANT TO BE THE QUEEN OF A HAPPY KINGDOM.
IT'S NOT THAT SIMPLE.
YOU'RE THE KING! MAKE A LAW AGAINST POVERTY! LET THEM ALL HAVE WHAT THEY NEED TO LIVE!
I PROMISE YOU THAT MISERY WILL NEVER AGAIN DISTURB YOUR GAZE. I CANNOT BEAR TO SEE YOU UNHAPPY.
THANKS.
I'M GOING TO GO TRY ON MY NEW DRESSES! IT'S ALL SO EXCITING!!

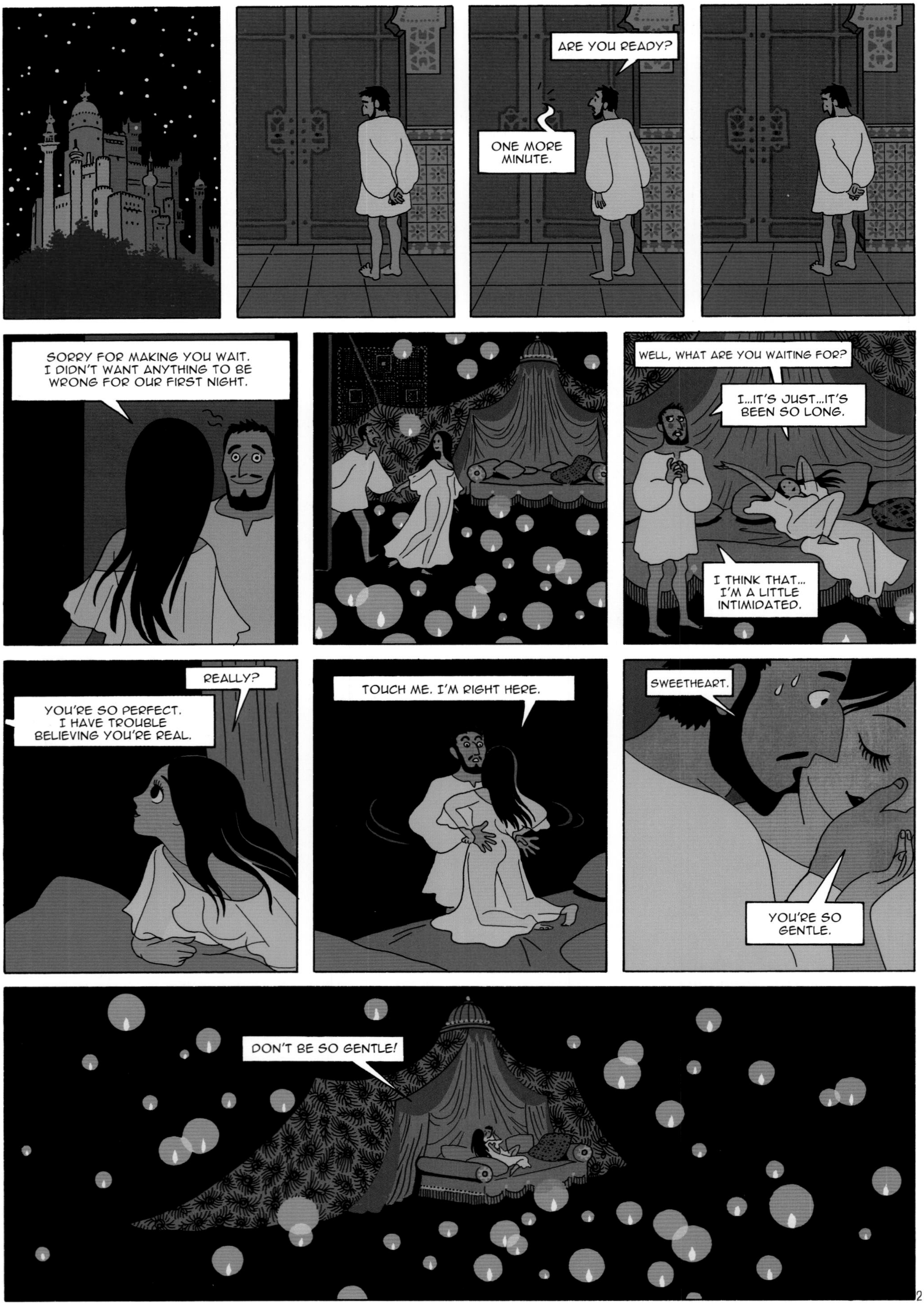
ARE YOU READY?
ONE MORE MINUTE.
SORRY FOR MAKING YOU WAIT. I DIDN'T WANT ANYTHING TO BE WRONG FOR OUR FIRST NIGHT.
WELL, WHAT ARE YOU WAITING FOR?
I...IT'S JUST...IT'S BEEN SO LONG.
I THINK THAT... I'M A LITTLE INTIMIDATED.
REALLY?
YOU'RE SO PERFECT. I HAVE TROUBLE BELIEVING YOU'RE REAL.
TOUCH ME. I'M RIGHT HERE.
SWEETHEART.
YOU'RE SO GENTLE.
DON'T BE SO GENTLE!

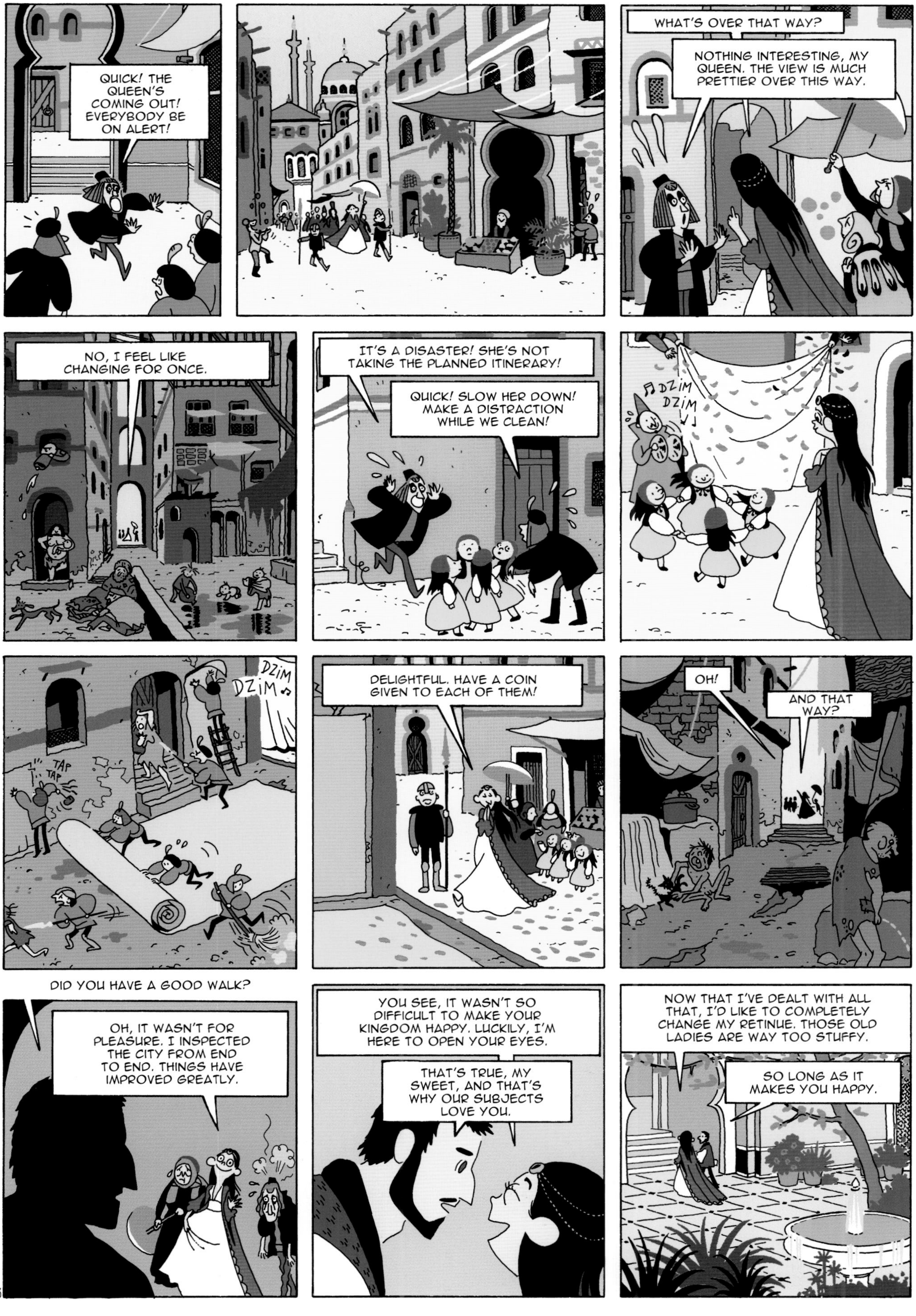

QUICK! THE QUEEN'S COMING OUT! EVERYBODY BE ON ALERT!
WHAT'S OVER THAT WAY?
NOTHING INTERESTING, MY QUEEN. THE VIEW IS MUCH PRETTIER OVER THIS WAY.
NO, I FEEL LIKE CHANGING FOR ONCE.
IT'S A DISASTER! SHE'S NOT TAKING THE PLANNED ITINERARY!
QUICK! SLOW HER DOWN! MAKE A DISTRACTION WHILE WE CLEAN!
DZIM DZIM
TAP TAP
DZIM DZIM
DELIGHTFUL. HAVE A COIN GIVEN TO EACH OF THEM!
OH!
AND THAT WAY?
DID YOU HAVE A GOOD WALK?
OH, IT WASN'T FOR PLEASURE. I INSPECTED THE CITY FROM END TO END. THINGS HAVE IMPROVED GREATLY.
YOU SEE, IT WASN'T SO DIFFICULT TO MAKE YOUR KINGDOM HAPPY. LUCKILY, I'M HERE TO OPEN YOUR EYES.
THAT'S TRUE, MY SWEET, AND THAT'S WHY OUR SUBJECTS LOVE YOU.
NOW THAT I'VE DEALT WITH ALL THAT, I'D LIKE TO COMPLETELY CHANGE MY RETINUE. THOSE OLD LADIES ARE WAY TOO STUFFY.
SO LONG AS IT MAKES YOU HAPPY.

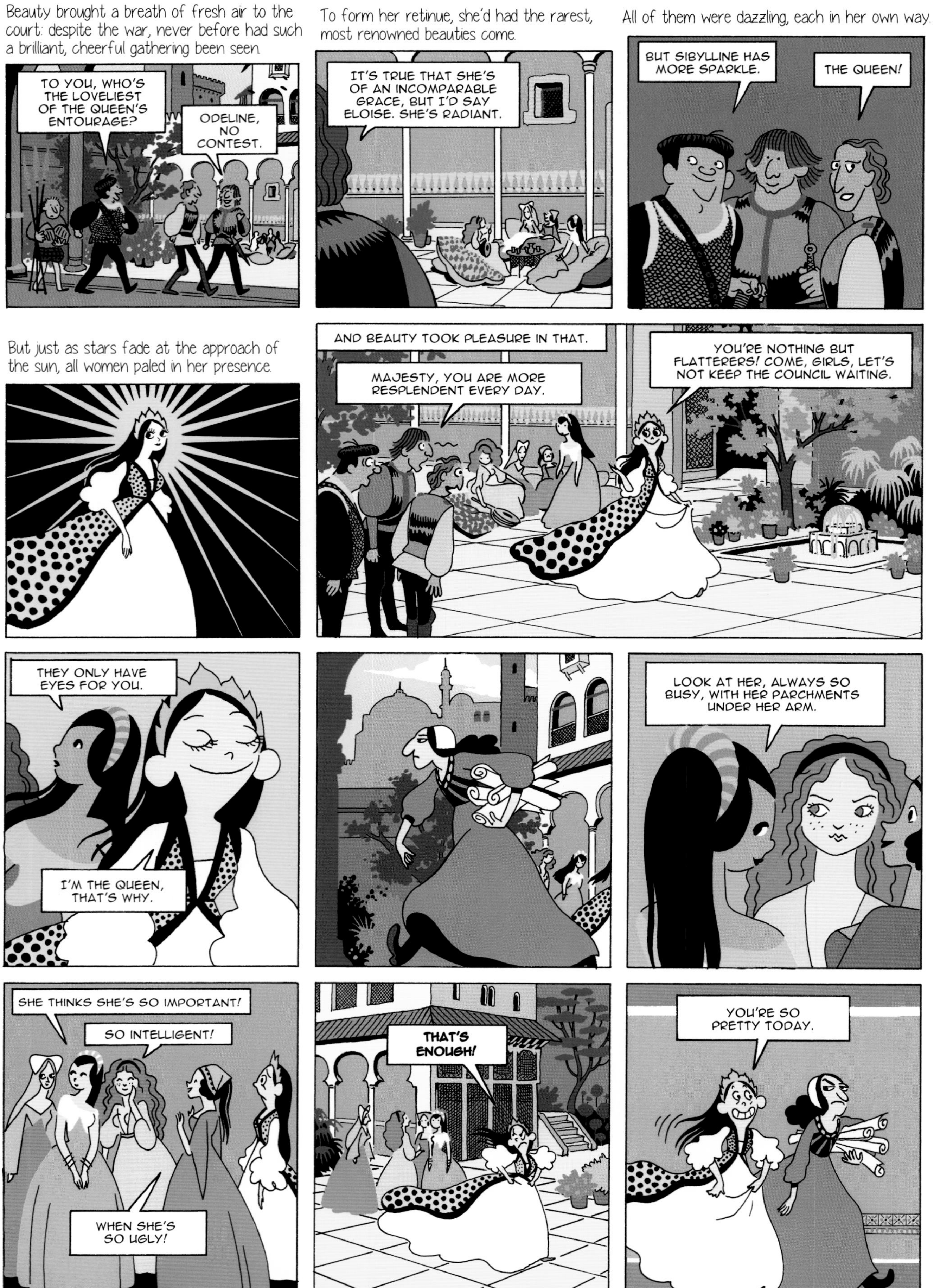
Beauty brought a breath of fresh air to the court: despite the war, never before had such a brilliant, cheerful gathering been seen.
TO YOU, WHO'S THE LOVELIEST OF THE QUEEN'S ENTOURAGE?
ODELINE, NO CONTEST.
To form her retinue, she'd had the rarest, most renowned beauties come.
IT'S TRUE THAT SHE'S OF AN INCOMPARABLE GRACE, BUT I'D SAY ELOISE. SHE'S RADIANT.
All of them were dazzling, each in her own way.
BUT SIBYLLINE HAS MORE SPARKLE.
THE QUEEN!
But just as stars fade at the approach of the sun, all women paled in her presence.
AND BEAUTY TOOK PLEASURE IN THAT.
MAJESTY, YOU ARE MORE RESPLENDENT EVERY DAY.
YOU'RE NOTHING BUT FLATTERERS! COME, GIRLS, LET'S NOT KEEP THE COUNCIL WAITING.
THEY ONLY HAVE EYES FOR YOU.
I'M THE QUEEN, THAT'S WHY.
LOOK AT HER, ALWAYS SO BUSY, WITH HER PARCHMENTS UNDER HER ARM.
SHE THINKS SHE'S SO IMPORTANT!
SO INTELLIGENT!
WHEN SHE'S SO UGLY!
THAT'S ENOUGH!
YOU'RE SO PRETTY TODAY.
4

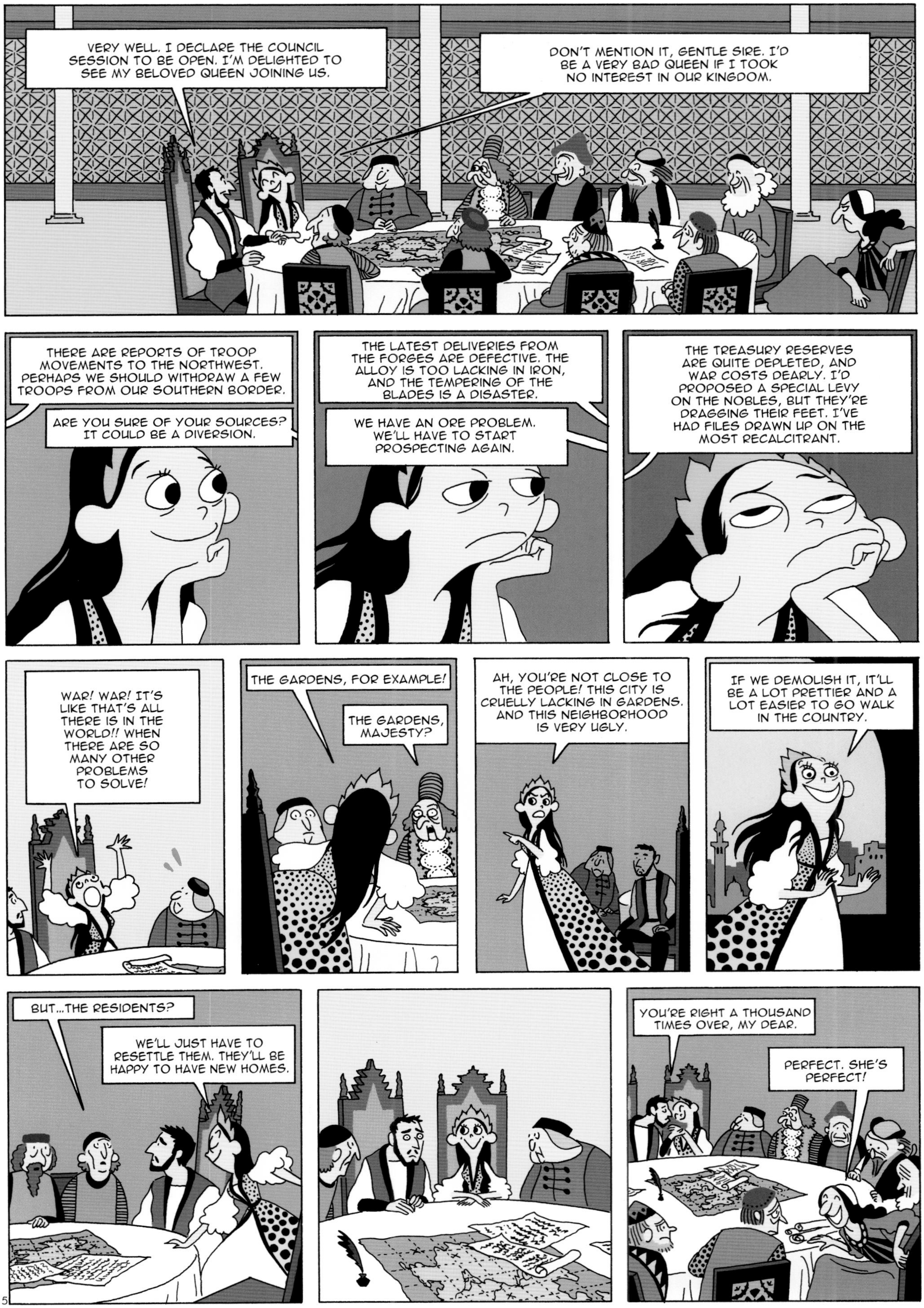
VERY WELL. I DECLARE THE COUNCIL SESSION TO BE OPEN. I'M DELIGHTED TO SEE MY BELOVED QUEEN JOINING US.
DON'T MENTION IT, GENTLE SIRE. I'D BE A VERY BAD QUEEN IF I TOOK NO INTEREST IN OUR KINGDOM.
THERE ARE REPORTS OF TROOP MOVEMENTS TO THE NORTHWEST. PERHAPS WE SHOULD WITHDRAW A FEW TROOPS FROM OUR SOUTHERN BORDER.
ARE YOU SURE OF YOUR SOURCES? IT COULD BE A DIVERSION.
THE LATEST DELIVERIES FROM THE FORGES ARE DEFECTIVE. THE ALLOY IS TOO LACKING IN IRON, AND THE TEMPERING OF THE BLADES IS A DISASTER.
WE HAVE AN ORE PROBLEM. WE'LL HAVE TO START PROSPECTING AGAIN.
THE TREASURY RESERVES ARE QUITE DEPLETED, AND WAR COSTS DEARLY. I'D PROPOSED A SPECIAL LEVY ON THE NOBLES, BUT THEY'RE DRAGGING THEIR FEET. I'VE HAD FILES DRAWN UP ON THE MOST RECALCITRANT.
WAR! WAR! IT'S LIKE THAT'S ALL THERE IS IN THE WORLD!! WHEN THERE ARE SO MANY OTHER PROBLEMS TO SOLVE!
THE GARDENS, FOR EXAMPLE!
THE GARDENS, MAJESTY?
AH, YOU'RE NOT CLOSE TO THE PEOPLE! THIS CITY IS CRUELLY LACKING IN GARDENS. AND THIS NEIGHBORHOOD IS VERY UGLY.
IF WE DEMOLISH IT, IT'LL BE A LOT PRETTIER AND A LOT EASIER TO GO WALK IN THE COUNTRY.
BUT...THE RESIDENTS?
WE'LL JUST HAVE TO RESETTLE THEM. THEY'LL BE HAPPY TO HAVE NEW HOMES.
YOU'RE RIGHT A THOUSAND TIMES OVER, MY DEAR.
PERFECT. SHE'S PERFECT!

To make Beauty happy, Otto had gone in search of riches.

But if fortune favors the bold, it's doesn't just fall into an impatient man's hands.

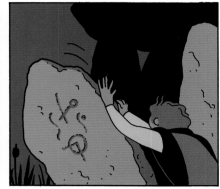

And Otto was impatient to the highest degree. At every moment, he burned to return to Beauty's arms.

BE CURSED! MAY THE FAIRIES NEVER GIVE ANY REST TO YOU WHO DISRESPECTS THE SLUMBER OF THE DEAD!

BEAUTY.

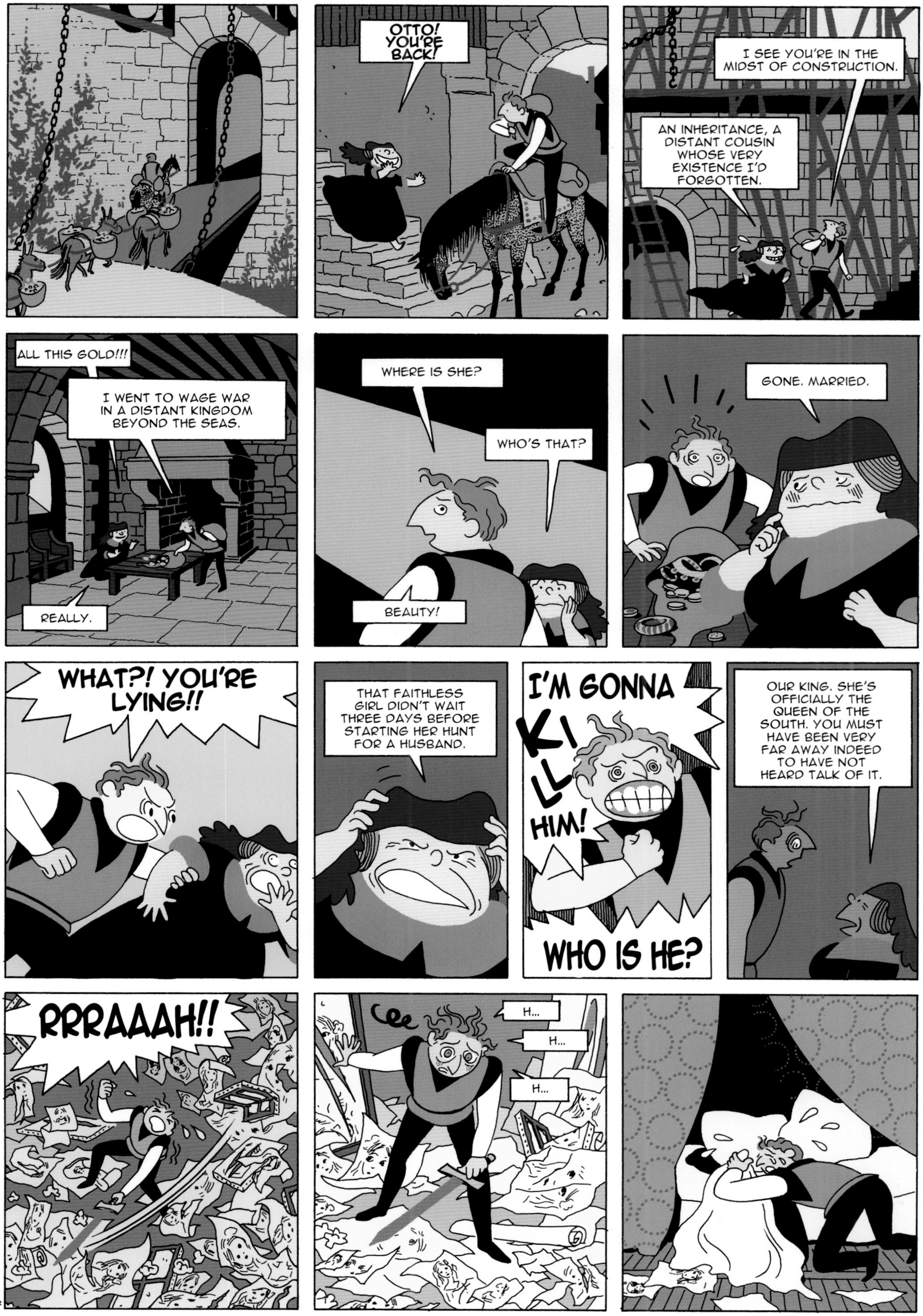
OTTO! YOU'RE BACK!
I SEE YOU'RE IN THE MIDST OF CONSTRUCTION.
AN INHERITANCE, A DISTANT COUSIN WHOSE VERY EXISTENCE I'D FORGOTTEN.
ALL THIS GOLD!!!
I WENT TO WAGE WAR IN A DISTANT KINGDOM BEYOND THE SEAS.
REALLY.
WHERE IS SHE?
WHO'S THAT?
BEAUTY!
GONE. MARRIED.
WHAT?! YOU'RE LYING!!
THAT FAITHLESS GIRL DIDN'T WAIT THREE DAYS BEFORE STARTING HER HUNT FOR A HUSBAND.
I'M GONNA KILL HIM!
WHO IS HE?
OUR KING. SHE'S OFFICIALLY THE QUEEN OF THE SOUTH. YOU MUST HAVE BEEN VERY FAR AWAY INDEED TO HAVE NOT HEARD TALK OF IT.
RRRAAAH!!
H...
H...
H...

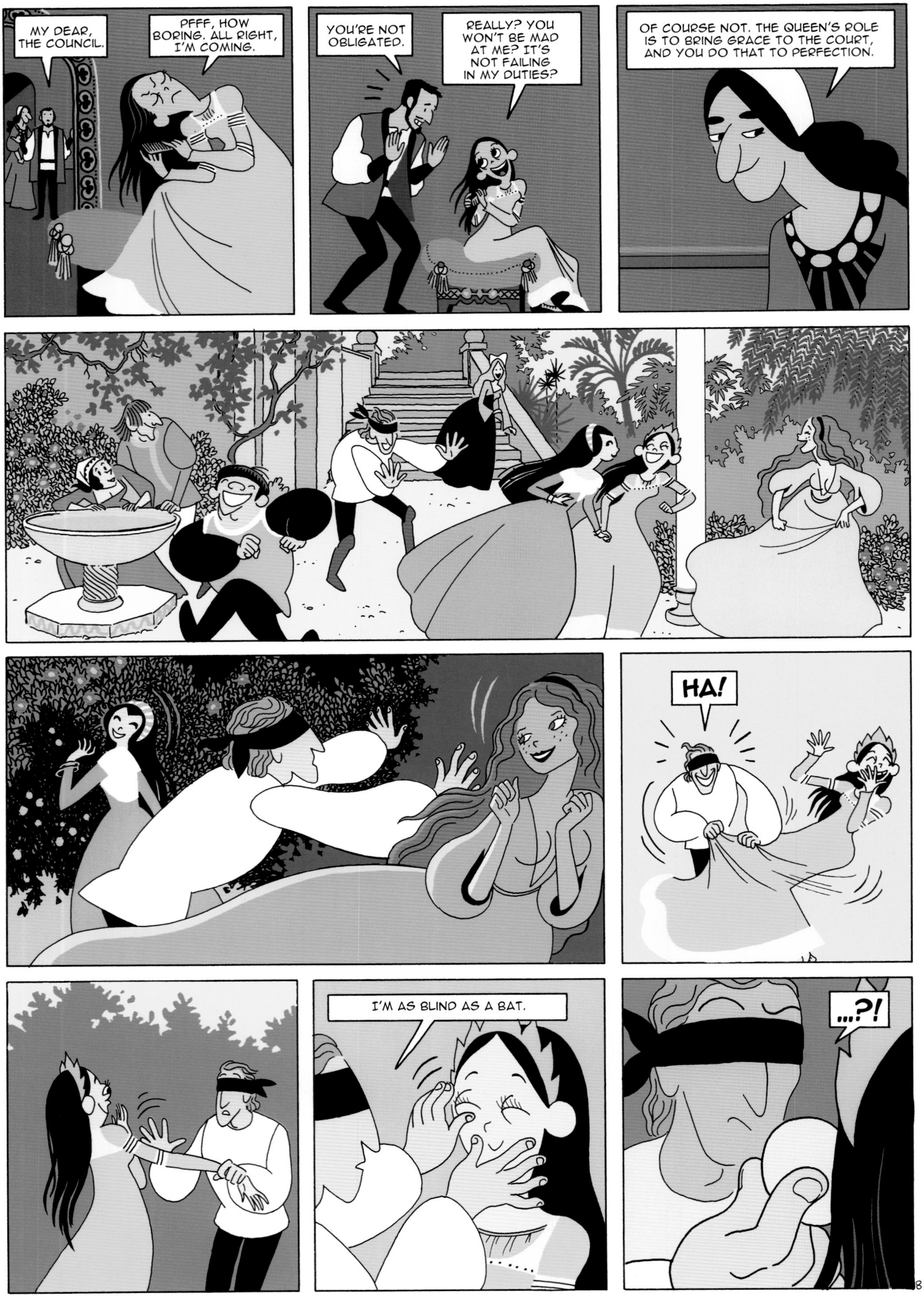
MY DEAR, THE COUNCIL.
PFFF, HOW BORING. ALL RIGHT, I'M COMING.
YOU'RE NOT OBLIGATED.
REALLY? YOU WON'T BE MAD AT ME? IT'S NOT FAILING IN MY DUTIES?
OF COURSE NOT. THE QUEEN'S ROLE IS TO BRING GRACE TO THE COURT, AND YOU DO THAT TO PERFECTION.
HA!
I'M AS BLIND AS A BAT.
...?!

THAT SCENT...THAT DELICATE IODIZED SCENT...

SNIF SNIF SNIF

MAJESTY!!

AS A REWARD, YOU CAN KISS MY HAND.

GENTLY, MILORD! I DIDN'T ALLOW YOU TO SNACK ON IT!

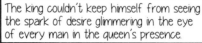

The king couldn't keep himself from seeing the spark of desire glimmering in the eye of every man in the queen's presence.

SIRE?

And although he had faith in her, that quickly hidden flash worried him.

SORRY? YOU WERE SAYING?

THE KNIGHTS ARE VERY GALLANT TOWARDS YOU.

COME NOW, IT'S ONLY A GAME! THEY ALL KNOW I'M YOUR QUEEN, AND NONE WILL LAY A HAND ON ME!

APART FROM YOU.

I DON'T THINK IT'S THAT CLEAR IN EVERYONE'S HEAD.

I'M HAVING FUN, THAT'S ALL! AND YOU'RE NEVER HERE EITHER. YOU JUST HAVE TO MAKE AN EFFORT.

THE KINGDOM'S NEEDS...

FRANKLY, YOU'RE NEVER ANY FUN. WHY DO YOU ALWAYS HAVE TO BE SO INHIBITED? LET YOURSELF GO A LITTLE!

COME NOW, IT'S NORMAL FOR MEN TO REVERE YOU. YOUR HUSBAND WOULD HAVE TO BE PRETTY WARPED TO SEE ANYTHING BAD IN IT WHEN YOU'RE PROTECTING YOUR VIRTUE.

THAT'S JUST WHAT I TOLD HIM.

ON THE CONTRARY, HE SHOULD BE FLATTERED: DESPITE ALL THE SUITORS CROWDING AT YOUR FEET, YOU REMAIN FAITHFUL TO HIM.

SO WHAT IF YOU'RE VIRTUOUS IF YOU'RE LIVING AS A RECLUSE, SHELTERED FROM TEMPTATIONS! IT'S BY PUTTING YOUR LOVE TO THE TEST THAT YOU PROVE YOUR STRENGTH AND COMMITMENT.

THAT'S NOT UNTRUE.

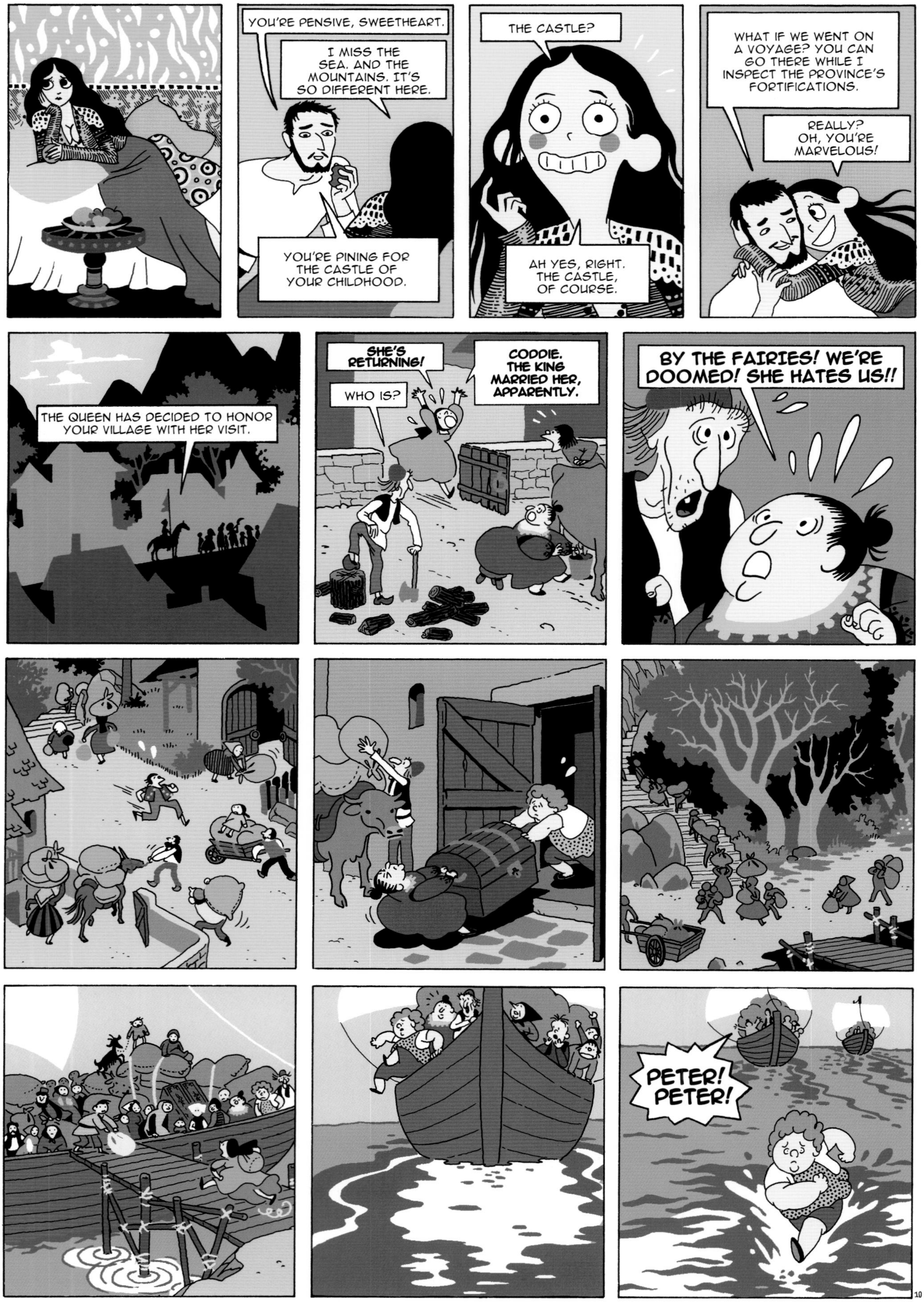
YOU'RE PENSIVE, SWEETHEART.
I MISS THE SEA. AND THE MOUNTAINS. IT'S SO DIFFERENT HERE.
YOU'RE PINING FOR THE CASTLE OF YOUR CHILDHOOD.
THE CASTLE?
AH YES, RIGHT. THE CASTLE, OF COURSE.
WHAT IF WE WENT ON A VOYAGE? YOU CAN GO THERE WHILE I INSPECT THE PROVINCE'S FORTIFICATIONS.
REALLY? OH, YOU'RE MARVELOUS!
THE QUEEN HAS DECIDED TO HONOR YOUR VILLAGE WITH HER VISIT.
SHE'S RETURNING!
WHO IS?
CODDIE. THE KING MARRIED HER, APPARENTLY.
BY THE FAIRIES! WE'RE DOOMED! SHE HATES US!!
PETER! PETER!
10

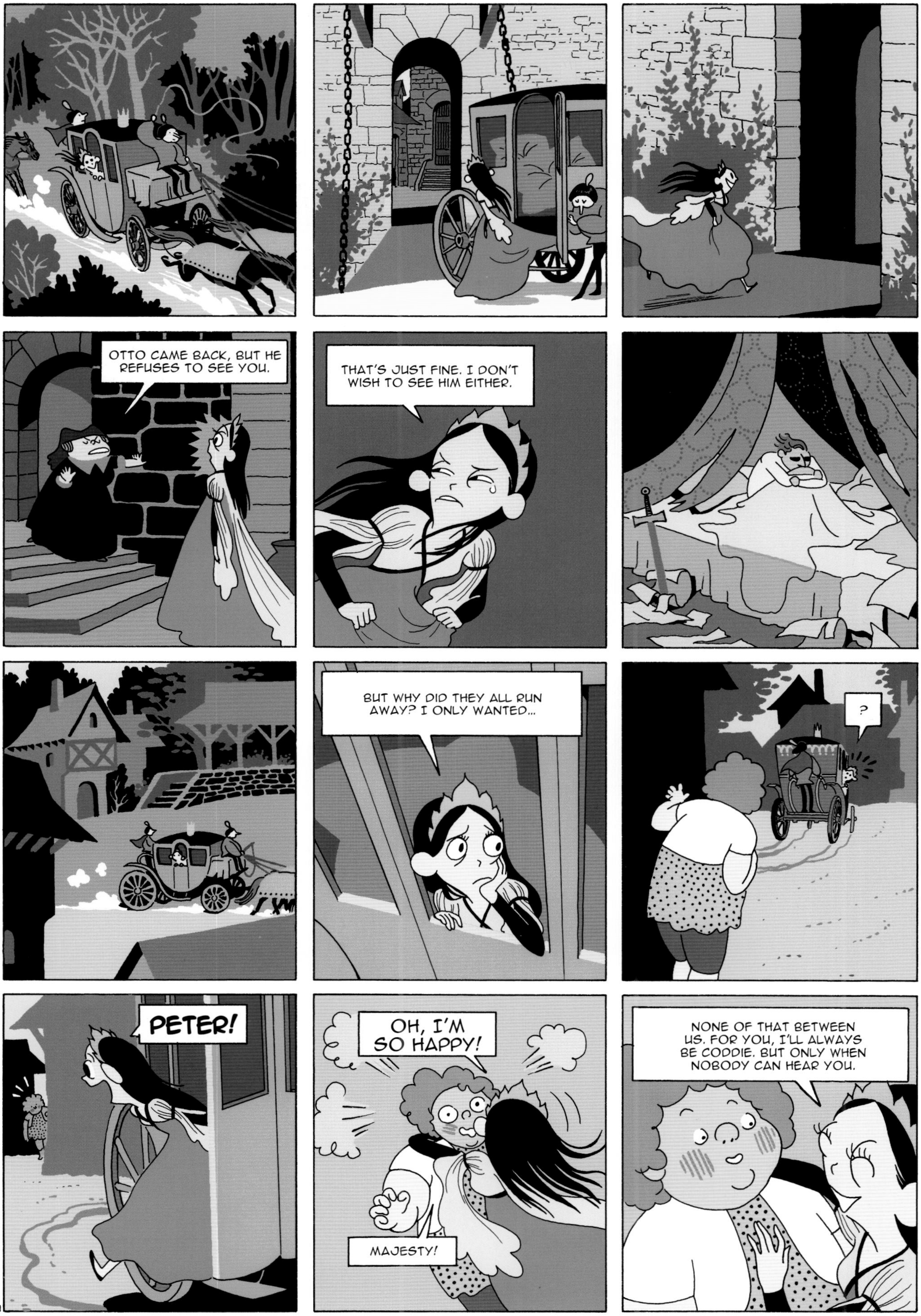
OTTO CAME BACK, BUT HE REFUSES TO SEE YOU.
THAT'S JUST FINE. I DON'T WISH TO SEE HIM EITHER.
BUT WHY DID THEY ALL RUN AWAY? I ONLY WANTED...
?
PETER!
OH, I'M SO HAPPY!
MAJESTY!
NONE OF THAT BETWEEN US. FOR YOU, I'LL ALWAYS BE CODDIE. BUT ONLY WHEN NOBODY CAN HEAR YOU.
11

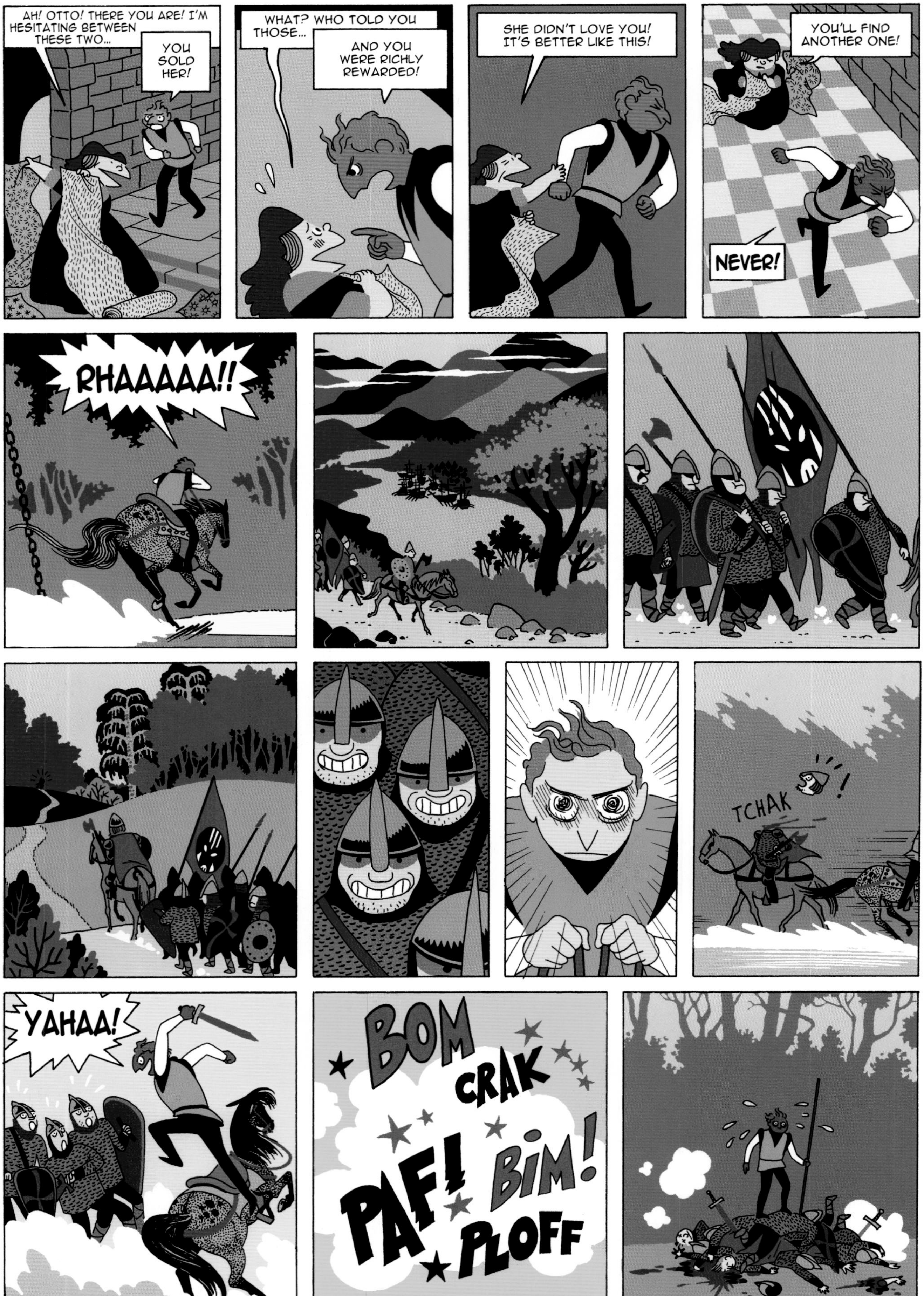

AH! OTTO! THERE YOU ARE! I'M HESITATING BETWEEN THESE TWO...
YOU SOLD HER!
WHAT? WHO TOLD YOU THOSE...
AND YOU WERE RICHLY REWARDED!
SHE DIDN'T LOVE YOU! IT'S BETTER LIKE THIS!
YOU'LL FIND ANOTHER ONE!
NEVER!
RHAAAAA!!
TCHAK
YAHAA!
BOM
CRAK
PAF!
BIM!
PLOFF
12

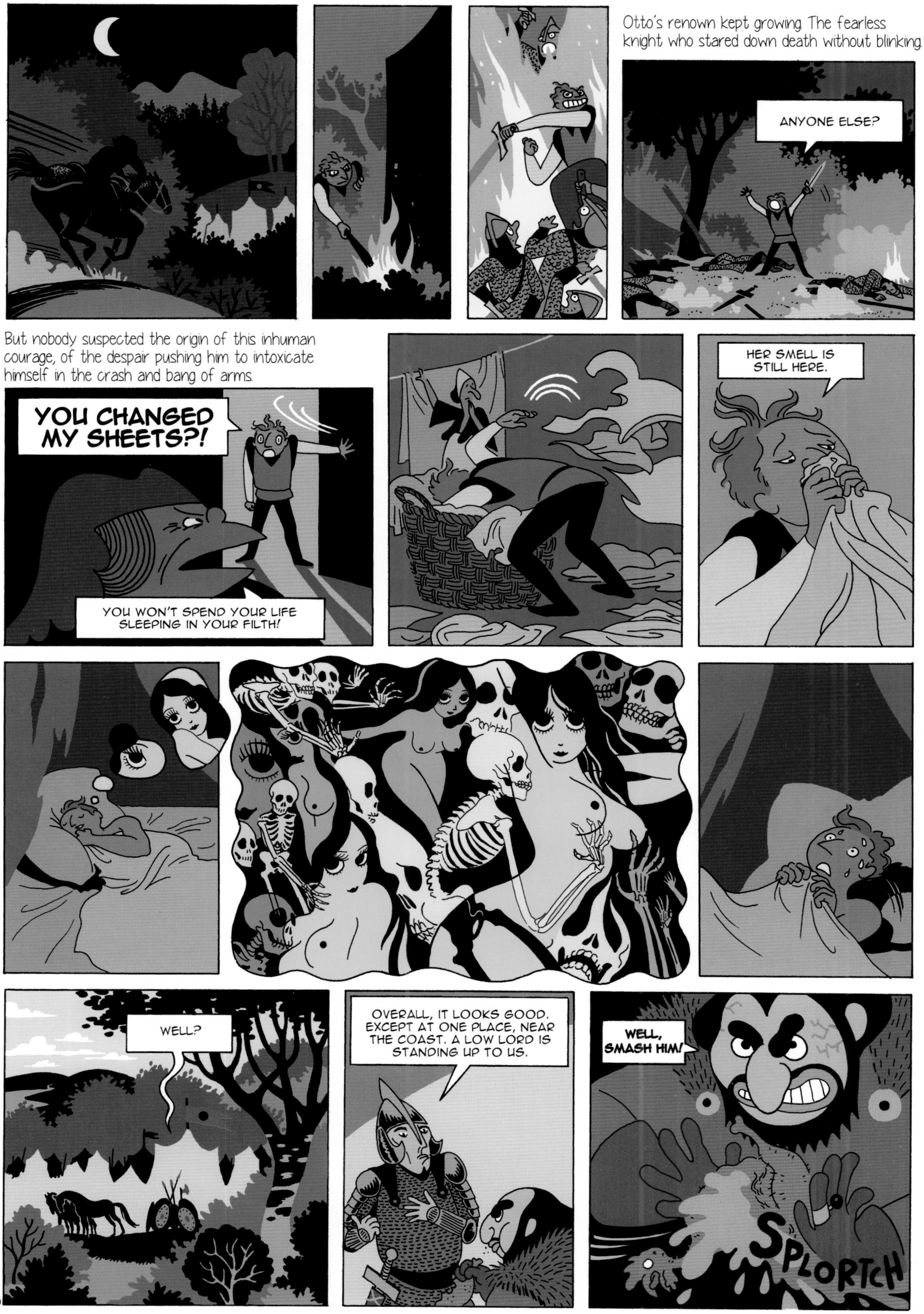
Otto's renown kept growing. The fearless knight who stared down death without blinking.
ANYONE ELSE?
But nobody suspected the origin of this inhuman courage, of the despair pushing him to intoxicate himself in the crash and bang of arms.
YOU CHANGED MY SHEETS?!
YOU WON'T SPEND YOUR LIFE SLEEPING IN YOUR FILTH!
HER SMELL IS STILL HERE.
WELL?
OVERALL, IT LOOKS GOOD. EXCEPT AT ONE PLACE, NEAR THE COAST. A LOW LORD IS STANDING UP TO US.
WELL, SMASH HIM!
SPLORTCH
13

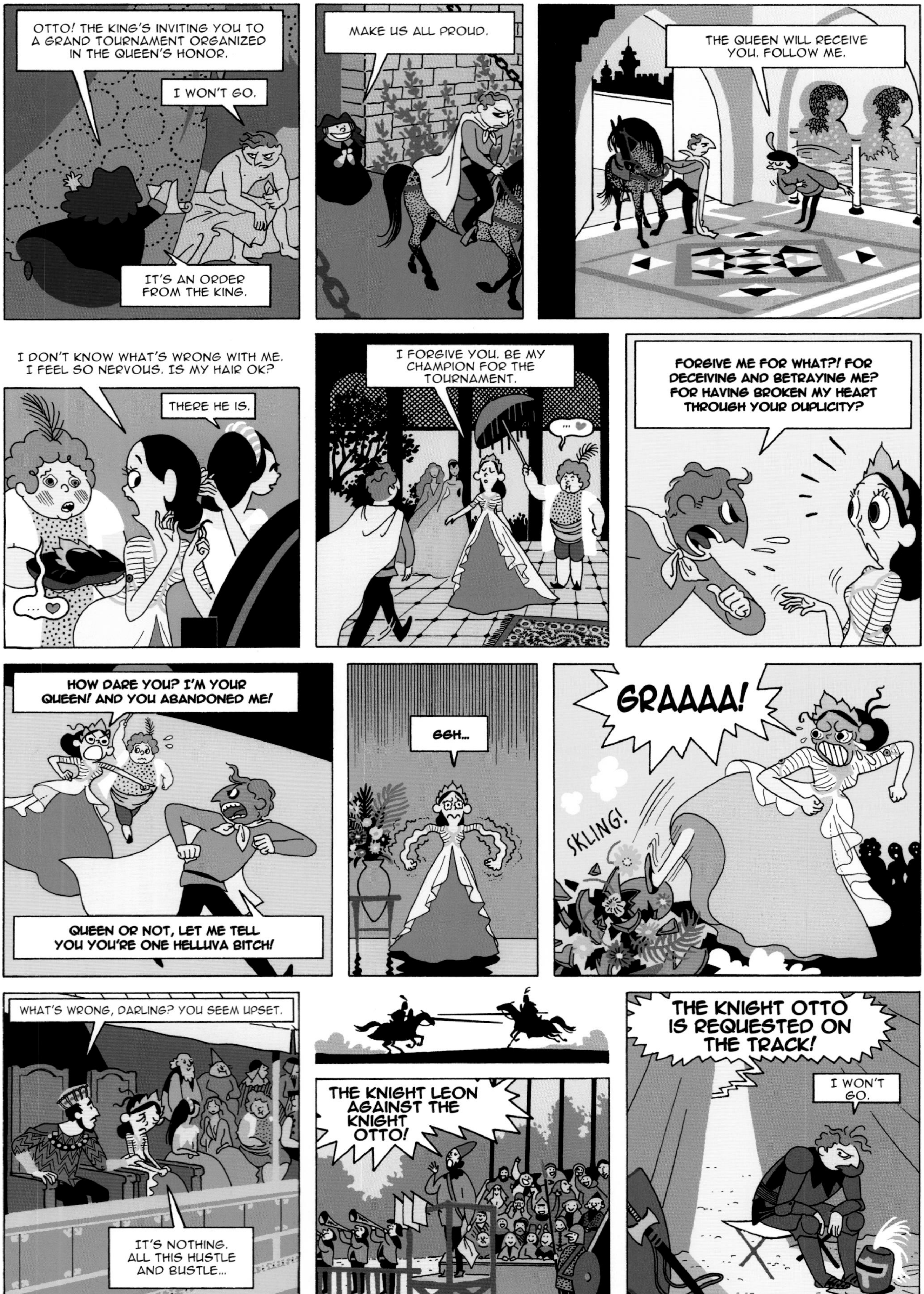
OTTO! THE KING'S INVITING YOU TO A GRAND TOURNAMENT ORGANIZED IN THE QUEEN'S HONOR.
I WON'T GO.
IT'S AN ORDER FROM THE KING.
MAKE US ALL PROUD.
THE QUEEN WILL RECEIVE YOU. FOLLOW ME.
I DON'T KNOW WHAT'S WRONG WITH ME. I FEEL SO NERVOUS. IS MY HAIR OK?
THERE HE IS.
...
I FORGIVE YOU. BE MY CHAMPION FOR THE TOURNAMENT.
...
FORGIVE ME FOR WHAT?! FOR DECEIVING AND BETRAYING ME? FOR HAVING BROKEN MY HEART THROUGH YOUR DUPLICITY?
HOW DARE YOU? I'M YOUR QUEEN! AND YOU ABANDONED ME!
QUEEN OR NOT, LET ME TELL YOU YOU'RE ONE HELLUVA BITCH!
GGH...
GRAAAA!
SKLING!
WHAT'S WRONG, DARLING? YOU SEEM UPSET.
IT'S NOTHING. ALL THIS HUSTLE AND BUSTLE...
THE KNIGHT LEON AGAINST THE KNIGHT OTTO!
THE KNIGHT OTTO IS REQUESTED ON THE TRACK!
I WON'T GO.

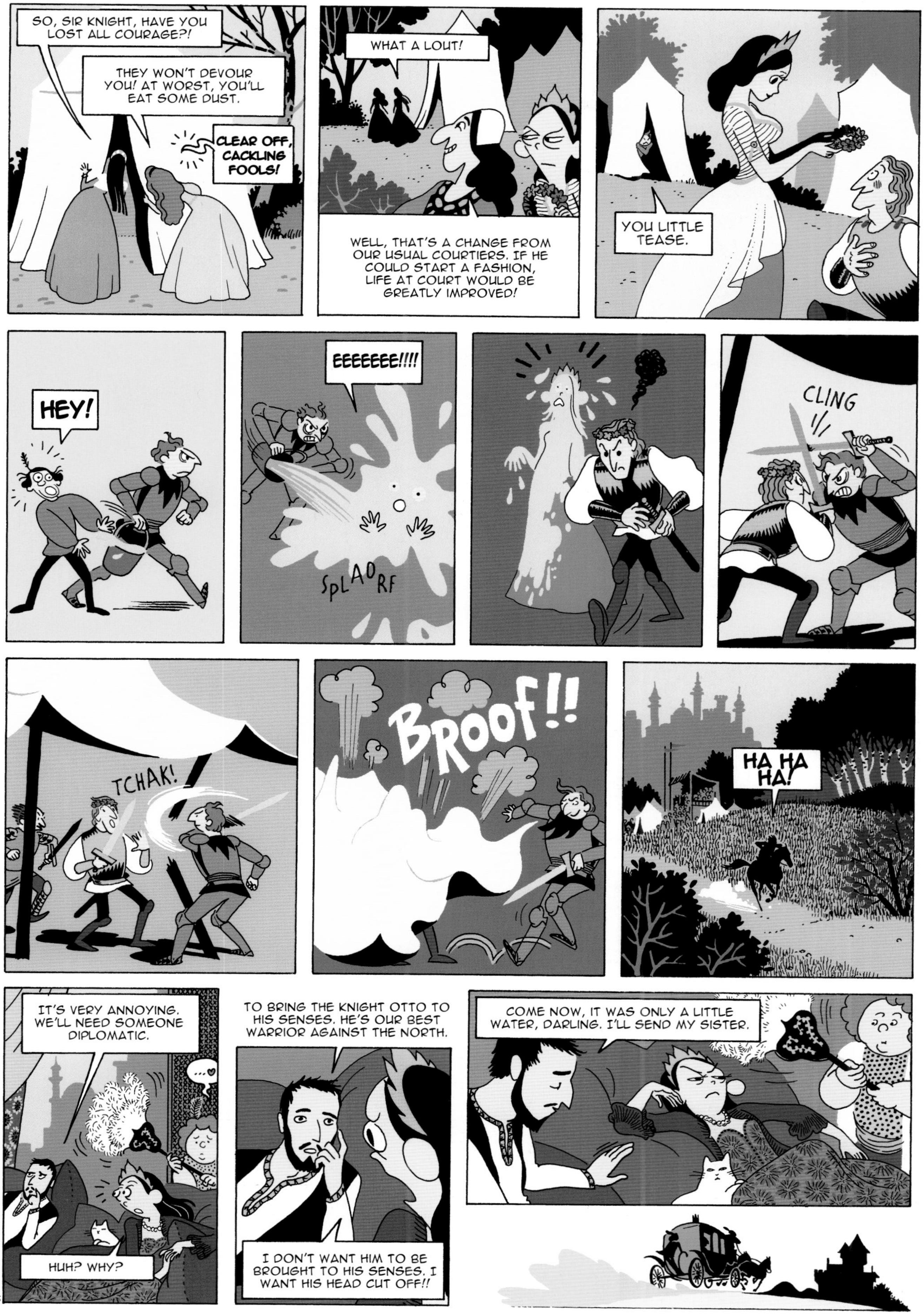
SO, SIR KNIGHT, HAVE YOU LOST ALL COURAGE?!
THEY WON'T DEVOUR YOU! AT WORST, YOU'LL EAT SOME DUST.
CLEAR OFF, CACKLING FOOLS!
WHAT A LOUT!
WELL, THAT'S A CHANGE FROM OUR USUAL COURTIERS. IF HE COULD START A FASHION, LIFE AT COURT WOULD BE GREATLY IMPROVED!
YOU LITTLE TEASE.
HEY!
EEEEEEE!!!!
SPLAORF
CLING
TCHAK!
BROOF!!
HA HA HA!
IT'S VERY ANNOYING. WE'LL NEED SOMEONE DIPLOMATIC.
HUH? WHY?
TO BRING THE KNIGHT OTTO TO HIS SENSES. HE'S OUR BEST WARRIOR AGAINST THE NORTH.
I DON'T WANT HIM TO BE BROUGHT TO HIS SENSES. I WANT HIS HEAD CUT OFF!!
COME NOW, IT WAS ONLY A LITTLE WATER, DARLING. I'LL SEND MY SISTER.

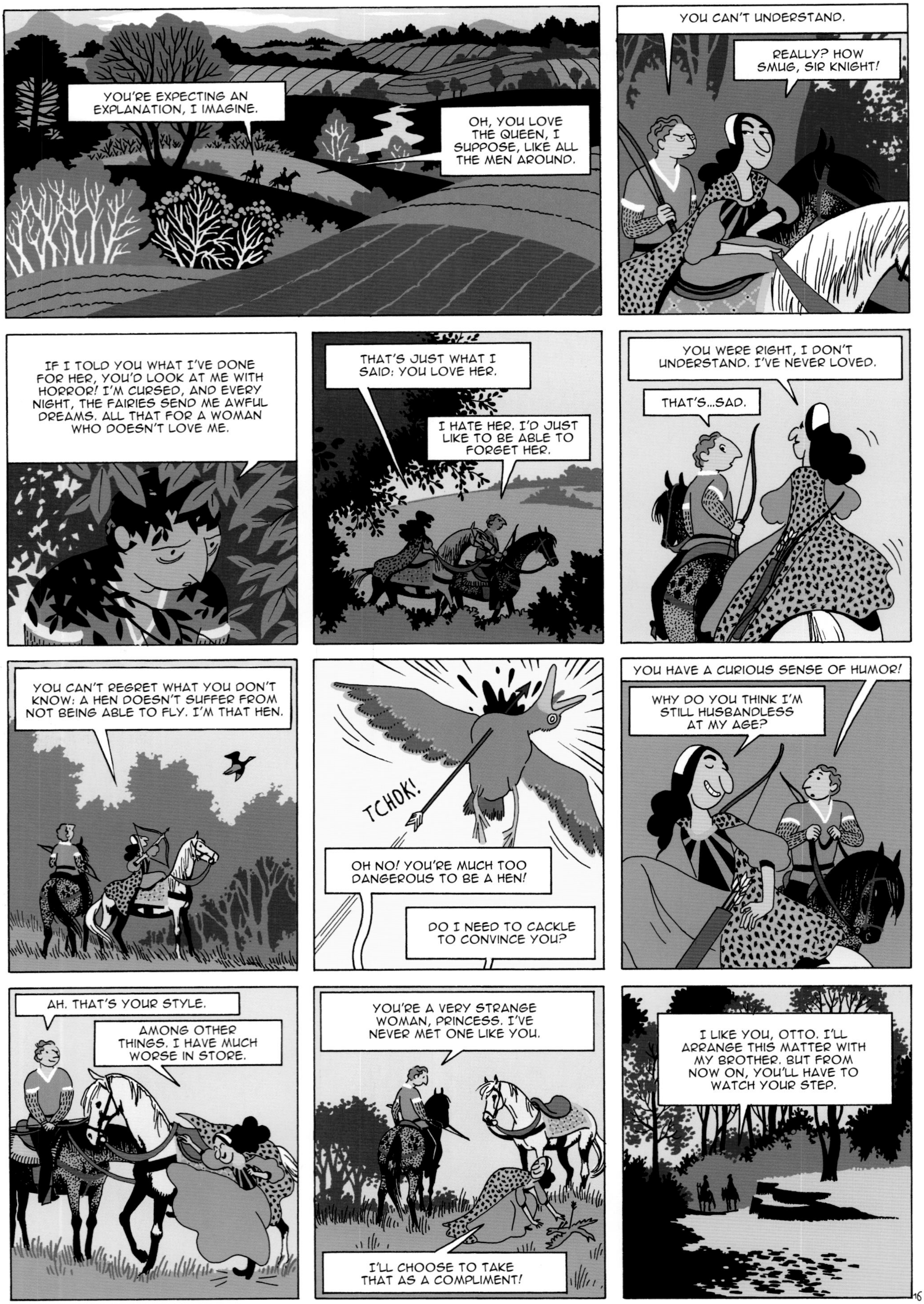
YOU'RE EXPECTING AN EXPLANATION, I IMAGINE.
OH, YOU LOVE THE QUEEN, I SUPPOSE, LIKE ALL THE MEN AROUND.
YOU CAN'T UNDERSTAND.
REALLY? HOW SMUG, SIR KNIGHT!
IF I TOLD YOU WHAT I'VE DONE FOR HER, YOU'D LOOK AT ME WITH HORROR! I'M CURSED, AND EVERY NIGHT, THE FAIRIES SEND ME AWFUL DREAMS. ALL THAT FOR A WOMAN WHO DOESN'T LOVE ME.
THAT'S JUST WHAT I SAID: YOU LOVE HER.
I HATE HER. I'D JUST LIKE TO BE ABLE TO FORGET HER.
YOU WERE RIGHT, I DON'T UNDERSTAND. I'VE NEVER LOVED.
THAT'S...SAD.
YOU CAN'T REGRET WHAT YOU DON'T KNOW: A HEN DOESN'T SUFFER FROM NOT BEING ABLE TO FLY. I'M THAT HEN.
TCHOK!
OH NO! YOU'RE MUCH TOO DANGEROUS TO BE A HEN!
DO I NEED TO CACKLE TO CONVINCE YOU?
YOU HAVE A CURIOUS SENSE OF HUMOR!
WHY DO YOU THINK I'M STILL HUSBANDLESS AT MY AGE?
AH. THAT'S YOUR STYLE.
AMONG OTHER THINGS. I HAVE MUCH WORSE IN STORE.
YOU'RE A VERY STRANGE WOMAN, PRINCESS. I'VE NEVER MET ONE LIKE YOU.
I'LL CHOOSE TO TAKE THAT AS A COMPLIMENT!
I LIKE YOU, OTTO. I'LL ARRANGE THIS MATTER WITH MY BROTHER. BUT FROM NOW ON, YOU'LL HAVE TO WATCH YOUR STEP.
16

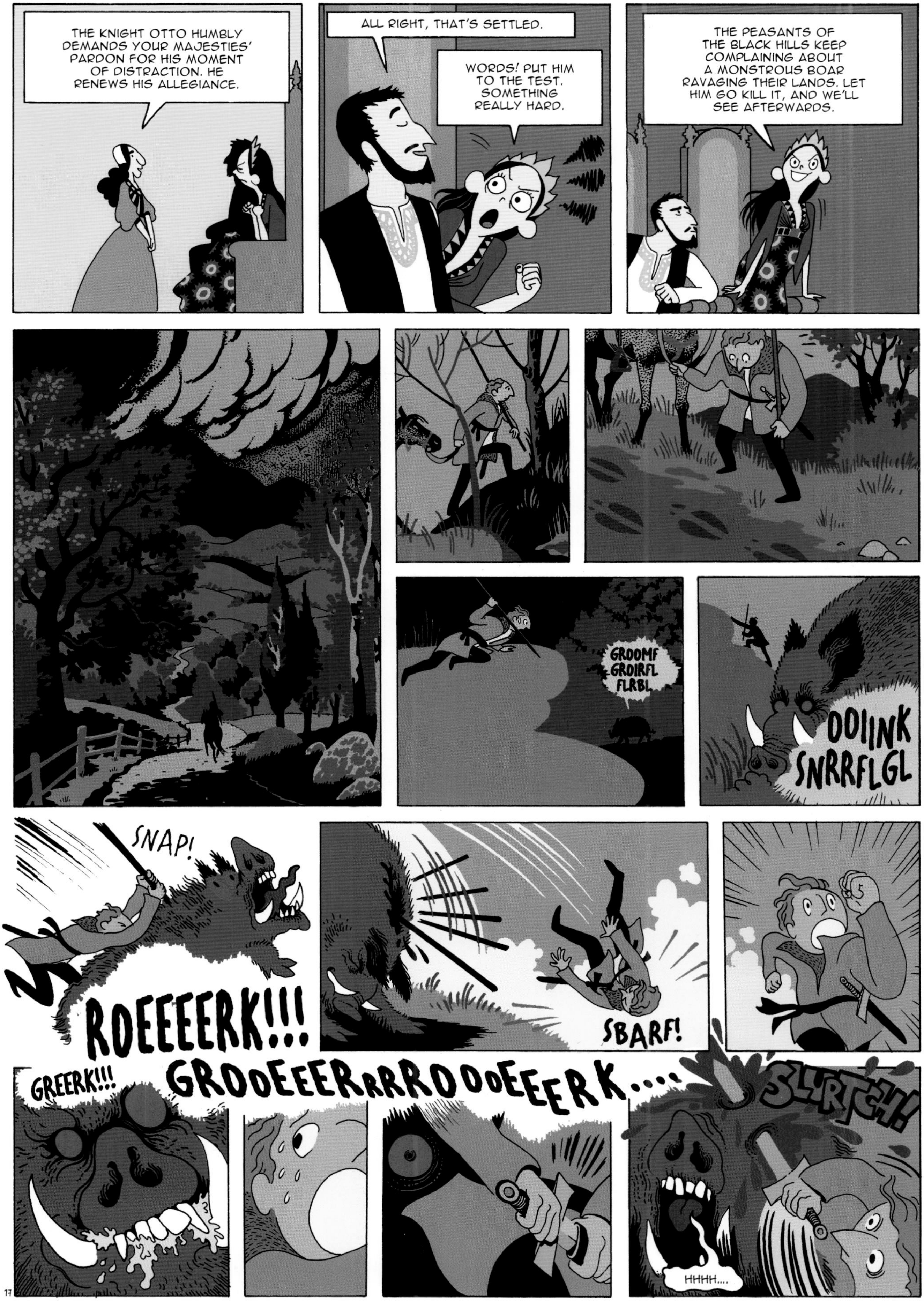
THE KNIGHT OTTO HUMBLY DEMANDS YOUR MAJESTIES' PARDON FOR HIS MOMENT OF DISTRACTION. HE RENEWS HIS ALLEGIANCE.
ALL RIGHT, THAT'S SETTLED.
WORDS! PUT HIM TO THE TEST. SOMETHING REALLY HARD.
THE PEASANTS OF THE BLACK HILLS KEEP COMPLAINING ABOUT A MONSTROUS BOAR RAVAGING THEIR LANDS. LET HIM GO KILL IT, AND WE'LL SEE AFTERWARDS.
GROOMF GROIRFL FLRBL
OOIINK SNRRFLGL
SNAP!
ROEEEERK!!!
SBARF!
GREERK!!!
GROOEEERRRROOOEEERK....
SLURTCH!
HHHH....

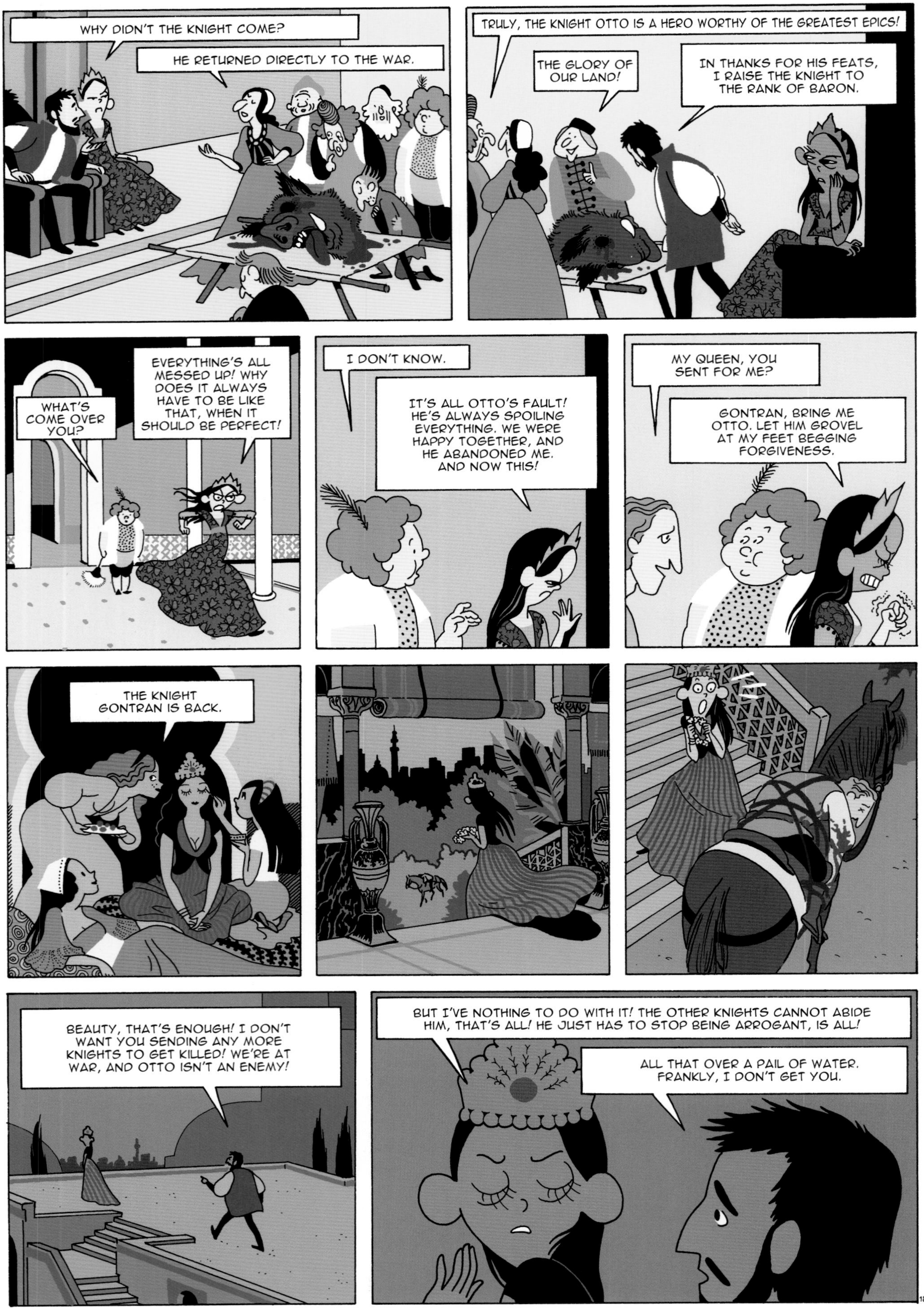
WHY DIDN'T THE KNIGHT COME?
HE RETURNED DIRECTLY TO THE WAR.
TRULY, THE KNIGHT OTTO IS A HERO WORTHY OF THE GREATEST EPICS!
THE GLORY OF OUR LAND!
IN THANKS FOR HIS FEATS, I RAISE THE KNIGHT TO THE RANK OF BARON.
EVERYTHING'S ALL MESSED UP! WHY DOES IT ALWAYS HAVE TO BE LIKE THAT, WHEN IT SHOULD BE PERFECT!
WHAT'S COME OVER YOU?
I DON'T KNOW.
IT'S ALL OTTO'S FAULT! HE'S ALWAYS SPOILING EVERYTHING. WE WERE HAPPY TOGETHER, AND HE ABANDONED ME. AND NOW THIS!
MY QUEEN, YOU SENT FOR ME?
GONTRAN, BRING ME OTTO. LET HIM GROVEL AT MY FEET BEGGING FORGIVENESS.
THE KNIGHT GONTRAN IS BACK.
BEAUTY, THAT'S ENOUGH! I DON'T WANT YOU SENDING ANY MORE KNIGHTS TO GET KILLED! WE'RE AT WAR, AND OTTO ISN'T AN ENEMY!
BUT I'VE NOTHING TO DO WITH IT! THE OTHER KNIGHTS CANNOT ABIDE HIM, THAT'S ALL! HE JUST HAS TO STOP BEING ARROGANT, IS ALL!
ALL THAT OVER A PAIL OF WATER. FRANKLY, I DON'T GET YOU.
18

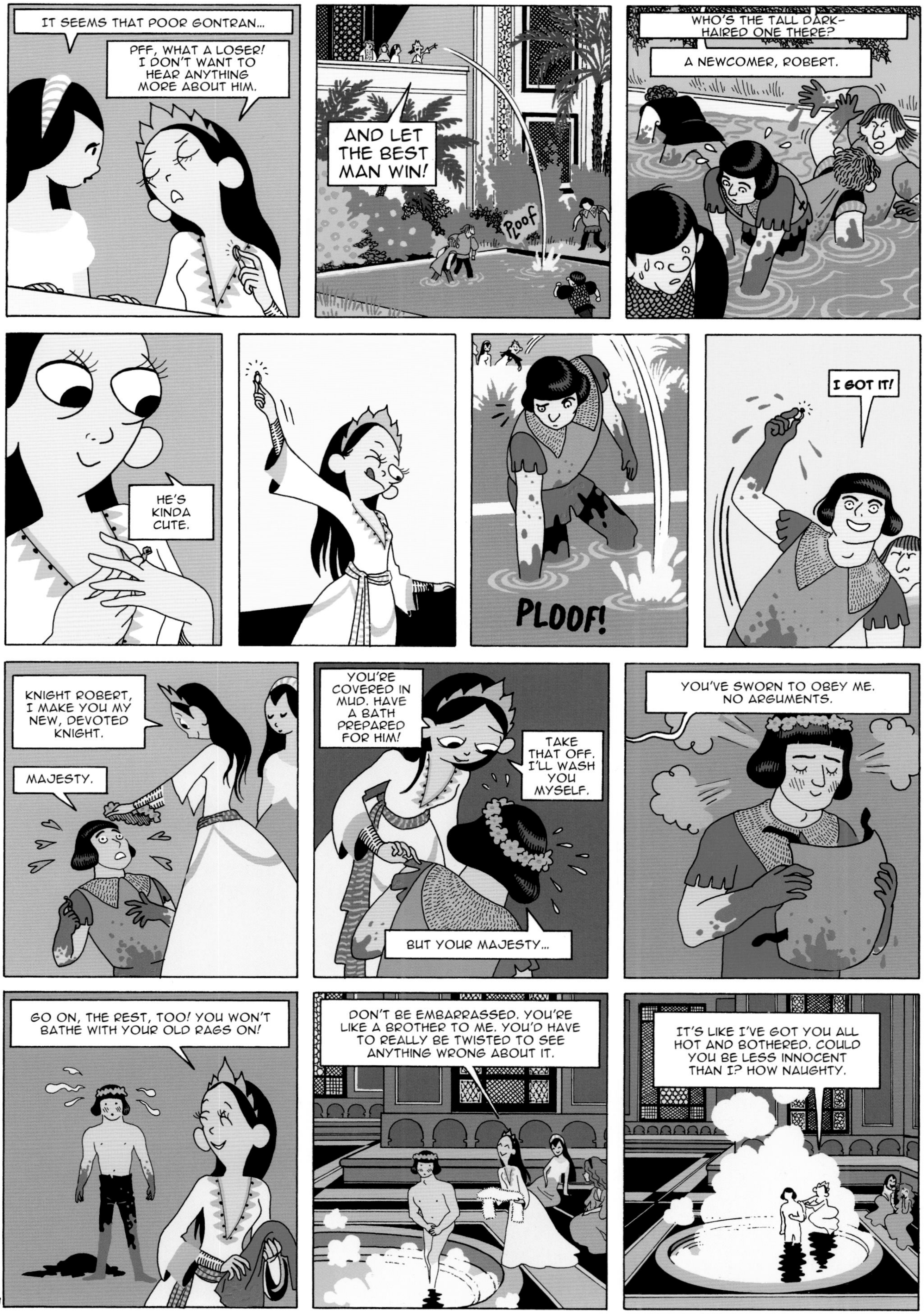

IT SEEMS THAT POOR GONTRAN...
PFF, WHAT A LOSER! I DON'T WANT TO HEAR ANYTHING MORE ABOUT HIM.
AND LET THE BEST MAN WIN!
PLOOF
WHO'S THE TALL DARK-HAIRED ONE THERE?
A NEWCOMER, ROBERT.
HE'S KINDA CUTE.
PLOOF!
I GOT IT!
KNIGHT ROBERT, I MAKE YOU MY NEW, DEVOTED KNIGHT.
MAJESTY.
YOU'RE COVERED IN MUD. HAVE A BATH PREPARED FOR HIM!
TAKE THAT OFF. I'LL WASH YOU MYSELF.
BUT YOUR MAJESTY...
YOU'VE SWORN TO OBEY ME. NO ARGUMENTS.
GO ON, THE REST, TOO! YOU WON'T BATHE WITH YOUR OLD RAGS ON!
19
DON'T BE EMBARRASSED. YOU'RE LIKE A BROTHER TO ME. YOU'D HAVE TO REALLY BE TWISTED TO SEE ANYTHING WRONG ABOUT IT.
IT'S LIKE I'VE GOT YOU ALL HOT AND BOTHERED. COULD YOU BE LESS INNOCENT THAN I? HOW NAUGHTY.

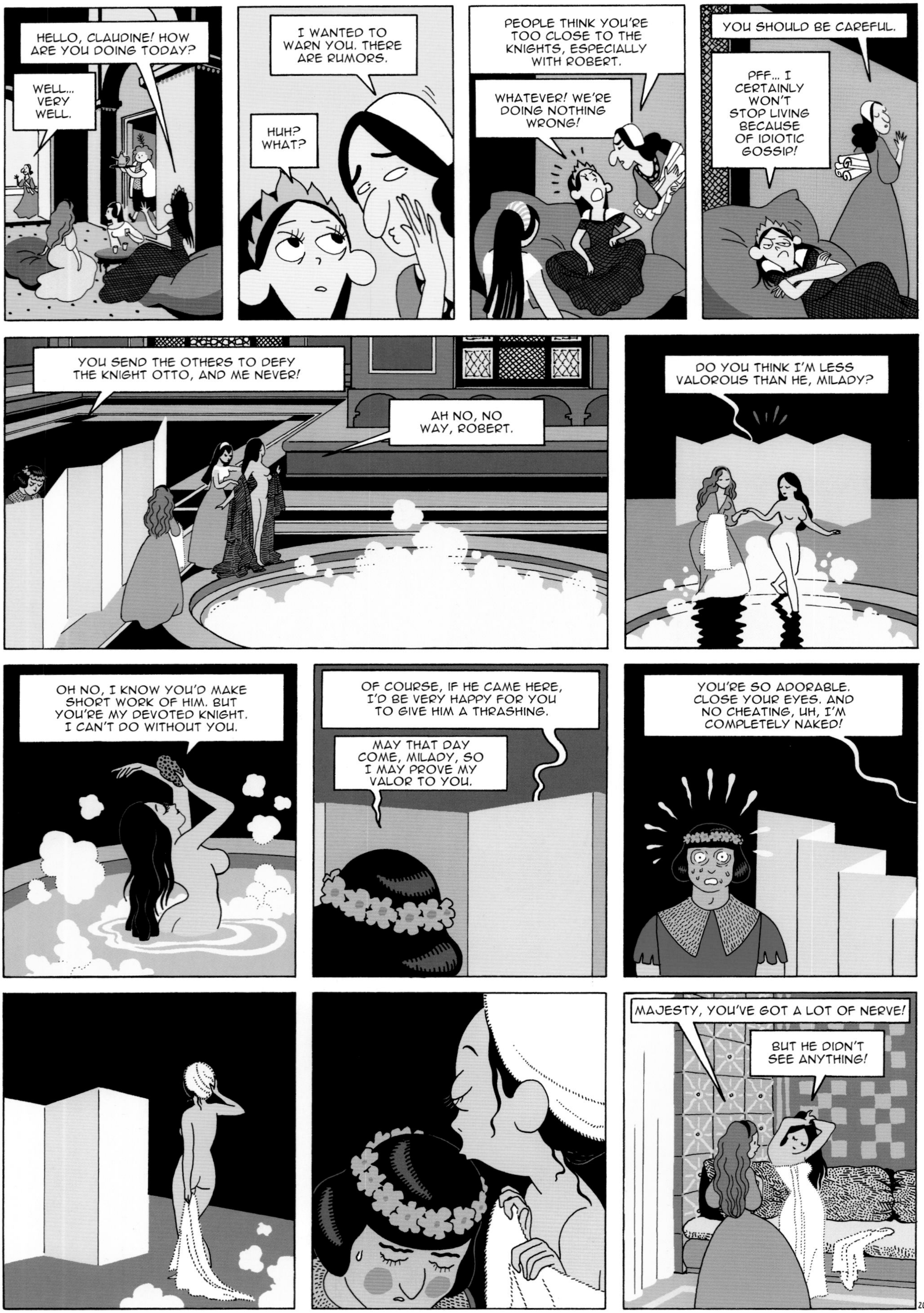
HELLO, CLAUDINE! HOW ARE YOU DOING TODAY?
WELL... VERY WELL.
I WANTED TO WARN YOU. THERE ARE RUMORS.
HUH? WHAT?
PEOPLE THINK YOU'RE TOO CLOSE TO THE KNIGHTS, ESPECIALLY WITH ROBERT.
WHATEVER! WE'RE DOING NOTHING WRONG!
YOU SHOULD BE CAREFUL.
PFF... I CERTAINLY WON'T STOP LIVING BECAUSE OF IDIOTIC GOSSIP!
YOU SEND THE OTHERS TO DEFY THE KNIGHT OTTO, AND ME NEVER!
AH NO, NO WAY, ROBERT.
DO YOU THINK I'M LESS VALOROUS THAN HE, MILADY?
OH NO, I KNOW YOU'D MAKE SHORT WORK OF HIM. BUT YOU'RE MY DEVOTED KNIGHT. I CAN'T DO WITHOUT YOU.
OF COURSE, IF HE CAME HERE, I'D BE VERY HAPPY FOR YOU TO GIVE HIM A THRASHING.
MAY THAT DAY COME, MILADY, SO I MAY PROVE MY VALOR TO YOU.
YOU'RE SO ADORABLE. CLOSE YOUR EYES. AND NO CHEATING, UH, I'M COMPLETELY NAKED!
MAJESTY, YOU'VE GOT A LOT OF NERVE!
BUT HE DIDN'T SEE ANYTHING!
20

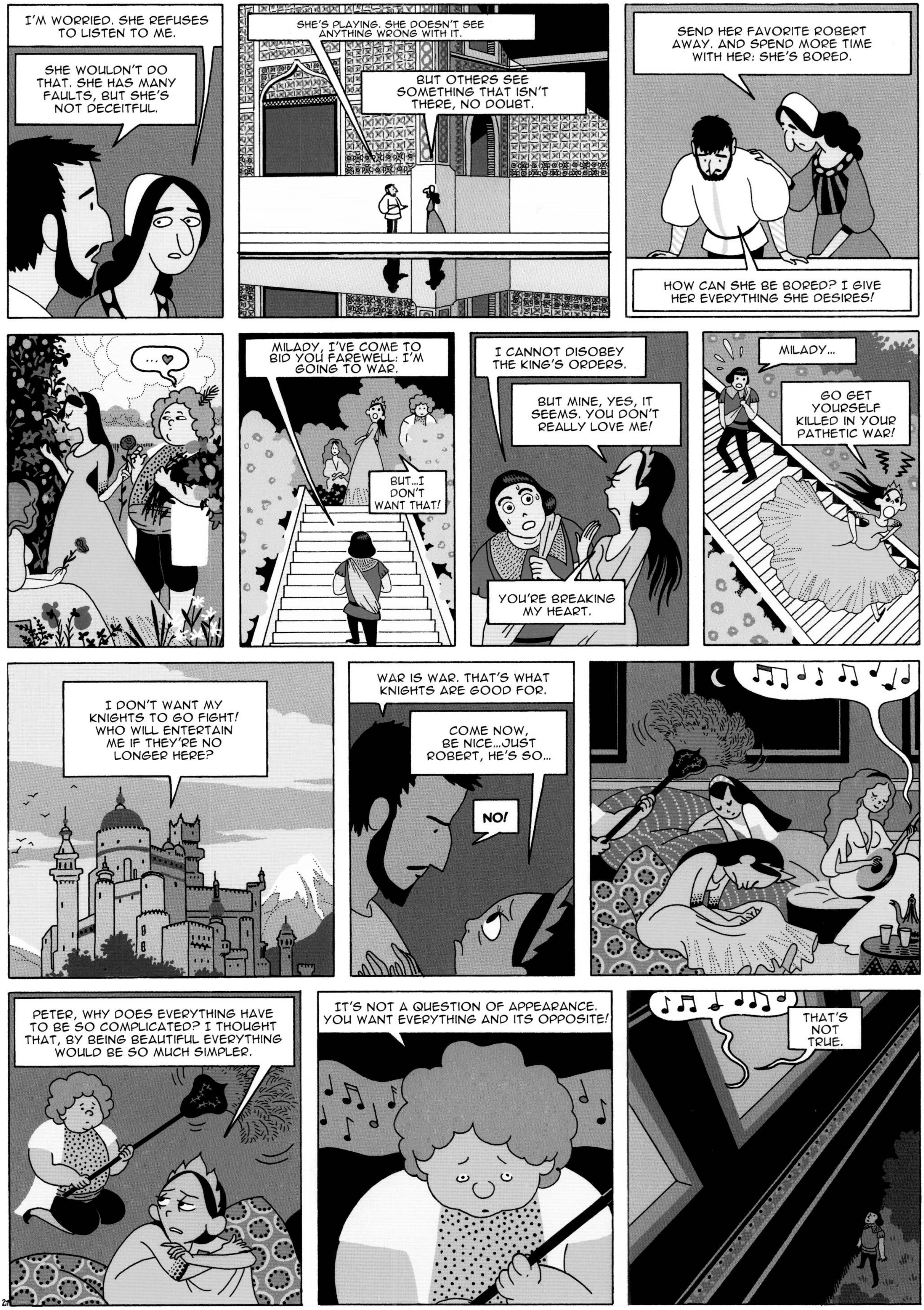
I'M WORRIED. SHE REFUSES TO LISTEN TO ME.
SHE WOULDN'T DO THAT. SHE HAS MANY FAULTS, BUT SHE'S NOT DECEITFUL.
SHE'S PLAYING. SHE DOESN'T SEE ANYTHING WRONG WITH IT.
BUT OTHERS SEE SOMETHING THAT ISN'T THERE, NO DOUBT.
SEND HER FAVORITE ROBERT AWAY. AND SPEND MORE TIME WITH HER: SHE'S BORED.
HOW CAN SHE BE BORED? I GIVE HER EVERYTHING SHE DESIRES!
...♥
MILADY, I'VE COME TO BID YOU FAREWELL: I'M GOING TO WAR.
BUT...I DON'T WANT THAT!
I CANNOT DISOBEY THE KING'S ORDERS.
BUT MINE, YES, IT SEEMS. YOU DON'T REALLY LOVE ME!
YOU'RE BREAKING MY HEART.
MILADY...
GO GET YOURSELF KILLED IN YOUR PATHETIC WAR!
I DON'T WANT MY KNIGHTS TO GO FIGHT! WHO WILL ENTERTAIN ME IF THEY'RE NO LONGER HERE?
WAR IS WAR. THAT'S WHAT KNIGHTS ARE GOOD FOR.
COME NOW, BE NICE...JUST ROBERT, HE'S SO...
NO!
PETER, WHY DOES EVERYTHING HAVE TO BE SO COMPLICATED? I THOUGHT THAT, BY BEING BEAUTIFUL EVERYTHING WOULD BE SO MUCH SIMPLER.
IT'S NOT A QUESTION OF APPEARANCE. YOU WANT EVERYTHING AND ITS OPPOSITE!
THAT'S NOT TRUE.

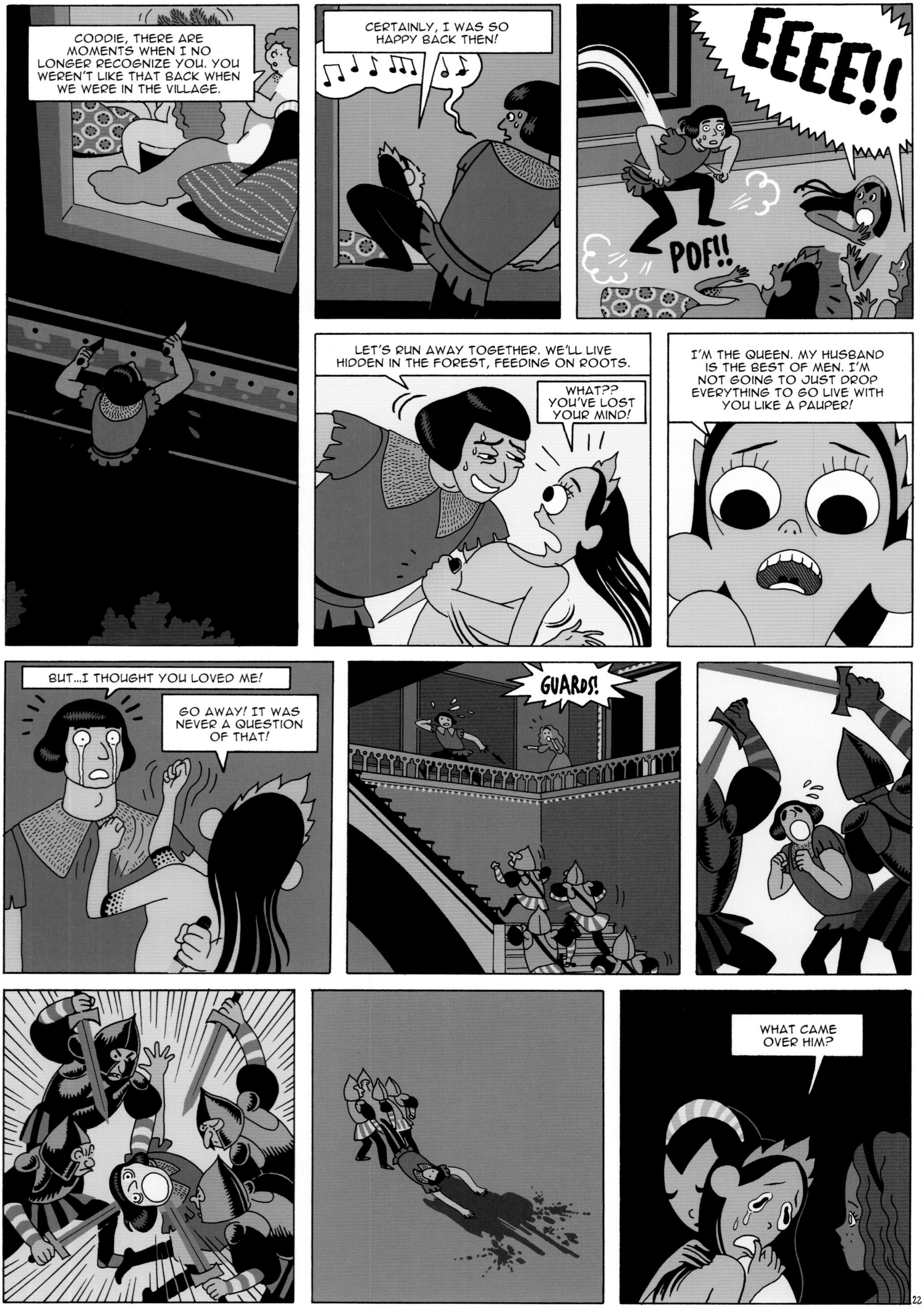

CODDIE, THERE ARE MOMENTS WHEN I NO LONGER RECOGNIZE YOU. YOU WEREN'T LIKE THAT BACK WHEN WE WERE IN THE VILLAGE.
CERTAINLY, I WAS SO HAPPY BACK THEN!
EEEE!!
POF!!
LET'S RUN AWAY TOGETHER. WE'LL LIVE HIDDEN IN THE FOREST, FEEDING ON ROOTS.
WHAT?? YOU'VE LOST YOUR MIND!
I'M THE QUEEN. MY HUSBAND IS THE BEST OF MEN. I'M NOT GOING TO JUST DROP EVERYTHING TO GO LIVE WITH YOU LIKE A PAUPER!
BUT...I THOUGHT YOU LOVED ME!
GO AWAY! IT WAS NEVER A QUESTION OF THAT!
GUARDS!
WHAT CAME OVER HIM?
22

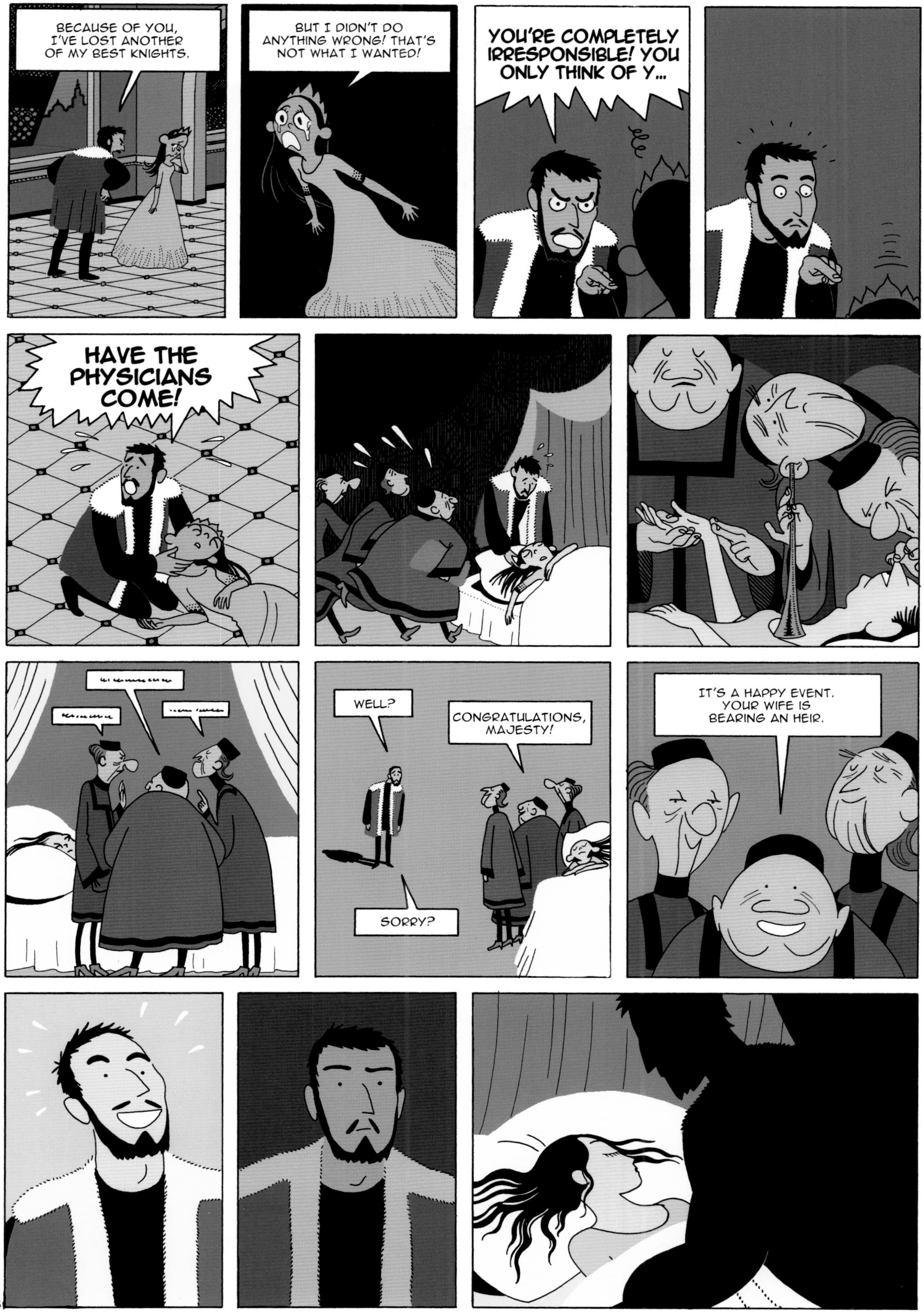
BECAUSE OF YOU, I'VE LOST ANOTHER OF MY BEST KNIGHTS.
BUT I DIDN'T DO ANYTHING WRONG! THAT'S NOT WHAT I WANTED!
YOU'RE COMPLETELY IRRESPONSIBLE! YOU ONLY THINK OF Y...
HAVE THE PHYSICIANS COME!
WELL?
CONGRATULATIONS, MAJESTY!
SORRY?
IT'S A HAPPY EVENT. YOUR WIFE IS BEARING AN HEIR.

23

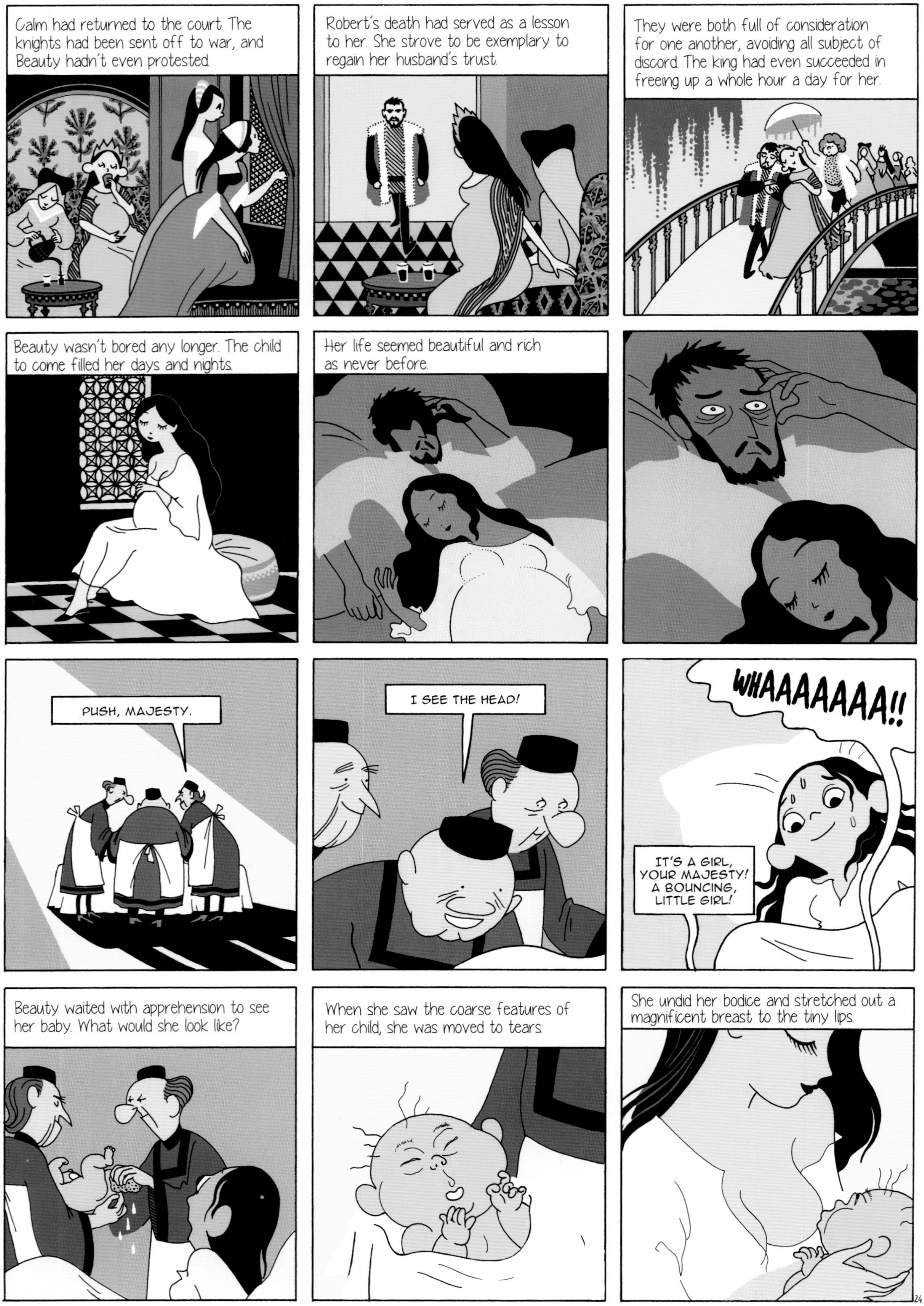

Calm had returned to the court. The knights had been sent off to war, and Beauty hadn't even protested.
Robert's death had served as a lesson to her. She strove to be exemplary to regain her husband's trust.
They were both full of consideration for one another, avoiding all subject of discord. The king had even succeeded in freeing up a whole hour a day for her.
Beauty wasn't bored any longer. The child to come filled her days and nights.
Her life seemed beautiful and rich as never before.
PUSH, MAJESTY.
I SEE THE HEAD!
WHAAAAAAA!!
IT'S A GIRL, YOUR MAJESTY! A BOUNCING, LITTLE GIRL!
Beauty waited with apprehension to see her baby. What would she look like?
When she saw the coarse features of her child, she was moved to tears.
She undid her bodice and stretched out a magnificent breast to the tiny lips.
24

Marine, she said to herself, daughter of Coddie.

ALL WILL BE WELL NOW THAT YOU'RE HERE.

ARE YOU HAPPY, MY DEAR?

YES! SURE!

YOU LOOK DESPONDENT. IS IT BECAUSE SHE'S NOT A BOY?

NO, NOT AT ALL! I... I'LL HAVE A PALACE BUILT FOR HER.

SHE LOOKS ADORABLE, DON'T YOU THINK?

MARINE LOOKS JUST LIKE YOU WHEN YOU WERE LITTLE. THE SAME EARS!

BUT SHE HAS MAXENCE'S EYES.

HE MUST BE OVERJOYED. I WOULD BE, IN HIS PLACE.

OH, YOU KNOW, HE'S RATHER RESERVED.

COOTCHYCOO! GIVE YOUR UNCLE PETER A LITTLE SMILE!

A horrid doubt had taken hold of the king's mind. Was he truly the father? Had the child been of an obvious beauty, that would have comforted him about its legitimacy. Wasn't he a rather handsome man himself?

He couldn't keep himself from seeking a resemblance to the child in the queen's male entourage.

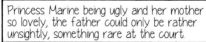

Princess Marine being ugly and her mother so lovely, the father could only be rather unsightly, something rare at the court.

.... ♥

25

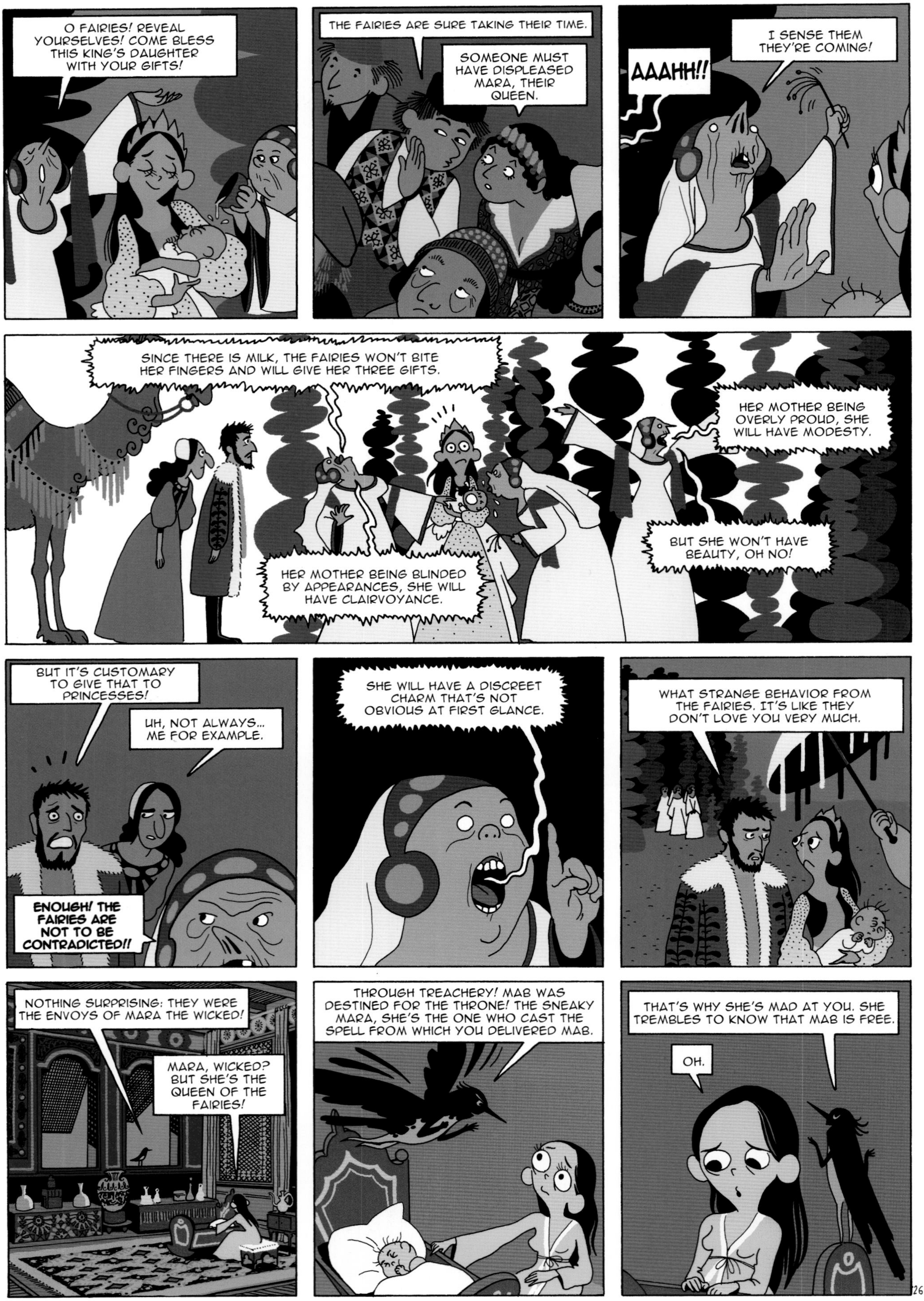

O FAIRIES! REVEAL YOURSELVES! COME BLESS THIS KING'S DAUGHTER WITH YOUR GIFTS!
THE FAIRIES ARE SURE TAKING THEIR TIME.
SOMEONE MUST HAVE DISPLEASED MARA, THEIR QUEEN.
AAAHH!!
I SENSE THEM THEY'RE COMING!
SINCE THERE IS MILK, THE FAIRIES WON'T BITE HER FINGERS AND WILL GIVE HER THREE GIFTS.
HER MOTHER BEING OVERLY PROUD, SHE WILL HAVE MODESTY.
HER MOTHER BEING BLINDED BY APPEARANCES, SHE WILL HAVE CLAIRVOYANCE.
BUT SHE WON'T HAVE BEAUTY, OH NO!
BUT IT'S CUSTOMARY TO GIVE THAT TO PRINCESSES!
UH, NOT ALWAYS... ME FOR EXAMPLE.
ENOUGH! THE FAIRIES ARE NOT TO BE CONTRADICTED!!
SHE WILL HAVE A DISCREET CHARM THAT'S NOT OBVIOUS AT FIRST GLANCE.
WHAT STRANGE BEHAVIOR FROM THE FAIRIES. IT'S LIKE THEY DON'T LOVE YOU VERY MUCH.
NOTHING SURPRISING: THEY WERE THE ENVOYS OF MARA THE WICKED!
MARA, WICKED? BUT SHE'S THE QUEEN OF THE FAIRIES!
THROUGH TREACHERY! MAB WAS DESTINED FOR THE THRONE! THE SNEAKY MARA, SHE'S THE ONE WHO CAST THE SPELL FROM WHICH YOU DELIVERED MAB.
THAT'S WHY SHE'S MAD AT YOU. SHE TREMBLES TO KNOW THAT MAB IS FREE.
OH.

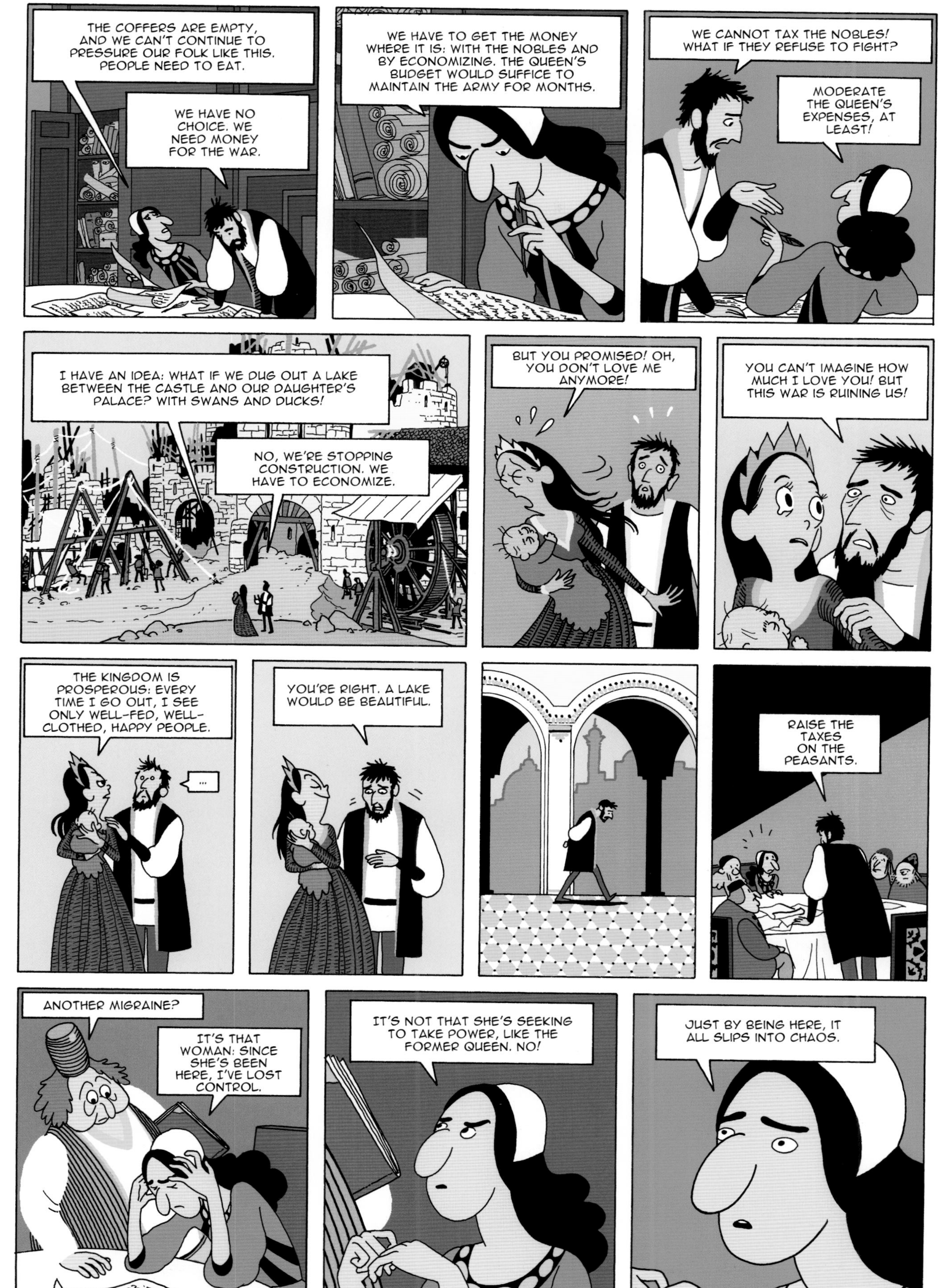
THE COFFERS ARE EMPTY, AND WE CAN'T CONTINUE TO PRESSURE OUR FOLK LIKE THIS. PEOPLE NEED TO EAT.
WE HAVE NO CHOICE. WE NEED MONEY FOR THE WAR.
WE HAVE TO GET THE MONEY WHERE IT IS: WITH THE NOBLES AND BY ECONOMIZING. THE QUEEN'S BUDGET WOULD SUFFICE TO MAINTAIN THE ARMY FOR MONTHS.
WE CANNOT TAX THE NOBLES! WHAT IF THEY REFUSE TO FIGHT?
MODERATE THE QUEEN'S EXPENSES, AT LEAST!
I HAVE AN IDEA: WHAT IF WE DUG OUT A LAKE BETWEEN THE CASTLE AND OUR DAUGHTER'S PALACE? WITH SWANS AND DUCKS!
NO, WE'RE STOPPING CONSTRUCTION. WE HAVE TO ECONOMIZE.
BUT YOU PROMISED! OH, YOU DON'T LOVE ME ANYMORE!
YOU CAN'T IMAGINE HOW MUCH I LOVE YOU! BUT THIS WAR IS RUINING US!
THE KINGDOM IS PROSPEROUS: EVERY TIME I GO OUT, I SEE ONLY WELL-FED, WELL-CLOTHED, HAPPY PEOPLE.
...
YOU'RE RIGHT. A LAKE WOULD BE BEAUTIFUL.
RAISE THE TAXES ON THE PEASANTS.
ANOTHER MIGRAINE?
IT'S THAT WOMAN: SINCE SHE'S BEEN HERE, I'VE LOST CONTROL.
IT'S NOT THAT SHE'S SEEKING TO TAKE POWER, LIKE THE FORMER QUEEN. NO!
JUST BY BEING HERE, IT ALL SLIPS INTO CHAOS.
27

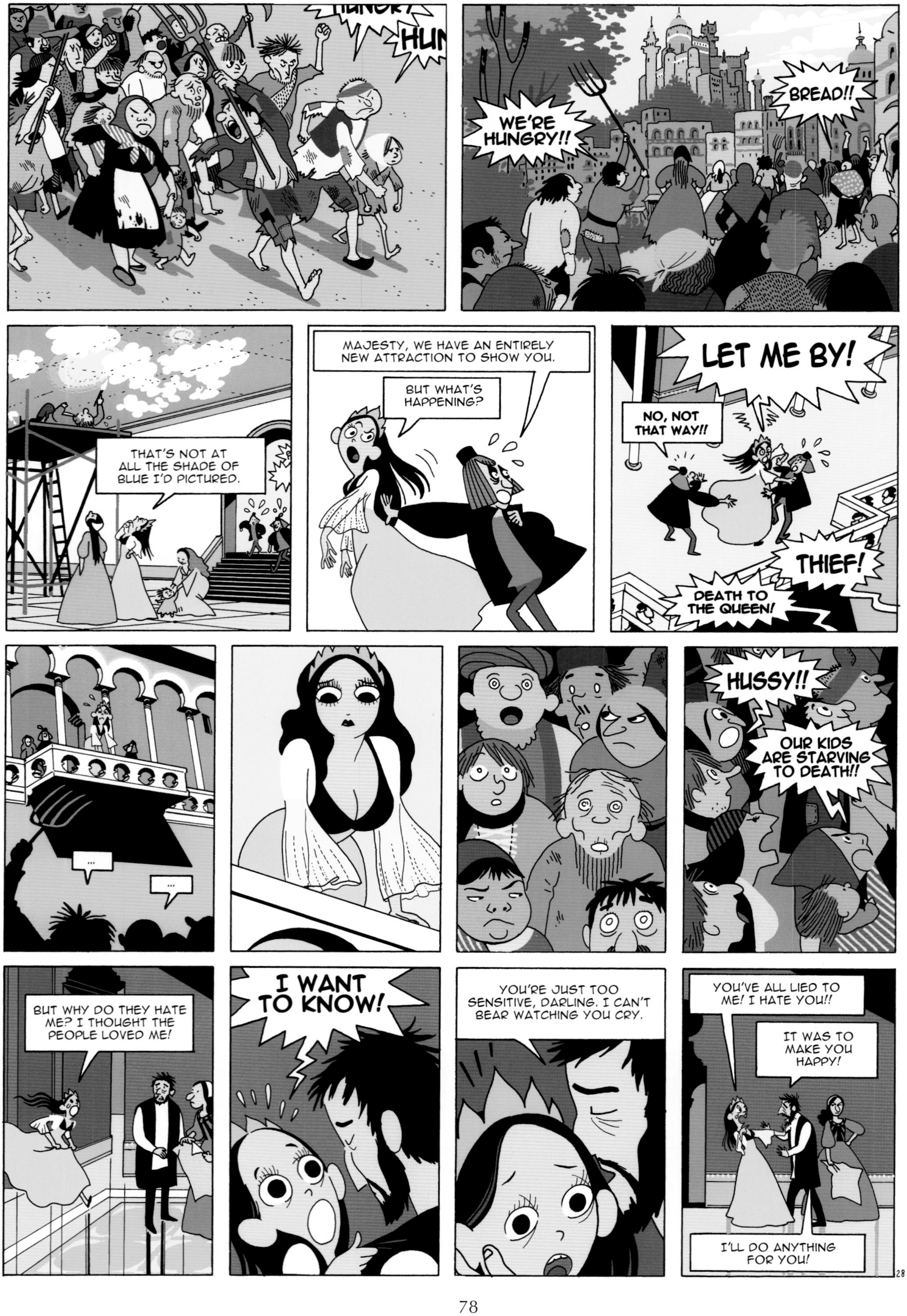
WE'RE HUNGRY!!
BREAD!!
THAT'S NOT AT ALL THE SHADE OF BLUE I'D PICTURED.
MAJESTY, WE HAVE AN ENTIRELY NEW ATTRACTION TO SHOW YOU.
BUT WHAT'S HAPPENING?
LET ME BY!
NO, NOT THAT WAY!!
THIEF!
DEATH TO THE QUEEN!
HUSSY!!
OUR KIDS ARE STARVING TO DEATH!!
BUT WHY DO THEY HATE ME? I THOUGHT THE PEOPLE LOVED ME!
I WANT TO KNOW!
YOU'RE JUST TOO SENSITIVE, DARLING. I CAN'T BEAR WATCHING YOU CRY.
YOU'VE ALL LIED TO ME! I HATE YOU!!
IT WAS TO MAKE YOU HAPPY!
I'LL DO ANYTHING FOR YOU!

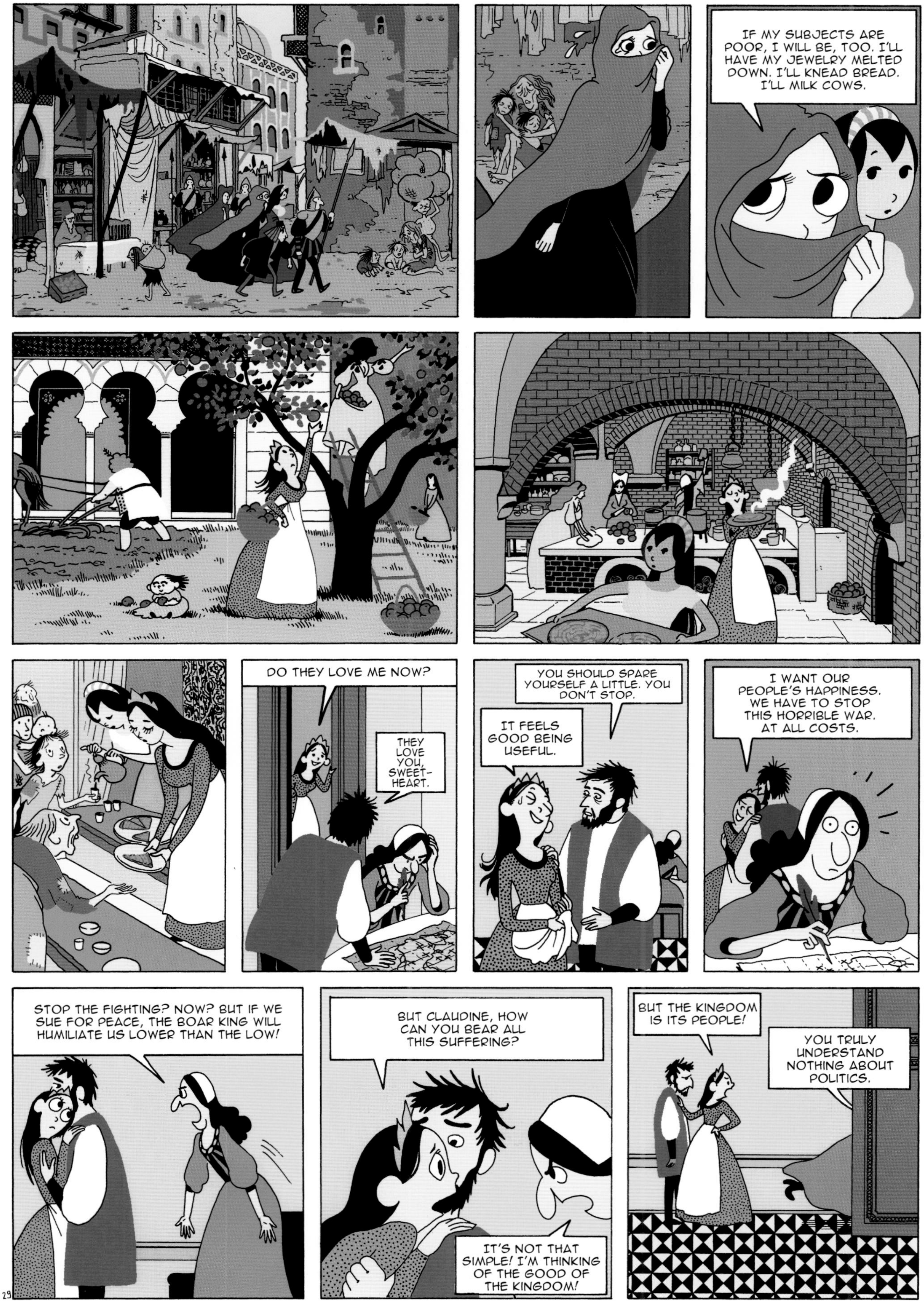
IF MY SUBJECTS ARE POOR, I WILL BE, TOO. I'LL HAVE MY JEWELRY MELTED DOWN. I'LL KNEAD BREAD. I'LL MILK COWS.
DO THEY LOVE ME NOW?
THEY LOVE YOU, SWEET-HEART.
YOU SHOULD SPARE YOURSELF A LITTLE. YOU DON'T STOP.
IT FEELS GOOD BEING USEFUL.
I WANT OUR PEOPLE'S HAPPINESS. WE HAVE TO STOP THIS HORRIBLE WAR. AT ALL COSTS.
STOP THE FIGHTING? NOW? BUT IF WE SUE FOR PEACE, THE BOAR KING WILL HUMILIATE US LOWER THAN THE LOW!
BUT CLAUDINE, HOW CAN YOU BEAR ALL THIS SUFFERING?
IT'S NOT THAT SIMPLE! I'M THINKING OF THE GOOD OF THE KINGDOM!
BUT THE KINGDOM IS ITS PEOPLE!
YOU TRULY UNDERSTAND NOTHING ABOUT POLITICS.
29

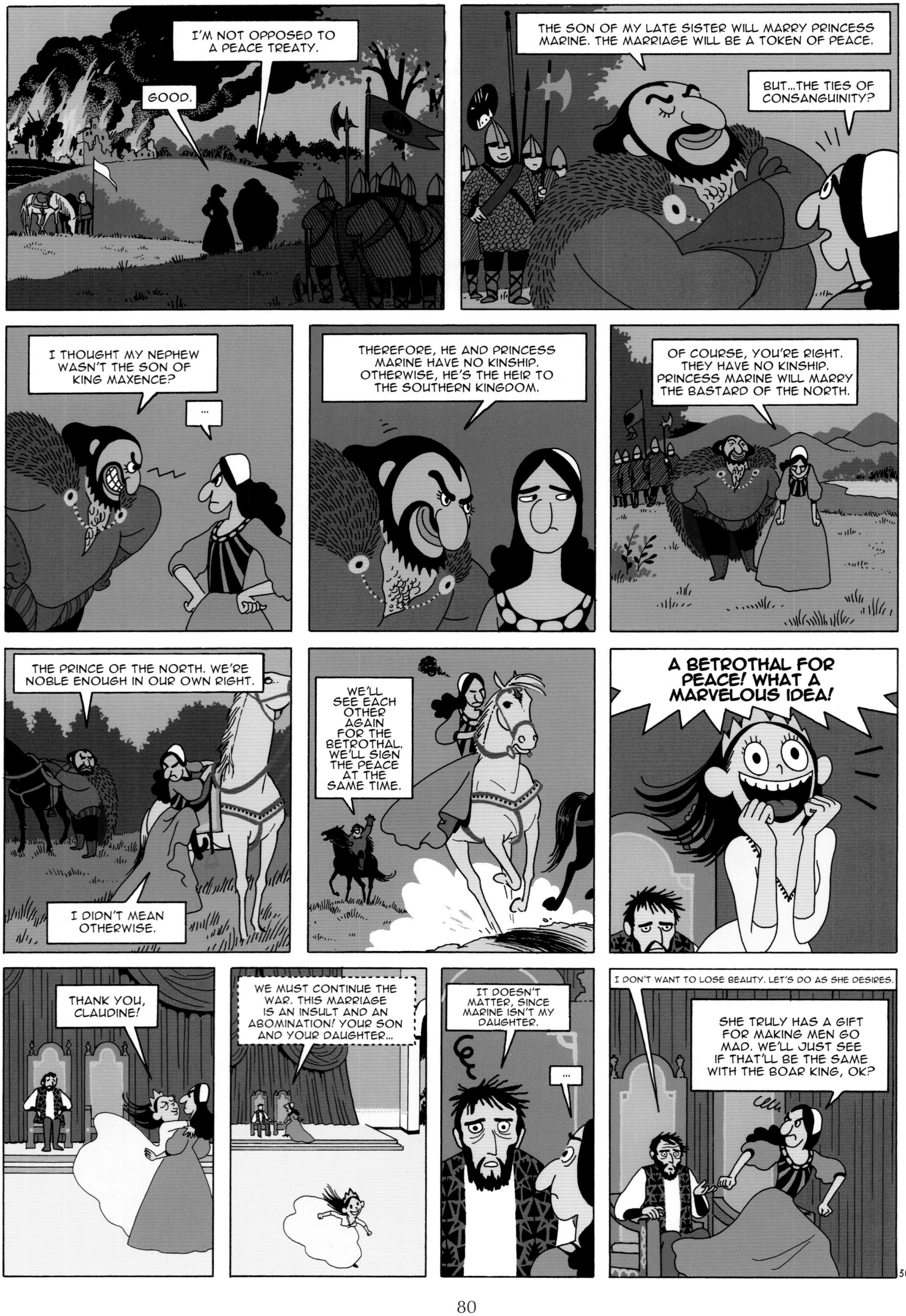

I'M NOT OPPOSED TO A PEACE TREATY.
GOOD.
THE SON OF MY LATE SISTER WILL MARRY PRINCESS MARINE. THE MARRIAGE WILL BE A TOKEN OF PEACE.
BUT...THE TIES OF CONSANGUINITY?
I THOUGHT MY NEPHEW WASN'T THE SON OF KING MAXENCE?
...
THEREFORE, HE AND PRINCESS MARINE HAVE NO KINSHIP. OTHERWISE, HE'S THE HEIR TO THE SOUTHERN KINGDOM.
OF COURSE, YOU'RE RIGHT. THEY HAVE NO KINSHIP. PRINCESS MARINE WILL MARRY THE BASTARD OF THE NORTH.
THE PRINCE OF THE NORTH. WE'RE NOBLE ENOUGH IN OUR OWN RIGHT.
I DIDN'T MEAN OTHERWISE.
WE'LL SEE EACH OTHER AGAIN FOR THE BETROTHAL. WE'LL SIGN THE PEACE AT THE SAME TIME.
A BETROTHAL FOR PEACE! WHAT A MARVELOUS IDEA!
THANK YOU, CLAUDINE!
WE MUST CONTINUE THE WAR. THIS MARRIAGE IS AN INSULT AND AN ABOMINATION! YOUR SON AND YOUR DAUGHTER...
IT DOESN'T MATTER, SINCE MARINE ISN'T MY DAUGHTER.
...
I DON'T WANT TO LOSE BEAUTY. LET'S DO AS SHE DESIRES.
SHE TRULY HAS A GIFT FOR MAKING MEN GO MAD. WE'LL JUST SEE IF THAT'LL BE THE SAME WITH THE BOAR KING, OK?
30

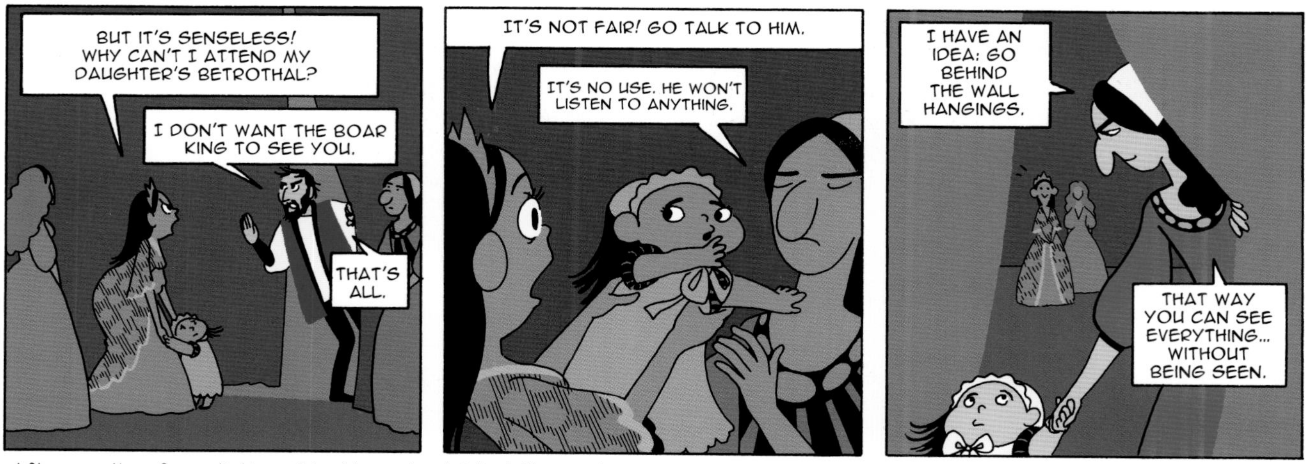
BUT IT'S SENSELESS! WHY CAN'T I ATTEND MY DAUGHTER'S BETROTHAL?
I DON'T WANT THE BOAR KING TO SEE YOU.
THAT'S ALL.
IT'S NOT FAIR! GO TALK TO HIM.
IT'S NO USE. HE WON'T LISTEN TO ANYTHING.
I HAVE AN IDEA: GO BEHIND THE WALL HANGINGS.
THAT WAY YOU CAN SEE EVERYTHING... WITHOUT BEING SEEN.

After months of negotiations, it had been decided that the meeting would take place on the front line, between the two armies. A city of tents had been built for the occasion.

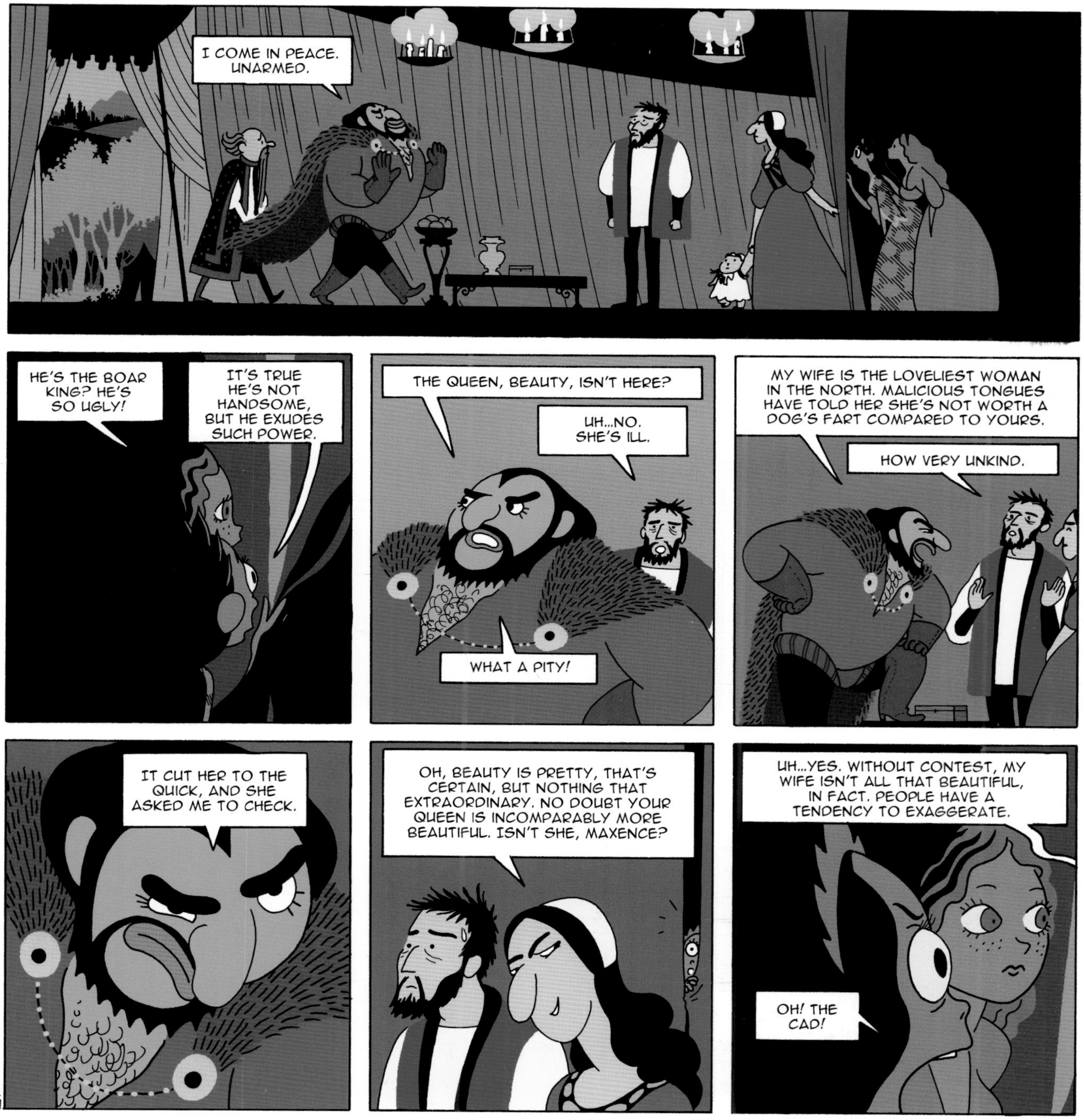
I COME IN PEACE. UNARMED.
HE'S THE BOAR KING? HE'S SO UGLY!
IT'S TRUE HE'S NOT HANDSOME, BUT HE EXUDES SUCH POWER.
THE QUEEN, BEAUTY, ISN'T HERE?
UH...NO. SHE'S ILL.
WHAT A PITY!
MY WIFE IS THE LOVELIEST WOMAN IN THE NORTH. MALICIOUS TONGUES HAVE TOLD HER SHE'S NOT WORTH A DOG'S FART COMPARED TO YOURS.
HOW VERY UNKIND.
IT CUT HER TO THE QUICK, AND SHE ASKED ME TO CHECK.
OH, BEAUTY IS PRETTY, THAT'S CERTAIN, BUT NOTHING THAT EXTRAORDINARY. NO DOUBT YOUR QUEEN IS INCOMPARABLY MORE BEAUTIFUL. ISN'T SHE, MAXENCE?
UH...YES. WITHOUT CONTEST, MY WIFE ISN'T ALL THAT BEAUTIFUL, IN FACT. PEOPLE HAVE A TENDENCY TO EXAGGERATE.
OH! THE CAD!

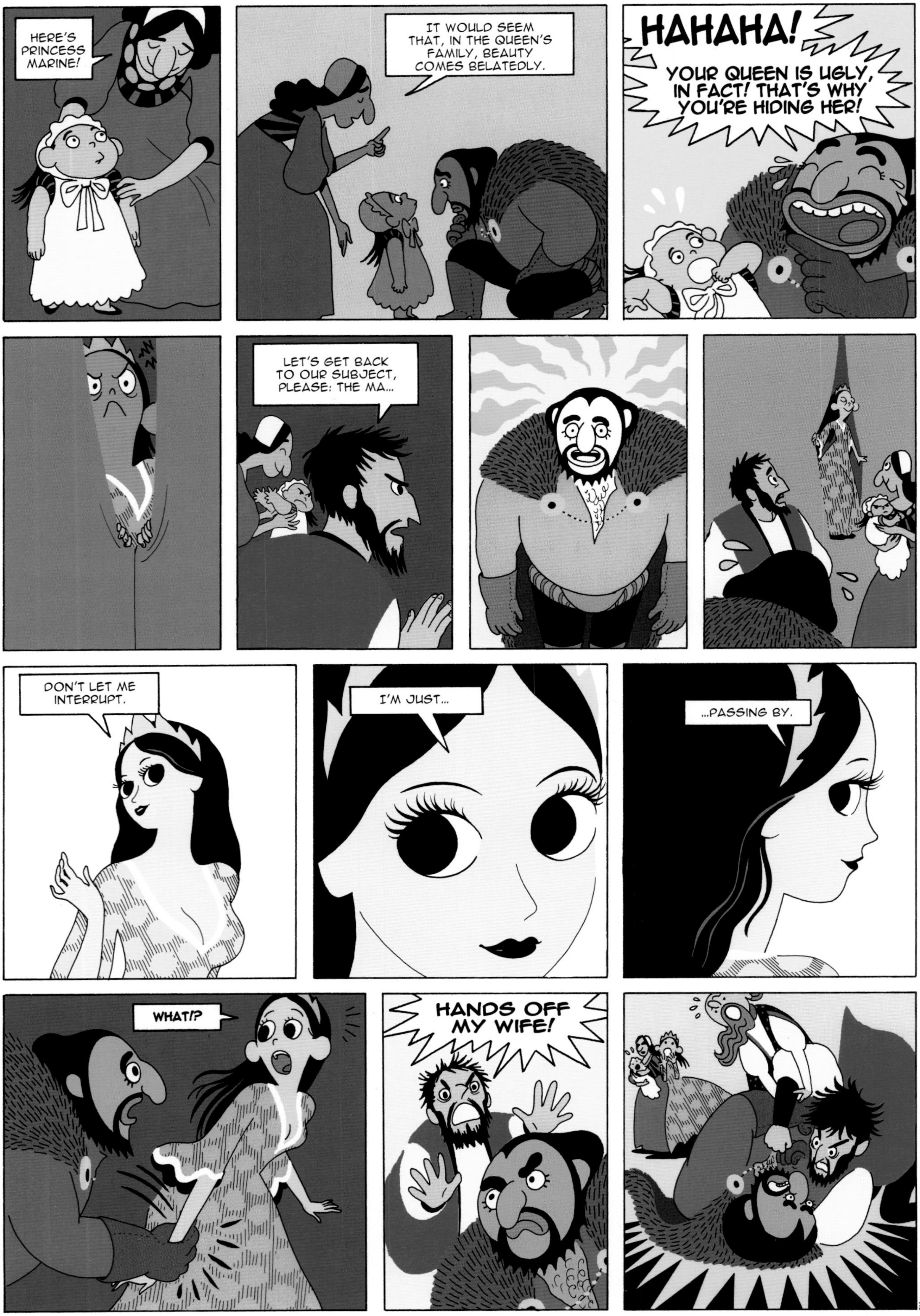
HERE'S PRINCESS MARINE!
IT WOULD SEEM THAT, IN THE QUEEN'S FAMILY, BEAUTY COMES BELATEDLY.
HAHAHA!
YOUR QUEEN IS UGLY, IN FACT! THAT'S WHY YOU'RE HIDING HER!
LET'S GET BACK TO OUR SUBJECT, PLEASE: THE MA...
DON'T LET ME INTERRUPT.
I'M JUST...
...PASSING BY.
WHAT!?
HANDS OFF MY WIFE!
2
32

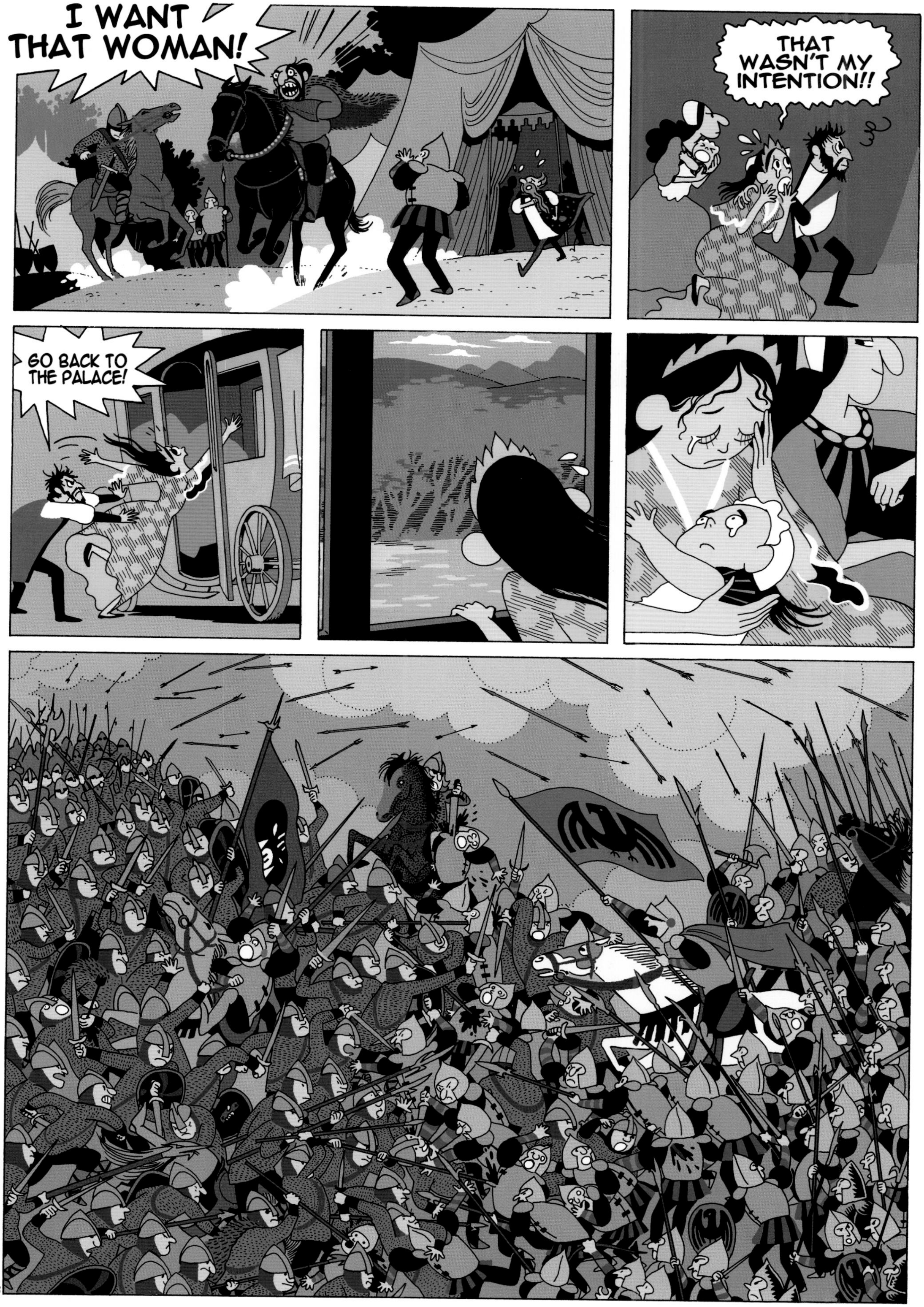
I WANT THAT WOMAN!
THAT WASN'T MY INTENTION!!
GO BACK TO THE PALACE!

The Southern Kingdom was tottering under the repeated attacks of the Boar King.

IT'S TOO SLOW! I NEED MORE SOLDIERS! MOBILIZE ALL ABLE MEN!!

THAT'S NOT POSSIBLE! YOU'LL RUIN YOUR KINGDOM! IT'S HARVEST TIME!

I DON'T WANT TO HEAR IT!! OBEY!

BUT THE MARRIAGE OF YOUR NEPHEW WITH PRINCESS MARINE SEEMED LIKE A SOLUTION.

BAF!!

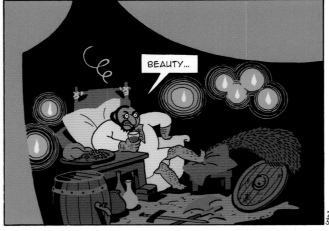

BEAUTY...

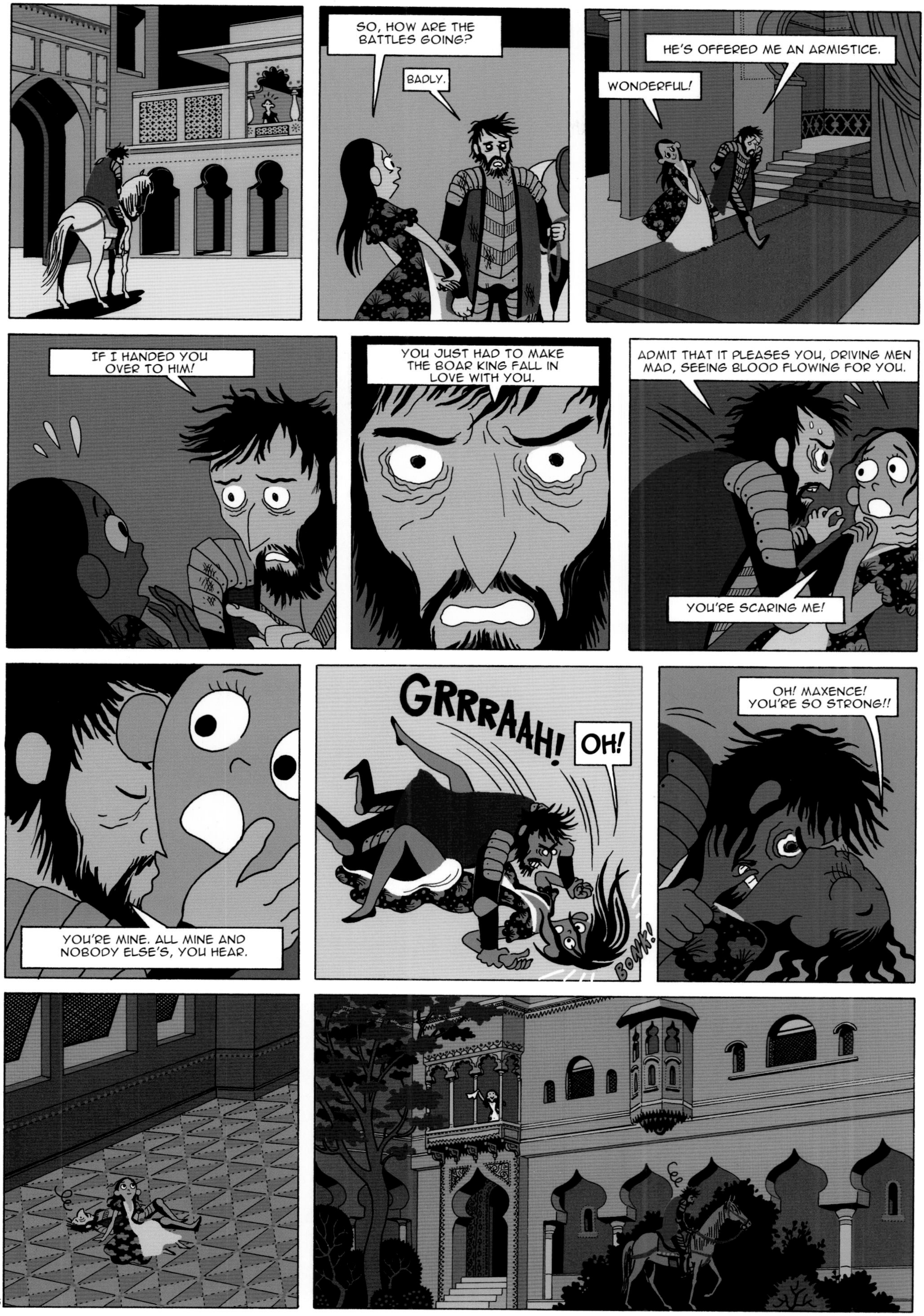
SO, HOW ARE THE BATTLES GOING?
BADLY.
HE'S OFFERED ME AN ARMISTICE.
WONDERFUL!
IF I HANDED YOU OVER TO HIM!
YOU JUST HAD TO MAKE THE BOAR KING FALL IN LOVE WITH YOU.
ADMIT THAT IT PLEASES YOU, DRIVING MEN MAD, SEEING BLOOD FLOWING FOR YOU.
YOU'RE SCARING ME!
YOU'RE MINE. ALL MINE AND NOBODY ELSE'S, YOU HEAR.
GRRRAAH!
OH!
BONK!
OH! MAXENCE! YOU'RE SO STRONG!!

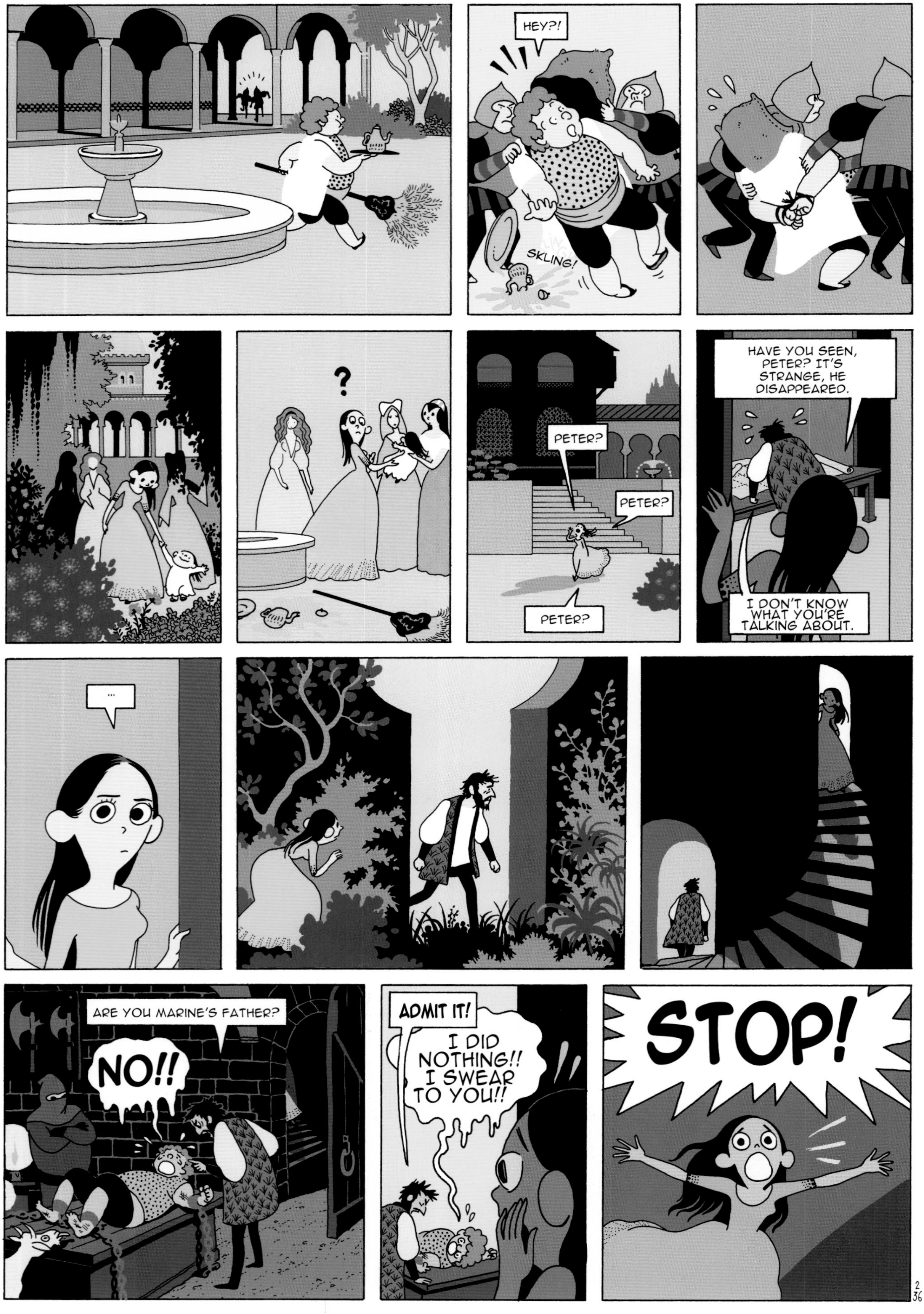
HEY?!
SKLING!
?
PETER?
PETER?
PETER?
HAVE YOU SEEN, PETER? IT'S STRANGE, HE DISAPPEARED.
I DON'T KNOW WHAT YOU'RE TALKING ABOUT.
...
ARE YOU MARINE'S FATHER?
NO!!
ADMIT IT!
I DID NOTHING!! I SWEAR TO YOU!!
STOP!
2
36

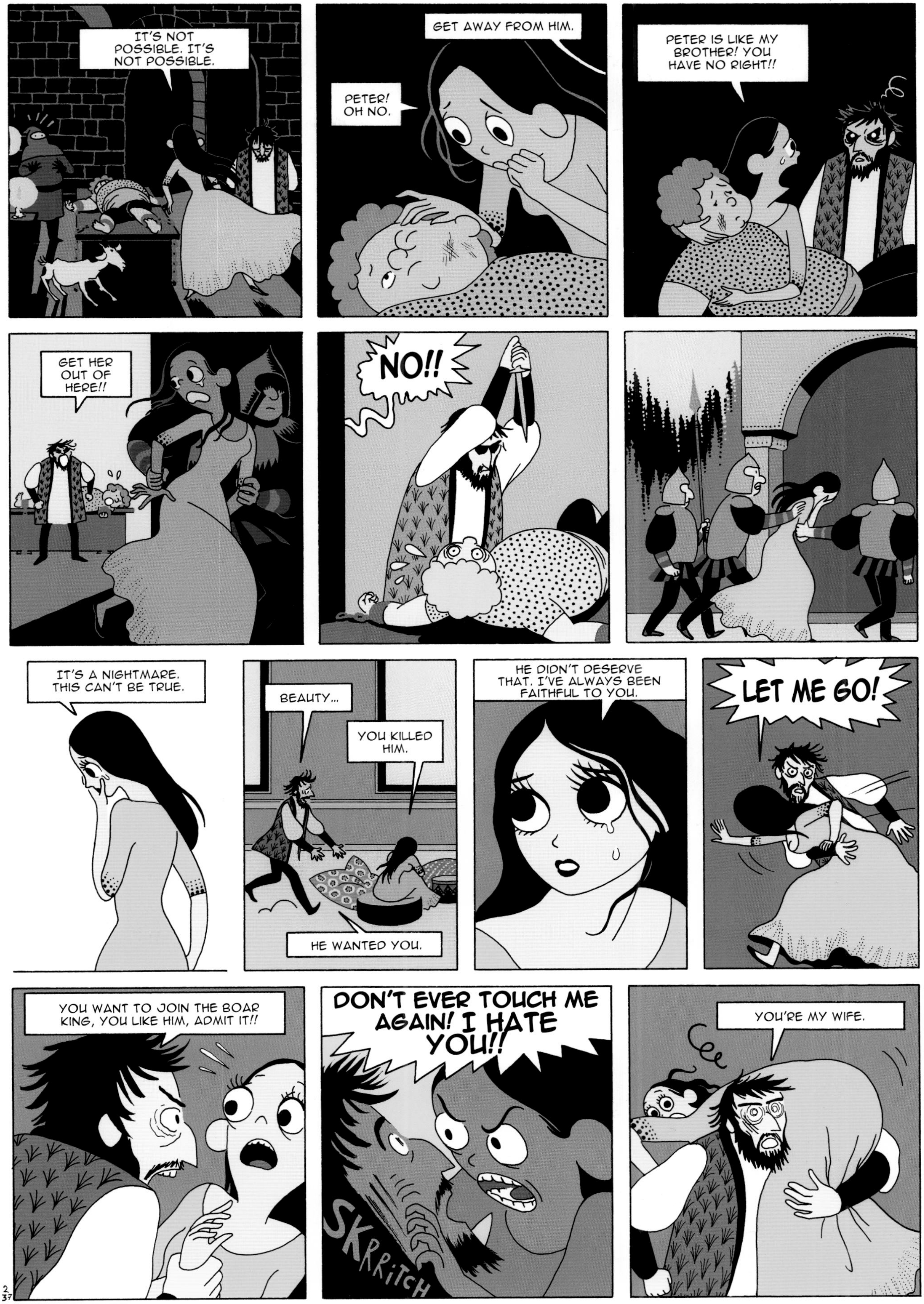
IT'S NOT POSSIBLE. IT'S NOT POSSIBLE.
GET AWAY FROM HIM.
PETER! OH NO.
PETER IS LIKE MY BROTHER! YOU HAVE NO RIGHT!!
GET HER OUT OF HERE!!
NO!!
IT'S A NIGHTMARE. THIS CAN'T BE TRUE.
BEAUTY...
YOU KILLED HIM.
HE WANTED YOU.
HE DIDN'T DESERVE THAT. I'VE ALWAYS BEEN FAITHFUL TO YOU.
LET ME GO!
YOU WANT TO JOIN THE BOAR KING, YOU LIKE HIM, ADMIT IT!!
DON'T EVER TOUCH ME AGAIN! I HATE YOU!!
SKRRITCH
YOU'RE MY WIFE.

MOMMY!

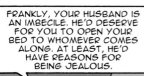

FRANKLY, YOUR HUSBAND IS AN IMBECILE. HE'D DESERVE FOR YOU TO OPEN YOUR BED TO WHOMEVER COMES ALONG. AT LEAST, HE'D HAVE REASONS FOR BEING JEALOUS.

SHUT UP.

YOU KNOW THE BOAR KING IS CRAZY ABOUT YOU? IT WOULD BE GOOD REVENGE.

NO!

WHY AM I NOT SIMPLY BEAUTIFUL? JUST AN ORDINARY BEAUTY, NICE, BUT A LITTLE ORDINARY? WHY DID YOU GIVE ME SUCH AN EXAGGERATED GIFT?

PFFFF, WHAT INGRATITUDE!

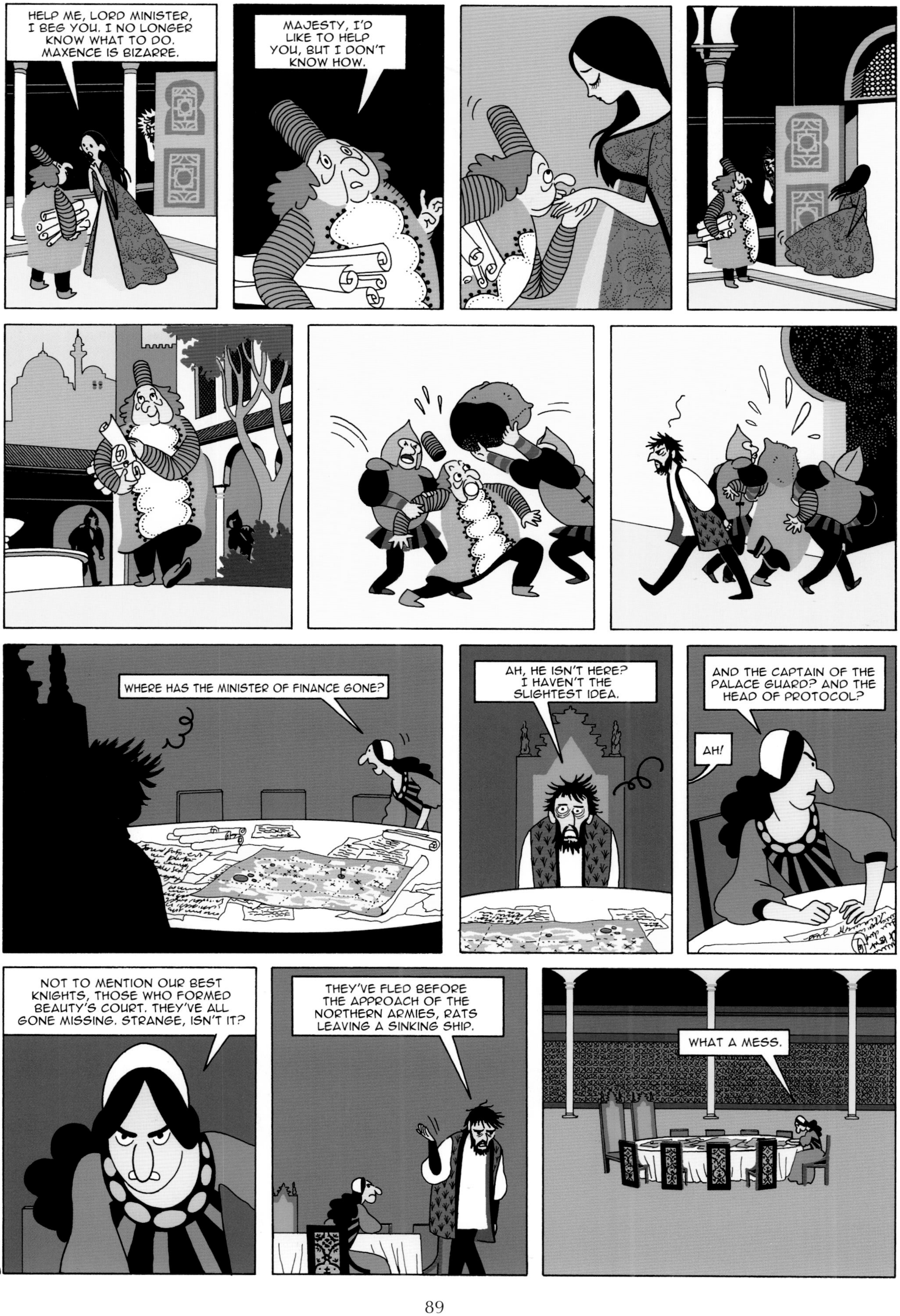

HELP ME, LORD MINISTER, I BEG YOU. I NO LONGER KNOW WHAT TO DO. MAXENCE IS BIZARRE.
MAJESTY, I'D LIKE TO HELP YOU, BUT I DON'T KNOW HOW.
WHERE HAS THE MINISTER OF FINANCE GONE?
AH, HE ISN'T HERE? I HAVEN'T THE SLIGHTEST IDEA.
AND THE CAPTAIN OF THE PALACE GUARD? AND THE HEAD OF PROTOCOL?
AH!
NOT TO MENTION OUR BEST KNIGHTS, THOSE WHO FORMED BEAUTY'S COURT. THEY'VE ALL GONE MISSING. STRANGE, ISN'T IT?
THEY'VE FLED BEFORE THE APPROACH OF THE NORTHERN ARMIES, RATS LEAVING A SINKING SHIP.
WHAT A MESS.
2
39

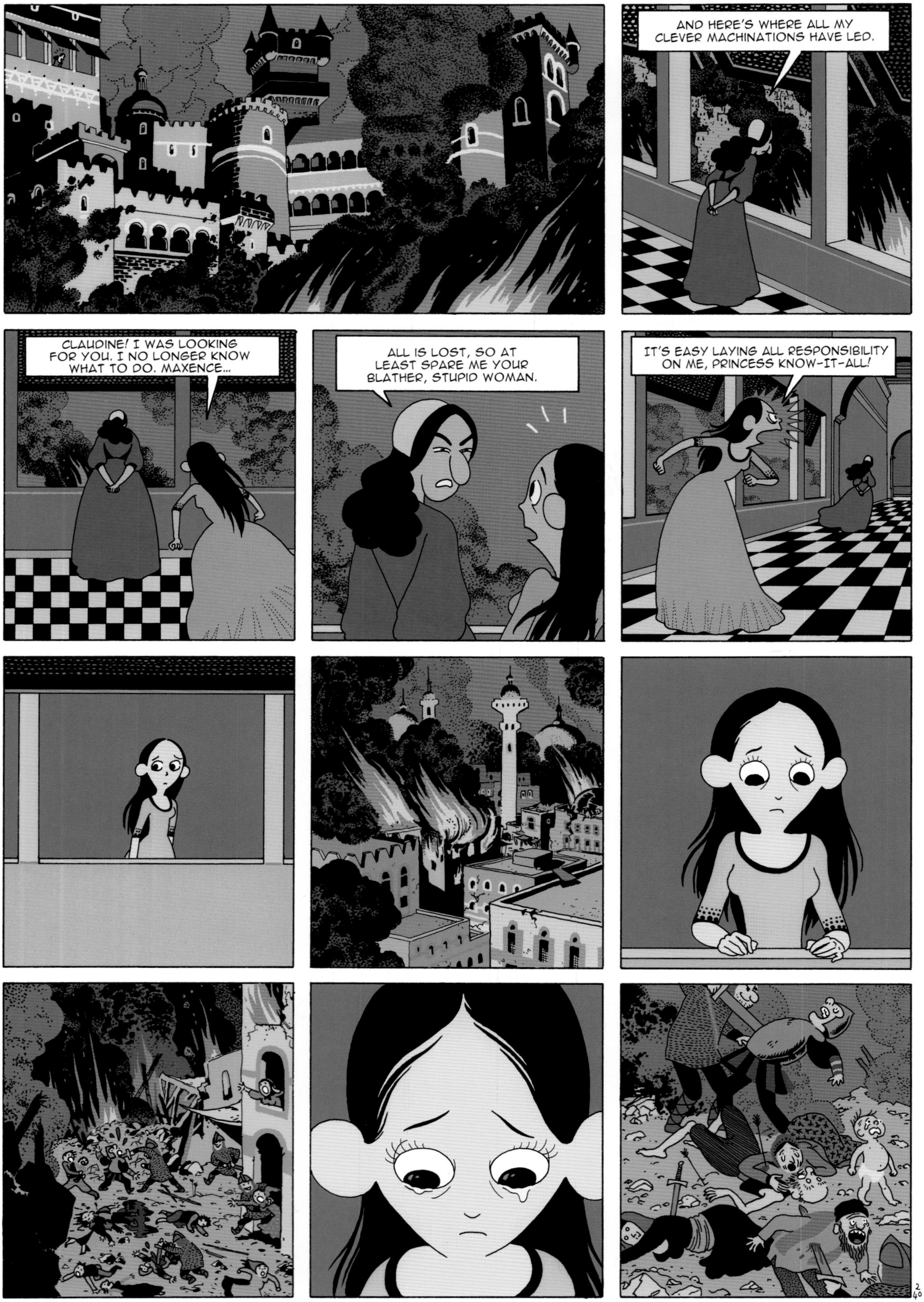
AND HERE'S WHERE ALL MY CLEVER MACHINATIONS HAVE LED.
CLAUDINE! I WAS LOOKING FOR YOU. I NO LONGER KNOW WHAT TO DO. MAXENCE...
ALL IS LOST, SO AT LEAST SPARE ME YOUR BLATHER, STUPID WOMAN.
IT'S EASY LAYING ALL RESPONSIBILITY ON ME, PRINCESS KNOW-IT-ALL!

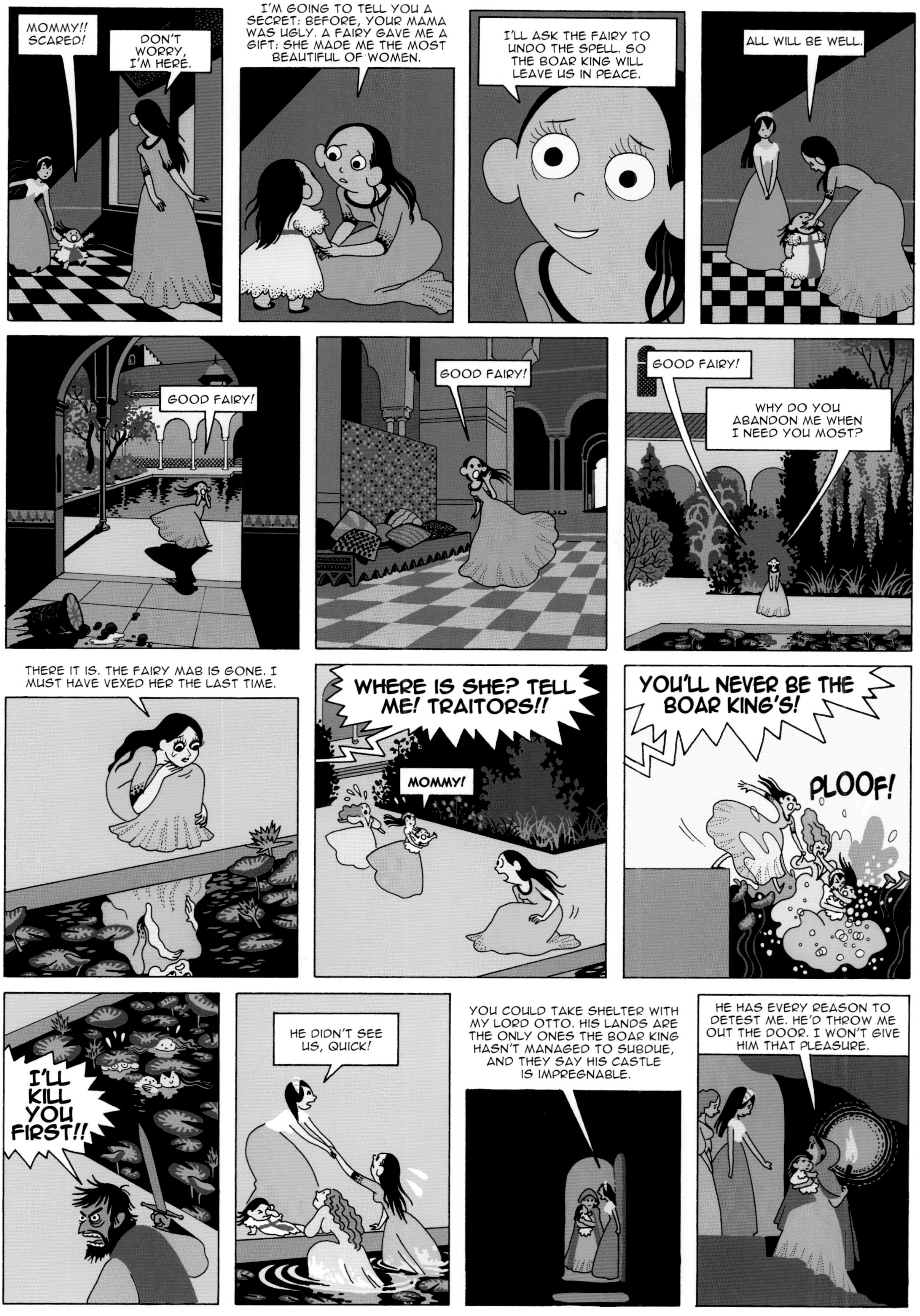
MOMMY!! SCARED!
DON'T WORRY, I'M HERE.
I'M GOING TO TELL YOU A SECRET: BEFORE, YOUR MAMA WAS UGLY. A FAIRY GAVE ME A GIFT: SHE MADE ME THE MOST BEAUTIFUL OF WOMEN.
I'LL ASK THE FAIRY TO UNDO THE SPELL. SO THE BOAR KING WILL LEAVE US IN PEACE.
ALL WILL BE WELL.
GOOD FAIRY!
GOOD FAIRY!
GOOD FAIRY!
WHY DO YOU ABANDON ME WHEN I NEED YOU MOST?
THERE IT IS. THE FAIRY MAB IS GONE. I MUST HAVE VEXED HER THE LAST TIME.
WHERE IS SHE? TELL ME! TRAITORS!!
MOMMY!
YOU'LL NEVER BE THE BOAR KING'S!
PLOOF!
I'LL KILL YOU FIRST!!
HE DIDN'T SEE US, QUICK!
YOU COULD TAKE SHELTER WITH MY LORD OTTO. HIS LANDS ARE THE ONLY ONES THE BOAR KING HASN'T MANAGED TO SUBDUE, AND THEY SAY HIS CASTLE IS IMPREGNABLE.
HE HAS EVERY REASON TO DETEST ME. HE'D THROW ME OUT THE DOOR. I WON'T GIVE HIM THAT PLEASURE.

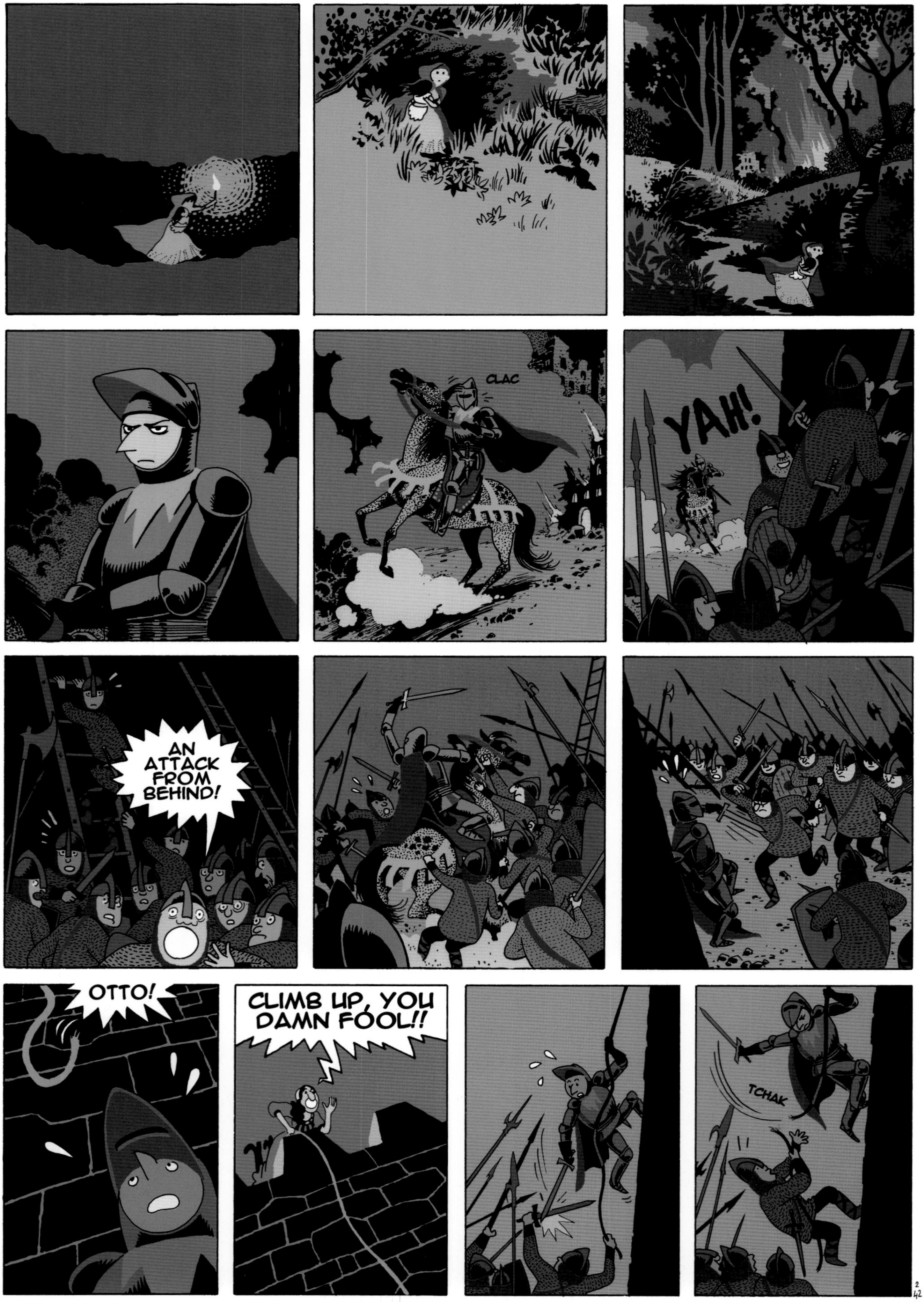
CLAC
YAH!
AN ATTACK FROM BEHIND!
OTTO!
CLIMB UP, YOU DAMN FOOL!!
TCHAK
2
42

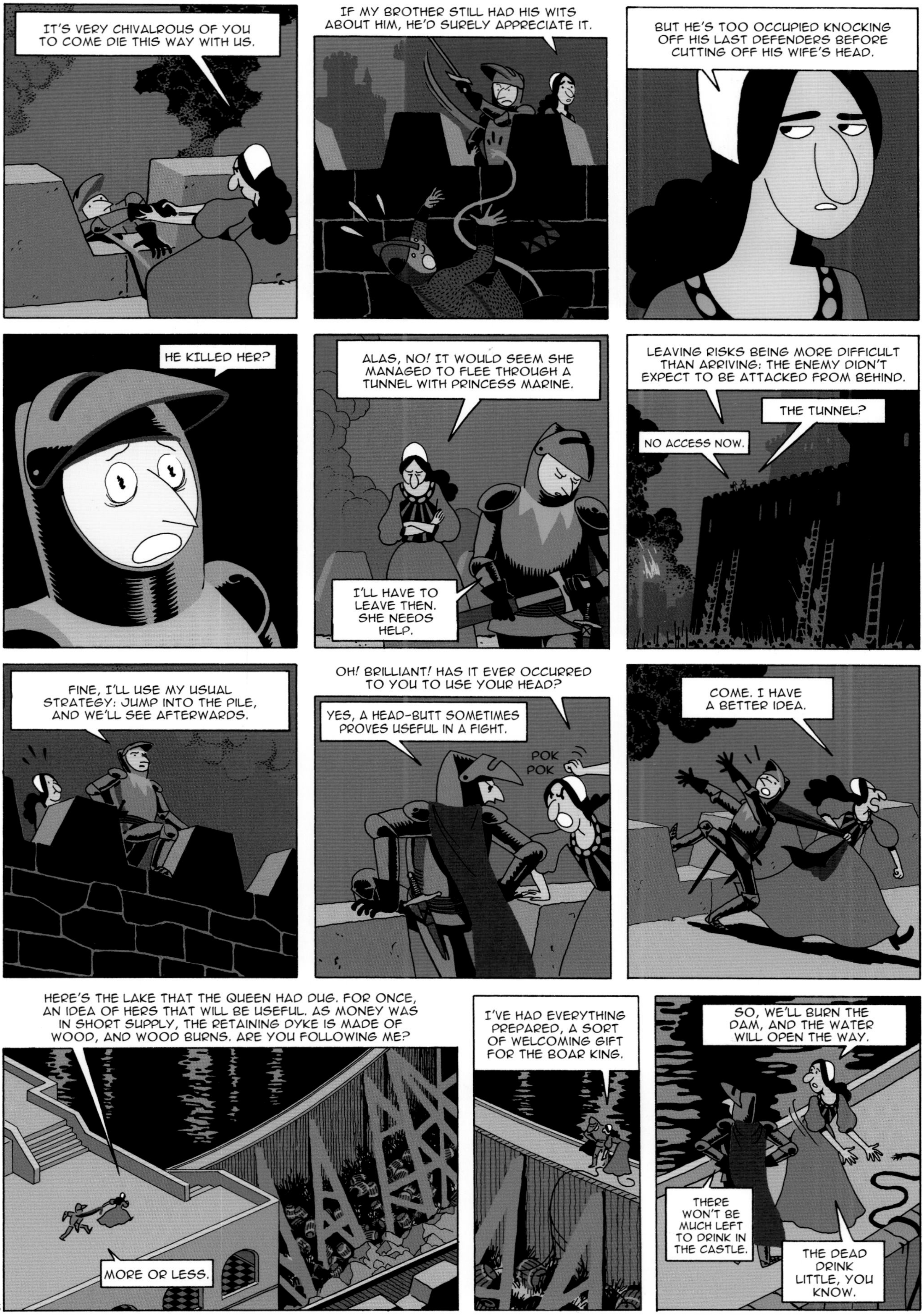

IT'S VERY CHIVALROUS OF YOU TO COME DIE THIS WAY WITH US.
IF MY BROTHER STILL HAD HIS WITS ABOUT HIM, HE'D SURELY APPRECIATE IT.
BUT HE'S TOO OCCUPIED KNOCKING OFF HIS LAST DEFENDERS BEFORE CUTTING OFF HIS WIFE'S HEAD.
HE KILLED HER?
ALAS, NO! IT WOULD SEEM SHE MANAGED TO FLEE THROUGH A TUNNEL WITH PRINCESS MARINE.
I'LL HAVE TO LEAVE THEN. SHE NEEDS HELP.
LEAVING RISKS BEING MORE DIFFICULT THAN ARRIVING: THE ENEMY DIDN'T EXPECT TO BE ATTACKED FROM BEHIND.
THE TUNNEL?
NO ACCESS NOW.
FINE, I'LL USE MY USUAL STRATEGY: JUMP INTO THE PILE, AND WE'LL SEE AFTERWARDS.
OH! BRILLIANT! HAS IT EVER OCCURRED TO YOU TO USE YOUR HEAD?
YES, A HEAD-BUTT SOMETIMES PROVES USEFUL IN A FIGHT.
POK POK
COME. I HAVE A BETTER IDEA.
HERE'S THE LAKE THAT THE QUEEN HAD DUG. FOR ONCE, AN IDEA OF HERS THAT WILL BE USEFUL. AS MONEY WAS IN SHORT SUPPLY, THE RETAINING DYKE IS MADE OF WOOD, AND WOOD BURNS. ARE YOU FOLLOWING ME?
MORE OR LESS.
2
43
I'VE HAD EVERYTHING PREPARED, A SORT OF WELCOMING GIFT FOR THE BOAR KING.
SO, WE'LL BURN THE DAM, AND THE WATER WILL OPEN THE WAY.
THERE WON'T BE MUCH LEFT TO DRINK IN THE CASTLE.
THE DEAD DRINK LITTLE, YOU KNOW.

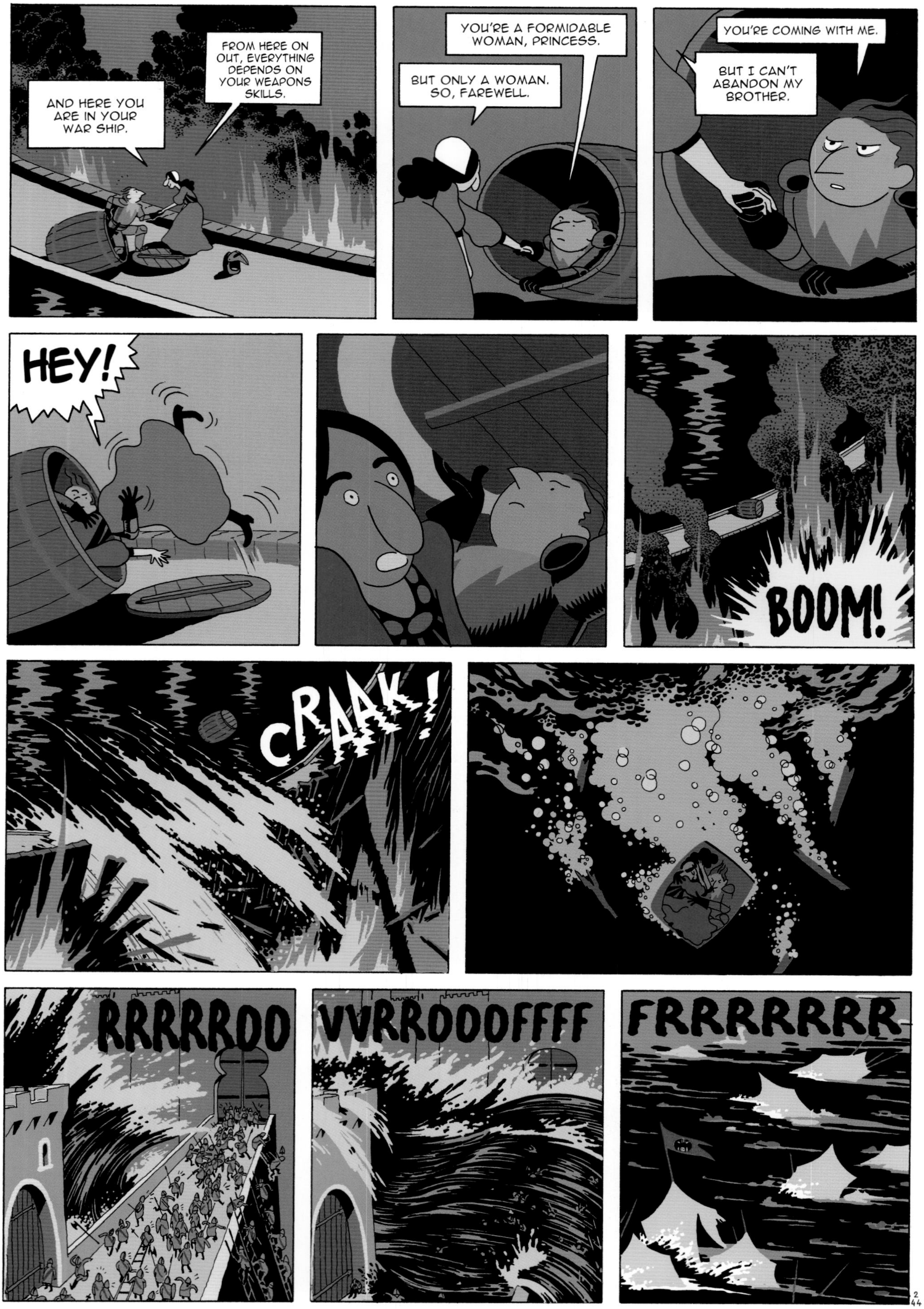
AND HERE YOU ARE IN YOUR WAR SHIP.
FROM HERE ON OUT, EVERYTHING DEPENDS ON YOUR WEAPONS SKILLS.
YOU'RE A FORMIDABLE WOMAN, PRINCESS.
BUT ONLY A WOMAN. SO, FAREWELL.
YOU'RE COMING WITH ME.
BUT I CAN'T ABANDON MY BROTHER.
HEY!
BOOM!
CRAAK!
RRRRROO
VVRROOOFFFF
FRRRRRRR
2
44

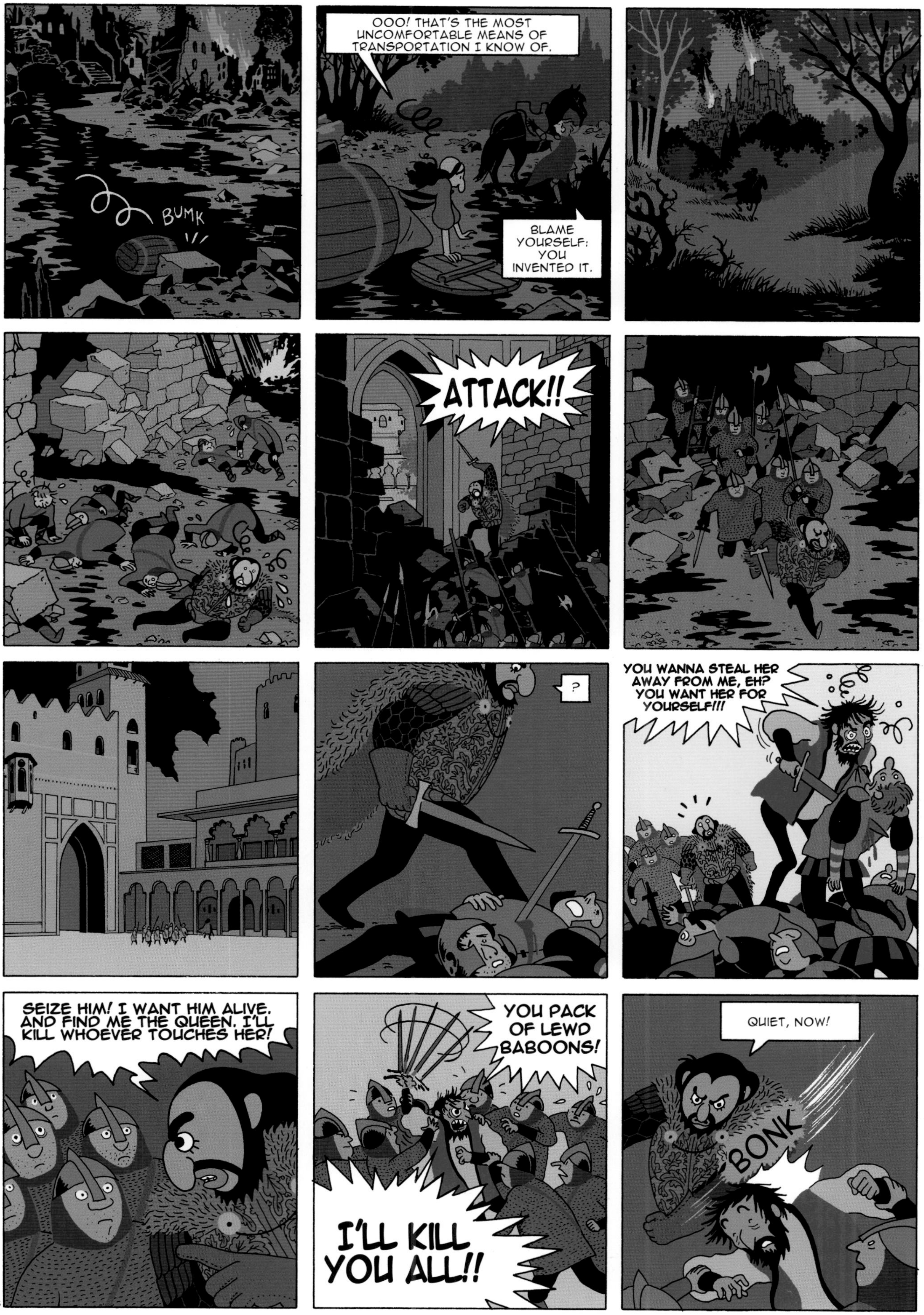
BUMK
OOO! THAT'S THE MOST UNCOMFORTABLE MEANS OF TRANSPORTATION I KNOW OF.
BLAME YOURSELF: YOU INVENTED IT.
ATTACK!!
?
YOU WANNA STEAL HER AWAY FROM ME, EH? YOU WANT HER FOR YOURSELF!!!
SEIZE HIM! I WANT HIM ALIVE. AND FIND ME THE QUEEN. I'LL KILL WHOEVER TOUCHES HER!
YOU PACK OF LEWD BABOONS!
I'LL KILL YOU ALL!!
QUIET, NOW!
BONK
2
45

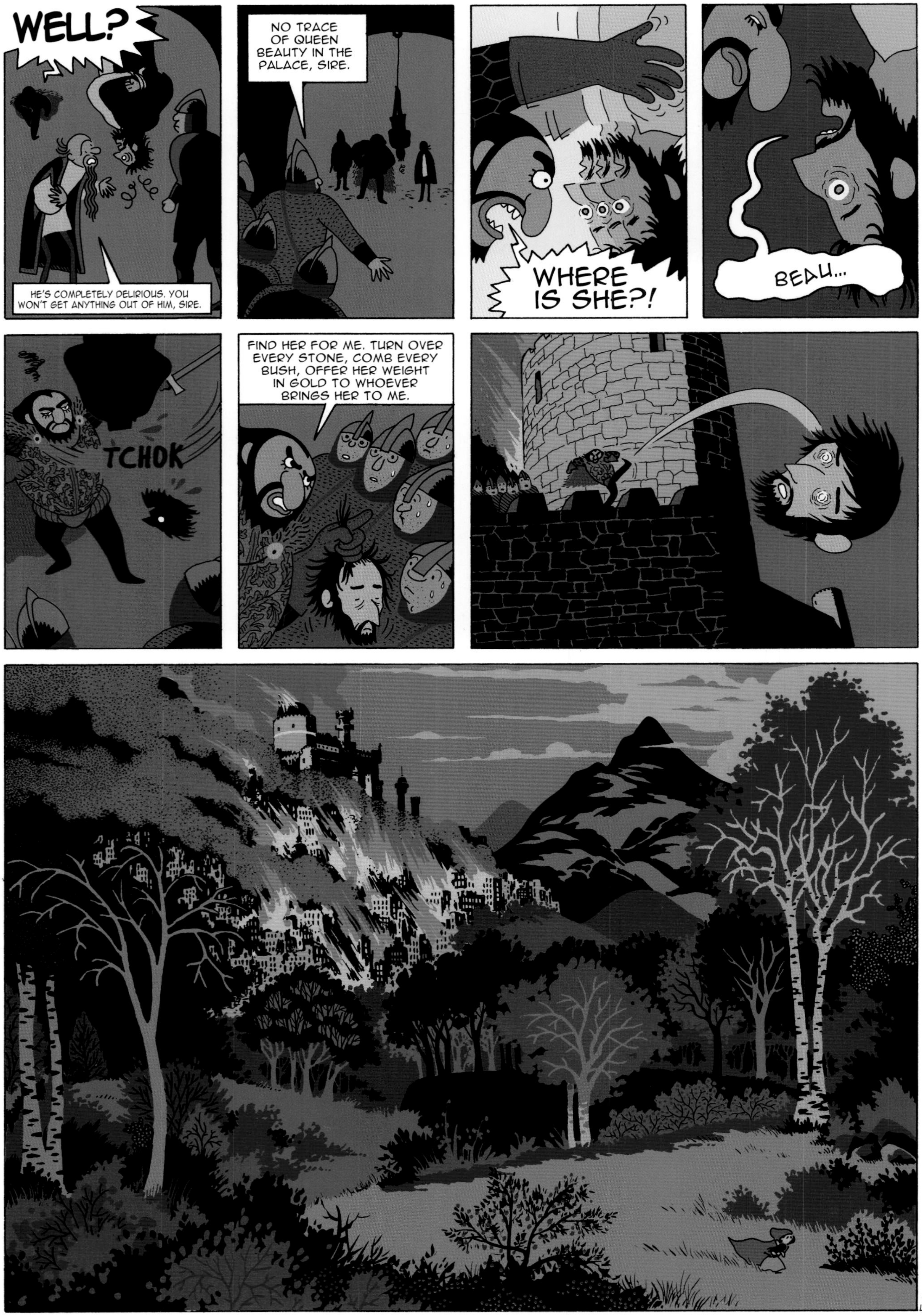
WELL?
HE'S COMPLETELY DELIRIOUS. YOU WON'T GET ANYTHING OUT OF HIM, SIRE.
NO TRACE OF QUEEN BEAUTY IN THE PALACE, SIRE.
WHERE IS SHE?!
BEAU...
TCHOK
FIND HER FOR ME. TURN OVER EVERY STONE, COMB EVERY BUSH, OFFER HER WEIGHT IN GOLD TO WHOEVER BRINGS HER TO ME.
2
46

And that's how Beauty lost her husband and her kingdom.

3 ~ Ordinary Mortals

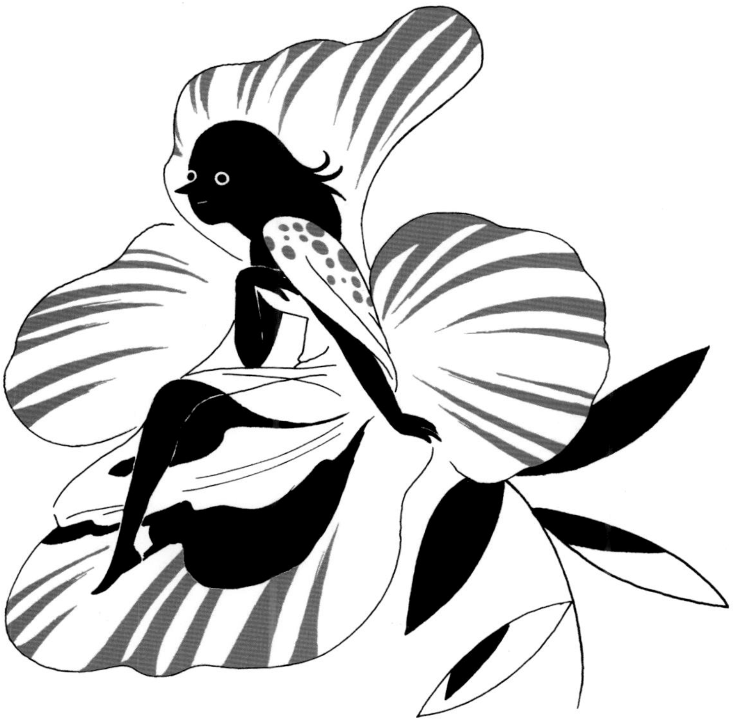

Everything had crumbled under Beauty. The only thing remaining from her former life was her daughter Marine, and the burdensome gift that Mab had given her.

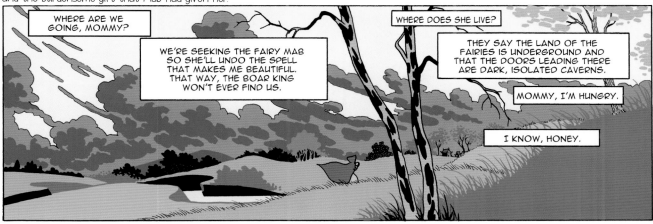

WHERE ARE WE GOING, MOMMY?

WE'RE SEEKING THE FAIRY MAB SO SHE'LL UNDO THE SPELL THAT MAKES ME BEAUTIFUL. THAT WAY, THE BOAR KING WON'T EVER FIND US.

WHERE DOES SHE LIVE?

THEY SAY THE LAND OF THE FAIRIES IS UNDERGROUND AND THAT THE DOORS LEADING THERE ARE DARK, ISOLATED CAVERNS.

MOMMY, I'M HUNGRY.

I KNOW, HONEY.

COULD YOU LOOK AFTER MY DAUGHTER? I'LL COME BACK SOON.

TIMES ARE HARD. OUR MEN WENT OFF TO WAR AND NEVER CAME BACK.

HERE. IT'S ALL THAT I POSSESS.

YOU'LL STAY WITH THESE KIND LADIES TILL I FIND MAB. YOU'LL BE SAFE.

WHEN I COME BACK, I WON'T LOOK LIKE I DO NOW ANY LONGER. BUT YOU'LL RECOGNIZE ME BY MY SMELL.

MAB?!

MAB?

MAB?

99

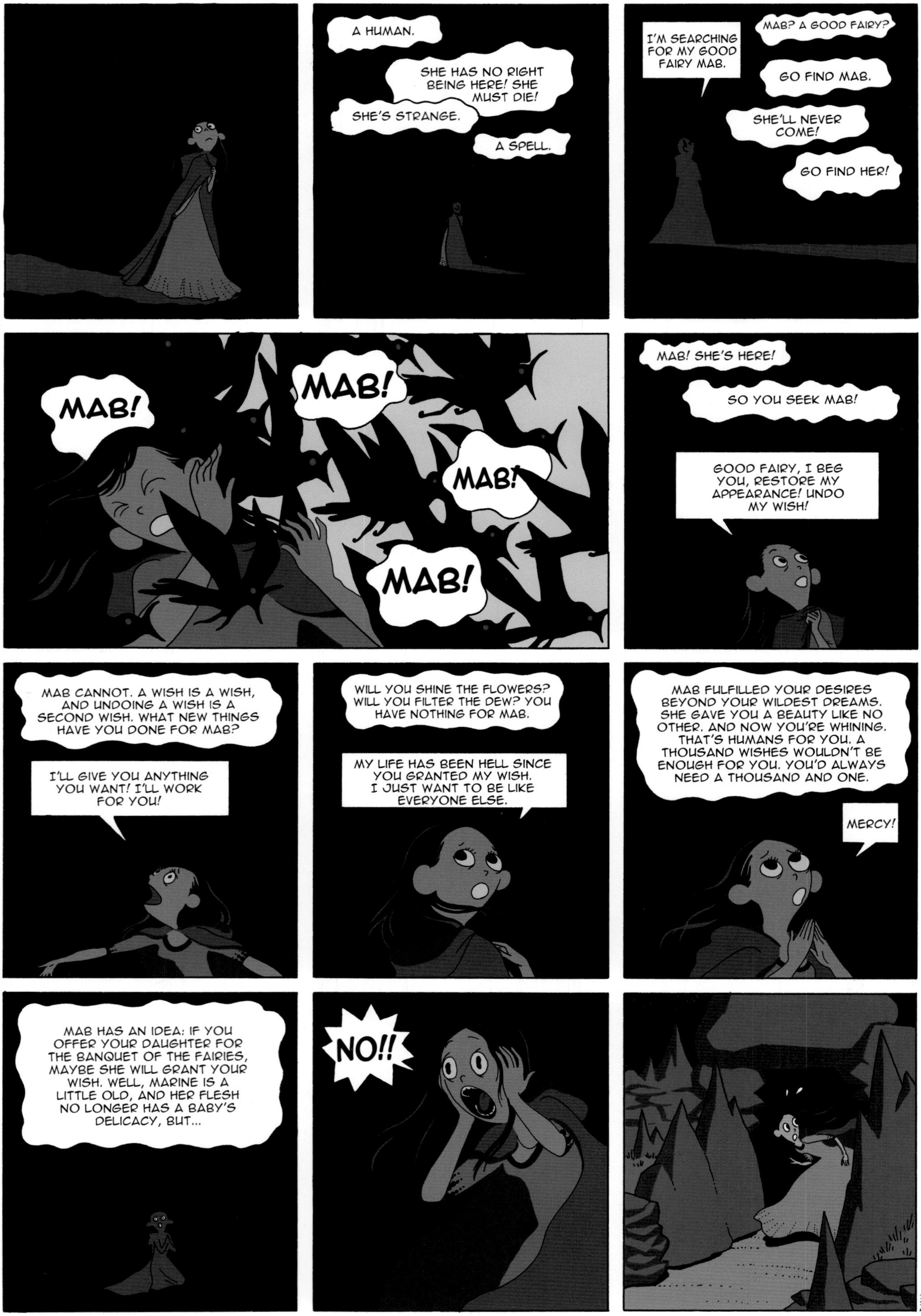
A HUMAN.
SHE HAS NO RIGHT BEING HERE! SHE MUST DIE!
SHE'S STRANGE.
A SPELL.
I'M SEARCHING FOR MY GOOD FAIRY MAB.
MAB? A GOOD FAIRY?
GO FIND MAB.
SHE'LL NEVER COME!
GO FIND HER!
MAB!
MAB!
MAB!
MAB!
MAB! SHE'S HERE!
SO YOU SEEK MAB!
GOOD FAIRY, I BEG YOU, RESTORE MY APPEARANCE! UNDO MY WISH!
MAB CANNOT. A WISH IS A WISH, AND UNDOING A WISH IS A SECOND WISH. WHAT NEW THINGS HAVE YOU DONE FOR MAB?
I'LL GIVE YOU ANYTHING YOU WANT! I'LL WORK FOR YOU!
WILL YOU SHINE THE FLOWERS? WILL YOU FILTER THE DEW? YOU HAVE NOTHING FOR MAB.
MY LIFE HAS BEEN HELL SINCE YOU GRANTED MY WISH. I JUST WANT TO BE LIKE EVERYONE ELSE.
MAB FULFILLED YOUR DESIRES BEYOND YOUR WILDEST DREAMS. SHE GAVE YOU A BEAUTY LIKE NO OTHER. AND NOW YOU'RE WHINING. THAT'S HUMANS FOR YOU. A THOUSAND WISHES WOULDN'T BE ENOUGH FOR YOU. YOU'D ALWAYS NEED A THOUSAND AND ONE.
MERCY!
MAB HAS AN IDEA: IF YOU OFFER YOUR DAUGHTER FOR THE BANQUET OF THE FAIRIES, MAYBE SHE WILL GRANT YOUR WISH. WELL, MARINE IS A LITTLE OLD, AND HER FLESH NO LONGER HAS A BABY'S DELICACY, BUT...
NO!!
32

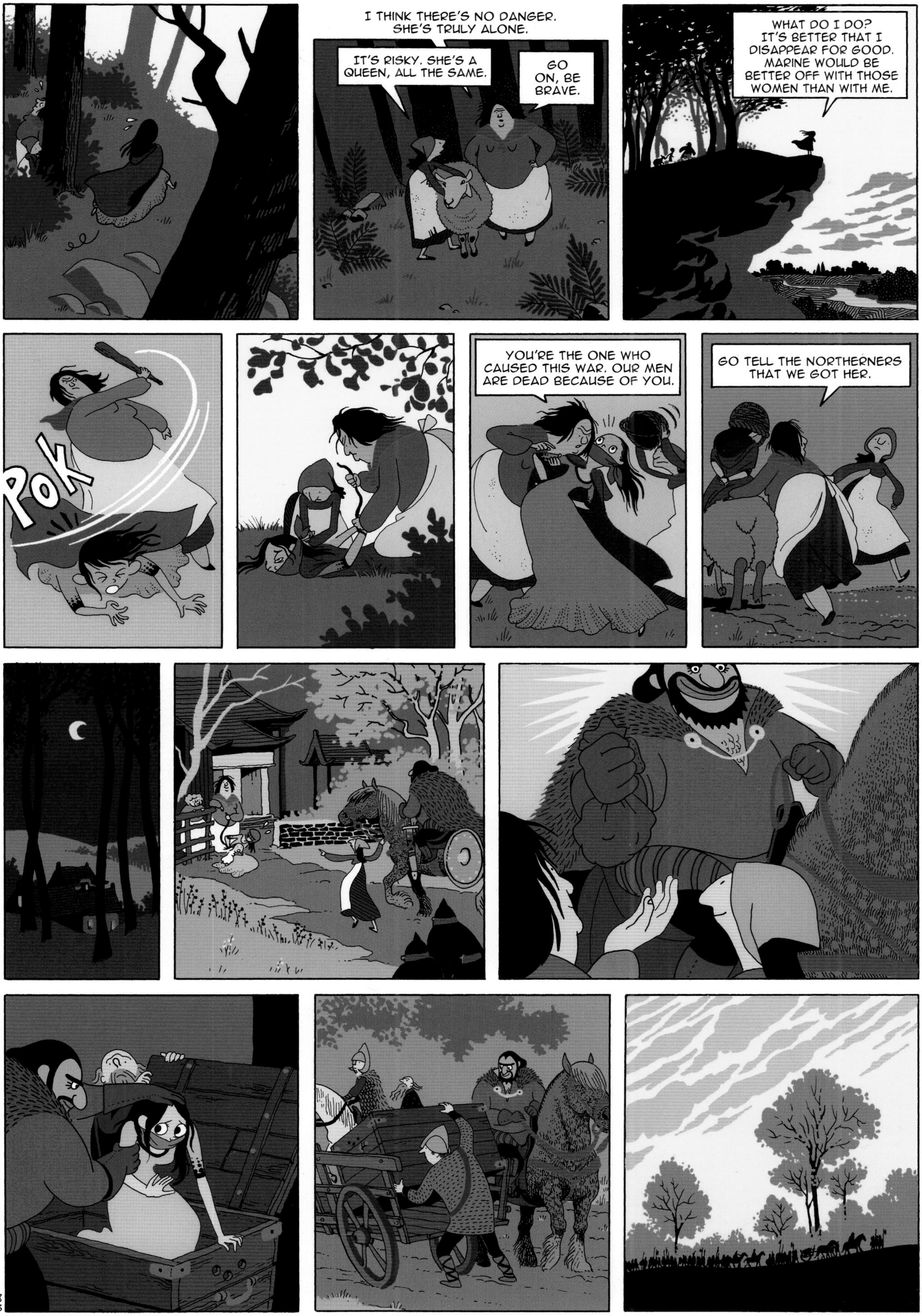
I THINK THERE'S NO DANGER. SHE'S TRULY ALONE.
IT'S RISKY. SHE'S A QUEEN, ALL THE SAME.
GO ON, BE BRAVE.
WHAT DO I DO? IT'S BETTER THAT I DISAPPEAR FOR GOOD. MARINE WOULD BE BETTER OFF WITH THOSE WOMEN THAN WITH ME.
POK
YOU'RE THE ONE WHO CAUSED THIS WAR. OUR MEN ARE DEAD BECAUSE OF YOU.
GO TELL THE NORTHERNERS THAT WE GOT HER.
33

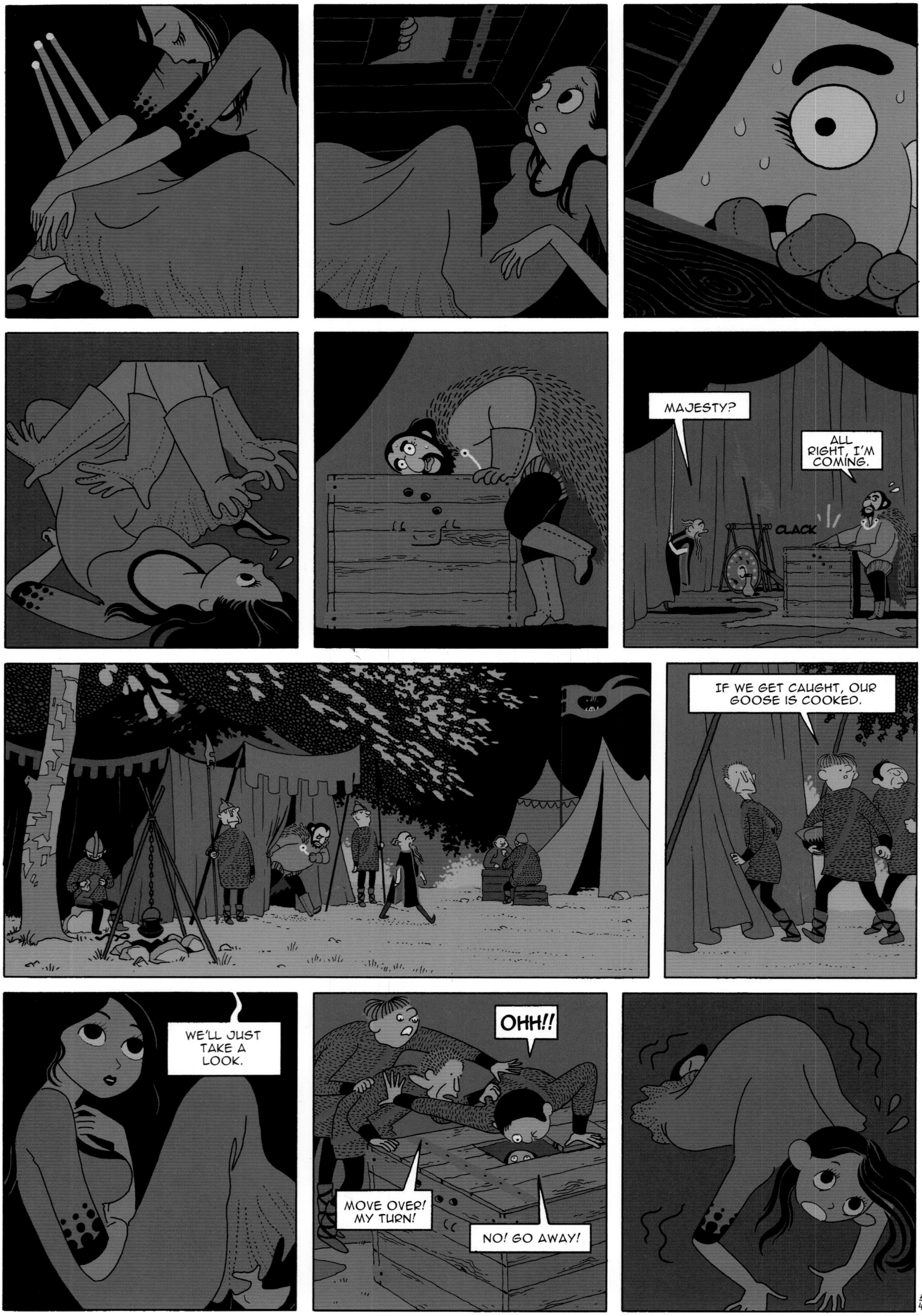
MAJESTY?
ALL RIGHT, I'M COMING.
CLACK
IF WE GET CAUGHT, OUR GOOSE IS COOKED.
WE'LL JUST TAKE A LOOK.
OHH!!
MOVE OVER! MY TURN!
NO! GO AWAY!
34

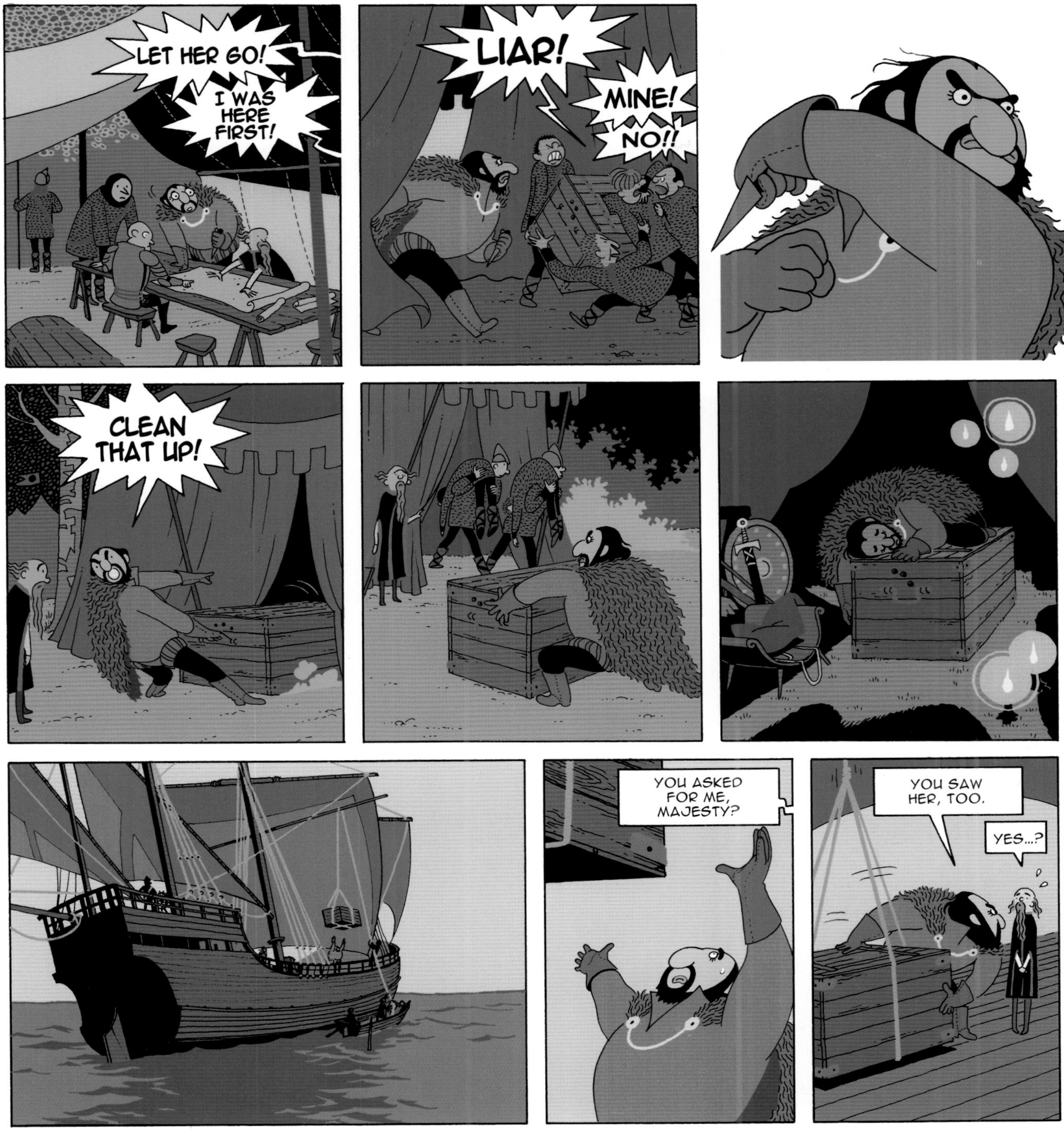
LET HER GO!
I WAS HERE FIRST!
LIAR!
MINE!
NO!!
CLEAN THAT UP!
YOU ASKED FOR ME, MAJESTY?
YOU SAW HER, TOO.
YES...?

AND HOW IS IT THAT SHE DOESN'T MAKE YOU LOSE YOUR MIND?

The councilor had a well-hidden secret: Beauty wasn't his type at all. For that, she'd be wider in the shoulders, endowed with a generous paunch, and have a handsome beard.

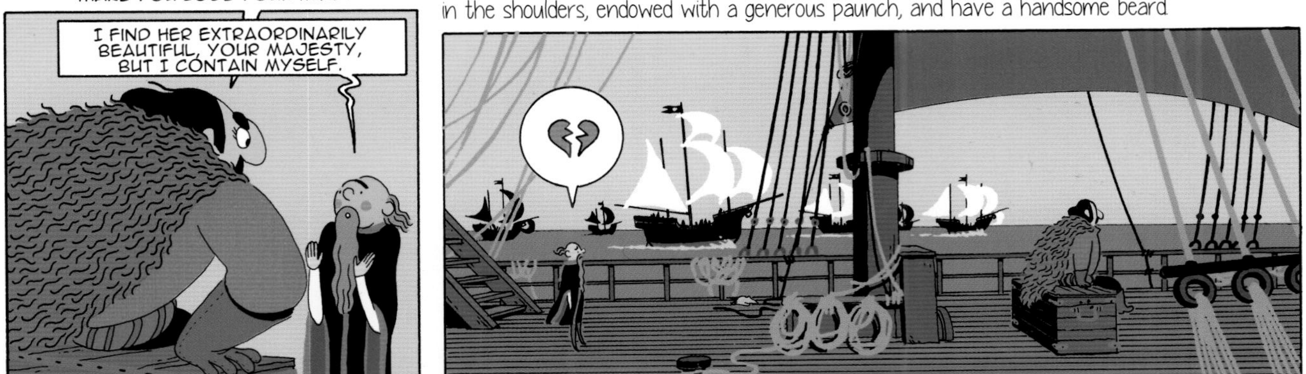
I FIND HER EXTRAORDINARILY BEAUTIFUL, YOUR MAJESTY, BUT I CONTAIN MYSELF.

35

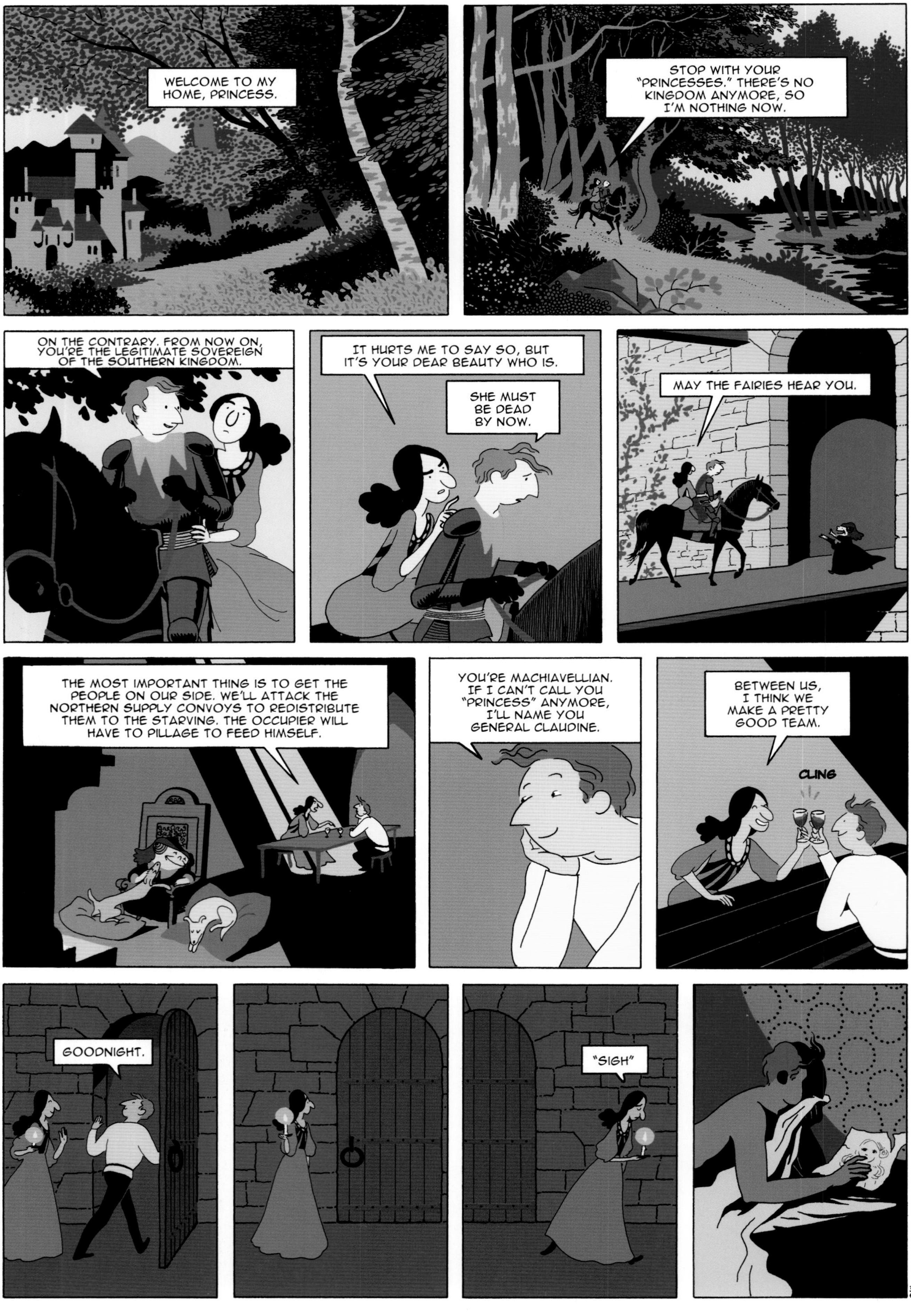
WELCOME TO MY HOME, PRINCESS.
STOP WITH YOUR "PRINCESSES." THERE'S NO KINGDOM ANYMORE, SO I'M NOTHING NOW.
ON THE CONTRARY. FROM NOW ON, YOU'RE THE LEGITIMATE SOVEREIGN OF THE SOUTHERN KINGDOM.
IT HURTS ME TO SAY SO, BUT IT'S YOUR DEAR BEAUTY WHO IS.
SHE MUST BE DEAD BY NOW.
MAY THE FAIRIES HEAR YOU.
THE MOST IMPORTANT THING IS TO GET THE PEOPLE ON OUR SIDE. WE'LL ATTACK THE NORTHERN SUPPLY CONVOYS TO REDISTRIBUTE THEM TO THE STARVING. THE OCCUPIER WILL HAVE TO PILLAGE TO FEED HIMSELF.
YOU'RE MACHIAVELLIAN. IF I CAN'T CALL YOU "PRINCESS" ANYMORE, I'LL NAME YOU GENERAL CLAUDINE.
BETWEEN US, I THINK WE MAKE A PRETTY GOOD TEAM.
CLING
GOODNIGHT.
"SIGH"
36

The Boar King felt larger than life. He'd crushed the Southern Kingdom, ravished the most beautiful woman of all, and his queen faithfully awaited him in the North. He was power incarnate, smashing any sign of resistance with his overwhelming strength.

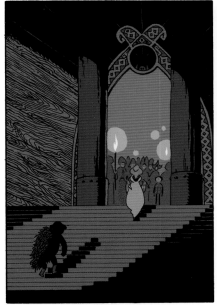

DARLING!

HELLO, SWEETIE.

YOU'RE HIDING SOMETHING FROM ME. IT'S ALL OVER YOUR FACE.

ME? NO.

URKAN! DON'T YOU REMEMBER ME? I'M YOUR UNCLE!

HOW YOU'VE GROWN. HOW OLD ARE YOU NOW?

SIX, UNCLE.

SIX ALREADY. HOW QUICKLY TIME PASSES.

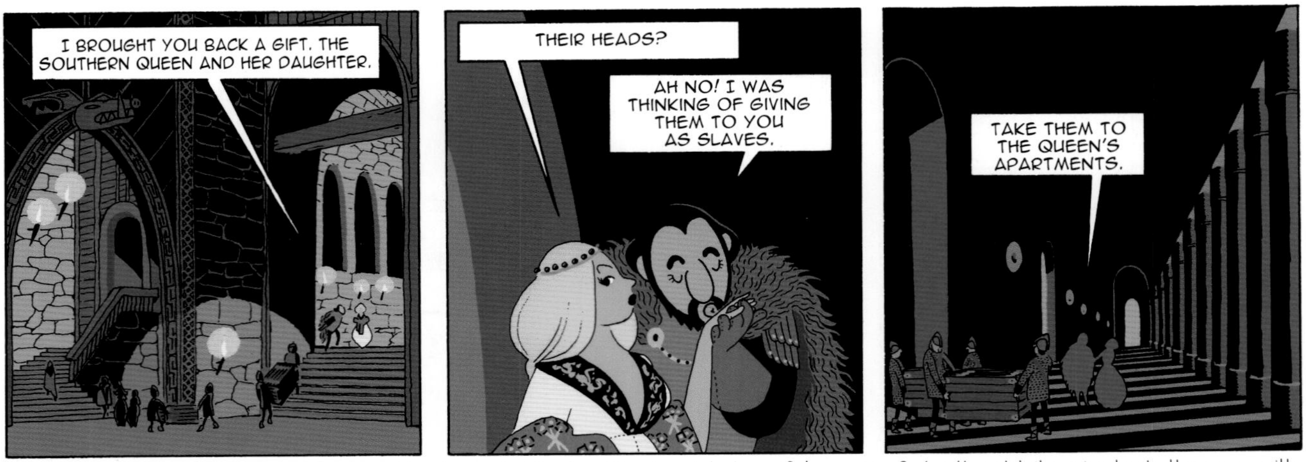
I BROUGHT YOU BACK A GIFT. THE SOUTHERN QUEEN AND HER DAUGHTER.
THEIR HEADS?
AH NO! I WAS THINKING OF GIVING THEM TO YOU AS SLAVES.
TAKE THEM TO THE QUEEN'S APARTMENTS.

Whenever a woman pleased him, the Boar King had a habit of putting her into his wife's service. So he thought it easier to do the same with Beauty. She'd be well guarded, far from the gaze of other men.

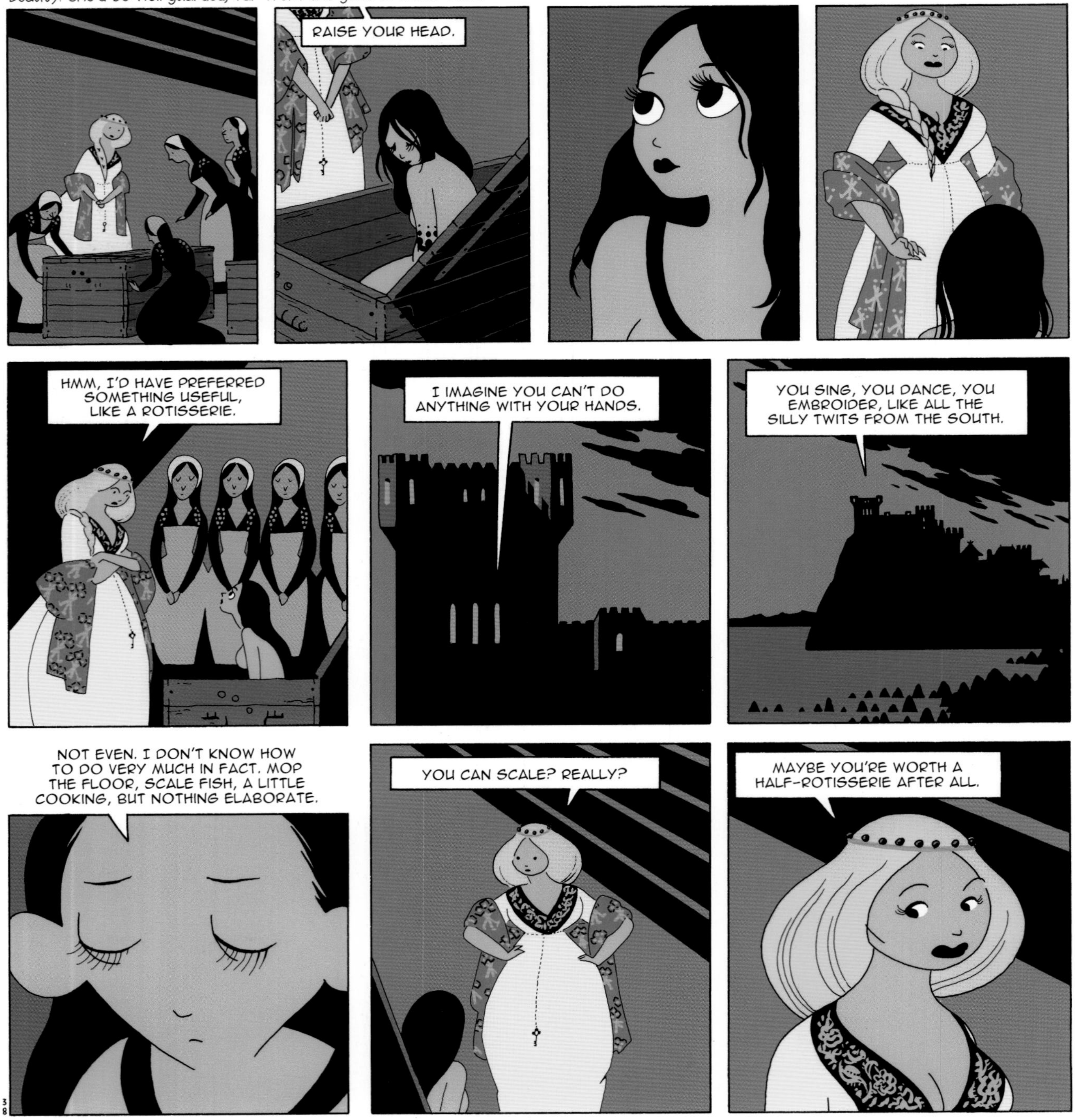
RAISE YOUR HEAD.
HMM, I'D HAVE PREFERRED SOMETHING USEFUL, LIKE A ROTISSERIE.
I IMAGINE YOU CAN'T DO ANYTHING WITH YOUR HANDS.
YOU SING, YOU DANCE, YOU EMBROIDER, LIKE ALL THE SILLY TWITS FROM THE SOUTH.
NOT EVEN. I DON'T KNOW HOW TO DO VERY MUCH IN FACT. MOP THE FLOOR, SCALE FISH, A LITTLE COOKING, BUT NOTHING ELABORATE.
YOU CAN SCALE? REALLY?
MAYBE YOU'RE WORTH A HALF-ROTISSERIE AFTER ALL.

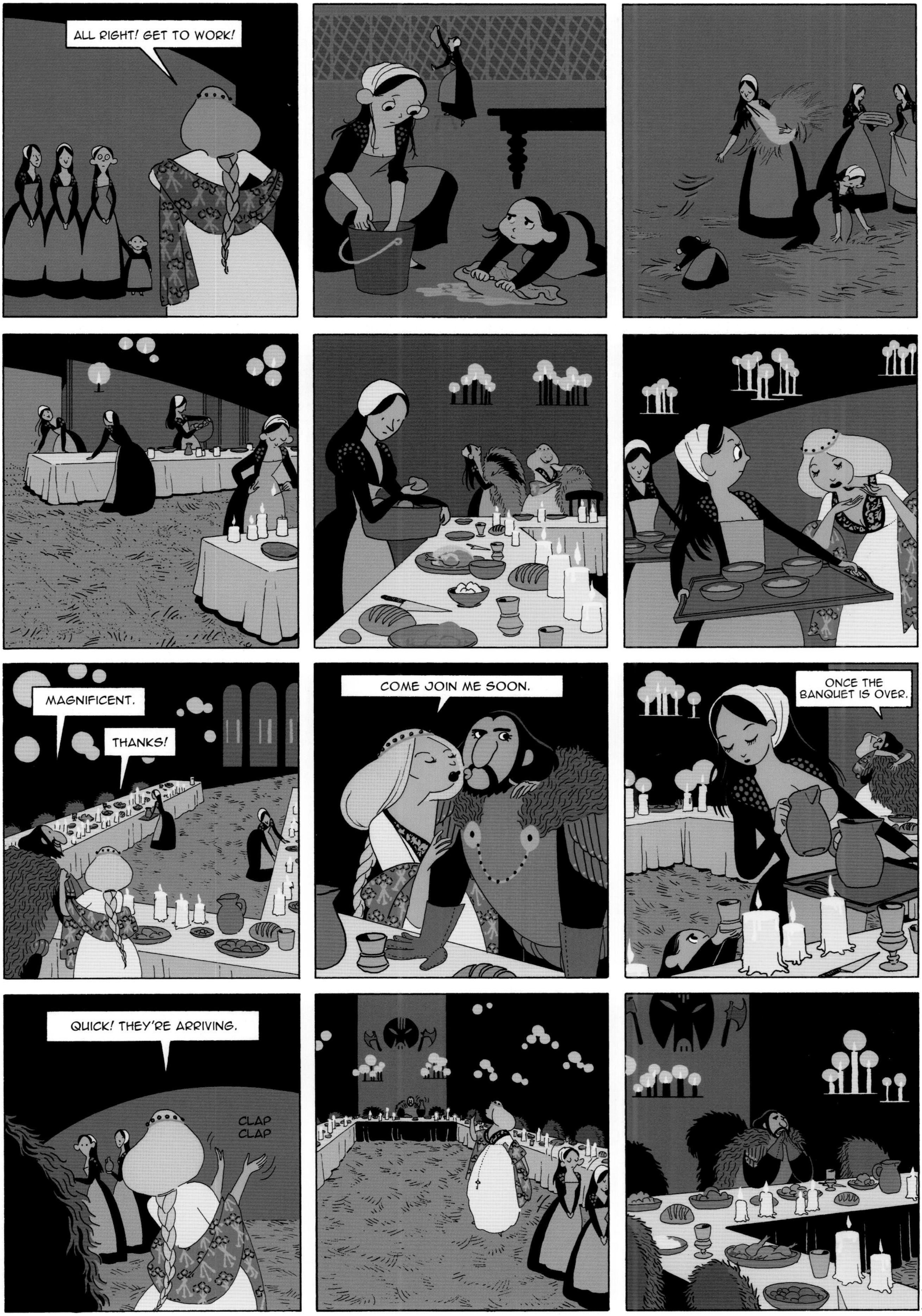
ALL RIGHT! GET TO WORK!
MAGNIFICENT.
THANKS!
COME JOIN ME SOON.
ONCE THE BANQUET IS OVER.
QUICK! THEY'RE ARRIVING.
CLAP CLAP
39

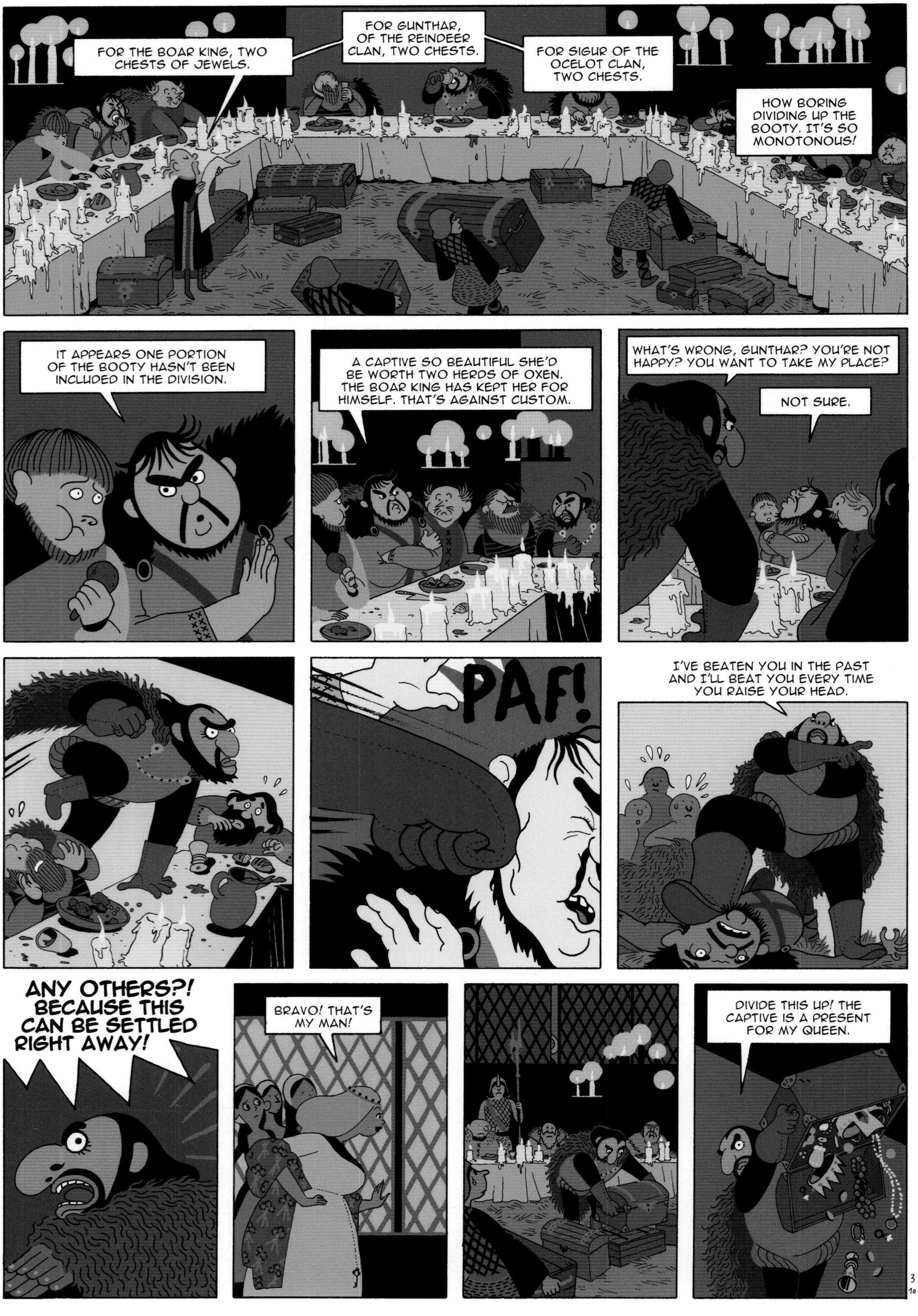
FOR THE BOAR KING, TWO CHESTS OF JEWELS.
FOR GUNTHAR, OF THE REINDEER CLAN, TWO CHESTS.
FOR SIGUR OF THE OCELOT CLAN, TWO CHESTS.
HOW BORING DIVIDING UP THE BOOTY. IT'S SO MONOTONOUS!
IT APPEARS ONE PORTION OF THE BOOTY HASN'T BEEN INCLUDED IN THE DIVISION.
A CAPTIVE SO BEAUTIFUL SHE'D BE WORTH TWO HERDS OF OXEN. THE BOAR KING HAS KEPT HER FOR HIMSELF. THAT'S AGAINST CUSTOM.
WHAT'S WRONG, GUNTHAR? YOU'RE NOT HAPPY? YOU WANT TO TAKE MY PLACE?
NOT SURE.
PAF!
I'VE BEATEN YOU IN THE PAST AND I'LL BEAT YOU EVERY TIME YOU RAISE YOUR HEAD.
ANY OTHERS?! BECAUSE THIS CAN BE SETTLED RIGHT AWAY!
BRAVO! THAT'S MY MAN!
DIVIDE THIS UP! THE CAPTIVE IS A PRESENT FOR MY QUEEN.
3
10

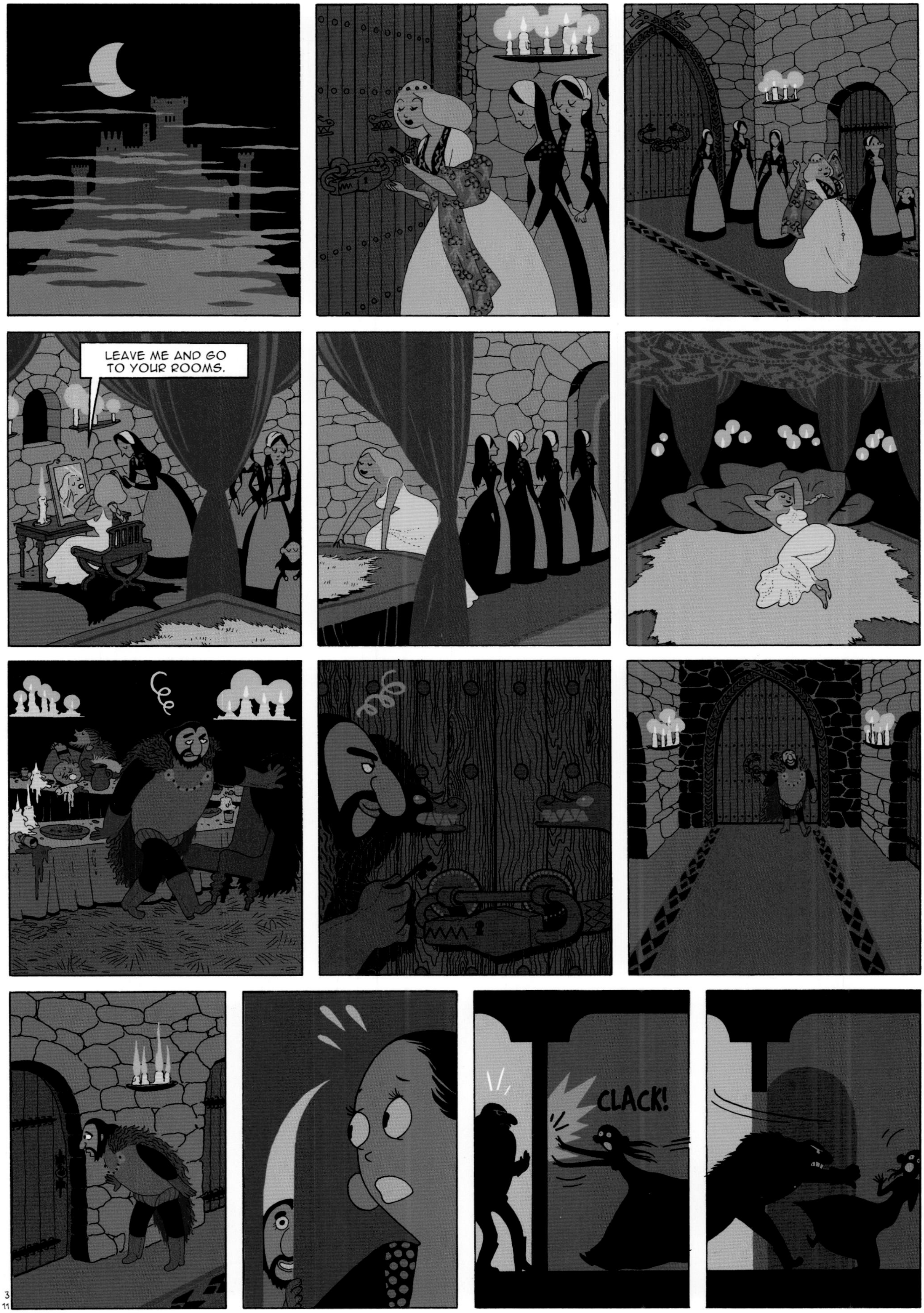
LEAVE ME AND GO TO YOUR ROOMS.
CLACK!

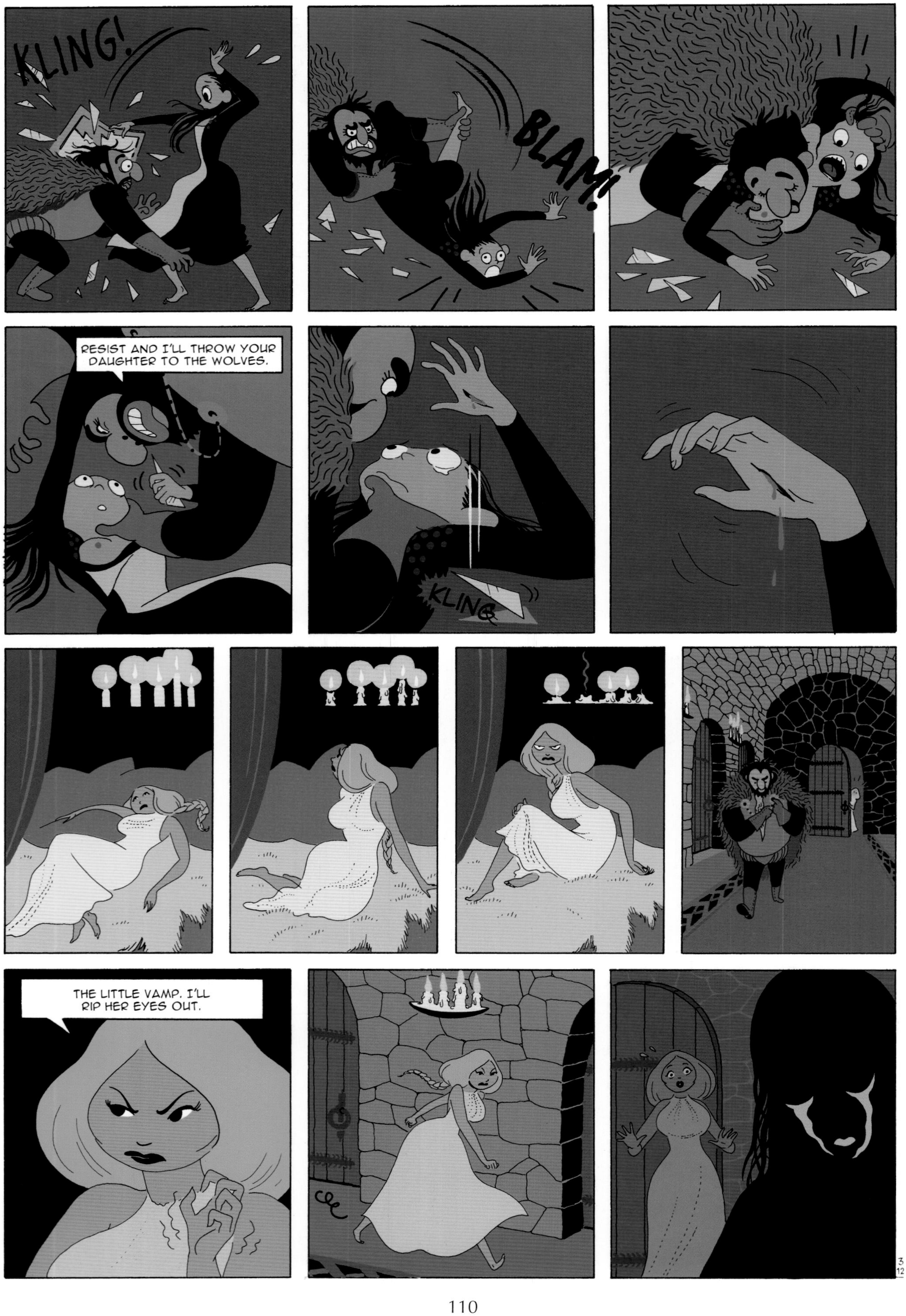
KLING!
BLAM!
RESIST AND I'LL THROW YOUR DAUGHTER TO THE WOLVES.
KLING
THE LITTLE VAMP. I'LL RIP HER EYES OUT.

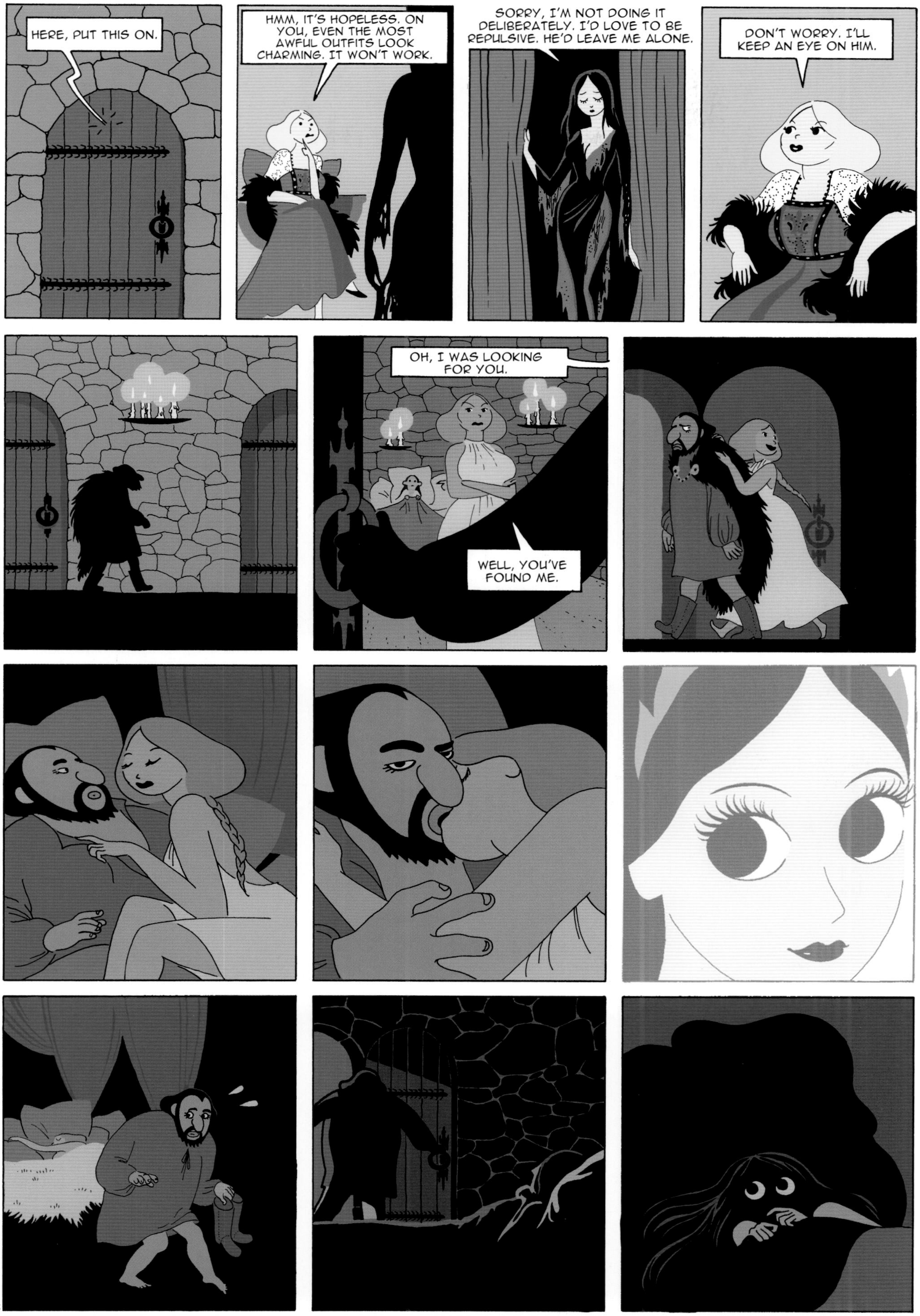
HERE, PUT THIS ON.
HMM, IT'S HOPELESS. ON YOU, EVEN THE MOST AWFUL OUTFITS LOOK CHARMING. IT WON'T WORK.
SORRY, I'M NOT DOING IT DELIBERATELY. I'D LOVE TO BE REPULSIVE. HE'D LEAVE ME ALONE.
DON'T WORRY. I'LL KEEP AN EYE ON HIM.
OH, I WAS LOOKING FOR YOU.
WELL, YOU'VE FOUND ME.

3
13

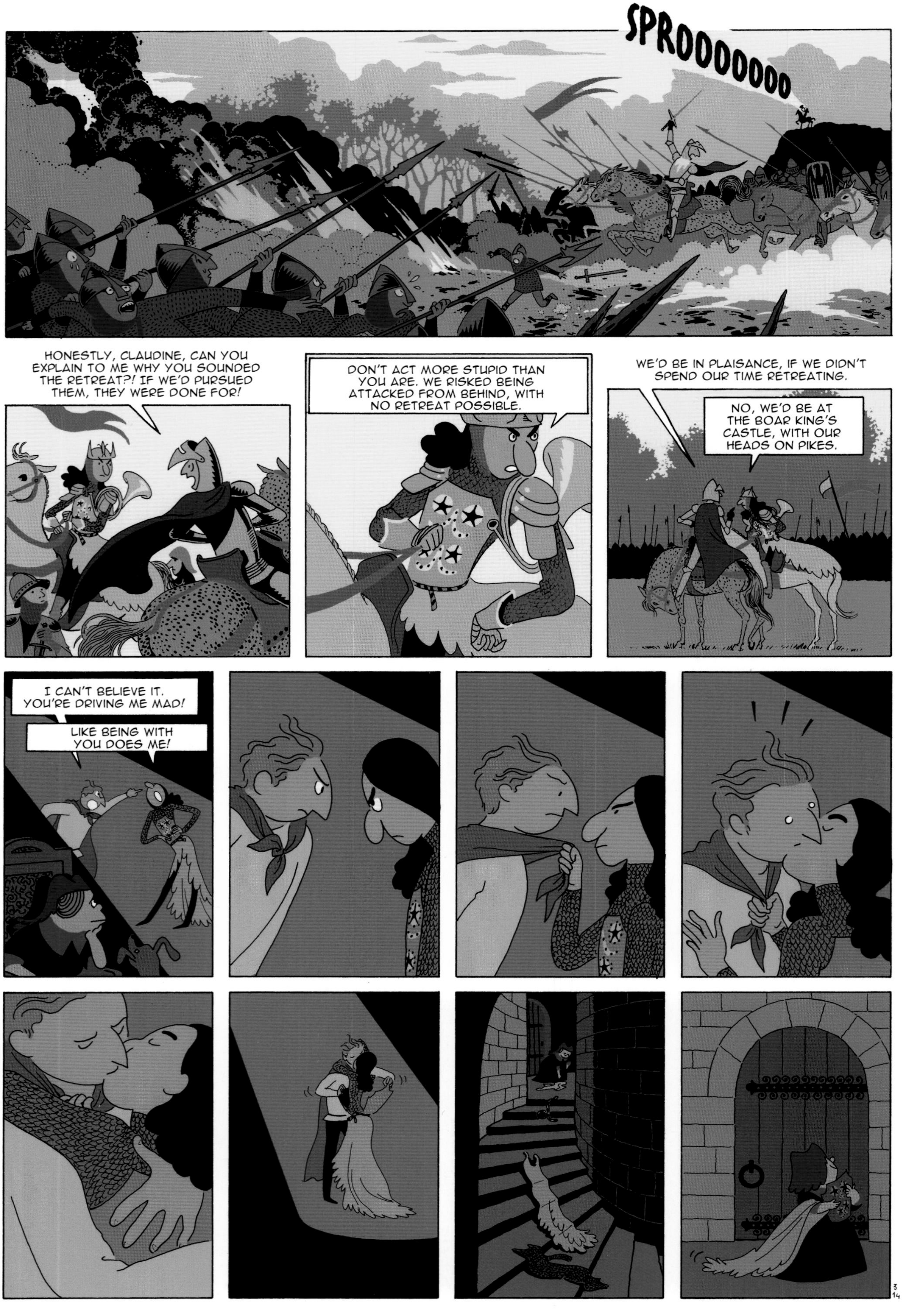
SPROOOOOOO
HONESTLY, CLAUDINE, CAN YOU EXPLAIN TO ME WHY YOU SOUNDED THE RETREAT?! IF WE'D PURSUED THEM, THEY WERE DONE FOR!
DON'T ACT MORE STUPID THAN YOU ARE. WE RISKED BEING ATTACKED FROM BEHIND, WITH NO RETREAT POSSIBLE.
WE'D BE IN PLAISANCE, IF WE DIDN'T SPEND OUR TIME RETREATING.
NO, WE'D BE AT THE BOAR KING'S CASTLE, WITH OUR HEADS ON PIKES.
I CAN'T BELIEVE IT. YOU'RE DRIVING ME MAD!
LIKE BEING WITH YOU DOES ME!
3
14

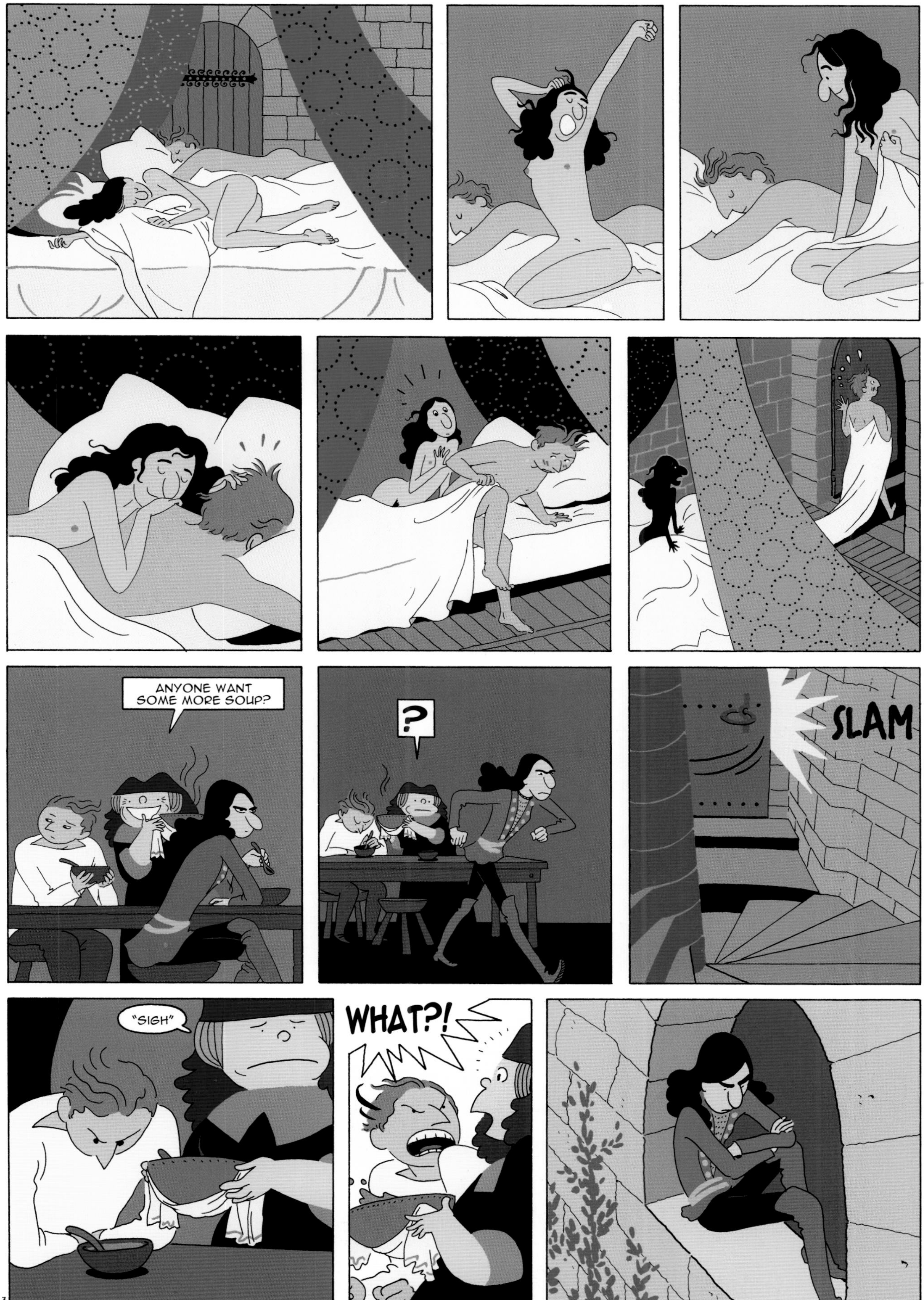
ANYONE WANT SOME MORE SOUP?
?
SLAM
"SIGH"
WHAT?!

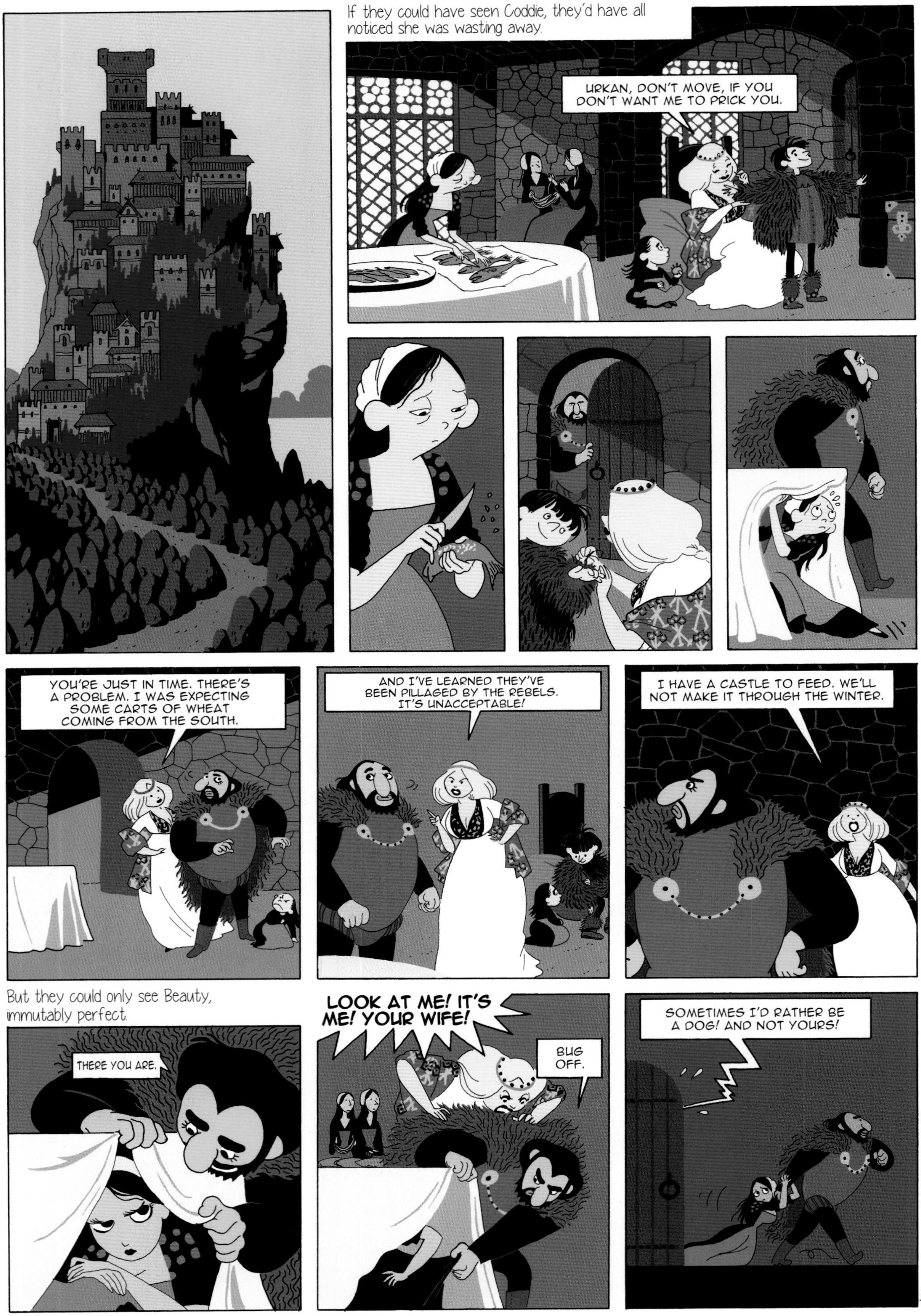

If they could have seen Coddie, they'd have all noticed she was wasting away.
URKAN, DON'T MOVE, IF YOU DON'T WANT ME TO PRICK YOU.
YOU'RE JUST IN TIME. THERE'S A PROBLEM. I WAS EXPECTING SOME CARTS OF WHEAT COMING FROM THE SOUTH.
AND I'VE LEARNED THEY'VE BEEN PILLAGED BY THE REBELS. IT'S UNACCEPTABLE!
I HAVE A CASTLE TO FEED. WE'LL NOT MAKE IT THROUGH THE WINTER.
But they could only see Beauty, immutably perfect.
THERE YOU ARE.
LOOK AT ME! IT'S ME! YOUR WIFE!
BUG OFF.
SOMETIMES I'D RATHER BE A DOG! AND NOT YOURS!

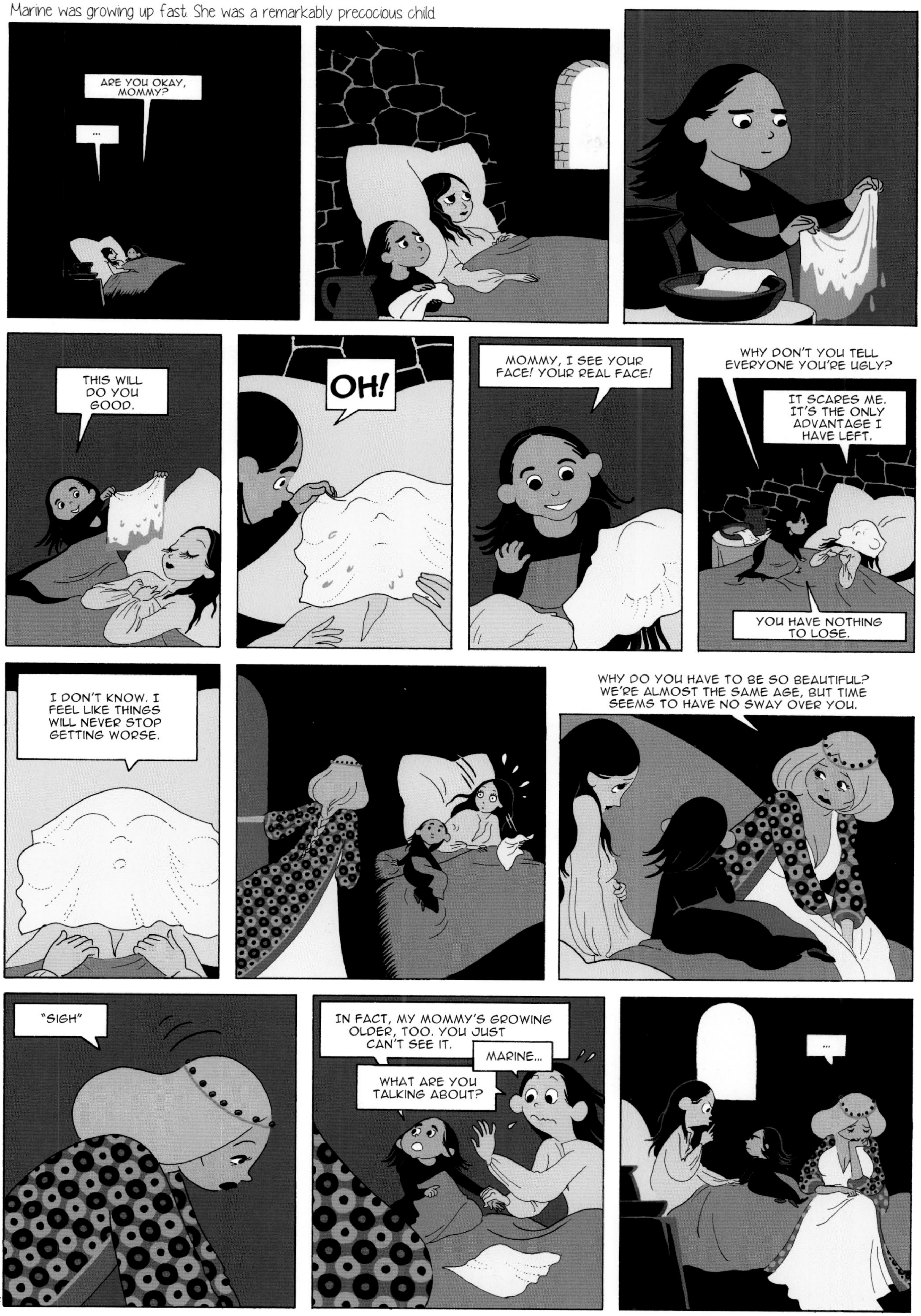

Marine was growing up fast. She was a remarkably precocious child.
ARE YOU OKAY, MOMMY?
...
THIS WILL DO YOU GOOD.
OH!
MOMMY, I SEE YOUR FACE! YOUR REAL FACE!
WHY DON'T YOU TELL EVERYONE YOU'RE UGLY?
IT SCARES ME. IT'S THE ONLY ADVANTAGE I HAVE LEFT.
YOU HAVE NOTHING TO LOSE.
I DON'T KNOW. I FEEL LIKE THINGS WILL NEVER STOP GETTING WORSE.
WHY DO YOU HAVE TO BE SO BEAUTIFUL? WE'RE ALMOST THE SAME AGE, BUT TIME SEEMS TO HAVE NO SWAY OVER YOU.
"SIGH"
IN FACT, MY MOMMY'S GROWING OLDER, TOO. YOU JUST CAN'T SEE IT.
MARINE...
WHAT ARE YOU TALKING ABOUT?
...

3
17

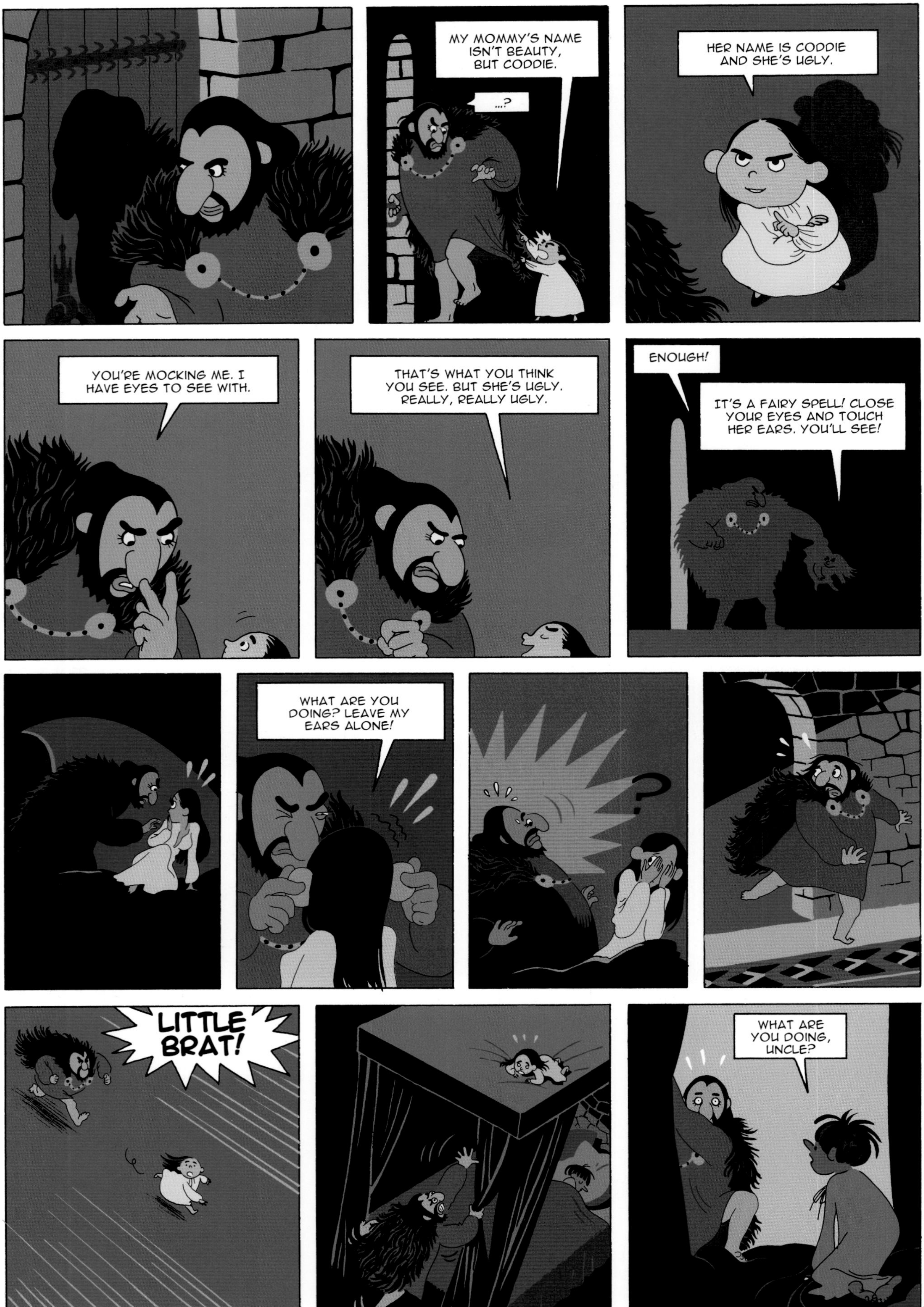
MY MOMMY'S NAME ISN'T BEAUTY, BUT CODDIE.
...?
HER NAME IS CODDIE AND SHE'S UGLY.
YOU'RE MOCKING ME. I HAVE EYES TO SEE WITH.
THAT'S WHAT YOU THINK YOU SEE. BUT SHE'S UGLY. REALLY, REALLY UGLY.
ENOUGH!
IT'S A FAIRY SPELL! CLOSE YOUR EYES AND TOUCH HER EARS. YOU'LL SEE!
WHAT ARE YOU DOING? LEAVE MY EARS ALONE!
?
LITTLE BRAT!
WHAT ARE YOU DOING, UNCLE?
3
18

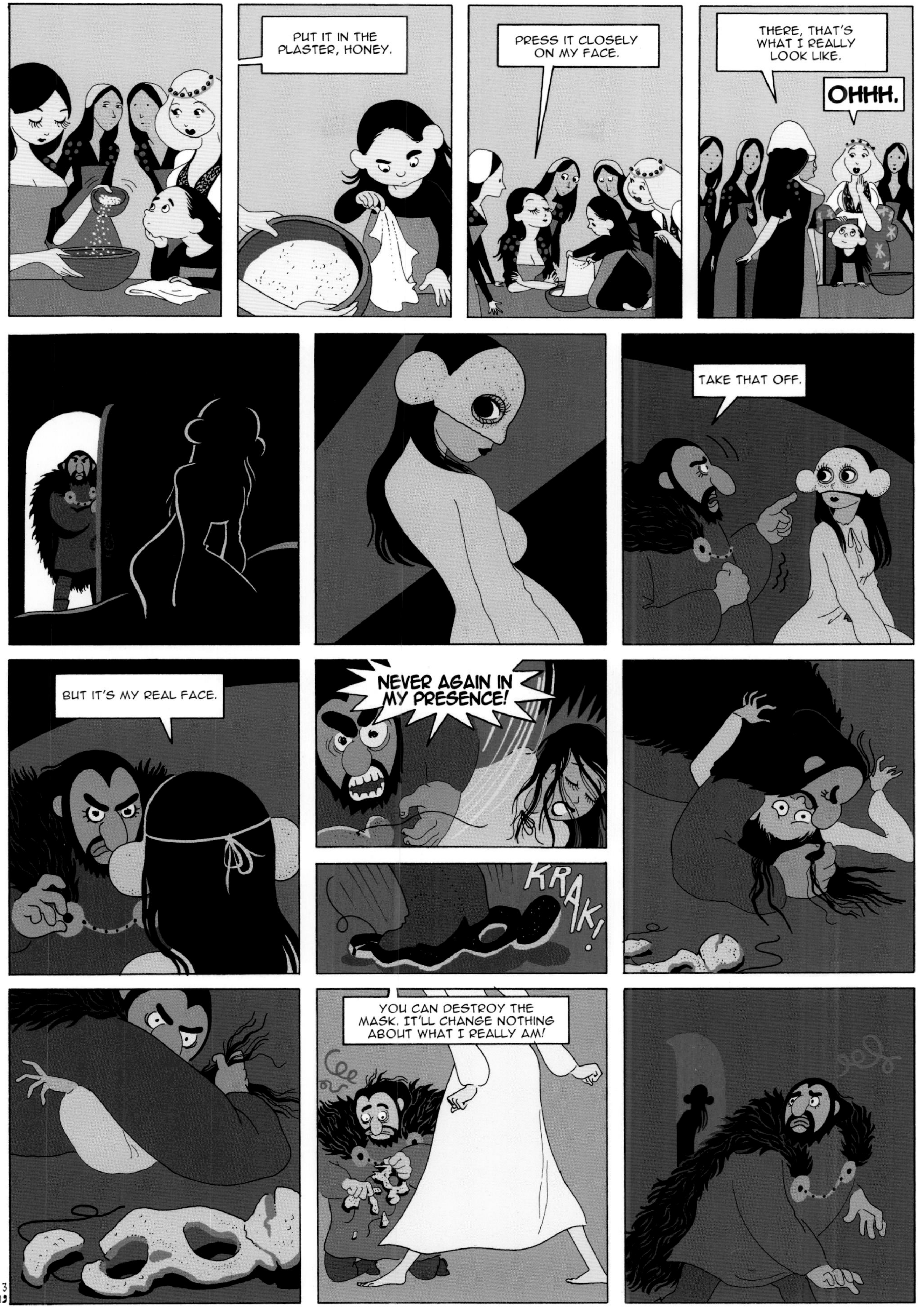
PUT IT IN THE PLASTER, HONEY.
PRESS IT CLOSELY ON MY FACE.
THERE, THAT'S WHAT I REALLY LOOK LIKE.
OHHH.
TAKE THAT OFF.
BUT IT'S MY REAL FACE.
NEVER AGAIN IN MY PRESENCE!
KRAK!
YOU CAN DESTROY THE MASK. IT'LL CHANGE NOTHING ABOUT WHAT I REALLY AM!

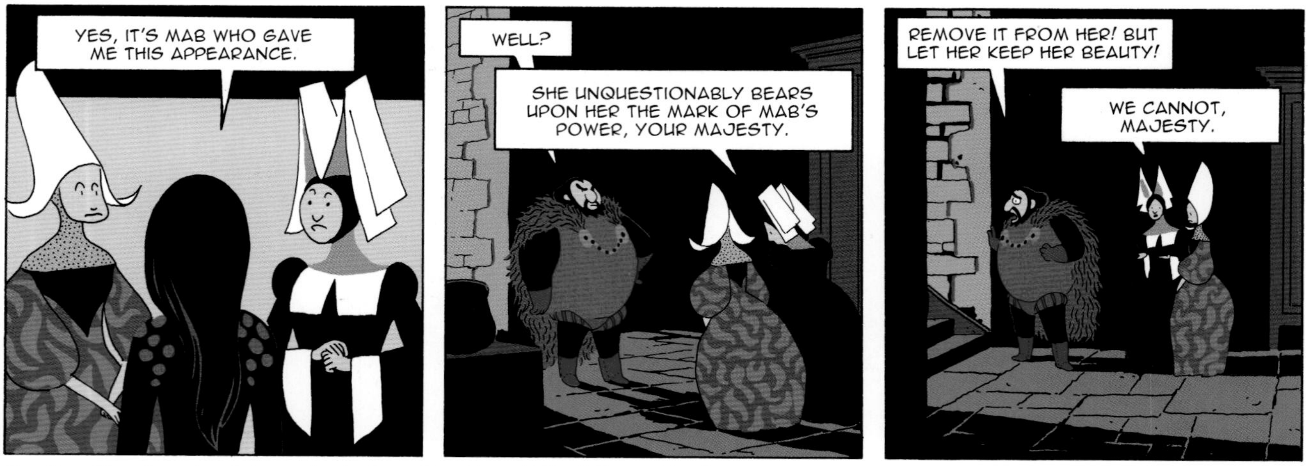
YES, IT'S MAB WHO GAVE ME THIS APPEARANCE.
WELL?
SHE UNQUESTIONABLY BEARS UPON HER THE MARK OF MAB'S POWER, YOUR MAJESTY.
REMOVE IT FROM HER! BUT LET HER KEEP HER BEAUTY!
WE CANNOT, MAJESTY.

The Boar King feared nothing and nobody in this old world. He felt capable of crushing anyone who might resist him.

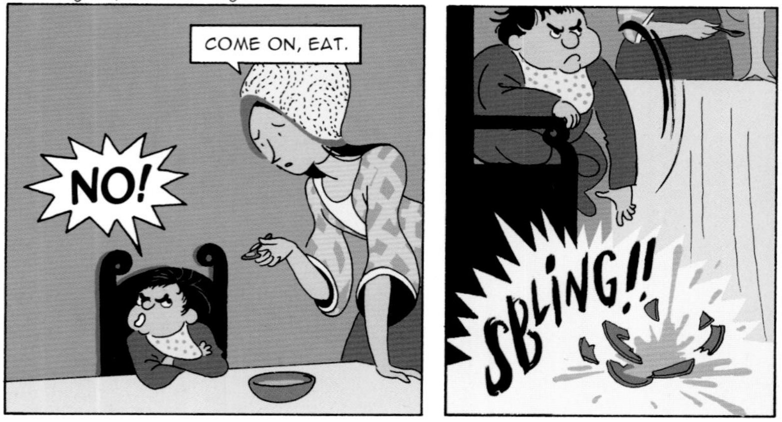
COME ON, EAT.
NO!
SBLING!!

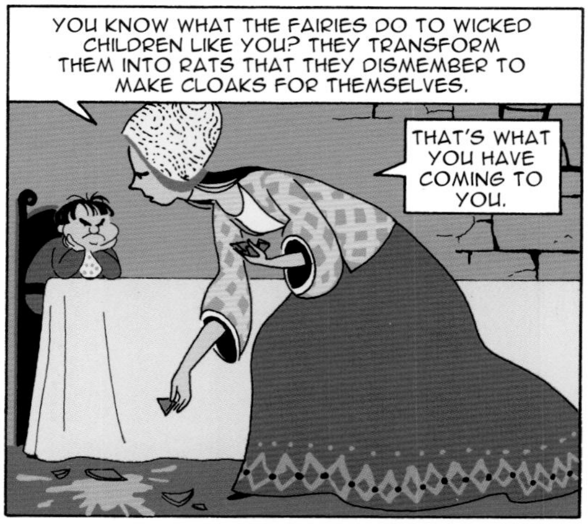
YOU KNOW WHAT THE FAIRIES DO TO WICKED CHILDREN LIKE YOU? THEY TRANSFORM THEM INTO RATS THAT THEY DISMEMBER TO MAKE CLOAKS FOR THEMSELVES.
THAT'S WHAT YOU HAVE COMING TO YOU.

But he was terrified of the Fairies' power. Against them, he felt powerless.

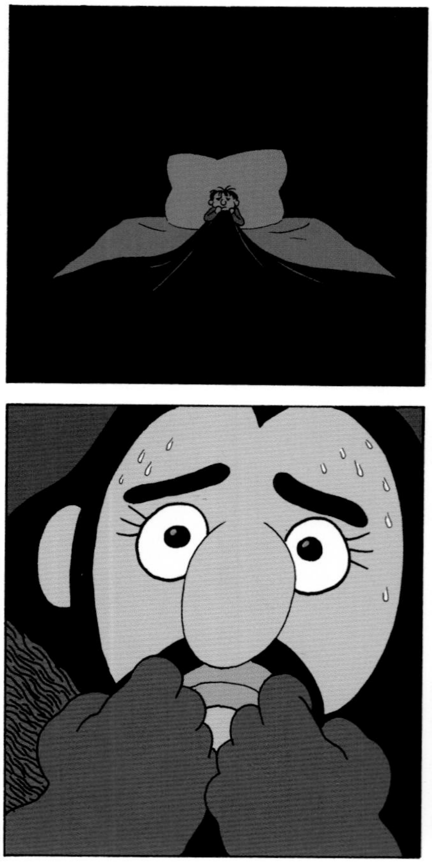

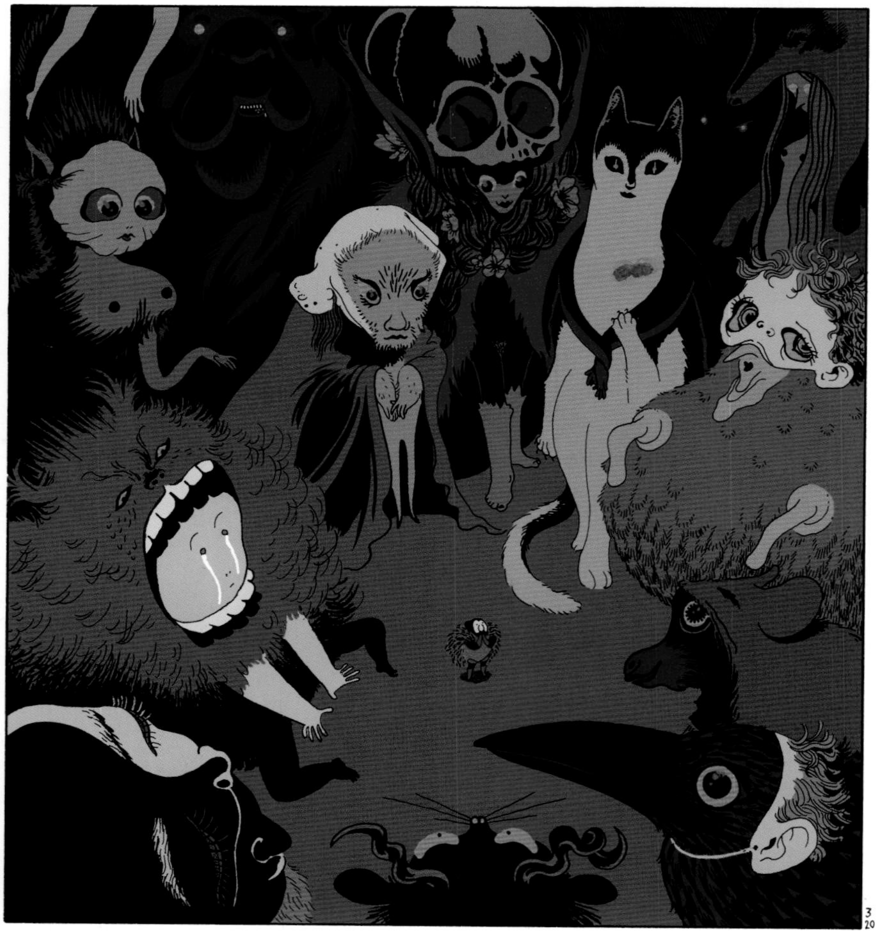

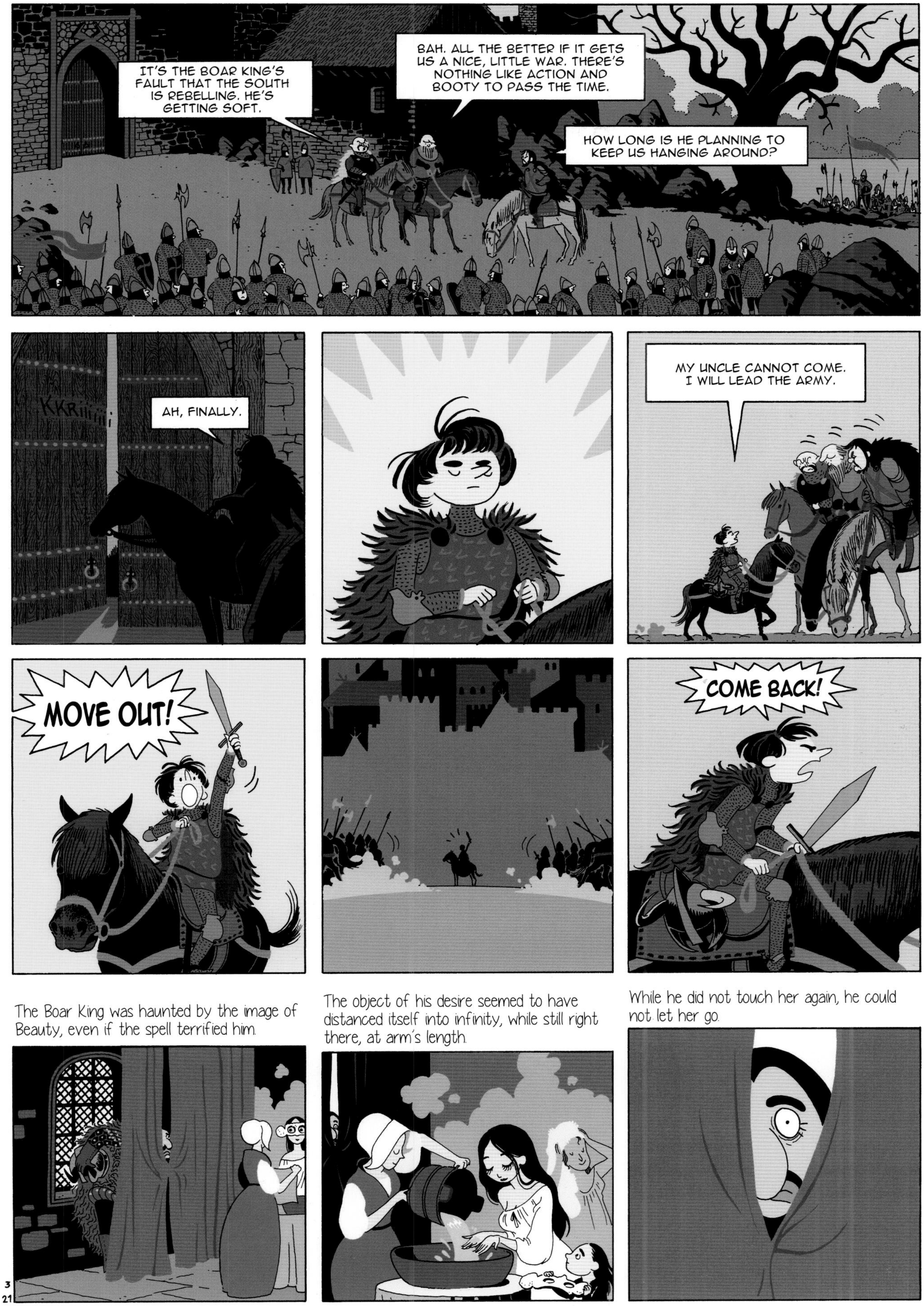
IT'S THE BOAR KING'S FAULT THAT THE SOUTH IS REBELLING. HE'S GETTING SOFT.
BAH. ALL THE BETTER IF IT GETS US A NICE, LITTLE WAR. THERE'S NOTHING LIKE ACTION AND BOOTY TO PASS THE TIME.
HOW LONG IS HE PLANNING TO KEEP US HANGING AROUND?
KKRiiiiiii
AH, FINALLY.
MY UNCLE CANNOT COME. I WILL LEAD THE ARMY.
MOVE OUT!
COME BACK!
The Boar King was haunted by the image of Beauty, even if the spell terrified him.
The object of his desire seemed to have distanced itself into infinity, while still right there, at arm's length.
While he did not touch her again, he could not let her go.

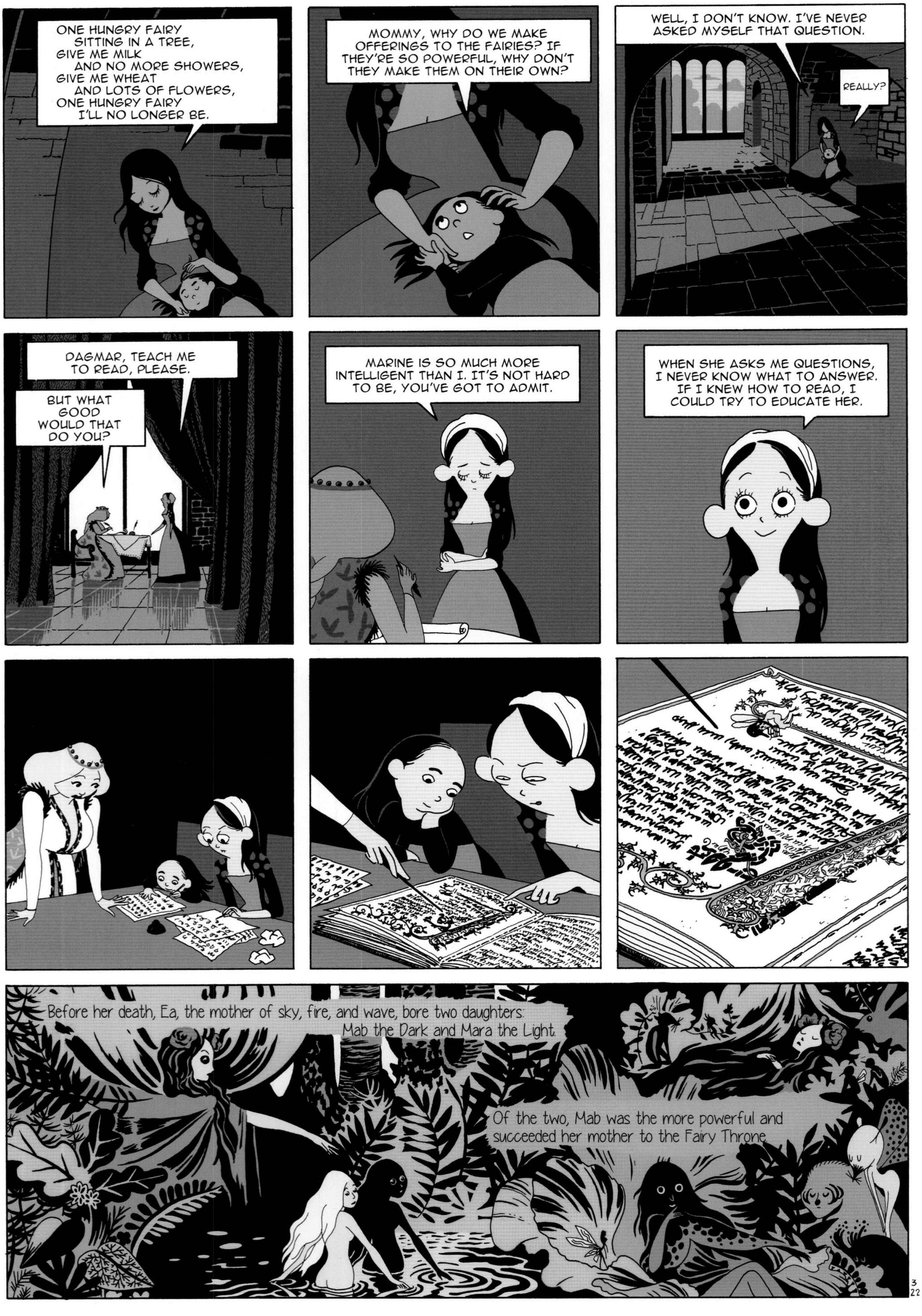
ONE HUNGRY FAIRY SITTING IN A TREE, GIVE ME MILK AND NO MORE SHOWERS, GIVE ME WHEAT AND LOTS OF FLOWERS, ONE HUNGRY FAIRY I'LL NO LONGER BE.
MOMMY, WHY DO WE MAKE OFFERINGS TO THE FAIRIES? IF THEY'RE SO POWERFUL, WHY DON'T THEY MAKE THEM ON THEIR OWN?
WELL, I DON'T KNOW. I'VE NEVER ASKED MYSELF THAT QUESTION.
REALLY?
DAGMAR, TEACH ME TO READ, PLEASE.
BUT WHAT GOOD WOULD THAT DO YOU?
MARINE IS SO MUCH MORE INTELLIGENT THAN I. IT'S NOT HARD TO BE, YOU'VE GOT TO ADMIT.
WHEN SHE ASKS ME QUESTIONS, I NEVER KNOW WHAT TO ANSWER. IF I KNEW HOW TO READ, I COULD TRY TO EDUCATE HER.
Before her death, Ea, the mother of sky, fire, and wave, bore two daughters: Mab the Dark and Mara the Light.
Of the two, Mab was the more powerful and succeeded her mother to the Fairy Throne.
3
22

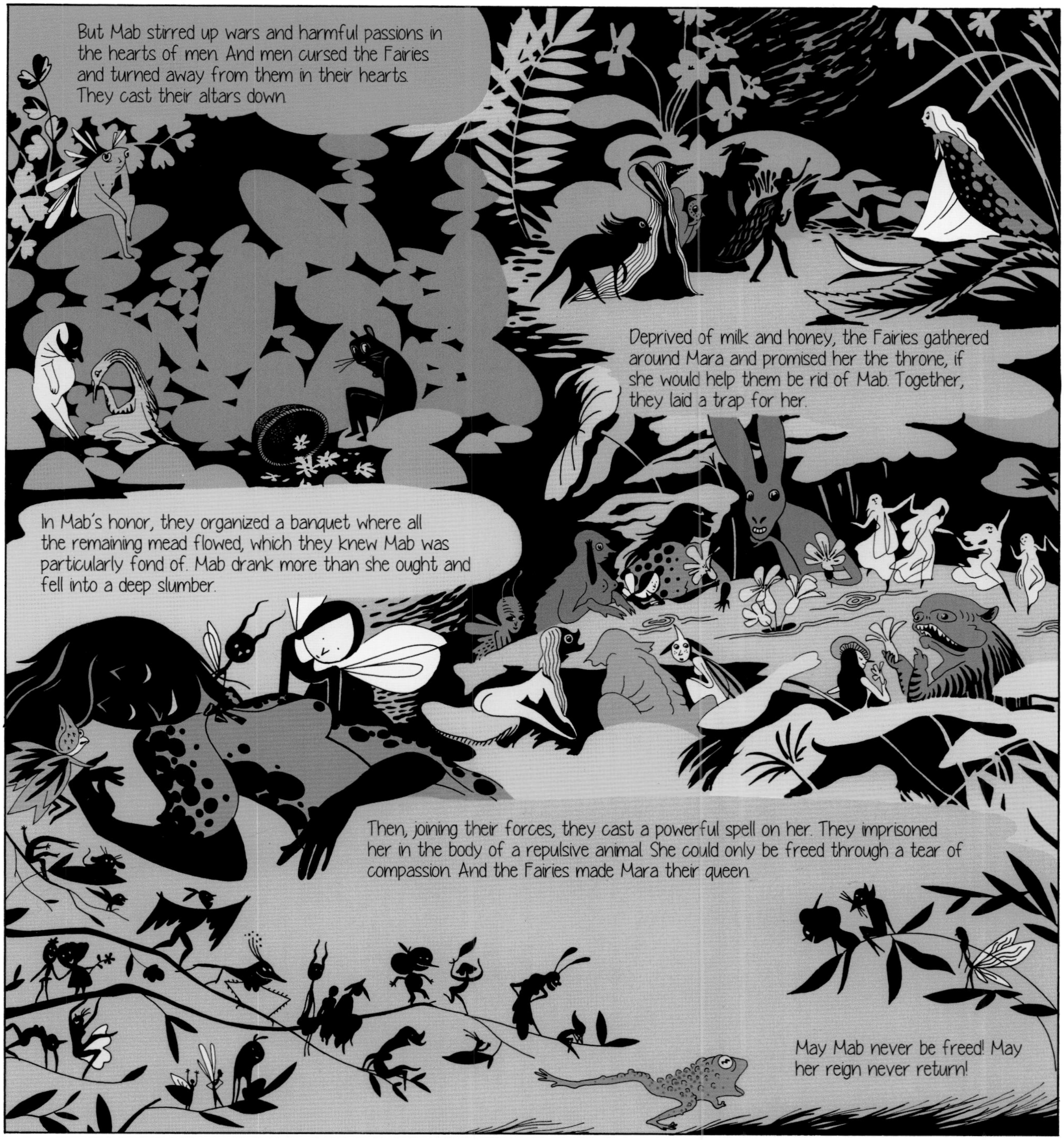
But Mab stirred up wars and harmful passions in the hearts of men. And men cursed the Fairies and turned away from them in their hearts. They cast their altars down.
Deprived of milk and honey, the Fairies gathered around Mara and promised her the throne, if she would help them be rid of Mab. Together, they laid a trap for her.
In Mab's honor, they organized a banquet where all the remaining mead flowed, which they knew Mab was particularly fond of. Mab drank more than she ought and fell into a deep slumber.
Then, joining their forces, they cast a powerful spell on her. They imprisoned her in the body of a repulsive animal. She could only be freed through a tear of compassion. And the Fairies made Mara their queen.
May Mab never be freed! May her reign never return!

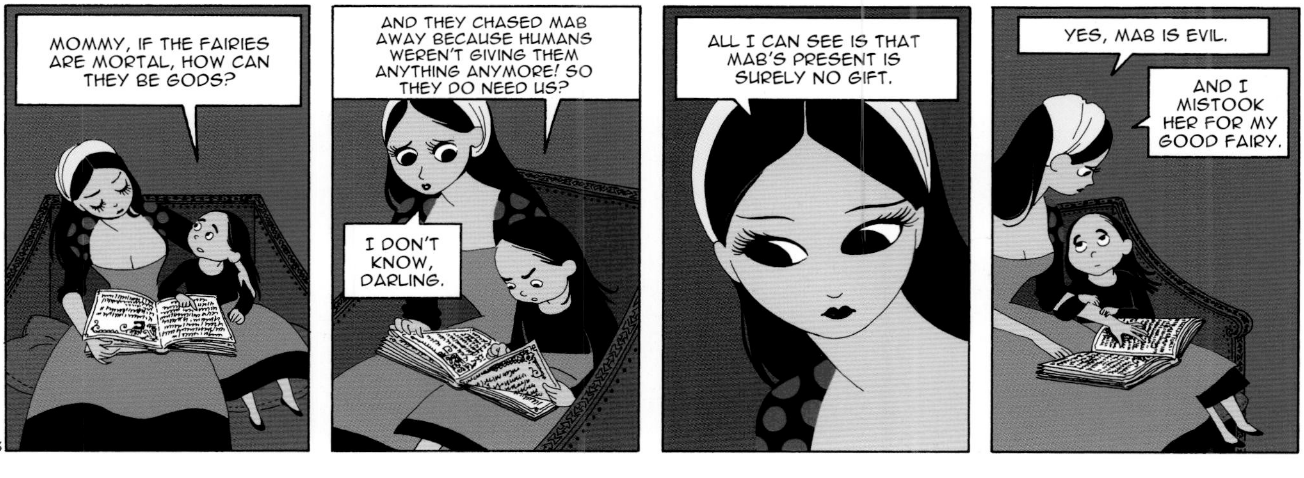
MOMMY, IF THE FAIRIES ARE MORTAL, HOW CAN THEY BE GODS?
AND THEY CHASED MAB AWAY BECAUSE HUMANS WEREN'T GIVING THEM ANYTHING ANYMORE! SO THEY DO NEED US?
I DON'T KNOW, DARLING.
ALL I CAN SEE IS THAT MAB'S PRESENT IS SURELY NO GIFT.
YES, MAB IS EVIL.
AND I MISTOOK HER FOR MY GOOD FAIRY.

3
23

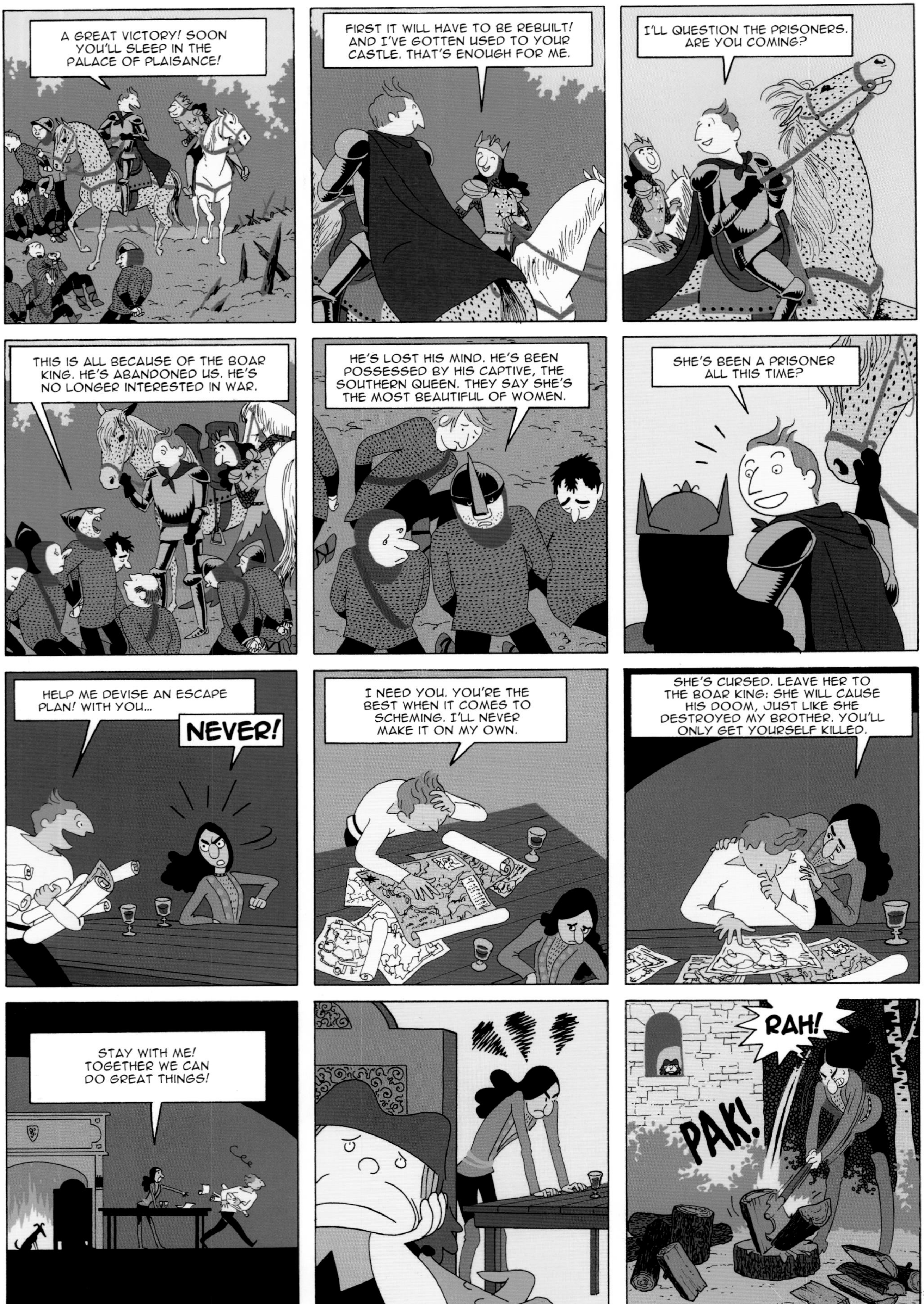
A GREAT VICTORY! SOON YOU'LL SLEEP IN THE PALACE OF PLAISANCE!
FIRST IT WILL HAVE TO BE REBUILT! AND I'VE GOTTEN USED TO YOUR CASTLE. THAT'S ENOUGH FOR ME.
I'LL QUESTION THE PRISONERS. ARE YOU COMING?
THIS IS ALL BECAUSE OF THE BOAR KING. HE'S ABANDONED US. HE'S NO LONGER INTERESTED IN WAR.
HE'S LOST HIS MIND. HE'S BEEN POSSESSED BY HIS CAPTIVE, THE SOUTHERN QUEEN. THEY SAY SHE'S THE MOST BEAUTIFUL OF WOMEN.
SHE'S BEEN A PRISONER ALL THIS TIME?
HELP ME DEVISE AN ESCAPE PLAN! WITH YOU...
NEVER!
I NEED YOU. YOU'RE THE BEST WHEN IT COMES TO SCHEMING. I'LL NEVER MAKE IT ON MY OWN.
SHE'S CURSED. LEAVE HER TO THE BOAR KING: SHE WILL CAUSE HIS DOOM, JUST LIKE SHE DESTROYED MY BROTHER. YOU'LL ONLY GET YOURSELF KILLED.
STAY WITH ME! TOGETHER WE CAN DO GREAT THINGS!
RAH!
PAK!
3
24

SO WHAT'S THE PLAN?

WELL...WE'LL SET THE CASTLE ON FIRE, ATTACK, AND RESCUE THE PRISONER.

BUT IF SHE'S IN THE CASTLE, DOESN'T SHE RISK GETTING BURNED?

... WE'LL ATTACK, FREE THE PRISONER, AND THEN SET THE CASTLE ON FIRE.

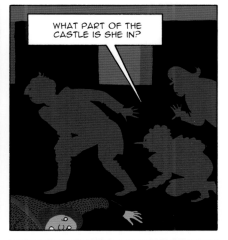

WHAT PART OF THE CASTLE IS SHE IN?

UH, I HAVEN'T THE SLIGHTEST CLUE.

YIKES...

SILENCE! I'M IN COMMAND HERE!

WE'LL ATTACK THAT WAY!

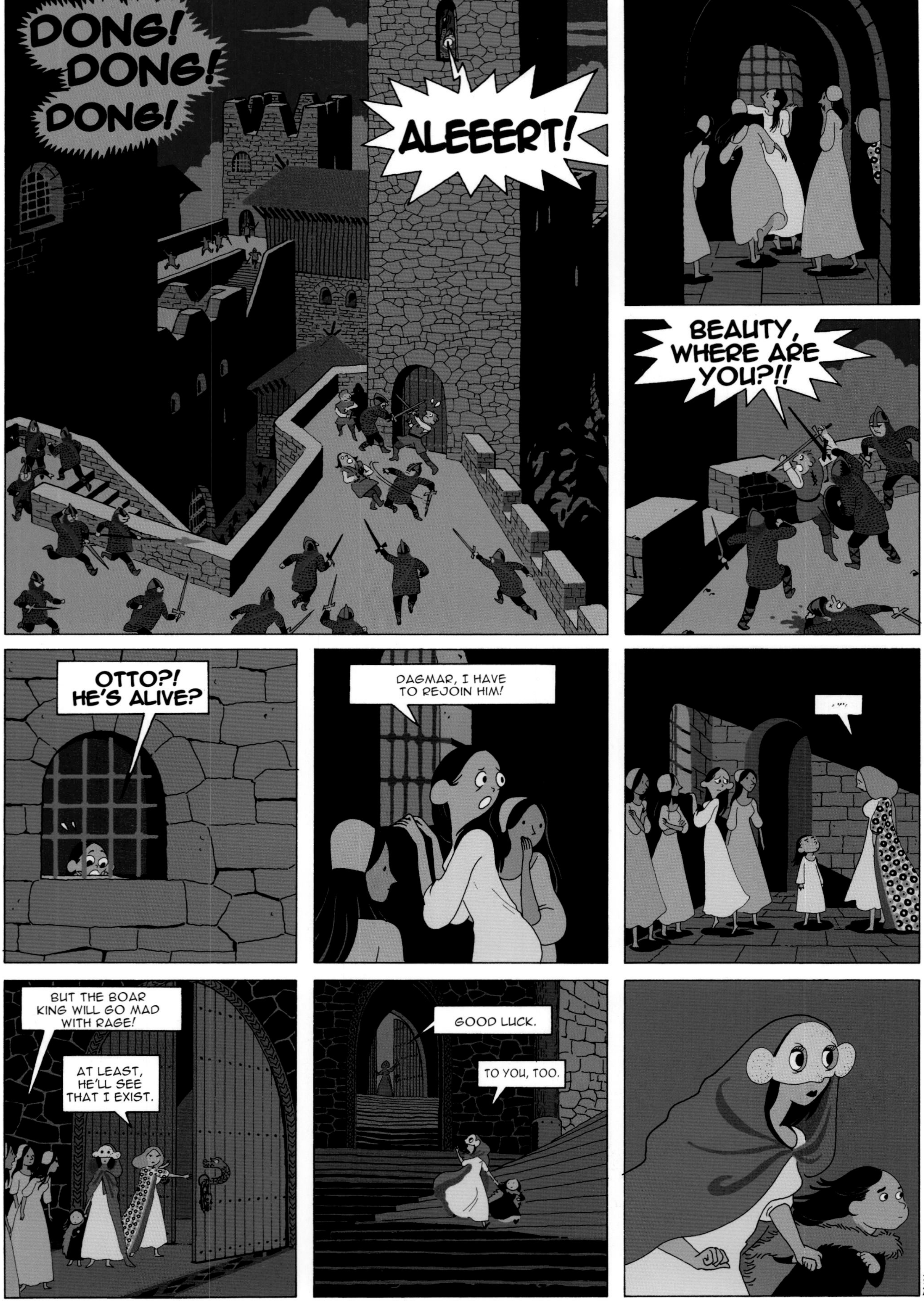
DONG! DONG! DONG!
ALEEERT!
BEAUTY, WHERE ARE YOU?!!
OTTO?! HE'S ALIVE?
DAGMAR, I HAVE TO REJOIN HIM!
BUT THE BOAR KING WILL GO MAD WITH RAGE!
AT LEAST, HE'LL SEE THAT I EXIST.
GOOD LUCK.
TO YOU, TOO.

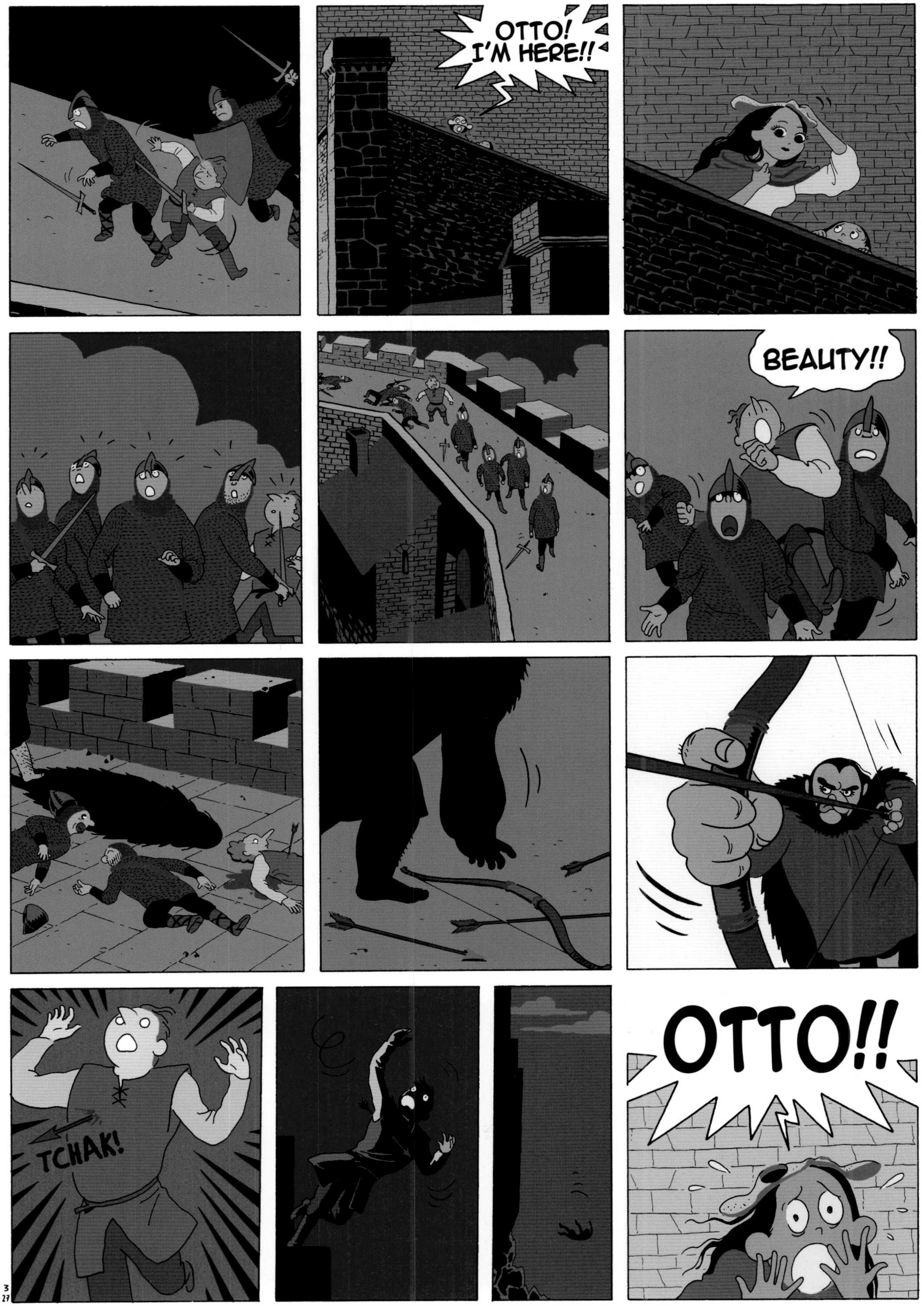
OTTO! I'M HERE!!
BEAUTY!!
TCHAK!
OTTO!!

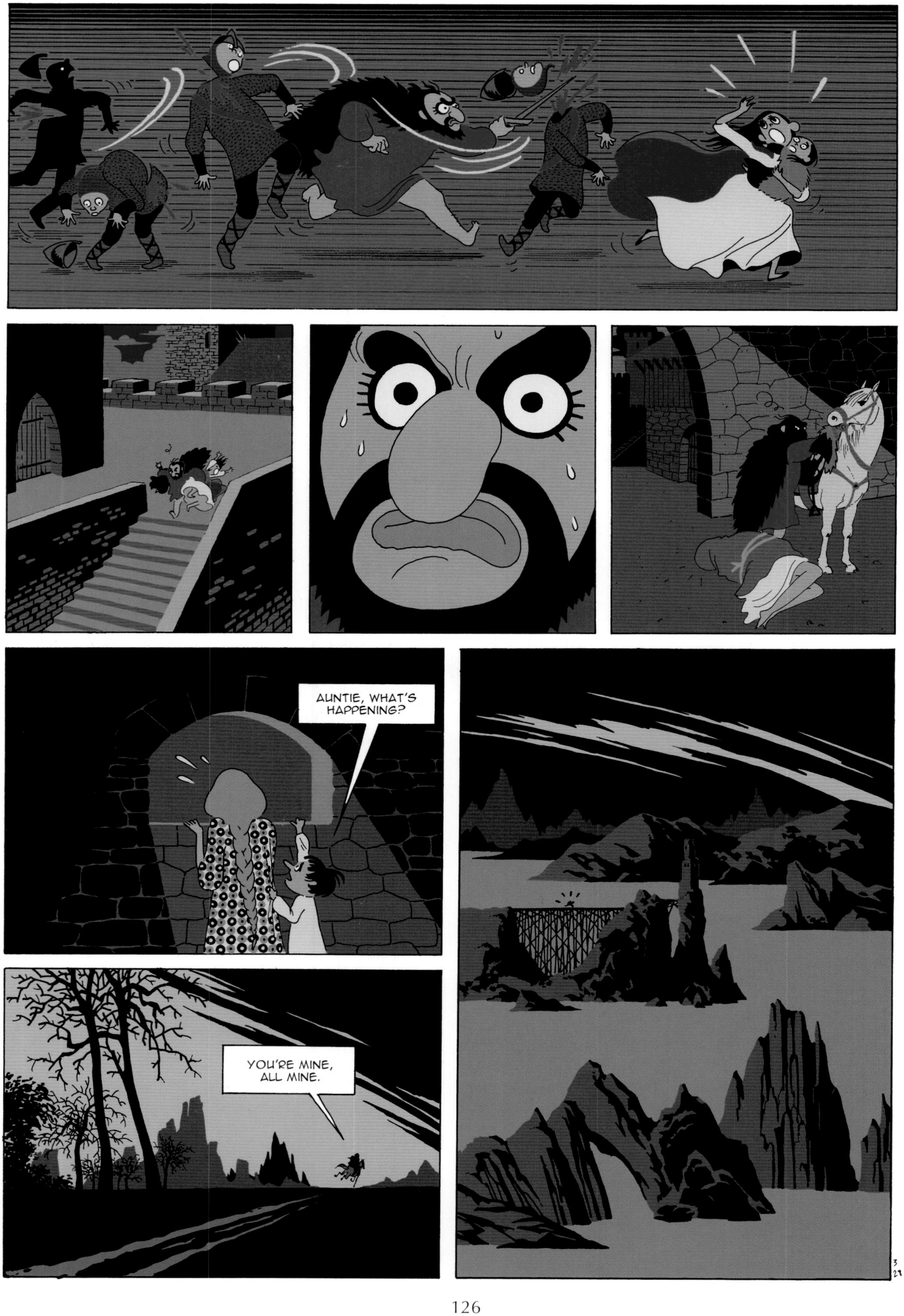
AUNTIE, WHAT'S HAPPENING?
YOU'RE MINE, ALL MINE.

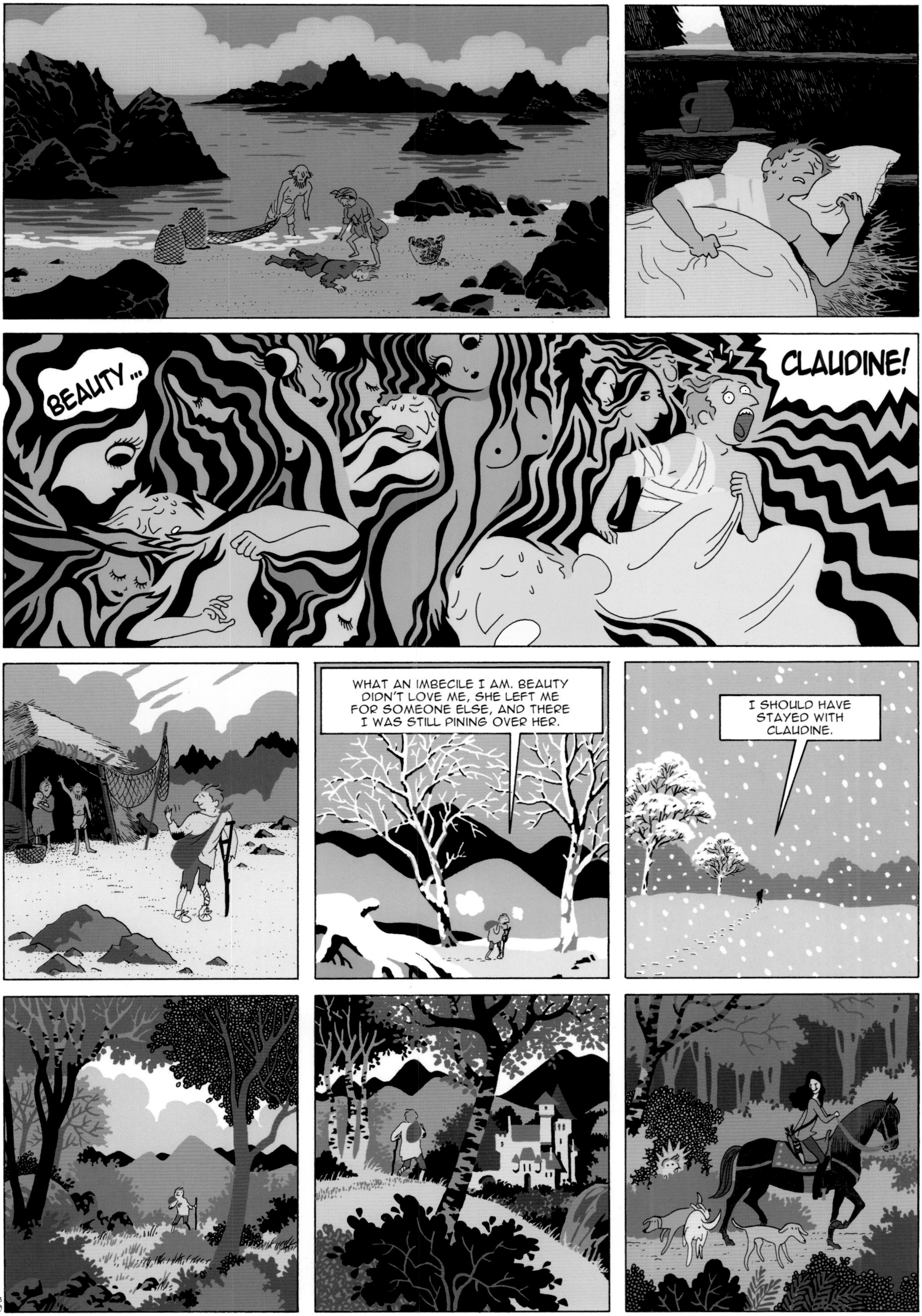
BEAUTY...
CLAUDINE!
WHAT AN IMBECILE I AM. BEAUTY DIDN'T LOVE ME, SHE LEFT ME FOR SOMEONE ELSE, AND THERE I WAS STILL PINING OVER HER.
I SHOULD HAVE STAYED WITH CLAUDINE.

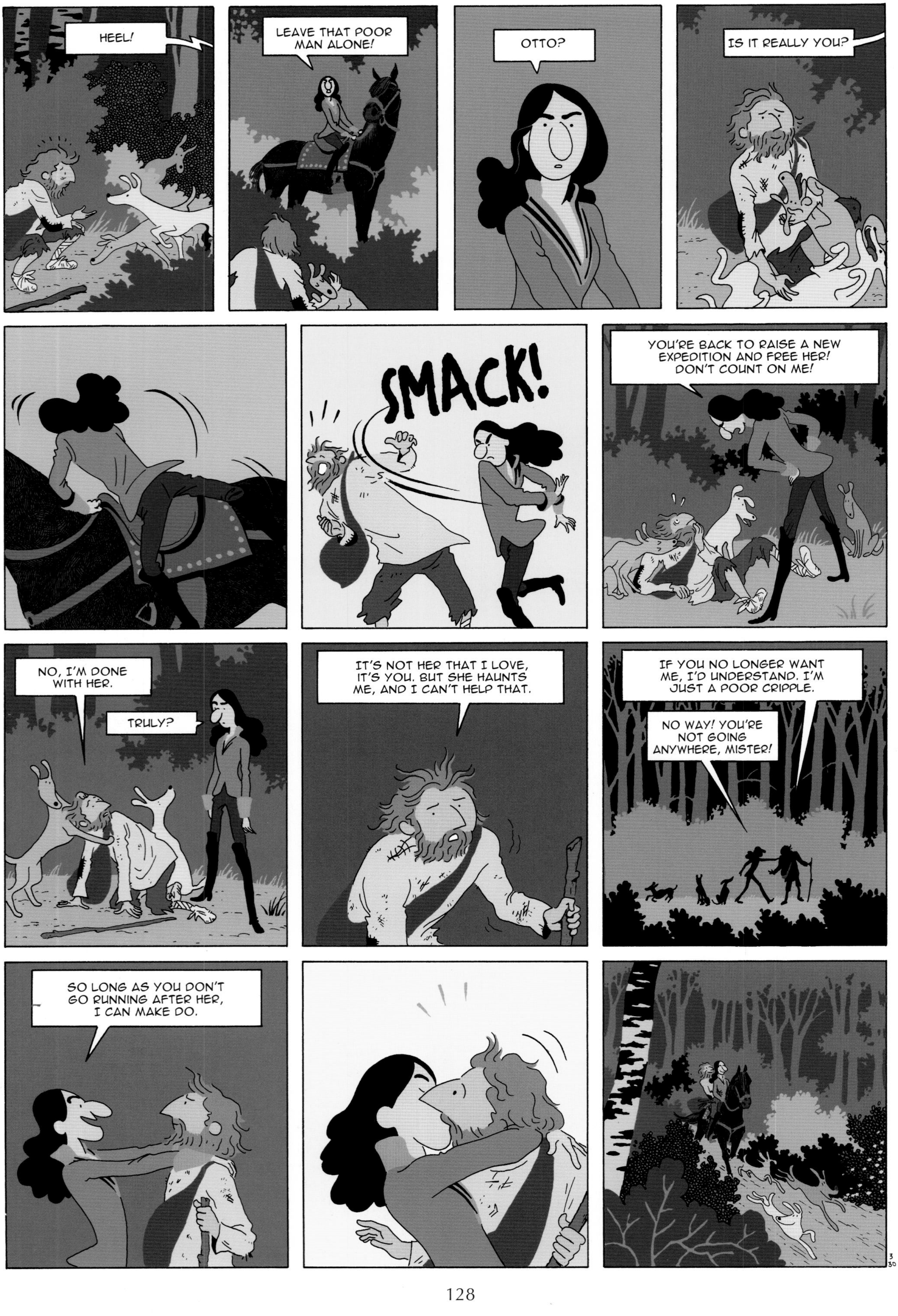
HEEL!
LEAVE THAT POOR MAN ALONE!
OTTO?
IS IT REALLY YOU?
SMACK!
YOU'RE BACK TO RAISE A NEW EXPEDITION AND FREE HER! DON'T COUNT ON ME!
NO, I'M DONE WITH HER.
TRULY?
IT'S NOT HER THAT I LOVE, IT'S YOU. BUT SHE HAUNTS ME, AND I CAN'T HELP THAT.
IF YOU NO LONGER WANT ME, I'D UNDERSTAND. I'M JUST A POOR CRIPPLE.
NO WAY! YOU'RE NOT GOING ANYWHERE, MISTER!
SO LONG AS YOU DON'T GO RUNNING AFTER HER, I CAN MAKE DO.
3 30

For a really long time now, no man except for the Boar King had seen Beauty. She'd become one of those legends recounted at evening gatherings, which sufficed to stoke the lust and desire for adventure of passing paladins.

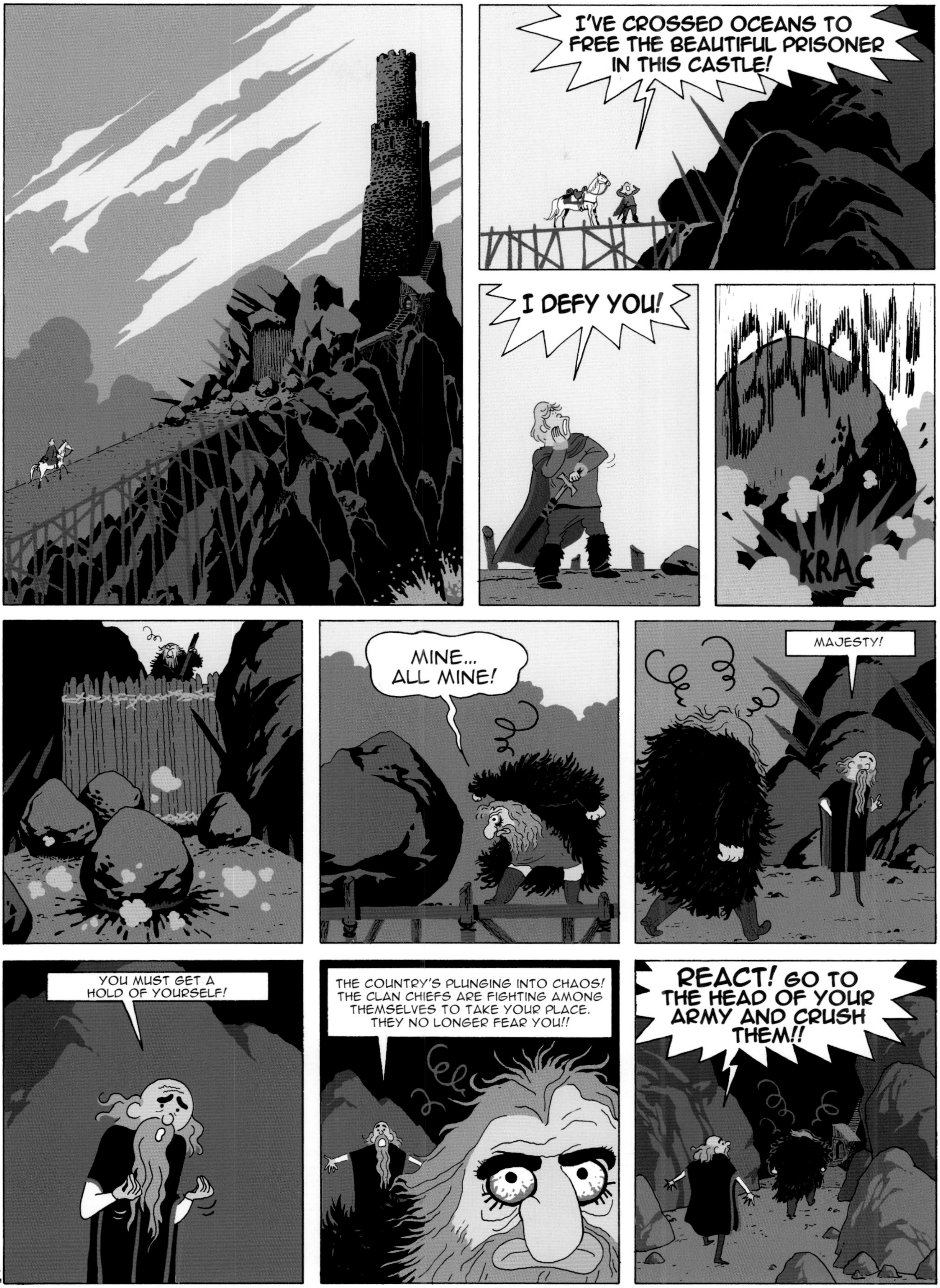
I'VE CROSSED OCEANS TO FREE THE BEAUTIFUL PRISONER IN THIS CASTLE!
I DEFY YOU!
BAOM!
KRAC
MINE... ALL MINE!
MAJESTY!
YOU MUST GET A HOLD OF YOURSELF!
THE COUNTRY'S PLUNGING INTO CHAOS! THE CLAN CHIEFS ARE FIGHTING AMONG THEMSELVES TO TAKE YOUR PLACE. THEY NO LONGER FEAR YOU!!
REACT! GO TO THE HEAD OF YOUR ARMY AND CRUSH THEM!!

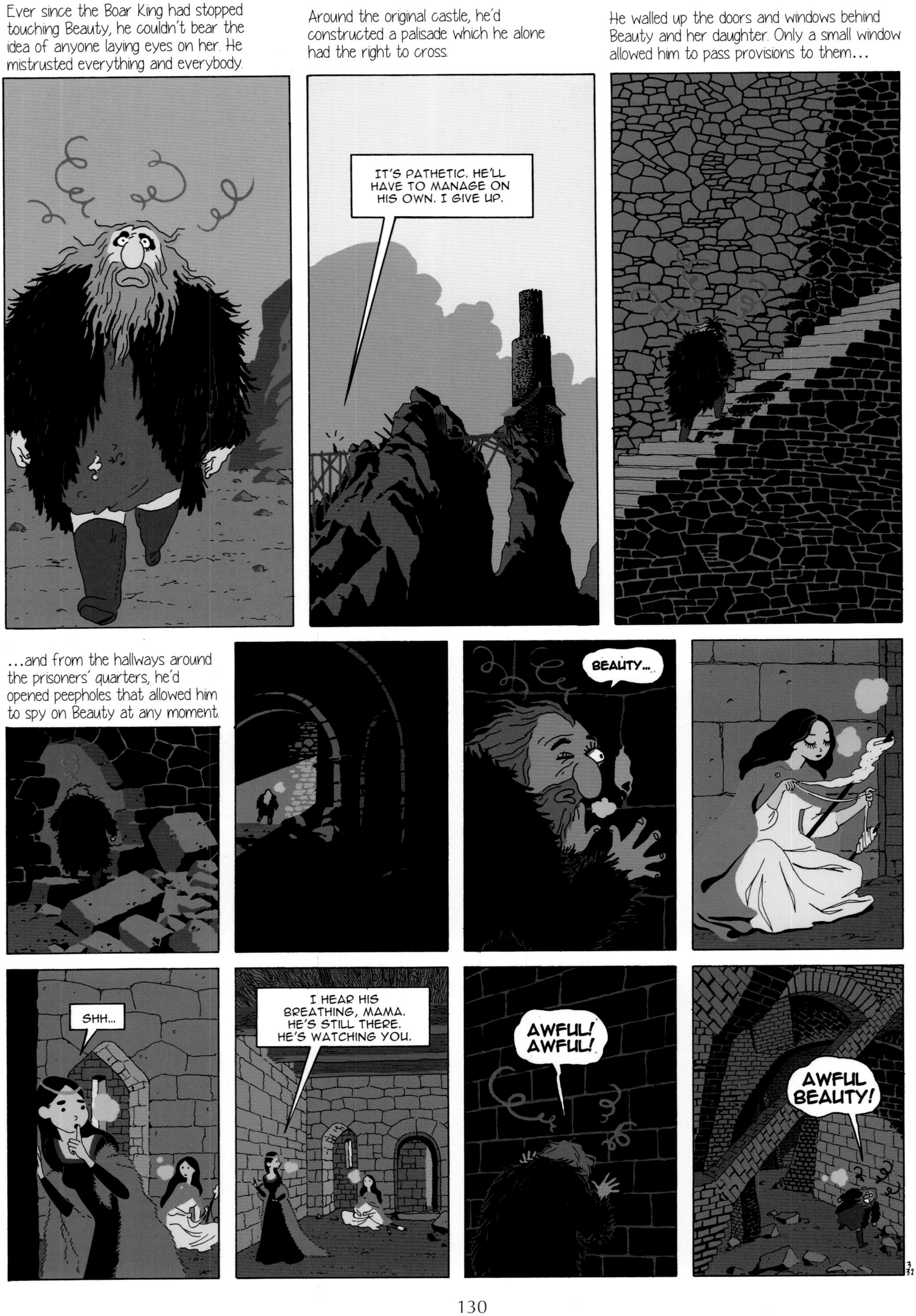
Ever since the Boar King had stopped touching Beauty, he couldn't bear the idea of anyone laying eyes on her. He mistrusted everything and everybody.
Around the original castle, he'd constructed a palisade which he alone had the right to cross.
IT'S PATHETIC. HE'LL HAVE TO MANAGE ON HIS OWN. I GIVE UP.
He walled up the doors and windows behind Beauty and her daughter. Only a small window allowed him to pass provisions to them...
...and from the hallways around the prisoners' quarters, he'd opened peepholes that allowed him to spy on Beauty at any moment.
BEAUTY...
SHH...
I HEAR HIS BREATHING, MAMA. HE'S STILL THERE. HE'S WATCHING YOU.
AWFUL! AWFUL!
AWFUL BEAUTY!

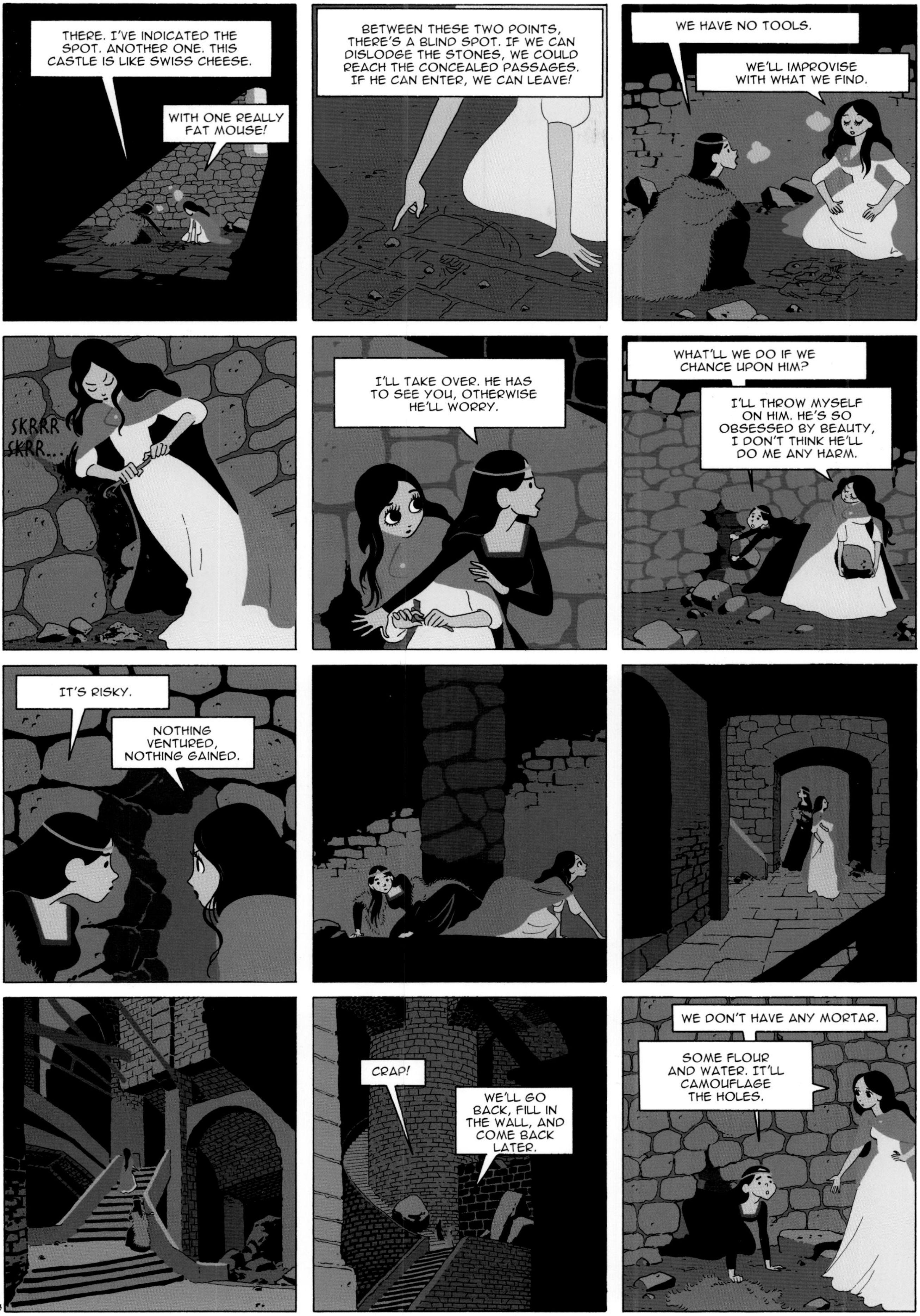
THERE. I'VE INDICATED THE SPOT. ANOTHER ONE. THIS CASTLE IS LIKE SWISS CHEESE.
WITH ONE REALLY FAT MOUSE!
BETWEEN THESE TWO POINTS, THERE'S A BLIND SPOT. IF WE CAN DISLODGE THE STONES, WE COULD REACH THE CONCEALED PASSAGES. IF HE CAN ENTER, WE CAN LEAVE!
WE HAVE NO TOOLS.
WE'LL IMPROVISE WITH WHAT WE FIND.
SKRRR SKRR...
I'LL TAKE OVER. HE HAS TO SEE YOU, OTHERWISE HE'LL WORRY.
WHAT'LL WE DO IF WE CHANCE UPON HIM?
I'LL THROW MYSELF ON HIM. HE'S SO OBSESSED BY BEAUTY, I DON'T THINK HE'LL DO ME ANY HARM.
IT'S RISKY.
NOTHING VENTURED, NOTHING GAINED.
CRAP!
WE'LL GO BACK, FILL IN THE WALL, AND COME BACK LATER.
WE DON'T HAVE ANY MORTAR.
SOME FLOUR AND WATER. IT'LL CAMOUFLAGE THE HOLES.
3 33

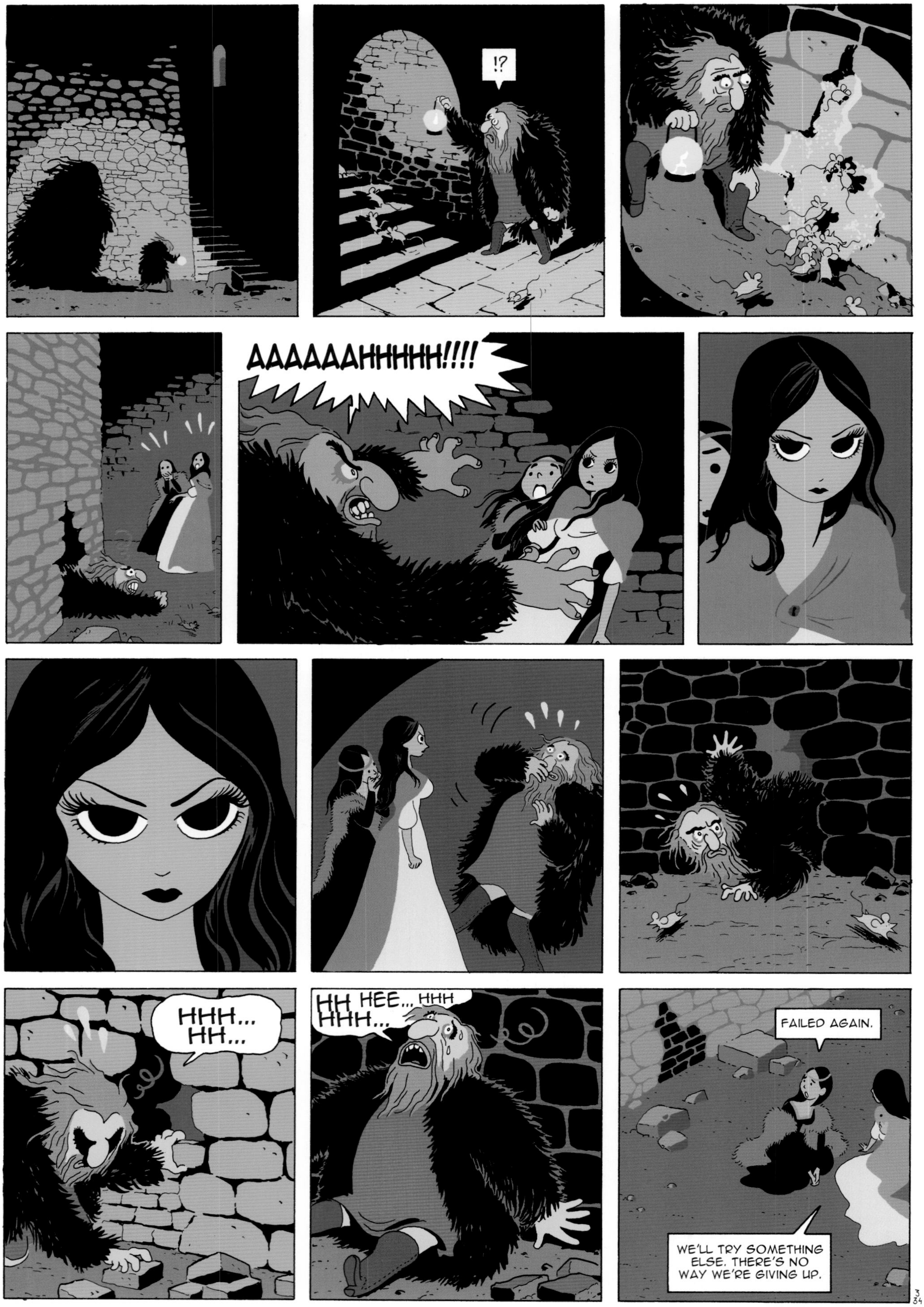
!?
AAAAAAHHHHH!!!!
HHH...
HH...
HH HEE... HHH
HHH...
FAILED AGAIN.
WE'LL TRY SOMETHING ELSE. THERE'S NO WAY WE'RE GIVING UP.

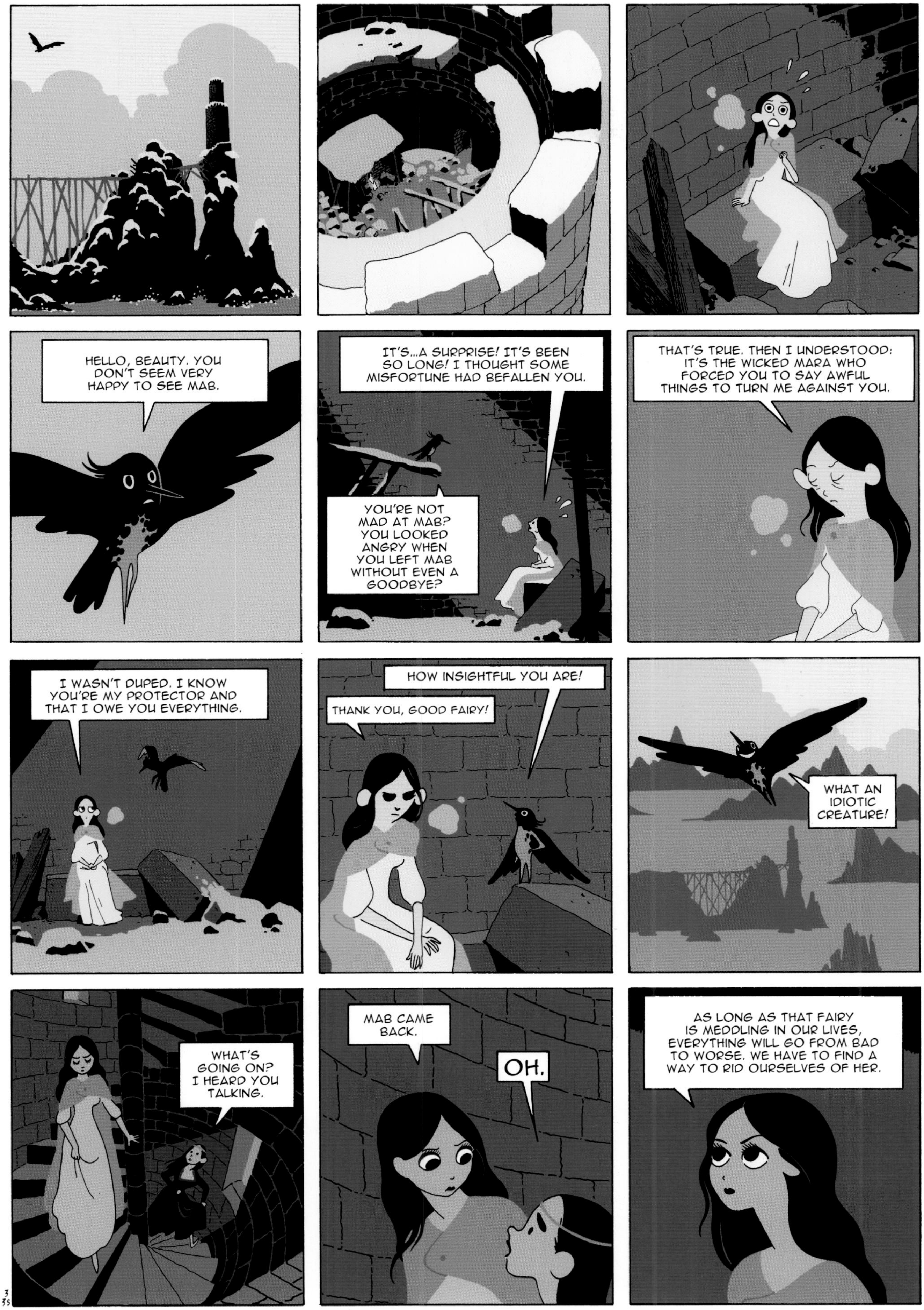
HELLO, BEAUTY. YOU DON'T SEEM VERY HAPPY TO SEE MAB.
IT'S...A SURPRISE! IT'S BEEN SO LONG! I THOUGHT SOME MISFORTUNE HAD BEFALLEN YOU.
YOU'RE NOT MAD AT MAB? YOU LOOKED ANGRY WHEN YOU LEFT MAB WITHOUT EVEN A GOODBYE?
THAT'S TRUE. THEN I UNDERSTOOD: IT'S THE WICKED MARA WHO FORCED YOU TO SAY AWFUL THINGS TO TURN ME AGAINST YOU.
I WASN'T DUPED. I KNOW YOU'RE MY PROTECTOR AND THAT I OWE YOU EVERYTHING.
HOW INSIGHTFUL YOU ARE!
THANK YOU, GOOD FAIRY!
WHAT AN IDIOTIC CREATURE!
WHAT'S GOING ON? I HEARD YOU TALKING.
MAB CAME BACK.
OH.
AS LONG AS THAT FAIRY IS MEDDLING IN OUR LIVES, EVERYTHING WILL GO FROM BAD TO WORSE. WE HAVE TO FIND A WAY TO RID OURSELVES OF HER.

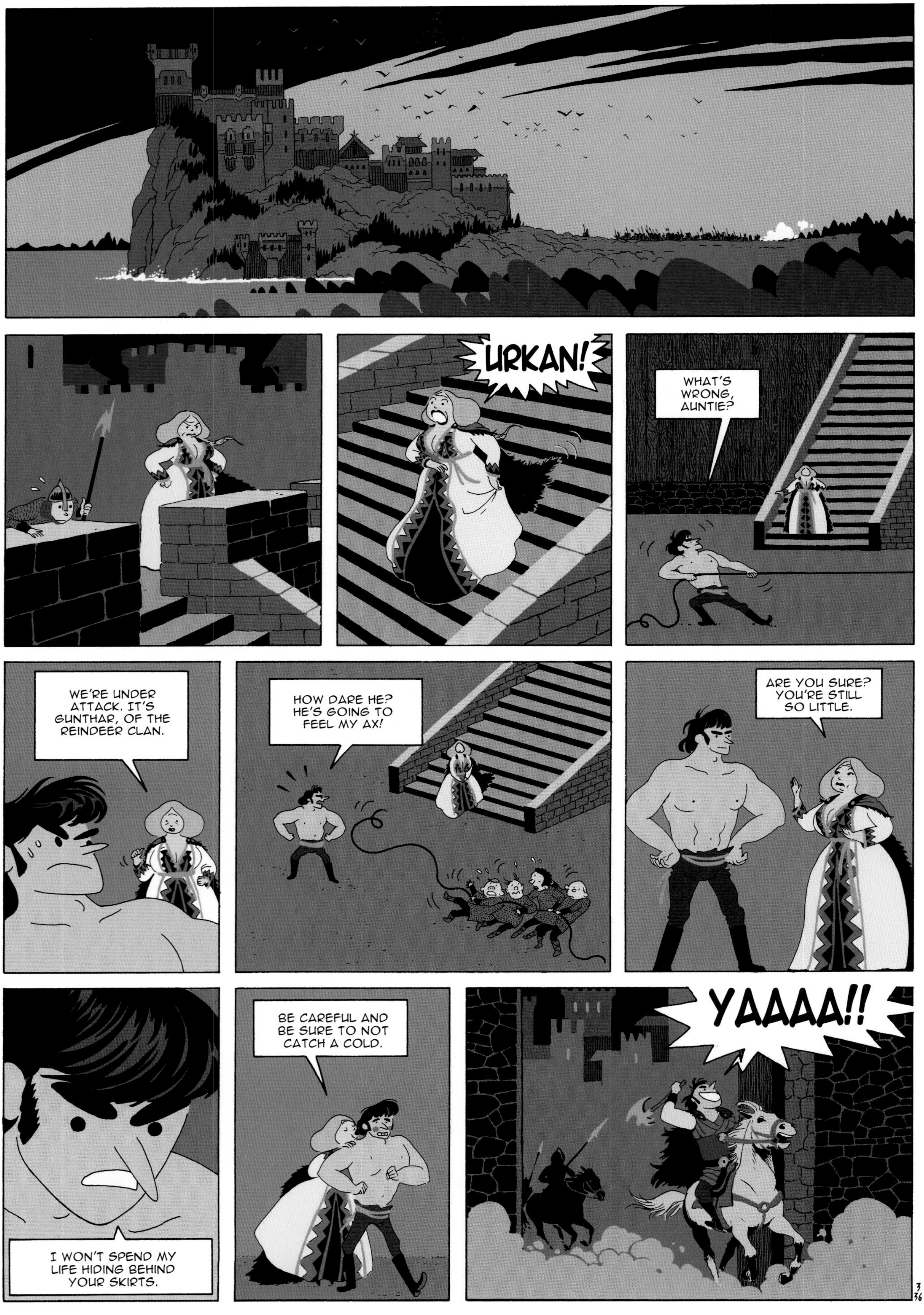
URKAN!
WHAT'S WRONG, AUNTIE?
WE'RE UNDER ATTACK. IT'S GUNTHAR, OF THE REINDEER CLAN.
HOW DARE HE? HE'S GOING TO FEEL MY AX!
ARE YOU SURE? YOU'RE STILL SO LITTLE.
I WON'T SPEND MY LIFE HIDING BEHIND YOUR SKIRTS.
BE CAREFUL AND BE SURE TO NOT CATCH A COLD.
YAAAA!!

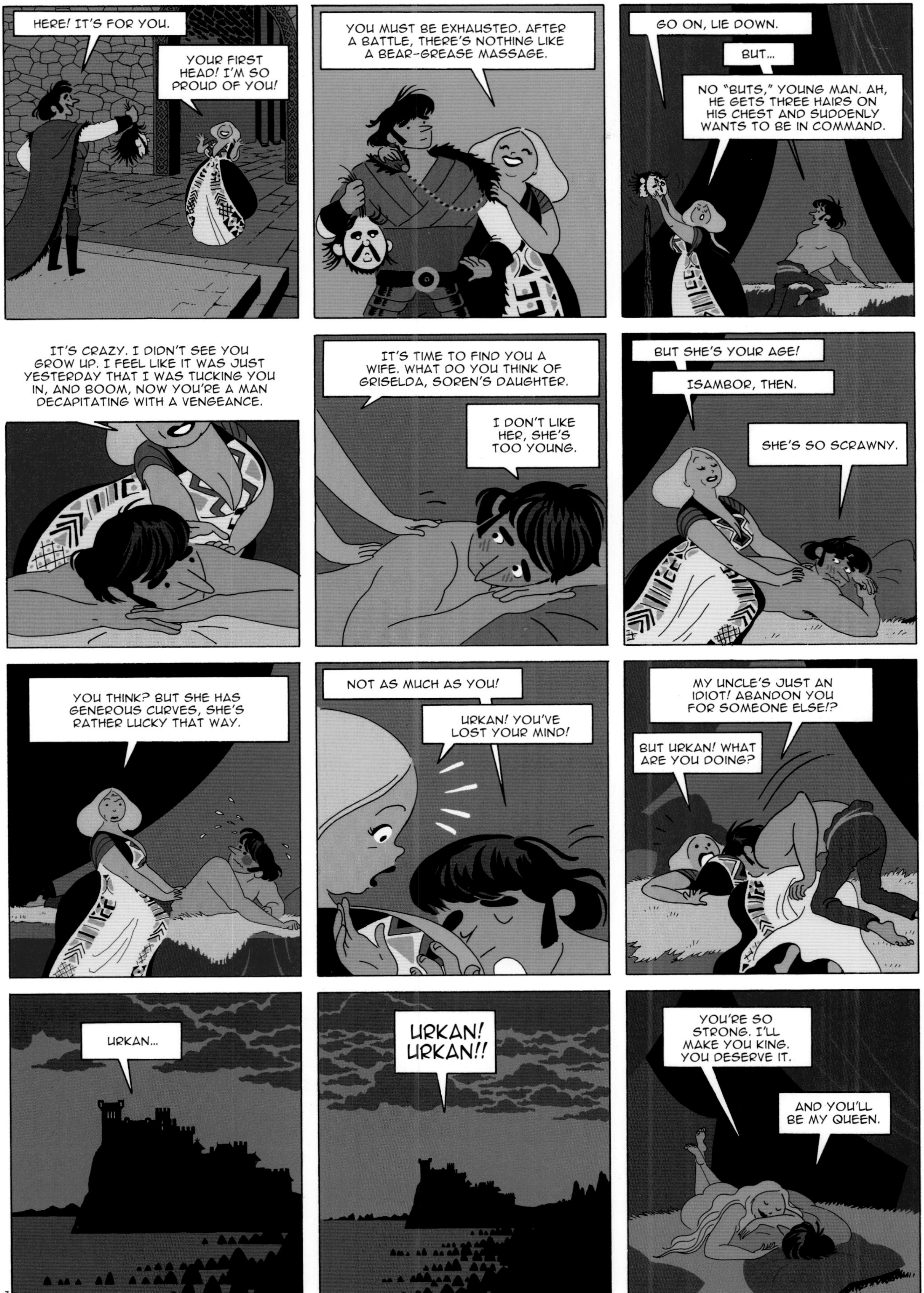
HERE! IT'S FOR YOU.
YOUR FIRST HEAD! I'M SO PROUD OF YOU!
YOU MUST BE EXHAUSTED. AFTER A BATTLE, THERE'S NOTHING LIKE A BEAR-GREASE MASSAGE.
GO ON, LIE DOWN.
BUT...
NO "BUTS," YOUNG MAN. AH, HE GETS THREE HAIRS ON HIS CHEST AND SUDDENLY WANTS TO BE IN COMMAND.
IT'S CRAZY. I DIDN'T SEE YOU GROW UP. I FEEL LIKE IT WAS JUST YESTERDAY THAT I WAS TUCKING YOU IN, AND BOOM, NOW YOU'RE A MAN DECAPITATING WITH A VENGEANCE.
IT'S TIME TO FIND YOU A WIFE. WHAT DO YOU THINK OF GRISELDA, SOREN'S DAUGHTER.
I DON'T LIKE HER, SHE'S TOO YOUNG.
BUT SHE'S YOUR AGE!
ISAMBOR, THEN.
SHE'S SO SCRAWNY.
YOU THINK? BUT SHE HAS GENEROUS CURVES, SHE'S RATHER LUCKY THAT WAY.
NOT AS MUCH AS YOU!
URKAN! YOU'VE LOST YOUR MIND!
MY UNCLE'S JUST AN IDIOT! ABANDON YOU FOR SOMEONE ELSE!?
BUT URKAN! WHAT ARE YOU DOING?
URKAN...
URKAN! URKAN!!
YOU'RE SO STRONG. I'LL MAKE YOU KING. YOU DESERVE IT.
AND YOU'LL BE MY QUEEN.

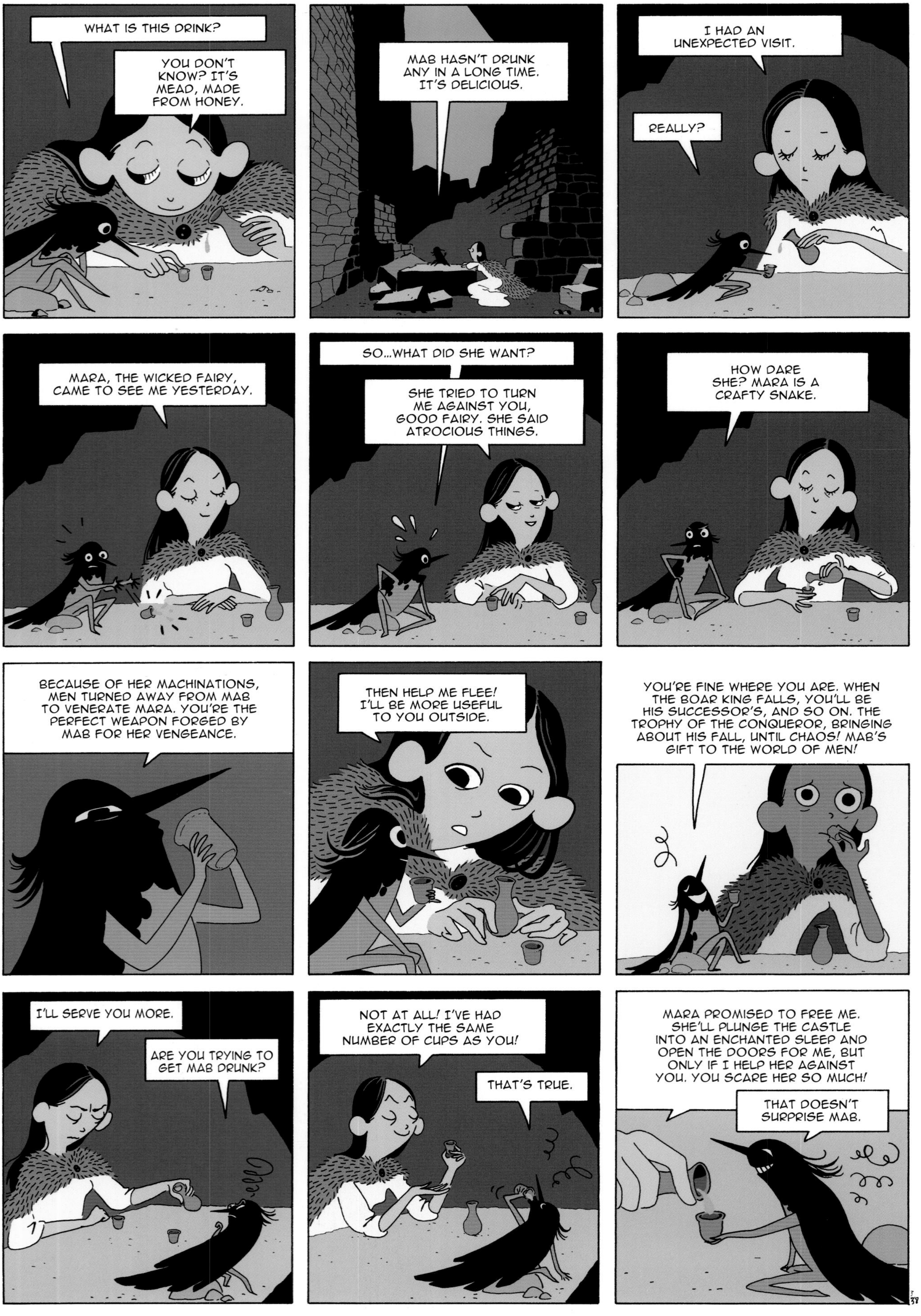
WHAT IS THIS DRINK?
YOU DON'T KNOW? IT'S MEAD, MADE FROM HONEY.
MAB HASN'T DRUNK ANY IN A LONG TIME. IT'S DELICIOUS.
I HAD AN UNEXPECTED VISIT.
REALLY?
MARA, THE WICKED FAIRY, CAME TO SEE ME YESTERDAY.
SO...WHAT DID SHE WANT?
SHE TRIED TO TURN ME AGAINST YOU, GOOD FAIRY. SHE SAID ATROCIOUS THINGS.
HOW DARE SHE? MARA IS A CRAFTY SNAKE.
BECAUSE OF HER MACHINATIONS, MEN TURNED AWAY FROM MAB TO VENERATE MARA. YOU'RE THE PERFECT WEAPON FORGED BY MAB FOR HER VENGEANCE.
THEN HELP ME FLEE! I'LL BE MORE USEFUL TO YOU OUTSIDE.
YOU'RE FINE WHERE YOU ARE. WHEN THE BOAR KING FALLS, YOU'LL BE HIS SUCCESSOR'S, AND SO ON. THE TROPHY OF THE CONQUEROR, BRINGING ABOUT HIS FALL, UNTIL CHAOS! MAB'S GIFT TO THE WORLD OF MEN!
I'LL SERVE YOU MORE.
ARE YOU TRYING TO GET MAB DRUNK?
NOT AT ALL! I'VE HAD EXACTLY THE SAME NUMBER OF CUPS AS YOU!
THAT'S TRUE.
MARA PROMISED TO FREE ME. SHE'LL PLUNGE THE CASTLE INTO AN ENCHANTED SLEEP AND OPEN THE DOORS FOR ME, BUT ONLY IF I HELP HER AGAINST YOU. YOU SCARE HER SO MUCH!
THAT DOESN'T SURPRISE MAB.

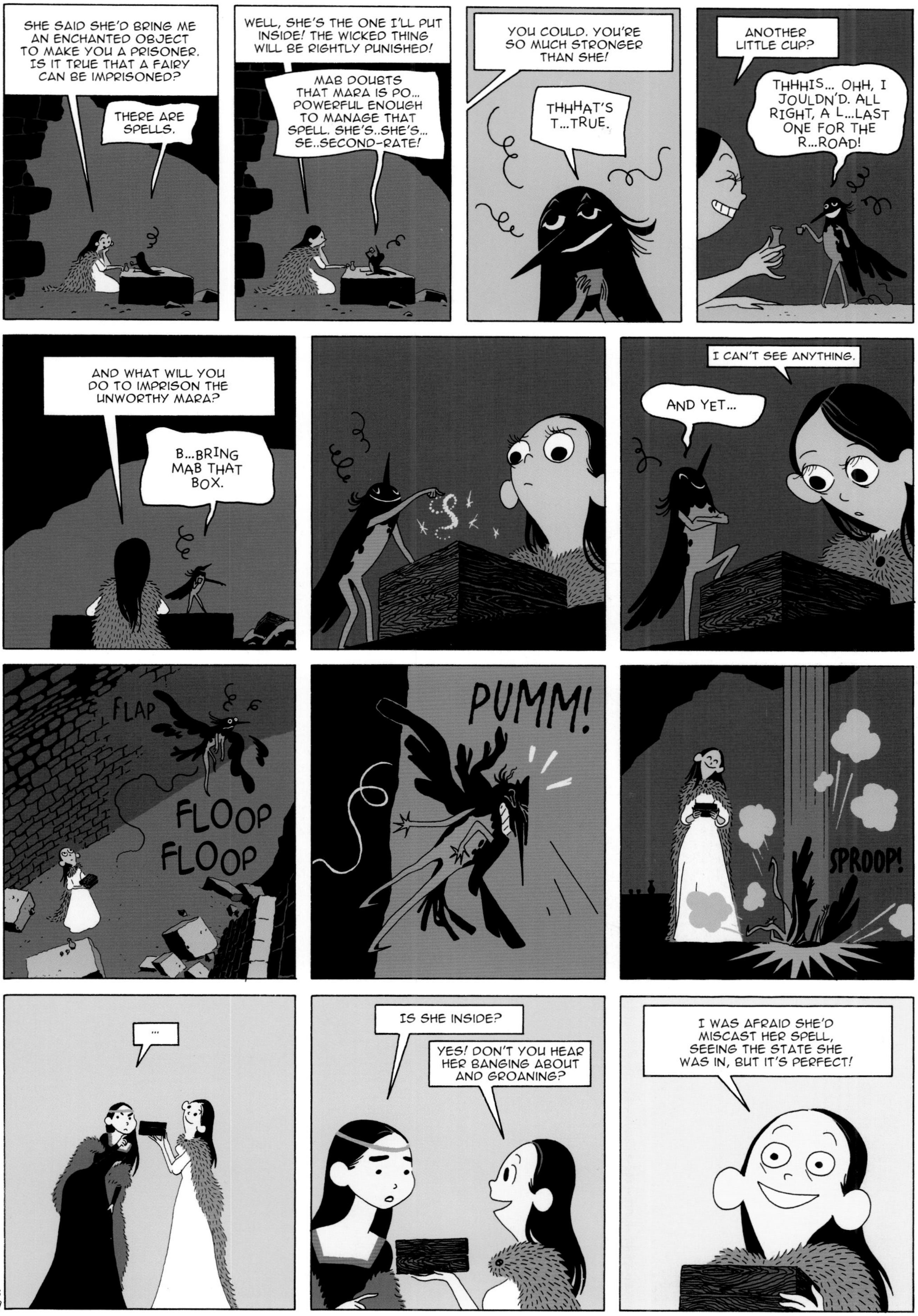
SHE SAID SHE'D BRING ME AN ENCHANTED OBJECT TO MAKE YOU A PRISONER. IS IT TRUE THAT A FAIRY CAN BE IMPRISONED?
THERE ARE SPELLS.
WELL, SHE'S THE ONE I'LL PUT INSIDE! THE WICKED THING WILL BE RIGHTLY PUNISHED!
MAB DOUBTS THAT MARA IS PO... POWERFUL ENOUGH TO MANAGE THAT SPELL. SHE'S..SHE'S... SE..SECOND-RATE!
YOU COULD. YOU'RE SO MUCH STRONGER THAN SHE!
THHHAT'S T...TRUE.
ANOTHER LITTLE CUP?
THHHIS... OHH, I JOULDN'D. ALL RIGHT, A L...LAST ONE FOR THE R...ROAD!
AND WHAT WILL YOU DO TO IMPRISON THE UNWORTHY MARA?
B...BRING MAB THAT BOX.
I CAN'T SEE ANYTHING.
AND YET...
FLAP
FLOOP FLOOP
PUMM!
SPROOP!
...
IS SHE INSIDE?
YES! DON'T YOU HEAR HER BANGING ABOUT AND GROANING?
I WAS AFRAID SHE'D MISCAST HER SPELL, SEEING THE STATE SHE WAS IN, BUT IT'S PERFECT!

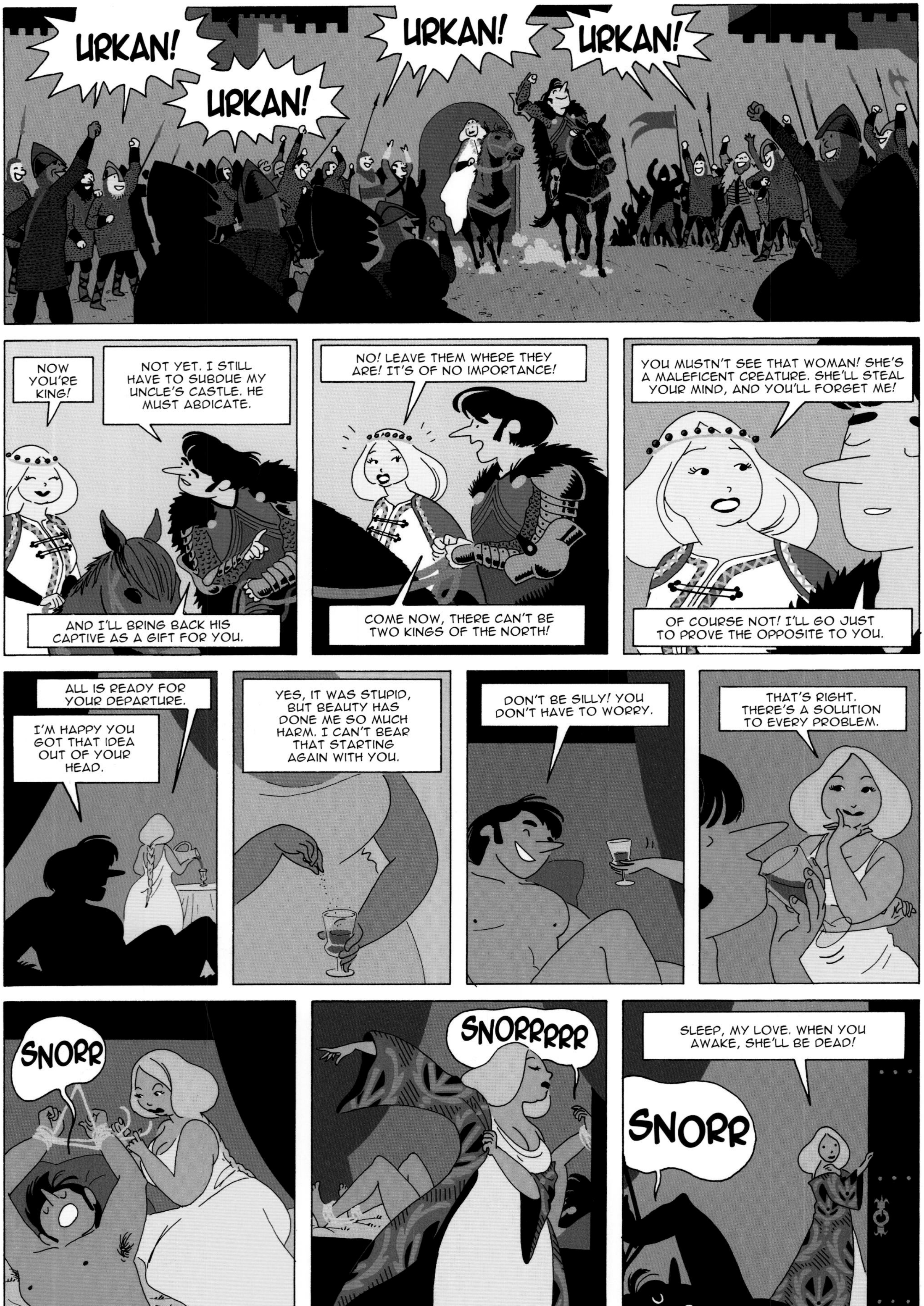
URKAN!
URKAN!
URKAN!
URKAN!
NOW YOU'RE KING!
NOT YET. I STILL HAVE TO SUBDUE MY UNCLE'S CASTLE. HE MUST ABDICATE.
AND I'LL BRING BACK HIS CAPTIVE AS A GIFT FOR YOU.
NO! LEAVE THEM WHERE THEY ARE! IT'S OF NO IMPORTANCE!
COME NOW, THERE CAN'T BE TWO KINGS OF THE NORTH!
YOU MUSTN'T SEE THAT WOMAN! SHE'S A MALEFICENT CREATURE. SHE'LL STEAL YOUR MIND, AND YOU'LL FORGET ME!
OF COURSE NOT! I'LL GO JUST TO PROVE THE OPPOSITE TO YOU.
ALL IS READY FOR YOUR DEPARTURE.
I'M HAPPY YOU GOT THAT IDEA OUT OF YOUR HEAD.
YES, IT WAS STUPID, BUT BEAUTY HAS DONE ME SO MUCH HARM. I CAN'T BEAR THAT STARTING AGAIN WITH YOU.
DON'T BE SILLY! YOU DON'T HAVE TO WORRY.
THAT'S RIGHT. THERE'S A SOLUTION TO EVERY PROBLEM.
SNORR
SNORRRRR
SLEEP, MY LOVE. WHEN YOU AWAKE, SHE'LL BE DEAD!
SNORR
3
40

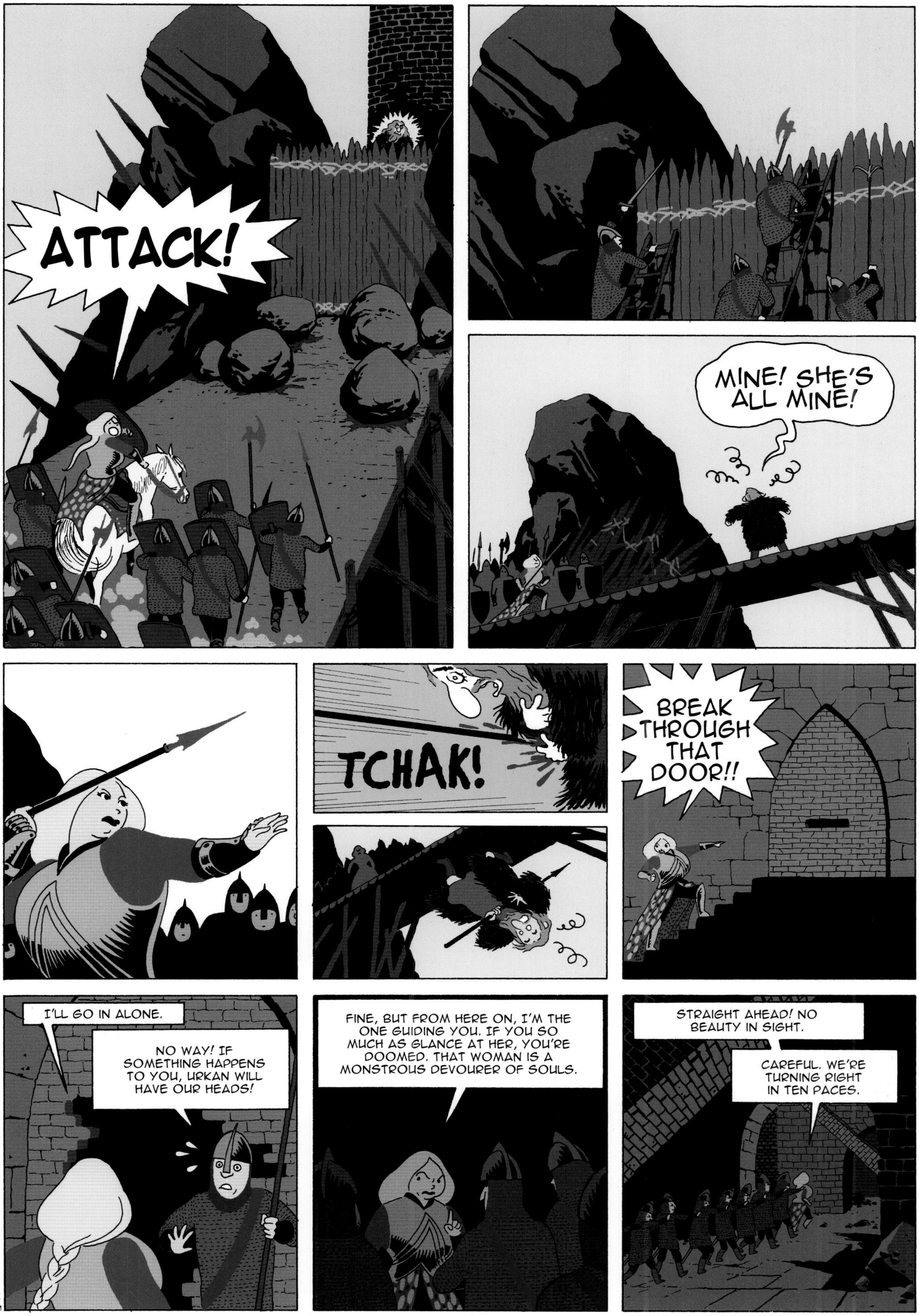
ATTACK!
MINE! SHE'S ALL MINE!
TCHAK!
BREAK THROUGH THAT DOOR!!
I'LL GO IN ALONE.
NO WAY! IF SOMETHING HAPPENS TO YOU, URKAN WILL HAVE OUR HEADS!
FINE, BUT FROM HERE ON, I'M THE ONE GUIDING YOU. IF YOU SO MUCH AS GLANCE AT HER, YOU'RE DOOMED. THAT WOMAN IS A MONSTROUS DEVOURER OF SOULS.
STRAIGHT AHEAD! NO BEAUTY IN SIGHT.
CAREFUL. WE'RE TURNING RIGHT IN TEN PACES.

MAMA! THEY'RE COMING!

I KNOW. I HEARD THEM.

OH, HELL!

BUT MAMA, WHAT ARE YOU DOING?

I'VE HAD ENOUGH! ENOUGH OF BEING AFRAID, OF RUNNING, AND TREMBLING. THEY'RE LOOKING FOR ME, WELL, THEY'LL SEE ME.

YOU'RE CRAZY! DON'T DO THAT!

THAT SPELL IS MY ONLY WEAPON AND I HAVE EVERY INTENTION OF USING IT.

HERE I AM!

When Dagmar saw Beauty approaching, her fear and hatred knew no further bounds.

THE MONSTER'S COMING! DON'T LOOK AT HER!

Beauty had changed in no way. The years had flowed over her without gaining any hold.

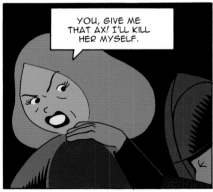

YOU, GIVE ME THAT AX! I'LL KILL HER MYSELF.

The soldier saw her coming towards him, like an unveiled goddess in her majesty.

Beyond her pure beauty, it was her eyes that weakened him, a look of such strength that it filled him with a sacred terror.

Imagining laying a hand on her seemed like an intolerable sacrilege.

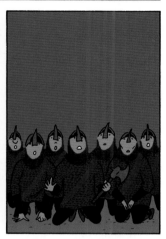

DEMON!!

SO THAT'S WHAT IS TO BE A SOVEREIGN.

COME, I STILL HAVE AN ENTIRE ARMY TO SUBDUE BEFORE WE'RE OUT OF THIS MESS.

Beauty's rise to power was a unique campaign in the chronicles of war: a woman marching alone at the head of an endlessly growing army adoring her on its knees.

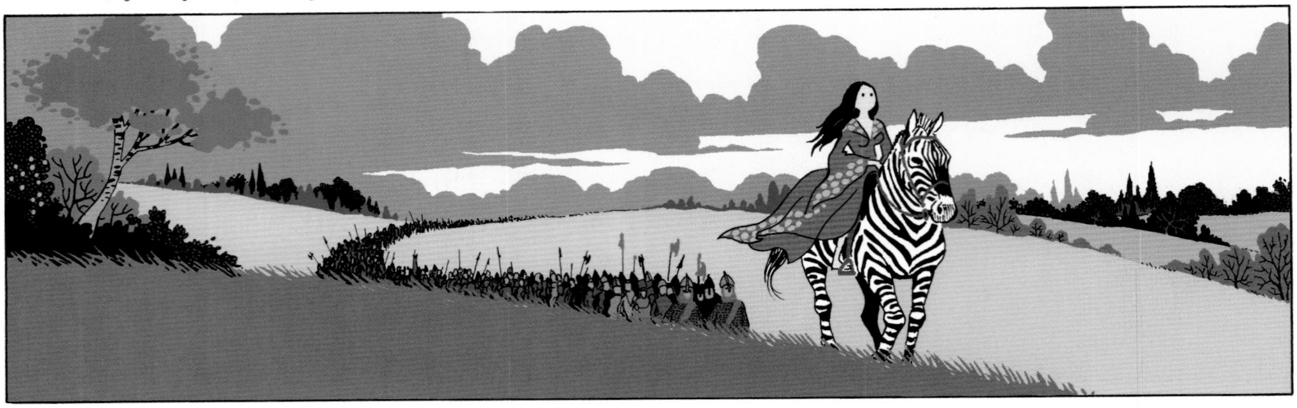

In less than two years, she subdued the North and then the South with no resistance.

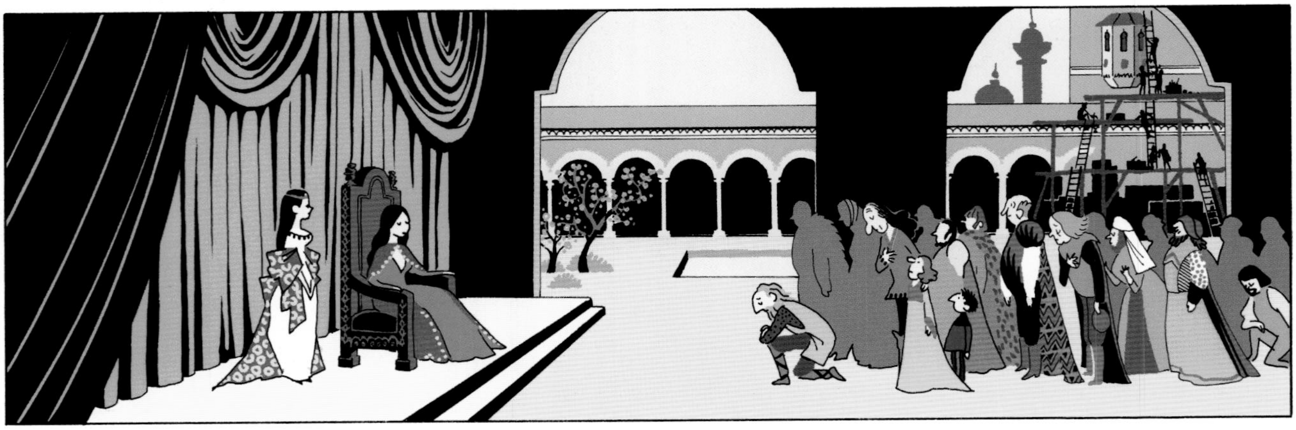

Counseled by her daughter, she reigned in an unequaled peace over her kingdoms. Her mere appearance sufficed to nip in the bud all conflict, all wish for rebellion.

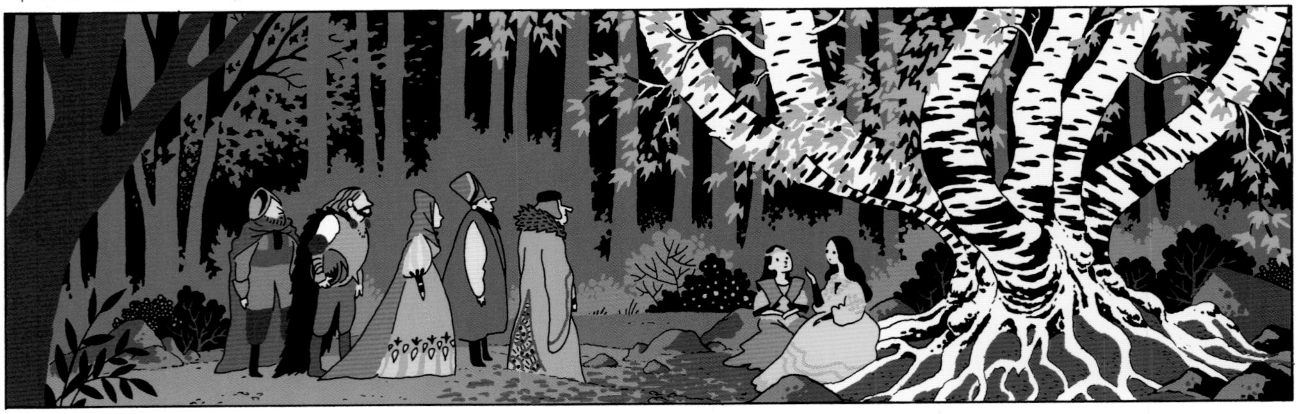

As the general fervor mounted, Beauty seemed to become disembodied. Nobody saw her anymore as a woman of flesh and blood, but as a supernatural being. Nobody would have dared lay a hand on her for fear of being instantly struck down.

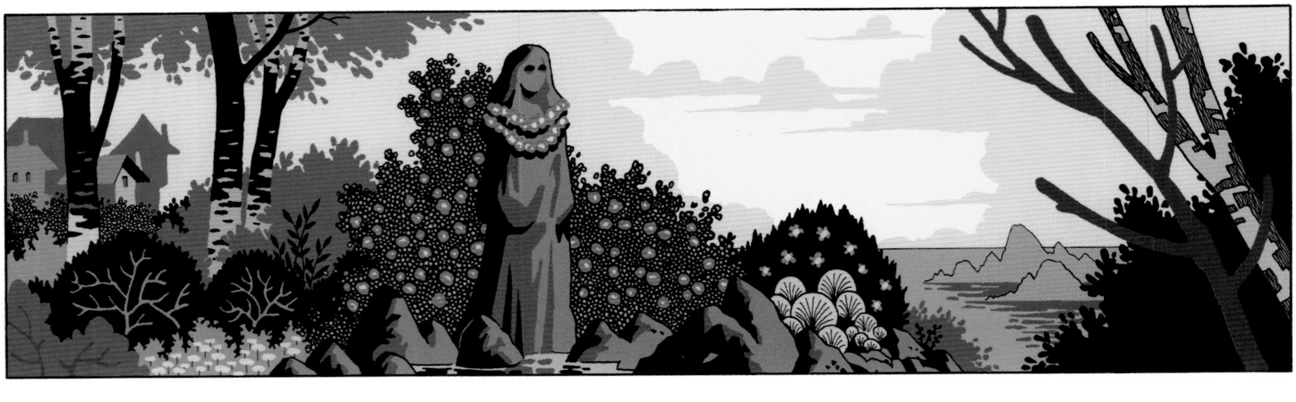

But Beauty's real war was the one she waged against the Fairies.

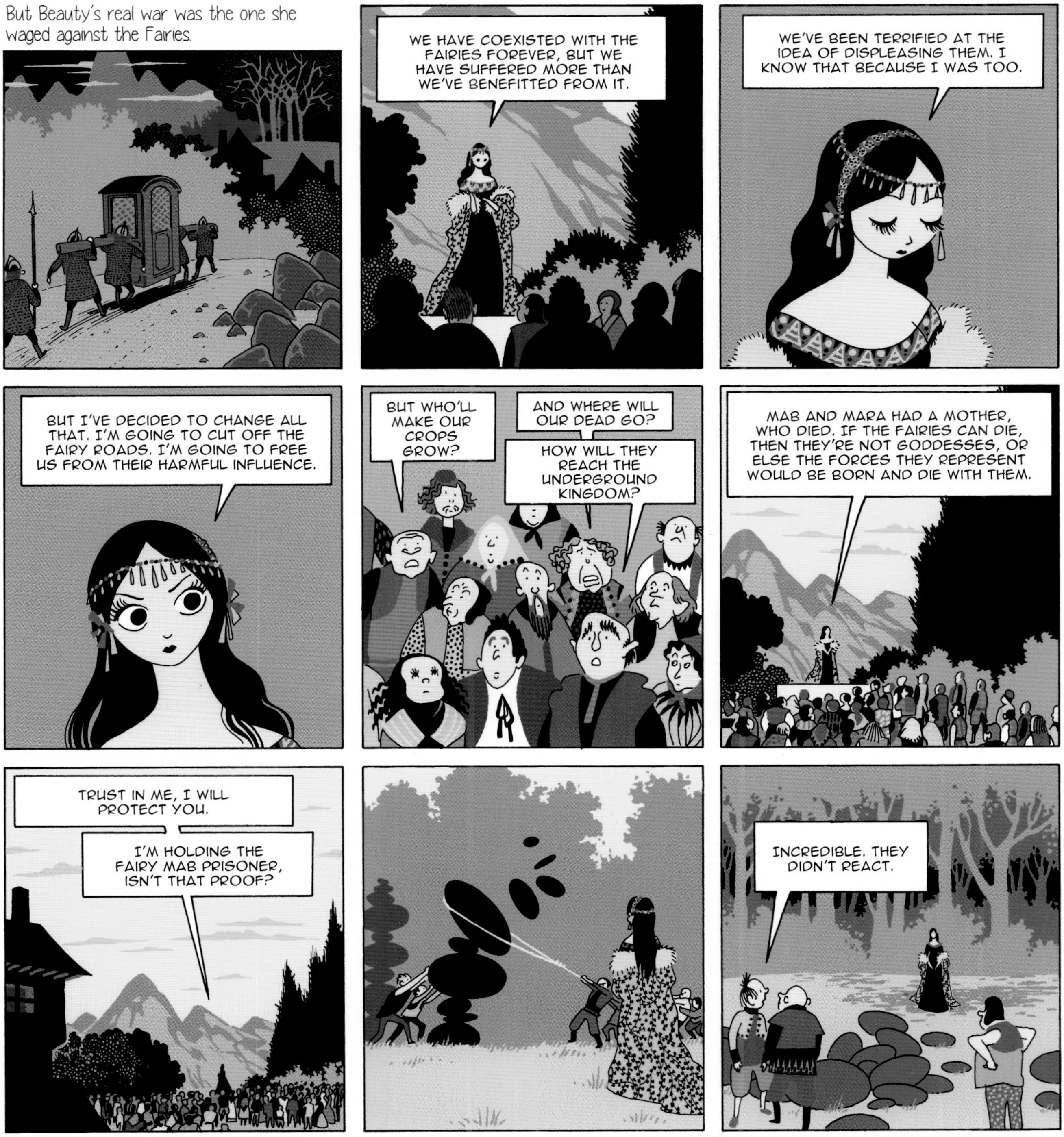
WE HAVE COEXISTED WITH THE FAIRIES FOREVER, BUT WE HAVE SUFFERED MORE THAN WE'VE BENEFITTED FROM IT.
WE'VE BEEN TERRIFIED AT THE IDEA OF DISPLEASING THEM. I KNOW THAT BECAUSE I WAS TOO.
BUT I'VE DECIDED TO CHANGE ALL THAT. I'M GOING TO CUT OFF THE FAIRY ROADS. I'M GOING TO FREE US FROM THEIR HARMFUL INFLUENCE.
BUT WHO'LL MAKE OUR CROPS GROW?
AND WHERE WILL OUR DEAD GO?
HOW WILL THEY REACH THE UNDERGROUND KINGDOM?
MAB AND MARA HAD A MOTHER, WHO DIED. IF THE FAIRIES CAN DIE, THEN THEY'RE NOT GODDESSES, OR ELSE THE FORCES THEY REPRESENT WOULD BE BORN AND DIE WITH THEM.
TRUST IN ME, I WILL PROTECT YOU.
I'M HOLDING THE FAIRY MAB PRISONER, ISN'T THAT PROOF?
INCREDIBLE. THEY DIDN'T REACT.

It took many years to find and wall up all the passages leading to the world of Fairies, and to everyone's surprise, nothing dire happened. Life continued its course as usual.

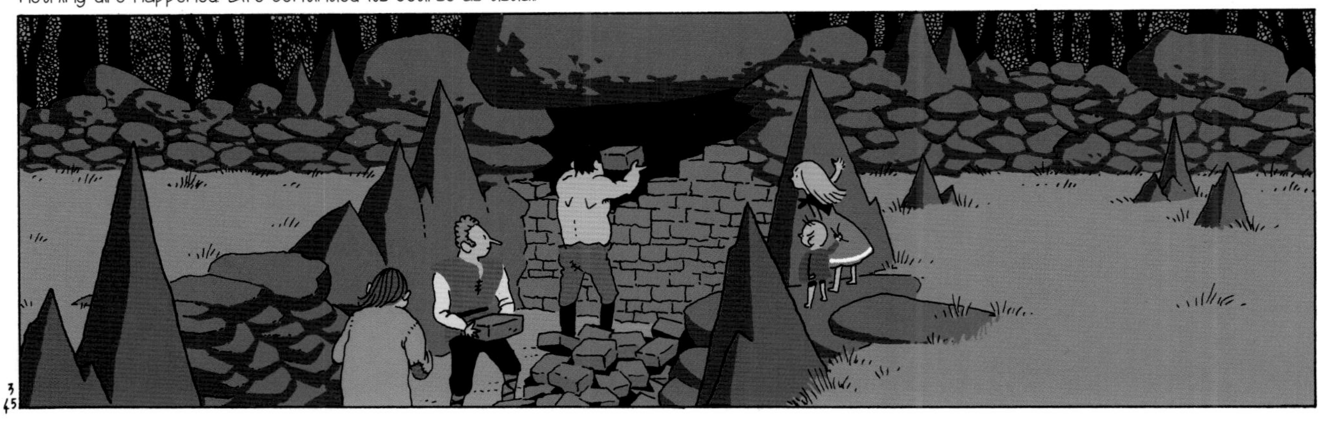

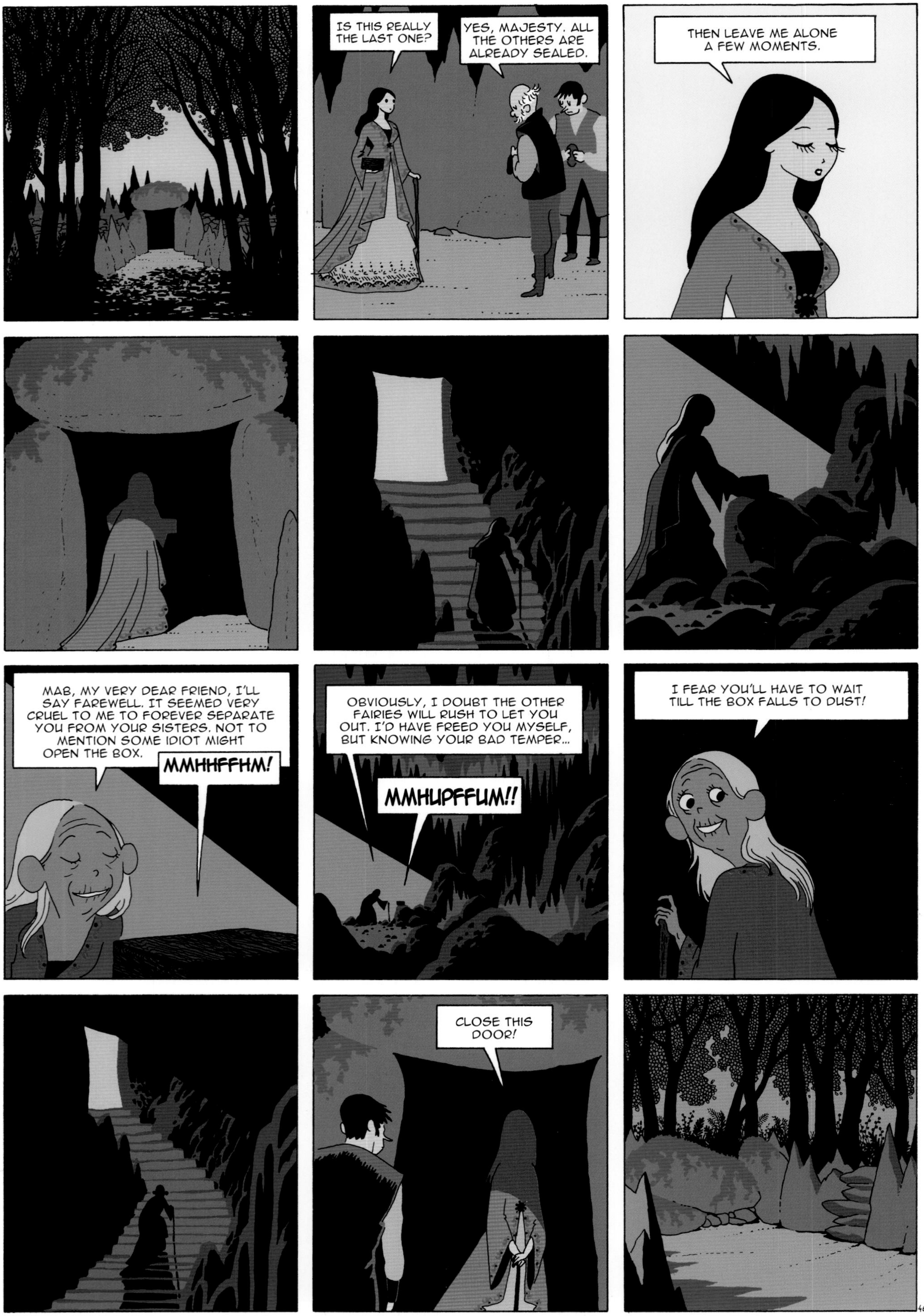
IS THIS REALLY THE LAST ONE?
YES, MAJESTY. ALL THE OTHERS ARE ALREADY SEALED.
THEN LEAVE ME ALONE A FEW MOMENTS.
MAB, MY VERY DEAR FRIEND, I'LL SAY FAREWELL. IT SEEMED VERY CRUEL TO ME TO FOREVER SEPARATE YOU FROM YOUR SISTERS. NOT TO MENTION SOME IDIOT MIGHT OPEN THE BOX.
MMHHFFHM!
OBVIOUSLY, I DOUBT THE OTHER FAIRIES WILL RUSH TO LET YOU OUT. I'D HAVE FREED YOU MYSELF, BUT KNOWING YOUR BAD TEMPER...
MMHUPFFUM!!
I FEAR YOU'LL HAVE TO WAIT TILL THE BOX FALLS TO DUST!
CLOSE THIS DOOR!

And that's how, from being a prisoner, Beauty became queen again, and remained on the throne until her final breath, and no one, ever, knew a more gracious sovereign.

EPILOGUE

One day, a strange group presented itself to the court to ask audience with Princess Marine. Queen Beauty had become quite aged and had retired from the world, entrusting the government of her realms to her daughter.

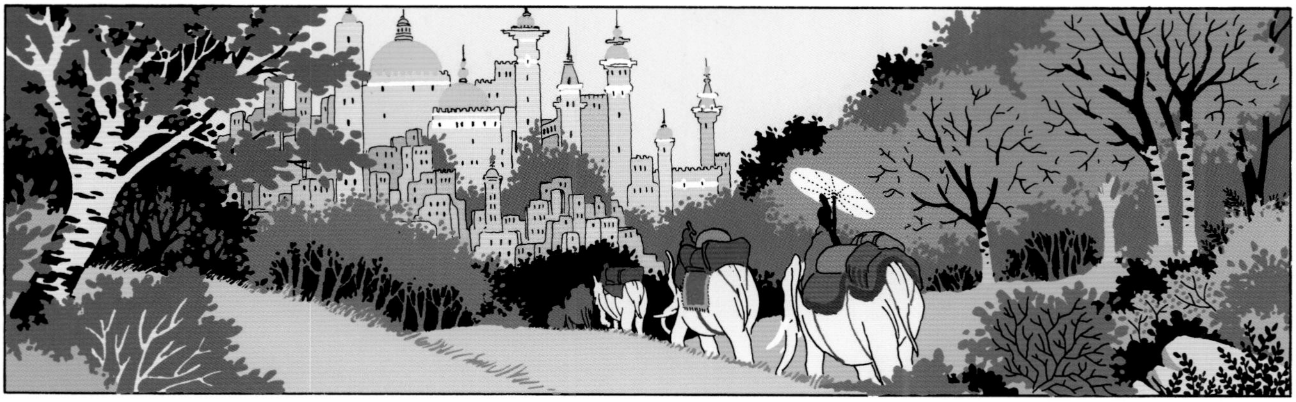

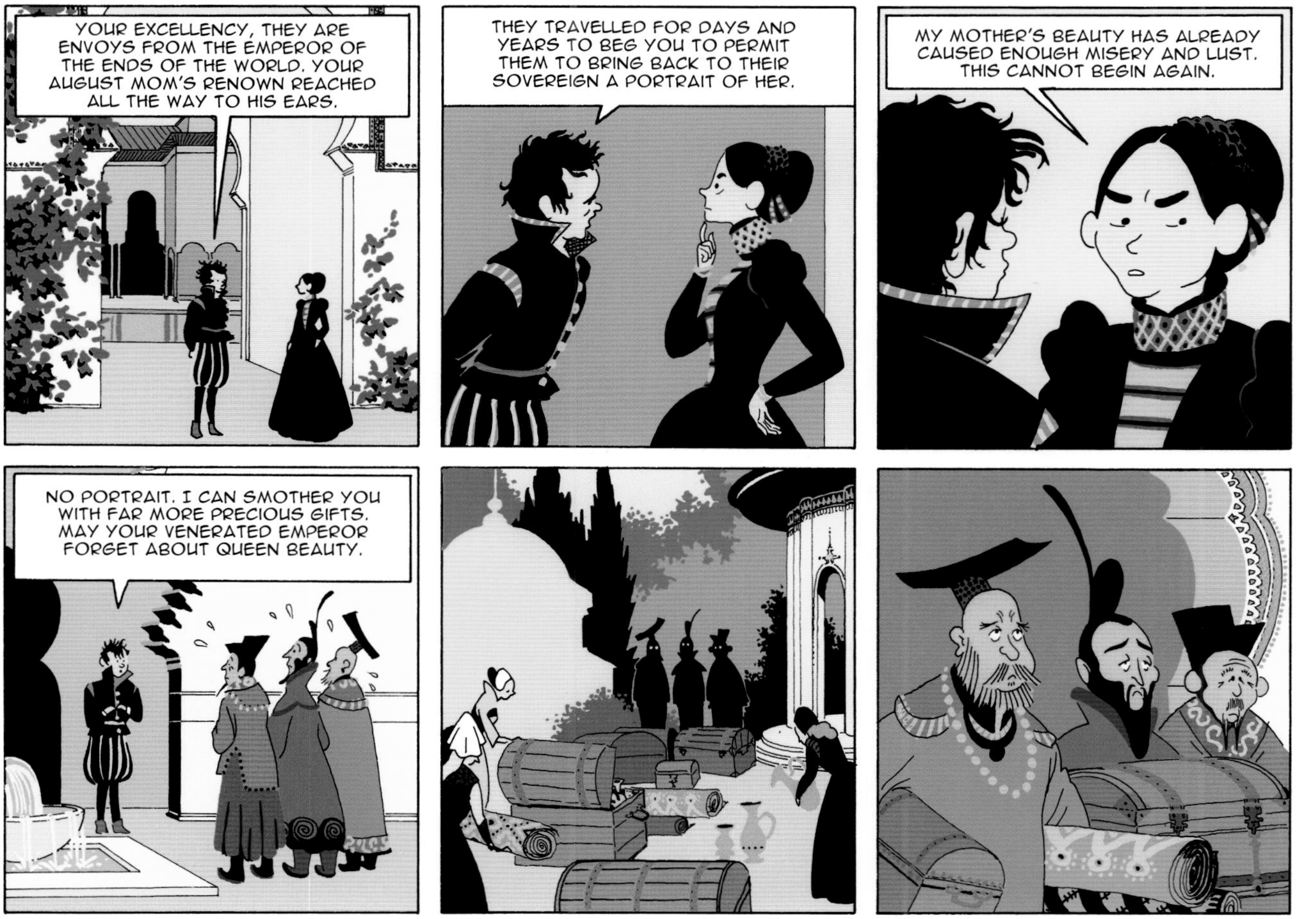
YOUR EXCELLENCY, THEY ARE ENVOYS FROM THE EMPEROR OF THE ENDS OF THE WORLD. YOUR AUGUST MOM'S RENOWN REACHED ALL THE WAY TO HIS EARS.
THEY TRAVELLED FOR DAYS AND YEARS TO BEG YOU TO PERMIT THEM TO BRING BACK TO THEIR SOVEREIGN A PORTRAIT OF HER.
MY MOTHER'S BEAUTY HAS ALREADY CAUSED ENOUGH MISERY AND LUST. THIS CANNOT BEGIN AGAIN.
NO PORTRAIT. I CAN SMOTHER YOU WITH FAR MORE PRECIOUS GIFTS. MAY YOUR VENERATED EMPEROR FORGET ABOUT QUEEN BEAUTY.

But the envoys knew the Emperor of the ends of the world would never forgive them such a failure.
So they stirred heaven and earth in search of a portrait of Beauty.

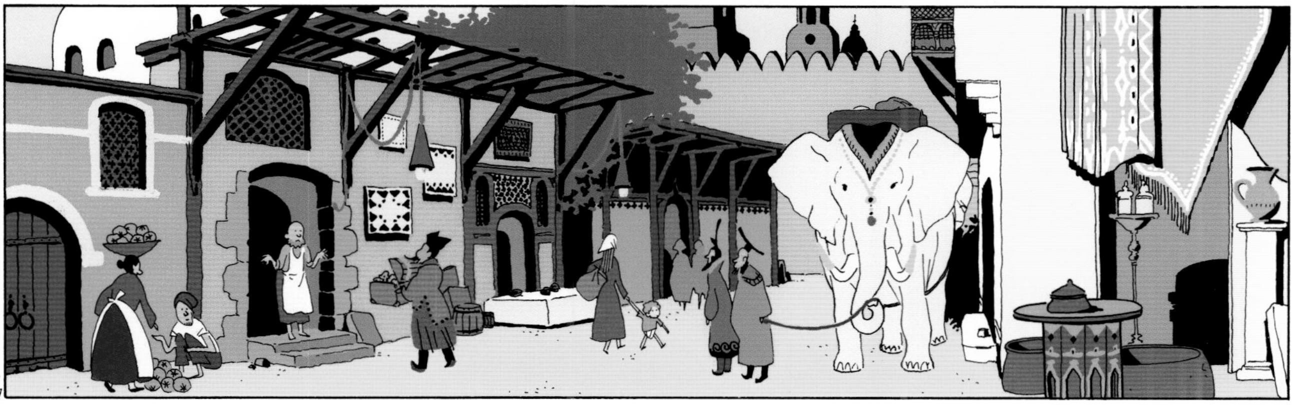

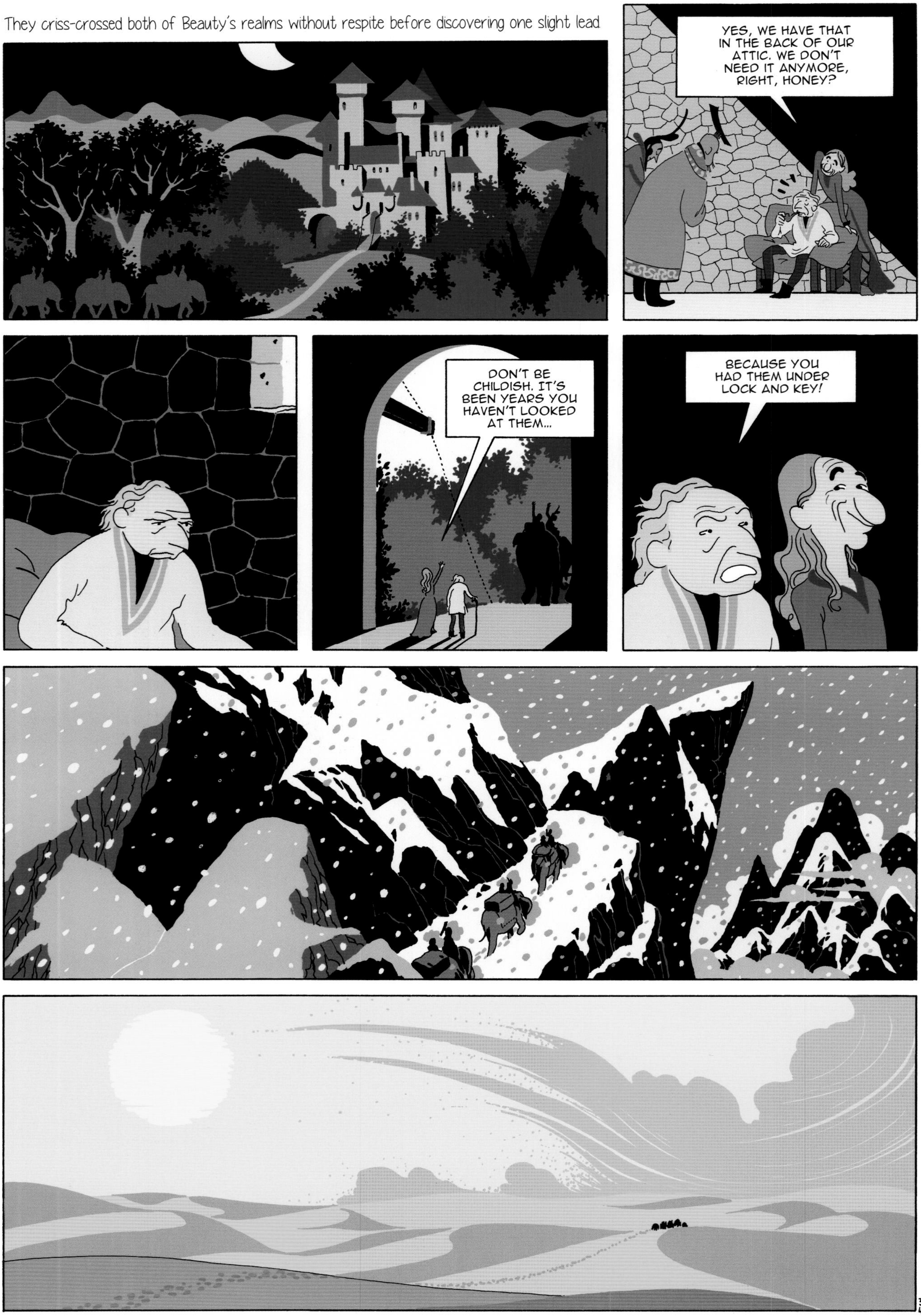
They criss-crossed both of Beauty's realms without respite before discovering one slight lead.
YES, WE HAVE THAT IN THE BACK OF OUR ATTIC. WE DON'T NEED IT ANYMORE, RIGHT, HONEY?
DON'T BE CHILDISH. IT'S BEEN YEARS YOU HAVEN'T LOOKED AT THEM...
BECAUSE YOU HAD THEM UNDER LOCK AND KEY!

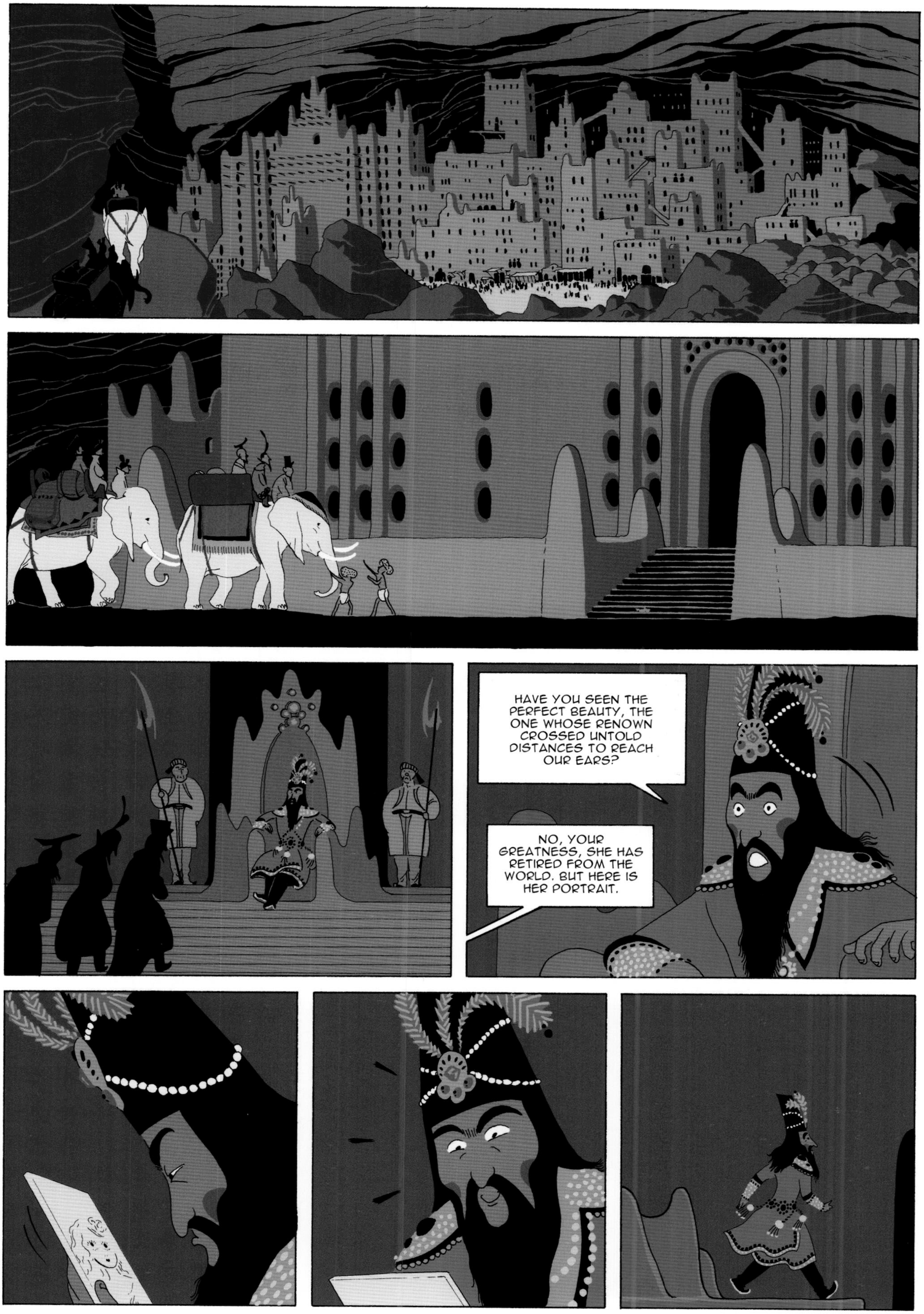
HAVE YOU SEEN THE PERFECT BEAUTY, THE ONE WHOSE RENOWN CROSSED UNTOLD DISTANCES TO REACH OUR EARS?
NO, YOUR GREATNESS, SHE HAS RETIRED FROM THE WORLD. BUT HERE IS HER PORTRAIT.

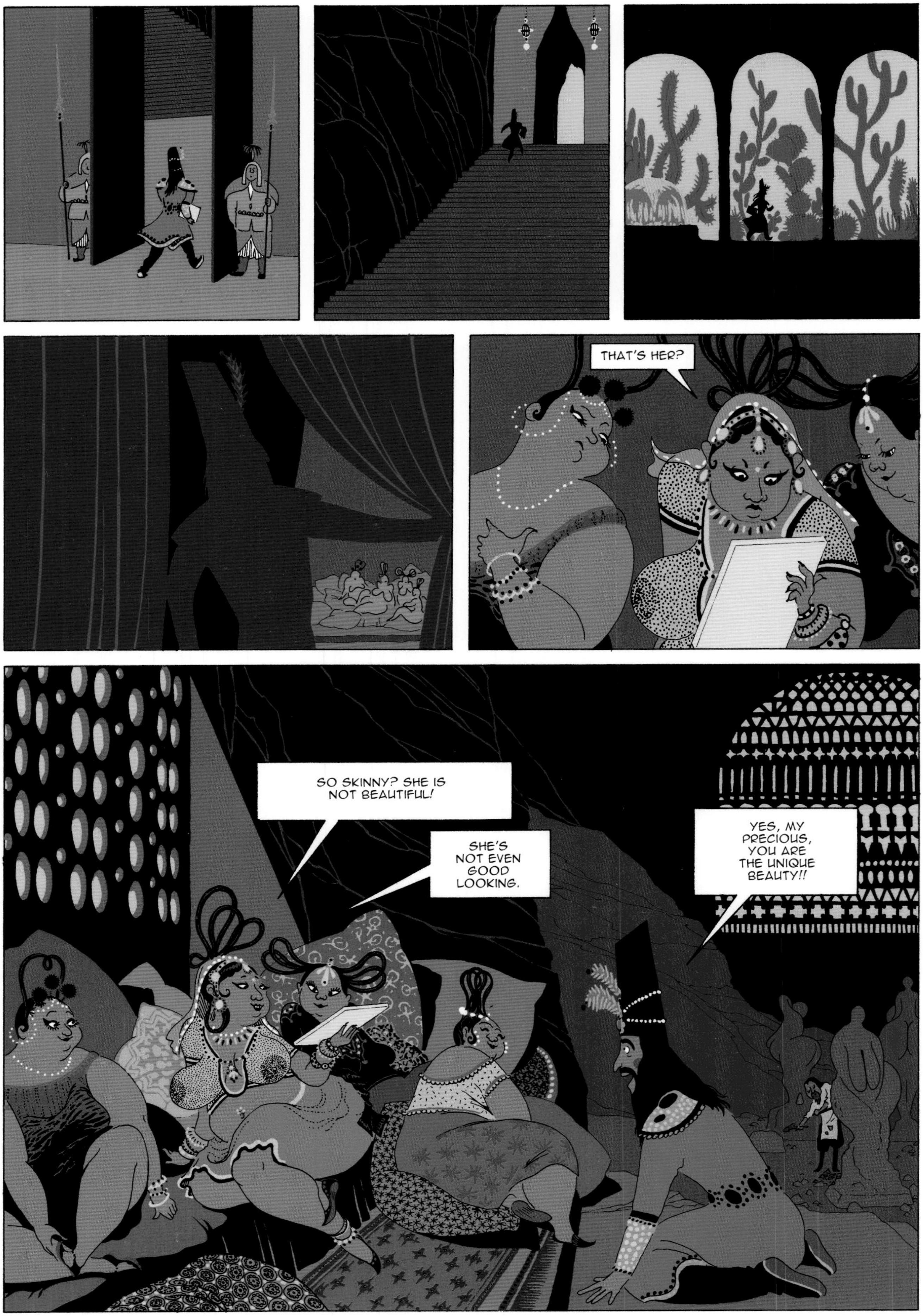
THAT'S HER?
SO SKINNY? SHE IS NOT BEAUTIFUL!
SHE'S NOT EVEN GOOD LOOKING.
YES, MY PRECIOUS, YOU ARE THE UNIQUE BEAUTY!!

Hubert & Kerascoet
MISS DON'T TOUCH ME
The Complete Story
A Graphic Novel

Dungeon
Twilight Vol. 2: Armageddon

SFAR • TRONDHEIM • KERASCOET • OBION
Dungeon
Twilight
Vol. 3: The New Centurions

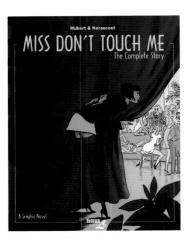

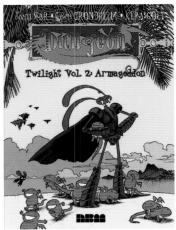

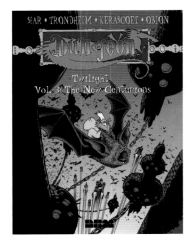

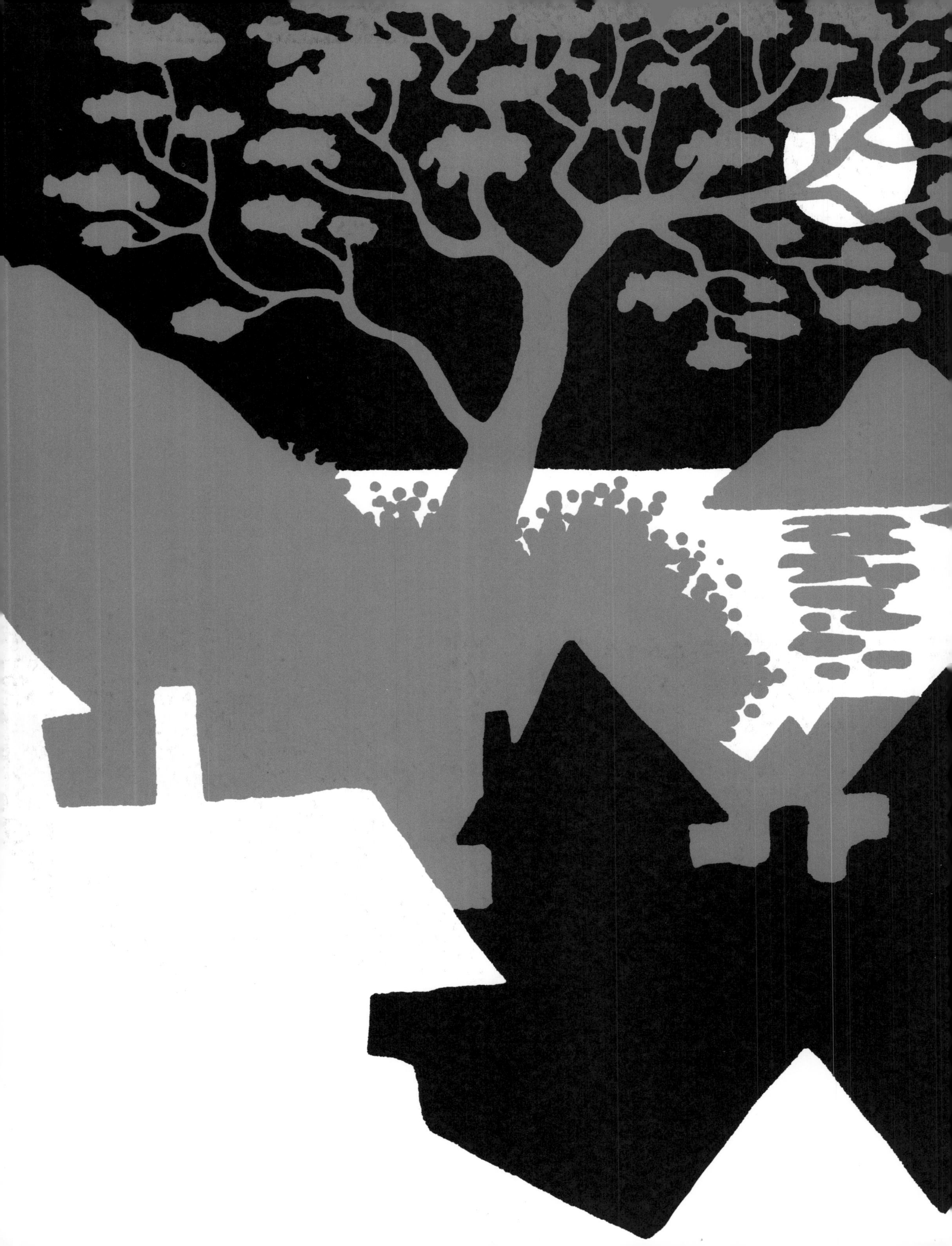